'It has become increasingly clear that W. G. Sebald is not just a very good writer, but quite simply one of the few essential writers of this generation . . . Nobody captures the epitaph quality of pastoral as well as he did' *Scotsman*

'Fascinating . . . A group portrait of a country and an empire in crisis . . . The reader will soon find not only Sebald's trademark concerns emerging but unexpected reflections on how we might navigate the end of empire and the rise of authoritarianism . . . For someone who may be feeling, in 2025, that their own homeland has become hostile and uncanny, there's much here to help make sense of that feeling of eeriness, and a repeated attempt to chart some kind of path forward' *New Republic*

'This book is full of strange and tender moments when Sebald's feeling for his subject translates into scenes and images that might have come straight from *Austerlitz* or *The Rings of Saturn* . . . Sebald push[es] past literary history, criticism or biography to another, visionary realm' *Art Review*

Also by W. G. Sebald in English translation

The Emigrants
The Rings of Saturn
Vertigo
Austerlitz
After Nature
On the Natural History of Destruction
Unrecounted
Campo Santo
Across the Land and the Water
A Place in the Country

Silent Catastrophes

W. G. SEBALD

Essays in Austrian Literature

Translated from the German and
with an introduction by Jo Catling

PENGUIN BOOKS

PENGUIN BOOKS

UK | USA | Canada | Ireland | Australia
India | New Zealand | South Africa

Penguin Books is part of the Penguin Random House group of companies
whose addresses can be found at global.penguinrandomhouse.com.

Penguin Random House UK,
One Embassy Gardens, 8 Viaduct Gardens, London SW11 7BW

penguin.co.uk

First published in German as *Die Beschreibung des Unglücks* (1985) and
Unheimliche Heimat (1991) by Residenz
This translation first published by Hamish Hamilton 2025
Published in Penguin Books 2026

001

Copyright © The estate of W. G. Sebald, 2025
Translation, introduction and notes © Jo Catling, 2025

The moral right of the author has been asserted

Illustration on page 452 by Alphonse Lévy (1843–1918), *Reading the London News*.

Extract from Barry Mitchell's translation of *Die Winterreise* by Wilhelm Müller,
English translation copyright © 2014 Barry Mitchell, courtesy of Theory of Music.

Penguin Random House values and supports copyright.
Copyright fuels creativity, encourages diverse voices, promotes freedom
of expression and supports a vibrant culture. Thank you for purchasing
an authorized edition of this book and for respecting intellectual property
laws by not reproducing, scanning or distributing any part of it by any
means without permission. You are supporting authors and enabling
Penguin Random House to continue to publish books for everyone.
No part of this book may be used or reproduced in any manner for the
purpose of training artificial intelligence technologies or systems. In accordance
with Article 4(3) of the DSM Directive 2019/790, Penguin Random House
expressly reserves this work from the text and data mining exception

Typeset by Jouve (UK), Milton Keynes
Printed and bound in Great Britain by Clays Ltd, Elcograf S.p.A.

The authorized representative in the EEA is Penguin Random House Ireland,
Morrison Chambers, 32 Nassau Street, Dublin D02 YH68

A CIP catalogue record for this book is available from the British Library

ISBN: 978–0–141–03702–8

Penguin Random House is committed to a sustainable future
for our business, our readers and our planet. This book is made from
Forest Stewardship Council® certified paper.

Contents

'Silent Catastrophes' – An Introduction (Jo Catling)   xiii

Part One
The Description of Misfortune – On Austrian Literature from Stifter to Handke

Foreword   3

To the Edge of Nature – An Essay on Stifter   9

> New aspects of Stifter reception – Stifter's agnosticism – His personal debacle – Pathological traits – Utopian structures – Space outside time – Description of nature – Entropy: everything in the world vanishes – Paedophilia – The ideal of feminine beauty – Clothes fetishism – Marriage and celibacy – No wished-for death

The Horror of Love – On Schnitzler's *Traumnovelle* [*Dream Story*]   36

> Myth of love and bourgeois literature – Schnitzler's critique of pure love – The Malthusian couple – The masturbating child and the body of the other – The hysterical woman – Classic hysteria: opera – Domestic hysteria: triviality of misery – Ideal masculine

type: chevalier in uniform – Duel and satisfaction, or otherwise – Promiscuity and prostitution – The spectre of syphilis – Youth in Vienna – The bourgeois as *hasardeur* – *Memento mori* – The pornographic scene – Sacrifice of the woman – Necrophilia

A Venetian Cryptogram – Hofmannsthal's *Andreas*   62

The Germanist myth of the unfinished *Bildungsroman* – Exploration of the taboo – Erotic libertinage of the Wiener Moderne – Hofmannsthal's monogamous ideal – The panic of the man of forty – Memory and hysteria – Impotence: the trials of male sexuality – *Aptitude à tous les excès* – *Horreur des femmes* – Homosexual violence and murder: Winckelmann in Trieste – *Wunderkind* Loris: consequences of adulation – St[efan]. George and the character of the Maltese: vampiric type – The son without a mother – Innocent perversion: Andreas and Romana as brother and sister – The dead Finazzer children – Maria and Mariquita: obsession with purity and dealings in love – The dog Fidèle – Techniques of *cruauté*: lives of the saints and pornography – *Le dernier mot du catholicisme* – Beauty of the fetish and the literary image

The Undiscover'd Country – The Death Motif in Kafka's *Castle*   82

Utopia and critique of death – Enigma of the blind images – The death of nature – *Winterreise* and journeying – Madame Lamort, the landlady of the Herrenhof and the completion of a fragment

Summa Scientiae – Systems and System Critique in
Elias Canetti   103

> Paranoia and system – Schreber – Hitler's architectural fantasies – Parasitic hierarchy of nature – Artificial order of fictions – Prison topos – Teaching and learning – Traditional Jewish vision of an open system

Wo die Dunkelheit den Strick zuzieht
[Where Darkness Draws Tight the Noose] –
Some Marginal Notes on Thomas Bernhard   114

> Rule and anarchy: madness of society – *Les malheurs de la nature* – The secret humorist – Bernhard as Rumpelstilzchen – Paranoia, cannibalism, satire – Bernhard and Swift – *Passing the test of sanity*

Beneath the Surface – Peter Handke's Story of the
Goalkeeper's Anxiety   133

> Schizophrenic perception and literary precision – Order and contingency – *Zugzwang* – Flight and paralysis – Transsubstantiation of the individual – Archaic behaviour patterns in illness: a prehistoric state – Aetiology of estrangement: childhood and early suffering – The mute schoolboy

A Small Traverse – The Poetry of Ernst Herbeck   152

> Backgrounds, principles of composition, representations of the 'condition-related' imagination – Missing life with precision – *Pensée sauvage*, *bricolage*, *art brut* – Schizophrenic ideals and images: seafaring, beautiful ladies, dwarf-like stature – Enigma of the alphabet – Detailed interpretation of an unintelligible text

The Man with the Overcoat — Gerhard Roth's
Winterreise 175

> The teacher plays truant — Problem of concentration in prose — Prose and pornography: impossible transition — The pornographic heresy — The Arctic explorer and *Frau Welt* ['Mistress World'] — The brown Austrian paralysis

Light Pictures and Dark — On the Dialectics of
Eschatology in Stifter and Handke 193

> Distant beauty, present horror — The order of things — Irruptions — Stifter's illness: eating mania — Pathological colours — Colour theory — Principles of depiction — Photography and description — Written image — Clarity — Flying and walking — The mountain of bliss — Virgil and Handke — Metaphysics of redemption — What is really white? — The Great Forest and the return from the dead

Part Two
Strange Homeland — Essays on Austrian Literature

Foreword 219

Introduction 220

Views from the New World — On Charles Sealsfield 227

> Outline of reception — Flight of the cleric — First stay in America — Sealsfield, the secret service agent — Austria as it is: looking back at the lost *Heimat* — Sealsfield and the 1848 Revolution — Theories of race — The higher meaning of extermination — German world

mission and reactionary republicanism – Subjugation and description of nature – Money fears and the bitter end

Westwards – Eastwards: Aporia of German-Language Tales from the Ghetto 253

Beginning of a new diaspora – Kompert and the ethnographic genre – The backward glance: sentimentality and aversion – Jerusalem and bourgeois reason – Kafka's children on the country road – Lightening the darkness – Karl Emil Franzos: cultural description as denunciation – Melanie Feiglstock, Friedrich Schiller and Aaron Tulpenblüh – Emancipation of emotions – Return from 'Americum' – *Historia calamitatum* – The Jewish cemetery as a metaphor of *Heimat* – Sacher-Masoch's tales from Jewish life – Caricature as the dark side of the sentimental genre – Joseph Roth's story of weights and measures

Peter Altenberg – *Le Paysan de Vienne* 281

Childhood, the one and only *Heimat*, *vie antérieure* – Separation from his adored Mama – Exiled to the metropolis – Fashion and the *Naturfreund* – Passion for collecting – The world in Vienna – The stationary *flâneur* – Eternal wandering – Flying by night: the poet as bat and aerobat – The waiting room of exile – Fear of *déclassement* – PA and money – The natural life – The worst turn of events – Alcohol, sleeping draughts, institutions – The martyr's death of PA, greatest of sinners – The Höllengebirge, pure seeing, the albatross

The Law of Ignominy – Authority, Messianism and
Exile in Kafka's *Castle*   306

> The legacy of power – Jewish Messianism – The wanderer –
> Cryptogram of the Land Surveyor – Powerlessness of Messianism
> and vulnerability of power – The crucial question, unasked from
> weariness – On the false Messiah – Exile and exclusion – The agent
> and the messenger from heaven

A Kaddish for Austria – On Joseph Roth   327

> The lost Fatherland – Experience of exile – Five minutes before
> the pogrom – Disillusionism – Allegoresis – Art of storytelling –
> Time and clocks – Waxworks – The modest ideal

Una montagna bruna – On Hermann Broch's
'Mountain Novel' [*Bergroman*]   344

> Trust in higher reason – Concepts on a grand scale – The sinister
> figure of Marius Ratti and its contradictory connotations – Narrator
> as inner emigrant – Inadvertent rightward shift – Inflationary land-
> scape painting – Narratological weaknesses – Kitsch, mystification
> and mythologism

A Lost Land – Jean Améry and Austria   359

> Biographical details – View of the Promised Land – Blindness of a
> threatened minority – Austrocentric view of the world – The *Wiener
> Kreis* – Last act, lost illusion, *Anschluß*, exile – Consumed by
> homesickness – Suicide and epilogue

In an Unknown Region – On Gerhard Roth's Novel *Landläufiger Tod* [*A Common or Garden Death*]   375

> The doctor and the dead child – Passive genii, aphoristic images – The mythopoetic method, or the opening of the beehive – Surreal fringes of reality – Paradigm of the end of human history – Catalogue of a past life – Sickness of the head – Violence: death enters into life – View from the Schneeberg – Against megalomania

Across the Border – Peter Handke's *Die Wiederholung* [*Repetition*]   394

> Handke and the critics – Crossing the border – True and false *Heimat* – Rinkenberg exile – The mission of the sons – Matriarchal utopia and the idea of *fraternité* – The secret king and the people without power – Under the sign of writing – Road mender and signwriter – Island of calm

Notes   413
Translator's Notes   473
Selected Bibliography   503
Acknowledgements   511

'Silent Catastrophes' – An Introduction

> The fascination of the particular narrative genre he developed lay in the absolutely innovative linguistic and imaginative precision with which [. . .] he relates and reflects upon the silent catastrophes continually occurring in the inner life of mankind.
>
> W. G. Sebald, *Strange Homeland*
> (on Peter Handke's *Repetition*)

Reflecting on his own origins towards the end of the long poem *Nach der Natur* (*After Nature*), his debut literary book publication, W. G. Sebald recalls how he 'grew up / despite the dreadful course / of events elsewhere, on the northern / edge of the Alps, so it seems / to me now, without any / idea of destruction'; and how nevertheless, beneath this outwardly idyllic rural childhood, there lurked an all-pervasive sense of 'a silent catastrophe that occurs / almost unperceived' ('die Vorstellung / von einer lautlosen Katastrophe, die sich / ohne ein Aufhebens vor dem Betrachter vollzieht'). This persistent theme, apostrophized as a 'natural history of destruction', runs through his literary and academic work alike, and seems particularly applicable to the essays translated here, in which, as in the later *Logis in einem Landhaus* (*A Place in the Country*), seemingly idyllic landscapes are juxtaposed with historical events and inward states which are anything but serene.

The present volume of 'Essays on Austrian Literature' 'From Stifter to Handke' – to cite in reverse order the subtitles of the two collections translated here – comprises two books of collected essays, *Die Beschreibung des Unglücks* (*The Description of Misfortune*) and *Unheimliche Heimat* (*Strange Homeland*), published by W. G. Sebald in 1985 and 1991 respectively with the Austrian literary publishing house Residenz. The nineteen essays in these two companion volumes, arranged chronologically in each volume, have as their subjects seventeen writers – all but one (the poet Ernst Herbeck) writers of prose. Like the essays in *A Place in the Country*, they span almost two centuries, an era which saw Austria evolve 'from the vastness of the Habsburg Empire to a diminutive Alpine republic' (below p. 220). Beginning in an age of colonial expansion and emigration (Sealsfield), via Biedermeier quietism (Stifter), the upheavals of the *Vormärz* and 1848 and the age of industrialization and concomitant urbanization, they reflect and document an era of deracination and transition, demonstrated most acutely, though by no means exclusively, in the successive waves of westward migration of the Jewish populations of Eastern Europe. In the twentieth century, the essays also reflect the crises of consciousness and identity, particularly bourgeois identity, in the age of Freud (Schnitzler, Hofmannsthal, Altenberg, Kafka), crises of identity and assimilation which, with the two world wars of the twentieth century and their consequent diasporic migrations, again become particularly acute for the many writers of Jewish extraction discussed – as experienced and evoked, in very different ways, by Elias Canetti, Hermann Broch, Joseph Roth and Jean Améry. The Second World War and its aftermath also leave traumatic traces in later generations of non-Jewish writers, such as Thomas Bernhard, Peter Handke, Gerhard Roth and indeed Sebald himself, fiercely critical of a social reality in which the spectre of the recent fascist past continues to lurk silently beneath the seemingly unruffled surface of the prosperous post-war present. Although the apparent idyllic Alpine setting, like that of Sebald's own childhood, might at first appear far removed from such historic turbulence, its seismic effects, as Sebald writes in the penultimate essay of this volume, affect 'even the remotest regions', striking 'just as much out of the blue as ever a lightning bolt did from the clearest of skies'. 'Indeed,' he continues, 'in the end it makes little difference whether the catastrophe is caused by nature or by the workings of history, which consumes and engulfs everything in exactly the same way as fire or water' (below p. 385).

Sebald of course was German, not Austrian; but, as the narrator of *Vertigo* demonstrates, the village of his childhood is situated within walking distance of the Austrian border, and this sense of being from the margins may go some way to explaining Sebald's interest in a literature beyond the borders of West (and East) Germany, with which of course it shares a language. In a 2001 interview with Michael Silverblatt, Sebald explains that one reason for his affinity with 'nineteenth-century prose writing' (in German) is 'not least' that 'the writers all hailed from the periphery of the German-speaking lands, where I also come from . . .'. Admiration for prose style aside, this sense of being from a 'regional backwater', as he puts it in another interview, 'a peripheral zone in which a dialect was spoken which was nearly as extreme as Swiss German', also suggests an identification with a contemporary generation of Austrian writers from modest backgrounds who 'in a topographical, social and psychological sense hailed from the periphery', as he writes in an article commemorating the thirtieth anniversary of the founding of the 'avant-garde' (or 'trans-garde') literary movement, the 'Grazer Gruppe' (Graz Group) and 'Forum Stadtpark', as well as its prime vehicle, the journal *manuskripte* founded by Alfred Kolleritsch in 1960 – a movement which, Sebald claims, inaugurated what amounted to a radical, and indeed polemical, 'reinvigoration of Austrian (and beyond that German) literature which in the 1960s was in a parlous not to say desolate state'.

The Graz journal *manuskripte*, bringing together linguistically and formally innovative work by progressive (mostly) Austrian authors with re-evaluations of (mostly) Austrian literature, in fact plays a key role in W. G. Sebald's emergence as a writer. Across nine issues, from 1981 to 1988, no fewer than ten pieces of Sebald's are published there, including two essays later collected in *Die Beschreibung des Unglücks* and two in *Unheimliche Heimat*. The first of these, in 1981, is the essay 'A Small Traverse' on Ernst Herbeck (the only essay on a poet in the present volume), followed in 1983 by an (as yet untranslated) essay on the Bavarian writer Herbert Achternbusch, and in 1984 by the final essay in *Die Beschreibung des Unglücks*, 'Light Pictures and Dark', bringing together the canonical nineteenth-century prose writer Adalbert Stifter with the later Nobel prizewinner from Graz, Sebald's near contemporary Peter Handke. The following issue of *manuskripte* sees the publication of what would become the central section of *Nach der Natur (After Nature)*, 'And If I Remained by the Outermost Sea' – his first literary publication since the publication of early poems in the journal *ZET* in 1974 and 1975. In 1985 there follows a German version of Sebald's second essay on Kafka, 'The Law of Ignominy', first published in English nine years earlier, and subsequently included in *Unheimliche Heimat* – Sebald's original English version of this essay is reprinted in the present volume. In 1986 there appears 'In an Unknown Region', also later included in *Unheimliche Heimat*, on Gerhard Roth's then recently published magnum opus *Landläufiger Tod* (1984), as well as – in the same issue of *manuskripte* – the long poem 'As the Snow on the Alps', which was to become the first part of *Nach der Natur*. This is followed the next year by 'Dark Night Sallies Forth', the third and final part of that 'Elementargedicht'. Sebald's two final publications in *manuskripte*, in successive issues in 1988, would later become the respective first sections of *Schwindel. Gefühle.* (*Vertigo*) and *Die Ausgewanderten* (*The Emigrants*). The story 'Berge oder das . . .' ('Mountains or the . . .'), episodes from the life of Henri Beyle – better known under his pen name Stendhal – is published in *Vertigo* under the title 'Beyle, or Love is a Madness Most Discreet'. Sebald's final contribution to *manuskripte*, in the 100th issue with the theme 'Über das Altern' ('On Ageing'), is the story 'Verzehret das letzte, die Erinnerung, nicht', which in *The Emigrants* becomes 'Henry Selwyn'. The last two pieces stand out for their inclusion of a number of photographic images, though these differ considerably from those in the subsequent book publications.

With the exception of the two essays on Kafka from the 1970s, both first published in English, the essays translated here as *Silent Catastrophes* date from this same period, between 1981 and 1991. For Sebald, who had in 1970 been appointed Lecturer in German at the University of East Anglia (UEA) at the age of twenty-six, this was an extraordinarily fruitful decade, which not only saw him promoted in 1988 to Professor of European Literature – thanks in part to the publication of *Die Beschreibung des Unglücks*

(Part One of the present volume), which also served as a *Habilitationsschrift*, giving him the option of applying for professorial positions at German universities – but also saw the publication of his first two books of, respectively, poetry and what he preferred to call 'prose fiction': the 'Elementargedicht' *Nach der Natur* in 1988, followed by *Schwindel. Gefühle.* in 1990. Thus the two volumes of essays on Austrian literature translated here bracket the crucial years in which Sebald – who had harboured literary ambitions from an early age – emerged on to the literary scene as an author in his own right; indeed it is in the contributors' biography of the 1990 Graz volume *Trans-Garde*, in which the above-mentioned article appeared, that Sebald describes himself for the first time as 'Autor sowie Professor' – 'author as well as professor' – a telling step on the journey from academic to author.

Given this 'Austrian' publication history, it is scarcely surprising that Jochen Jung of Residenz, who would go on to publish both *Die Beschreibung des Unglücks* and *Unheimliche Heimat*, should have thought the author of these essays an Austrian when, in January 1984, he invited him to contribute an essay on Stifter to the volume *Österreichische Porträts* (*Austrian Portraits*), a collection of essays aiming to portray the lives and works of notable Austrians of the past from the point of view of 'the most significant and brightest' Austrian authors of the present, stipulating that it be 'not academic research but also not a journalistic piece': the resulting essay, 'To the Edge of Nature', forms the first essay in the present volume. However, as the correspondence from Jung, preserved among Sebald's papers in the Deutsches Literaturarchiv Marbach (DLA), makes clear, Sebald had by 1983 already approached him with the idea of a volume of collected essays or academic articles, an idea rejected by Jung on the grounds that such volumes did not form part of the Residenz publishing programme (in other words, unlikely to sell). That notwithstanding, it clearly provides the basis for a fruitful collaboration; Jung, curious about this new – as he supposes – Austrian author, is quick to appreciate his talent, writing that he scarcely knows of 'another author in this country whose textual interpretations and illuminations are so acutely perceptive, and at the same time so little academically boring as yours'. Thus encouraged, Sebald continued to submit essays to Jung, and by January 1985, having been particularly impressed by the essay on Hofmannsthal's *Andreas* ('A Venetian Cryptogram'), Jung is finally convinced: *Die Beschreibung des Unglücks* is published almost simultaneously with the longer-planned *Österreichische Porträts*, allowing Sebald to give it pride of place among his publications in his contributor's biography in that work. By the time *Unheimliche Heimat* is published six years later, Sebald has already made a name for himself as a writer with *Nach der Natur* (*After Nature*) and *Schwindel. Gefühle.* (*Vertigo*), and reviewers of the essay volume are quick to note the connections, reading the essays in this light, rather than as a purely academic work – as Sebald no doubt intended.

Thus although the essays in *Silent Catastrophes*, in common with Sebald's other articles on German and Austrian authors published in conference volumes, academic journals and indeed broadsheets in the 1970s and 1980s, may be seen as the products of an ambitious academic *Wunderkind*, following on as they do from the two books based on his MA and PhD theses on Carl Sternheim and Alfred Döblin respectively, nevertheless the boundaries between the essays and the 'prose fiction' for which Sebald later became justly famous are more porous than might at first appear. It is clear that, especially when it came to the essays in *Unheimliche Heimat* (*Strange Homeland*), for which he deliberately chose the subtitle

'Essays zur österreichischen Literatur' ('Essays on Austrian Literature'), Sebald was keen that these be received as *Literaturkritik* – what he thought of as the Anglo-Saxon genre of literary criticism, or belles-lettres – rather than as examples of *Literaturwissenschaft* (literature as an academic discipline) or as traditional *Germanistik*, with which, following his early student years in Freiburg, he had a decidedly ambivalent, not to say polemical, relationship. As he notes in a funding application, preserved among his papers in DLA, for his next, still rather vague, 'prose project' ('eine Prosaarbeit mit Bildern' – 'a prose work with images'), 'my literary-critical works represent an attempt to uphold the genre of essay vis-à-vis the strictures of academic literary studies' – something that one might paraphrase as 'putting the literary back into literary criticism' (N. C. Pages).

In this vein, an early review of *Schwindel. Gefühle.* (*Vertigo*) poses the pertinent question as to whether the author is 'ein dichtender Dozent oder ein dozierender Dichter' – 'a (university) teacher who writes, or a writer who teaches'; and reviews of *Unheimliche Heimat*, published the following year, tend to focus on the empathetic quality of the writing, and the way in which it succeeds in capturing and at times echoing the tone of the authors, such as Peter Altenberg and Joseph Roth, discussed. Anticipating the more self-consciously literary essays in *A Place in the Country*, these essays on Austrian literature can be read as both critical appreciations and biographical 'narratives', a quality noted approvingly by Jochen Jung. Impressed by Sebald's 'willingness to take risks on the most solid of foundations' in the 'absolutely brilliant' Stifter essay, he comments on Sebald's gift for seizing on the heart of the matter (the '*nervus rerum*') while showing 'the whole man' without feeling the need to 'fill in all the details of his life'.

The quasi-biographical approach of the essays – albeit deeply unfashionable in the critical discourse of the time – is identified by Neil Christian Pages as 'a critical turn to the kind of literary biography that readers familiar with Sebald's literary work will recognize', suggesting that, in the essays on Stifter, Sebald 'attempts to describe a kind of disappearing act and thus to give an account of the artist's life through his writing in the face of the conspicuous lack of overt autobiographical material. At the same time, this representation of the convergence of life and work relies on the depiction of an image that occupies a particular imagination, namely that of the reader Sebald.' Martin Swales, meanwhile, considers the way the essays show 'the need to define the world portrayed in any particular fiction and to extrapolate from this some sense of the universe of discourse and signification which the writer in question inhabits and to which he gives expression'.

This emphasis on reading, and a fascination with, and reimagining of, the often painful processes of creativity, the problematic interaction of life and work, suggests that Sebald's essays and literary work are in fact two sides of the same coin: moreover, as the publication history in *manuskripte* shows, their genesis (*Entstehungsgeschichte*) is tightly interwoven. While *After Nature* sets out in its three sections the reimagined lives of the painter Mathias Grünewald, the explorer Vitus Bering and an unnamed narrator, *Vertigo* intersperses episodes in 1813 and 1913, from the lives of the writers Henri Beyle (that is, Stendhal) and Kafka ('Dr K.') respectively, with the semi-autobiographical adventures of the unnamed narrator abroad and *in patria*. The four stories of *The Emigrants*, too, in common with the later *Austerlitz*, all centre around the reimagined, remembered or reconstructed lives of their respective protagonists. *Vertigo* in particular, with its Austrian and what may loosely be termed Austro-Hungarian settings, overlaps geographically with *Silent Catastrophes*: Ernst Herbeck's and Franz Kafka's affiliations to Klosterneuburg just outside Vienna; the excursion of the former and the *Vertigo* narrator to Altenberg, the town on the Danube which Peter Altenberg adopted as his own elective *Heimat*; Vienna itself, where he and so many of these authors spent their days pacing the streets or sitting in cafés; and Venice, where, arguably, all these intersect.

This overlap of fiction and research is supported by evidence of several research trips funded by the British Academy undertaken by Sebald during periods of research leave in the 1980s. In the autumn term of 1980, a field trip to research 'problems of literature and psychopathology' took in Klosterneuburg, Vienna, Venice, Sonthofen, Innsbruck and Wertach, dovetailing neatly with the narrator's travels in 'All'estero' and 'Ritorno in patria' in *Vertigo*, where the narrator recounts a visit to Ernst Herbeck; indeed, the essay on Herbeck in the present volume dates from late 1980. In the summer of 1983, a further grant from the British Academy took Sebald to Linz and Graz for research on Stifter and visits to Peter Handke and Gerhard Roth. In the summer of 1987, a further grant to research 'Heimat and Exil. Austrian Literature of the 19th and 20th centuries' – in other words, *Unheimliche Heimat* – again traced a similar itinerary, taking in Salzburg, Vienna, Milan, Verona, Riva and Innsbruck, as well as Sonthofen and Munich. Research for the essays and the settings of the contemporaneous fictional work thus appear as inextricably linked.

Although, as the early publication history in *manuskripte* shows, the genesis of the stories in *Vertigo* and *The Emigrants* overlaps – there is evidence to suggest they originally formed part of a single 'prose project' – parallels may nonetheless be drawn between the preoccupations of the essays in the earlier volume, *Die Beschreibung des Unglücks*, with their focus on what Sebald calls 'das Unglück des schreibenden Subjekts' ('the unhappiness or misfortune of the writing subject': below p. 6) and *Schwindel. Gefühle.* (*Vertigo*) with its stories from the lives of Stendhal and Kafka, and its disoriented first-person narrator adrift in Vienna and Venice. The second volume of essays, *Unheimliche Heimat*, published the following year, with its focus on writers 'far from home', more closely mirrors the overarching theme of *Die Ausgewanderten* (*The Emigrants*). However, as the final story in *Vertigo* 'Ritorno in patria' shows, even – or especially – at 'home' one may feel far more estranged than 'All'estero' – abroad. As Sebald writes in his Introduction to *Die Beschreibung des Unglücks*, 'It may be that it is precisely the narrowness and provincialism of the home country, the *Heimat*, which actively incites emigration to the most far-flung corners of the earth' (below p. 4); and the sense of being an 'expatriate' or 'emigrant' remains all-pervasive, even, or especially, when at home, in 'die fremdgewordene Heimat' ('the home country grown strange'), as Sebald writes in *A Place in the Country* of the protagonists in Keller's 'A Village Romeo and Juliet'. Indeed, in the twentieth century the Austrian *Heimat* becomes 'unheimlich' – not just 'unhomely' but both hostile and uncanny, strange in both senses, both for writers of Jewish extraction (featured in ten of the nineteen essays here) and for those of the post-war generation; something of course even more true of Germany, which Sebald himself chose to leave, first for Switzerland, then for England, at an early age. 'How much home does a person need?' asks the displaced Jean Améry, while Kolleritsch, founder of *manuskripte*, argues that home, *Heimat*, is 'a mirage' – a place, Sebald writes in the essay in the *Trans-Garde* volume, 'where none has ever been' and yet which 'those of us who have left it still believe we are on the point of returning to. [. . .] The imaginary or illusory status the idea of home necessarily entails came about, historically speaking, from the fact that remembering it was always a matter for those who had had to leave it.' In this sense, the essays in *Silent Catastrophes* may be said to trace an alternative Austrian literary tradition of what Sebald calls 'extraterritorial writing', 'from Altenberg and Schnitzler, Kafka and Wittgenstein down to Broch and Musil', and on down to the contemporary writers from the Grazer Gruppe with whom he identifies: a 'vaterlandslose Literatur' – a literature without a Fatherland.

In his Introduction to *Unheimliche Heimat*, Sebald rationalizes the differences between the two essay volumes thus: 'Whereas [*Die Beschreibung des Unglücks*] was more preoccupied with the psychological factors which govern writing, [*Unheimliche Heimat*] is concerned more with the social determinants of the literary world view, although naturally the one can never be completely separated from the other' (below p. 219). And while the preoccupation with 'ill-starred lives', victims of catastrophes individual and historical – as Sebald writes, 'the high incidence of ill-starred lives in the history of Austrian literature is, to say the least, somewhat uncanny' – may seem at first to suggest, as noted above, a broadly biographical approach, this is of course not to suggest that Sebald's critical and methodological approach is of a 'one size fits all' variety which would 'force everything into a single critical or theoretical mould' (below p. 3). Reflecting his own interest in interdisciplinarity and different theoretical and critical approaches, and in common with 'that conscious insouciance with which Austrian literature is so often pleased to disregard traditional boundaries', in these essays he draws on a wide, indeed 'eclectic' range of methodologies, citing authorities from Freud to Foucault, from Benjamin (ever-present in Sebald's work) to Hans Blumenberg, Lévi-Strauss to Deleuze and Guattari.

Indeed, the writers focused on in what one might term Sebald's 'case studies', for all that many are now canonical, tend to be themselves in one way or another 'on the margins', 'liminal figures' (N. C. Pages), cast as outsiders either socially or psychologically, exiles literal and metaphorical: though, as the example of Kafka shows, it is perfectly possible for their works to be both classed as *littérature mineure* and co-opted into the canon at one and the same time. As with, say, Henry Selwyn in *The Emigrants*, both essays and prose fiction lay bare the ways in which the veneer of bourgeois respectability can conceal a deep inner estrangement from the milieu, as true of Stifter as, for different reasons, of Kafka. The struggle to assimilate and the literal expatriation of many of the writers from their original *Heimat* during the last two centuries naturally plays a part. Moreover, *Die Beschreibung des Unglücks* in particular presents a critique of the bourgeois conventions of heteronormative love and marriage, a state compared unfavourably, for example in the essays on Stifter, to the celibate state of the bachelor (or widower), whose 'single state represents the positive contrast to the frustrations and tensions of marriage' (below p. 35). Indeed, the bachelor, as Deleuze and Guattari write, citing Kafka, is 'the deterritorialized, the one who has neither "centre" nor "any great complex of possessions"' (below p. 173). However, Sebald's essay on Herbeck does concede that 'all that is left for the unhappy victim of unrequited love is to retreat into a life of celibacy' (below p. 172), a fate of many of the writers – or their subjects – here. That these essays deal exclusively with male authors – a reference to Ingeborg Bachmann in the essay on Jean Améry aside – is, however, not something particularly unusual given the still male-dominated outlook of the Austrian literary scene – and indeed of *Germanistik* – at the time. Nevertheless, an early draft of the Contents list for *Unheimliche Heimat* in Sebald's archive (*Nachlass*) in DLA does suggest the possible inclusion of Marianne Fritz (as well as Christoph Ransmayr) in the final chapter.

The description of the unhappiness and misfortunes of the writing subject, 'that peculiar behavioural disturbance which causes every emotion to be transformed into letters on the page', as he writes in the Foreword to *Logis in einem Landhaus* (*A Place in the Country*), is, then, a constant theme of both Sebald's academic and creative work: unlucky in love, tortured by the business of writing – for 'there seems to be no remedy for the vice of literature' – a clouded picture indeed. Yet Jochen Jung, the perceptive first reader and publisher of these essays, describes Sebald's letters, written on the ancient typewriter 'with its letters bouncing merrily up and down', on which many of the essays here were composed, as characterized by a 'heitere Melancholie' – a cheerful melancholy. Echoes of this quality may surely also be discerned in the essays which, for all the seriousness of the subject matter, are shot through with flashes of Sebald's characteristic dry wit, revealed in a turn of phrase here, a lapse into French there, or on occasion, when the subject of the essay proves rebarbatively resistant to his usual empathetic approach, a – borderline sarcastic – polemical attack.

Although they date in the main from the 1980s, an era before the all-too-brief glimmers of hope offered by the events of 1989, these essays speak urgently to current issues of migration, displacement, environmental catastrophe and existential crisis. Yet while the brooding presence of Dürer's *Melencolia* seems inescapable, the melancholic stance – which is also a distance – is a contemplative one, a counsel not of despair but of 'resistance' (*Widerstand*), as Sebald writes in the Foreword to *Die Beschreibung des Unglücks* [below p. 7]:

> Melancholy, the contemplation of disaster in progress, has, however, nothing in common with a desire for death. It is a form of resistance. And on the level of art, in particular, its function is anything but reactive or reactionary. When, with a fixed stare, Melancholy considers once more how things could have come to this, it becomes clear that the mechanics of hopelessness are identical to those which drive our knowledge and insight. The description of misfortune contains within it the possibility of its overcoming.

A note on the text and translation

W. G. Sebald called translation – about which he cared deeply, having set up and directed the British Centre for Literary Translation at UEA in 1988 – an 'infernally complicated business'; and the translator of Sebald's essays faces a set of challenges which both intersects with and differs from those of translating his prose fiction. If the essays in *Logis in einem Landhaus* (*A Place in the Country*) offer a glimpse into the writer's workshop, with passages from favourite writers and considerations of how they achieve their effects of 'light and dark', the narrative thrust, carried in the prose fiction and to an extent in the essays in *Logis* by 'the unrolling of the narrative sentence after lovely sentence', as Sebald writes of Gottfried Keller, is replaced in his earlier, more 'academic' essays – his own literary ambitions for them notwithstanding – by the often idiosyncratic, indeed iconoclastic twists and turns of the argument and a highly selective, not to say eclectic, use of quotation and paraphrase from the texts discussed, as well as from secondary literature and theory. There are many dense and complex passages, freighted with technical terms (not to mention occasional jargon) from psychology, sociology, anthropology, philosophy and critical theory; nevertheless, where Sebald examines the prose style of an admired author, for example Adalbert Stifter (one of his favourite authors, as he says in more than one interview, precisely on the basis of what is achieved by the style) or Joseph Roth, it is possible to hear what in his fiction is later identified as the 'Sebald Sound' coming through in the cadencing of the sentences and the placing of words. As his last PhD student Florian Radvan notes, 'the Sebald Sound also characterizes many of his academic texts.'

All this can make for a sometimes uneven register; what is more, Sebald's is a polyphonic text, sprinkled with Gallicisms and quotations from French, English and Italian, as one might perhaps expect from one who has spent his professional life abroad (indeed, three of the essays here are reproduced in his own original English versions). Academic German also makes liberal use of *Fremdwörter*, loan words, which present a particular challenge to the translator, as not only are they often used to reinforce something which has already been stated in German (famous for its abstract and compound nouns), but they also rarely correspond exactly to what appears to be an almost identical term in English. The essays are also generously illustrated with quotations from the texts discussed; and as frequently with paraphrases, as Sebald adapts the phrasing of the text to fit his German sentence – and sometimes his argument – not always, it has to be said, completely accurately. As with Sebald's prose fiction, so in the essays these different 'voices' of the text need to be retained in the translation. While there are no such finely modulated distinctions as are found, for example, between the narratorial and protagonist's voice in *Austerlitz* – themselves made up of an intarsia of literary resonances and quotations – the essays nevertheless also echo the subtle contrasts between the authorial voice, the voice of the author quoted and the – sometimes heavily ironized – language of earlier or contemporary criticism.

One way of attempting to preserve this layering in the translated text is by quoting from an existing English translation (always assuming that one exists), a method which has however to be deployed with caution, as some of the stylistic features which Sebald so admires, and which indeed form an intrinsic part of the attraction the subjects of the essays hold for him, do not necessarily carry the same emphasis or resonance within the overall context of a given published translation. In the present volume, where a published translation of a given text is accessible, I have used this translation. However, it has sometimes been necessary to adapt the published translation so as to reflect more accurately the point Sebald is making in the German; this has been indicated in the relevant endnote. Where Sebald quotes in English, this has been noted; in the case of works having both an English and a German version, as is the case with Charles Sealsfield, I have followed the English version where possible, noting where it – and Sebald's quotation – diverges from the German version he quotes. In the case of the not infrequent quotations and mottos in French and Italian, which Sebald on the whole does not translate, a translation has been included in the Translator's Notes. These latter are indicated in the text by note cues, usually lower-case roman numerals but in a few cases alphabetic. Sebald's own endnotes also need a word of explanation: in the strictly analogue age to which he resolutely adhered, he sometimes economized on reference notes by simply repeating the number where more than one quotation is from the same page of the source, so that, for example, one may find two notes numbered 30, an idiosyncrasy to which none of his journal or Residenz editors seem, in those pre-digital days, to have had any objection, and which has been retained here to maintain consistency with the German text.

Three of the essays in the present volume are reproduced in Sebald's original English versions: the two essays on Kafka, 'The Undiscover'd Country – The Death Motif in Kafka's *Castle*' and 'The Law of Ignominy – Authority, Messianism and Exile in Kafka's *Castle*', first published in English in the 1970s, and the essay on Bernhard, 'Wo die Dunkelheit den Strick zuzieht [Where Darkness Draws Tight the Noose] – Some Marginal Notes on Thomas Bernhard', an English typescript of which, presumably a conference paper, I discovered in his *Nachlass* in DLA Marbach and which is published here in English for the first time. In the case of this last essay, in order to preserve the integrity of Sebald's text, translations of the original German quotations have been included as footnotes. In general, however, quotations are provided only in translation, references to which have been silently added to Sebald's own references in the endnotes, separated by a semi-colon (in such cases, as will be evident, 'Ibid.' refers only to Sebald's reference). The sole exception is the essay 'A Small Traverse', where the highly idiosyncratic poems by Ernst Herbeck are quoted first in the original

German, followed by an English translation. In all cases where no published English translations are referenced in the endnotes, the translations are my own. For clarity, further details, for example headings or section numbers, have on occasion been added to Sebald's references in the endnotes. Inaccurate quotation, as sometimes occurs, has either been silently corrected, or noted in square brackets in the endnotes, as the occasion demands.

Finally, to end at the beginning, mention should be made of the first and perhaps greatest obstacle to the translation of these essays, namely the German titles of the two respective volumes. Happy the French translator who can render *Die Beschreibung des Unglücks* without further ado as *La Description du malheur*. As with the equivalent French terms *malheur* and *bonheur*, 'Unglück' – the opposite of 'Glück', meaning happiness, luck or (good) fortune – covers a range of meanings, from unhappiness through misfortune to disaster; often all three meanings can resonate in the German text. For this reason, although 'misfortune' is the most common translation used, I have sometimes flagged the reference to 'Unglück', which runs like a leitmotif through the essays of the first volume in particular; from time to time, in keeping with the title of the present volume, I have also used 'catastrophe'. A pencil note in his papers in the DLA *Nachlass* shows Sebald trying out numerous variations of the title, most featuring 'Unglück', each more untranslatable than the last. For the second volume, *Unheimliche Heimat*, Sebald was, as other notes suggest, until quite a late stage working with the – if anything even less translatable – title 'Ungute Heimat'. 'Ungut', literally un-good, but not quite as definite as bad – was one of Sebald's characteristic phrases: 'eine ungute Sache' or 'eine ungute Geschichte', he might comment ironically on, for example, a particularly heinous aspect of university affairs, where in English one might say 'a bad business'. 'Heimat' (home, homeland) is so specific to the German-speaking situation that it has mainly been left in German, while 'unheimlich' literally means 'unhomely', though it also has the sense of 'strange' or uncanny. Although 'unhomely' could capture the pun and alliteration, it seemed to the present translator in fact too homely; the air of strangeness and estrangement in 'strange' seemed to capture the paradox inherent in the title better. As for the other possible titles suggested in Sebald's manuscript notes in the *Nachlass*, neither 'Ausserfern' – a dialect word for the region of Austria in the Tyrol just over the border from Sebald's native Wertach, but literally meaning 'outer (or outside) far' – nor the more straightforward 'Heimatlos' ('homeless') offer the translator better prospects. While the Spanish and Portuguese translations, compiling selections from both volumes, opt to preserve the alliteration with *Pútrida Patria* and *Pátria Apátrida* respectively, the prize must go to the French translation for the stroke of utter genius which is *Amère patrie*; literally bitter homeland, but containing within it the implicit contrast of mother country and fatherland.

Jo Catling
Norwich, June 2024

PART ONE
The Description of Misfortune
On Austrian Literature from Stifter to Handke

PART ONE

Foreword

The essays collected in the present volume make no claims to offer a new panoramic survey of Austrian literature, nor is there any intention to force everything into a single critical or theoretical mould. Rather, the various analyses aim to focus on some of the specific complexities which seem to be a defining feature of Austrian literature – if indeed such a thing can be said to exist. This eclectic method, which does not hesitate to alter its critical approach according to the particular difficulties of each case, is in keeping with that conscious insouciance with which Austrian literature is so often pleased to disregard traditional boundaries, such as, for example, those which divide its own domain from, say, that of science. Austrian literature, then, is not merely a pre-school[1] for psychology; around the turn of the century, and in the decades which follow, its psychological insights, even if not systematically formulated, are in many ways equal to, and indeed at times ahead of, those of psychoanalysis. What the works of Hofmannsthal and Schnitzler have to offer by way of case studies to the investigation of psychological development and disturbance goes far beyond mere illustration, presenting a nuanced range of psychological insights such as are all too easily stifled by the dogmatic tendencies so characteristic of science. If it is true that one should not read Schnitzler without Freud, then the reverse is equally true. No less important, it seems to me, is

Canetti's contribution to our understanding of paranoid structures, or Peter Handke's microscopically accurate descriptions of acute schizophrenic states. The precision of observation and language with which these authors operate shines such an intense spotlight on the nature of human *dérangement* that the traditional teachings of psychology, being first and foremost concerned with the classification and administration of suffering, appear by comparison a relatively superficial and soulless affair.

It is difficult to determine where the interest in border crossings, so prevalent in Austrian literature, originates, and whether it might be related to the fact that what remains of Austria – as the end result of a protracted historical debacle – is, as Herzmanovsky-Orlando cryptically remarks, 'the one and only neighbouring state [*Nachbarland*] in the world': a statement which should roughly be interpreted as meaning that, in Austria, if one but makes a start on the business of thinking, it is not long before the point is reached where familiar territory is left behind and one is confronted with a whole different set of systems. It may be that it is precisely the narrowness and provincialism of the home country, the *Heimat*, which actively incites emigration to the most far-flung corners of the earth – a recurring theme in Austrian literature from the time of Charles Sealsfield onwards.[ii] Whether those who disappear[iii] in this fashion end up in the Jacinto, as landscape painters in the Andes or as extras in the *Naturtheater* of Oklahoma[iv] – or, after a spell in the far north, set out on a slow homecoming[v] via the South of France – is another story. Either way, though, the first crossing of the border brings with it the irrevocable loss of all that is familiar.

In this context it should also be remembered that Austria – or at least Vienna – was for a long time also a place of immigration, representing as it did the first entrepôt and emporium en route from the provinces to the wider world. And even those immigrants most willing to assimilate brought with them a quantum of that weighty and difficult quality of distance and strangeness, which is never quite resolved but becomes a ferment in a constantly shifting social and psychological system of values which is at the same time permeated by a number of archaic taboos.

From 1896 to 1907, the Kafka family lived in an apartment in the Zeltnergasse in Prague. One of the windows in this apartment looked out, not on to the outside world, but into the interior of the Teynkirche[vi] which contained, it was said, the grave of a Jewish boy named Simon Abeles, killed by his father because he wished to convert to Christianity. If one tries to imagine the mixed feelings with which, from this singular vantage point, the young Franz Kafka may have followed, say, the lugubrious rituals of the Good Friday services, one can perhaps get an idea of how acute — extreme proximity notwithstanding — a sense of foreignness could be in the process of assimilation.

Frictions of this kind are what gave rise both to so-called Austrian culture and to its discontents — a culture whose defining characteristic was the fact that it made self-criticism into its guiding principle. This resulted, at the turn of the century, in an aesthetic and ethical calculation of the utmost complexity, designed to compensate for the deficit incurred as a result of endorsing bourgeois society with all its intrinsic authority, value systems and works of art. How challenging were the demands of this scenario is demonstrated not only in the cabbalistic imbroglios of Kafka's oeuvre, but also in the fact that not even Hofmannsthal, a number of significant compromises notwithstanding, really succeeded in achieving recognition as a figure of national importance. Like Kafka, in the end he too remained an outsider.

Related to the set of problems outlined here is another subject central to my investigations, namely the unhappiness or misfortune [*Unglück*][vii] of the writing subject – something often remarked upon as a fundamental characteristic of Austrian literature. Now of course those who take up the profession of writing are not, as a general rule, the most lighthearted of folk. How else would they come to be involved in the impossible business of trying to find the truth? Nevertheless, the high incidence of ill-starred lives in the history of Austrian literature is, to say the least, somewhat uncanny. Raimund's premature phobia of dying, Nestroy's fear of being buried alive, Grillparzer's bouts of depression, the case of Stifter, Schnitzler's references on almost every page of his journal to his fits of melancholy, Hofmannsthal's feelings of alienation, the suicide of poor Weininger, Kafka's forty-year-long tactical withdrawal from life, Musil's solipsism, Roth's addiction to alcohol, Horvath's apparently so logical end – all this has frequently led to an emphasis on the seemingly intrinsic negative tendencies of Austrian literature. The theory that a melancholic disposition is the correlative of a peculiarly protracted political decline, and thus identical with the inability to accept the changing times – identical with the wish to prolong Habsburg rule in a Habsburg myth[viii] – is, while in many respects plausible, in the end rather a blinkered view.

Certainly, authors such as Grillparzer, Stifter, Hofmannsthal, Kafka and Bernhard consider progress to be a loss-making business. It would, however, be wrong to use this as grounds for moral or political reproach. Kafka's insight that all our inventions are devised at the moment of crashing[ix] can no longer be readily dismissed. The slow death of nature, then as now our sole means of survival, is the ever more obvious confirmation of this view. Melancholy, the contemplation of disaster[x] in progress, has, however, nothing in common with a desire for death. It is a form of resistance. And on the level of art, in particular, its function is anything but reactive or reactionary. When, with a fixed stare, Melancholy considers once more how things could have come to this, it becomes clear that the mechanics of hopelessness are identical to those which drive our knowledge and insight. The description of misfortune[xi] contains within it the possibility of its overcoming. There could be no clearer example of this than the two apparently so different authors, Bernhard and Handke. Each is, in his own way, of good cheer, notwithstanding the most acute of insights into the *historia calamitatum*. Neither Bernhard's peculiar brand of humour nor Handke's high seriousness could be realized as counterweights to the experience of misfortune and calamity[xii] other than through the medium of writing. Here we may refer to the story of Rabbi Chanoch, recalling the advice given by the teacher at the elementary school to a small boy who had started to cry during the lesson: 'Look at your book. If you look inside, you won't cry.'[xiii]

This parable of the bridge of letters spanning misery and consolation brings us to the category of teaching and learning, so important – in contrast to Imperial Germany – in the Austrian literary tradition; a subject to which, as far as I know, no one has yet drawn attention, probably because it stands in such glaring contrast to the far more conspicuous and – apparently – defeatist trait of melancholy. Stifter's provincial pedagogy; Karl Kraus, repetiteur to the nation; Kafka's didactic science; the wonderful scene in *Das Schloss* [*The Castle*] in which K. and the young boy Hans are learning from each other in the classroom; Canetti, who became a great teacher and remained a humble pupil; the hopes Wittgenstein pinned on life as a village schoolteacher; Bernhard's memories of his grandfather's philosophy; and Peter Handke's apprenticeship, always extended just that little bit longer: these are all aspects of an attitude which holds fast to the idea that it is worthwhile passing something on. Seen from this perspective, the expression of our personal unhappiness and collective misfortune[xiv] also places at our disposal an experience by means of which its opposite can be attained – even if only by the skin of our teeth.

It remains for me – *pénétré d'amitié et de reconnaissance* – to thank all those who have been more or less closely involved with the making of this book. They will know who they are. In particular I wish to express my thanks to the British Academy, who through their various grants have greatly facilitated the work on this book.

W. G. Sebald
Norwich, Spring 1985

To the Edge of Nature

An Essay on Stifter

> Sehen und Denken sind zwei Verrichtungen,
> deren eine nicht die andere erklärt.
>
> Seeing and thinking are two different things,
> the one does not explain the other.
>
> Franz von Baader

Much has been written about Adalbert Stifter, both hagiographical and disparaging, without however making the difficult beauty of his works any more accessible. At first it seemed as if Stifter was destined to go down in literary history as a Biedermeier poet of flowers and beetles. That, at least, was the role the Viennese salons of the *Vormärz*[1] had assigned him. Nowhere is the tone of sentimental reverence clearer than in the *billets doux* which Jenny Lind, the Swedish nightingale, sent to Stifter in the early spring of 1847, where she speaks of 'the wonderful evenings at my dear Frau Jager's house' and muses, somewhat theatrically, 'how strange that people are fated to find each other, understand and esteem each other – and then immediately have to part for ever! My dear Herr von Stifter! as long as I live I shall never forget you!'[1]

How far the thus ennobled 'Herr von Stifter' was affected by this touching declaration need not concern us here. At any rate, the sense of social incompatibility hinted at in Jenny Lind's words corresponds closely with Stifter's own feelings of inferiority, which, as he says, always made him feel rather apprehensive in the salons of the educated classes. 'Every time I enter polite society, I feel like a schoolboy in the presence of the headmaster, the priest, or indeed the bishop.'[2] The sense of constraint Stifter describes here is, no doubt, one of the reasons he never really made a name for himself among the better classes of society; however, this same discomfiture was also the prerequisite for the creation of an oeuvre in which human beings are depicted as strangers not only in society, but also in their first home, nature.

The profound seriousness of Stifter's work was a consequence of the progressive withdrawal from society of an author constitutionally incapable, either socially or psychologically, of living up to its expectations. During his time in Vienna, and particularly later, in Linz, in the Bavarian Forest, and up on the mountain at Kirchschlag, Stifter is writing in a kind of exile, and it is this which casts the long shadows across his prose, this the source of the melancholy that lifts him far above the gilt-edged volumes of the late bourgeois era. Stifter's affirmatory gestures were of no avail against the implicit vote of no confidence his stories contain. If, towards the end of his life and right up to the time of the First World War, Stifter was largely forgotten, this had less to do with exclusion by society – which would have liked to cultivate him – than with his own self-imposed isolation.

The rediscovery of Stifter took place in a literary climate filled with conviction as to its own poetic mission, which hailed the reserved prose writer as a kind of saint. It was Karl Kraus who set this in motion — albeit, as one might expect, in his own uniquely backhanded way — when, in 1916, he urged the 'novelist mercenaries and buccaneers of opinion and the word' to immolate themselves on Stifter's grave, 'upon the pyre of their grubby papers and quill pens'. Bahr saw in Stifter a successor to Goethe; Hesse in 1923 speaks of 'an ardent soul', 'the essence of true humanity', of 'seeking and finding' and 'the spirit of true reverence'; Hofmannsthal, two years later, of the 'crystal clear form' of Stifter's 'delicately sketched characters' and the 'secret spiral of European intellectual life'. [Stefan] George's disciple Bertram, in a speech given in 1928, cites qualities of 'simplicity and strength', 'loyalty and dream', 'peasant-like and Benedictine', 'folk-like and aristocratic', 'loyal to the tribe and pan-German', and a whole string of such and similar adjectival combinations.[3]

Views of this kind set the pattern and direction of Stifter reception for years to come. With their proverbial industriousness, the philologists set about perpetrating a conservative hagiography, a process which continued up to the 1960s and reached a dubious apotheosis in the pious paraphrasings of Emil Staiger and Walter Rehm. As Peter [J. P.] Stern has shown,[4] the paradox of this usurpation of Stifter by an affirmatory secondary literature is that it confers upon Stifter's work a veneer of timelessness, while itself remaining utterly in thrall to the prevailing *Zeitgeist*. For this reason, the almost infinite shelves of secondary literature contain little that might enlighten us as to the conflicts underlying the very deliberate order of Stifter's prose.[5] Thus it is that, after decades of oblivion — after being commandeered as the spirit of German Literature and the German Nation, forced into the mould of an Austrian *Heimat*-poet and principal witness to a culture of renunciation – only now, perhaps, can Stifter be read properly for the first time.

Some of the first obstacles to a reinterpretation of Stifter are the interpretations, as misleading as they are unavoidable, which he in all naïvety insisted on imposing on his texts, their hermetic tendencies notwithstanding. It is striking, though, that nowhere in his work does Stifter consciously explore or analyse the affirmative constructs of his work – for example his oft-quoted Christian humility, his pious secular pantheism, the assertion of the gentle law of nature, not to mention the strict moralism of his stories. Last vestiges of a philosophy of salvation embracing both nature and history, they can be preserved from dissolution solely by a process of constant and invariable reiteration. But the meaning thus explicitly proclaimed has little to do with the inherent truth of an oeuvre whose actual focus is, by contrast, a profound agnosticism, and a pessimism extending to the cosmos as a whole. In Stifter's description of the world, there exists from the outset the uneasy suspicion that – as Kafka's fictional dog driven by a perverse desire for knowledge later puts it – 'something was not quite right from the very beginning, a small rift in the fabric of things,'[6] and that this rift opens up to reveal the whole insanity of natural and social life. And if Kafka's restless protagonist admits that 'in the middle of the most solemn public functions'[6] he is gripped by a sense of discomfort, then this is no less true of the author of *Witiko*, whose attempt at a grandiose *mise-en-scène* of our collective history would turn out to be the most strange and hollow of all his works. Here there can no longer be any question of the concordance between secular and sacred history so dramatically enacted in the *Haupt- und Staatsaktionen* [chief and state plays] of baroque theatre.

Stifter is writing at a point in history where the notion of universal meaning is beginning to atrophy. And if – as Emil Staiger suggested – Stifter was actually a priest celebrating one last time the liturgy of an absolute order, then – like the poor priest in Kafka's *Ein Landarzt* [*A Country Doctor*] – he was one who had long been secretly engaged in plucking his vestments to pieces.

The dissolution of the metaphysical world order is reflected in the shattering materialism, pervading the whole of Stifter's work, in which, perhaps, by sheer force of observation, something of the former meaning of the world may yet be salvaged. The scrupulous registering of the most minute details, the endless enumeration of what – strangely enough – is actually there: all bear the signs of a lack of belief, and mark the point at which even the bourgeois doctrine of salvation could no longer be sustained by the progressive unfolding of the *Weltgeist* [World Spirit]. The singular objectivism of Stifter's prose – which finds a more self-conscious equivalent in the work of his contemporary, Flaubert – places its faith in objects in the hope of lasting existence, and yet, precisely through this identification, makes apparent within them the force of time's decay. The houses, the furnishings, the household implements, the clothes, the faded letters, all these minutely described objects which form such a striking contrast to the monotone economy of Stifter's prose, in the end bear witness to nothing more than their own existence. And how little this can be relied upon is demonstrated in the story *Das alte Siegel* [*The Ancient Seal*], when Hugo, who for many weeks has paid daily visits to the extraordinarily beautiful woman in the little white house surrounded by linden trees, suddenly finds the locus of his erotic dreams and desires abandoned and empty. Everything is open, but there is nothing left. On the stairs lie dust and refuse, and 'the air from the open sky blew through the rooms . . . and the walls along which furniture, the marble table, the mirror and other things had been ranged now stood bare.'[7] The allegory of the deserted interior, with nothing remaining but the bitterness of disappointment, is the hidden side of Stifter's materialism, where, beneath the sober description of the visible world, there always lurks the fear that tomorrow all might be lost – not only love for another person, but also everything with which we have surrounded ourselves, even Nature in all her greenery, and the mountains 'in their ancient splendour and glory', and 'perhaps even this beauteous, congenial earth which now seems to us so firmly grounded and built for all eternity'.[8]

Doubtless the reason for Stifter's extreme emotional attachment in his writing to what he most feared to lose can be found in his own psychological and social predispositions, something which, however, he seems scarcely to have reflected upon. It is significant that his attempts at autobiography never went beyond a few preliminary sketches. The exception, his curious recollection of his early childhood memories, is itself only fragmentary. Similarly, he never addresses his repeated failure to become established in bourgeois society, whether critically – with regard to the hierarchical organization of society – or self-critically. Although he sometimes appears to have emancipated himself from the limitations of his – by comparison with the cultured classes – relatively underprivileged origins, he never completely succeeded in banishing the spectres of poverty and *déclassement* which haunted him from the age of twelve, on account of the altered circumstances brought about by the early death of his father. It is especially difficult to grasp why the ambitious, and in many respects exceedingly talented and adaptable, young scholar never manages to bring his studies to any regular conclusion, nor why he continually contrives, at the decisive moment, to thwart his own strenuous efforts to achieve social recognition. Until the age of forty-five, when he is appointed *Oberschulrat* [Inspector of Schools] for Upper Austria, his financial situation was so precarious that he was continually beleaguered by creditors, and on several occasions had his assets seized. The years of service as a private tutor, which circumstances obliged him to undertake during his time in Vienna, will also have had a lasting effect on his self-esteem, ensuring that, in common with so many writers from the lower-middle classes, he remained – out of a combination of humiliation and envy – in thrall to a class to which he himself did not belong. Stifter's appointment as Inspector of Schools had little effect on his malaise, since, as he himself soon realized, this office, and the recognition and respectability it implied, was achieved at the cost of what was in effect a banishment to the provinces. Nor – because of the higher expenses associated with his post – did he succeed in achieving anything like financial security. The hopes he from time to time pinned on the state lottery were just as ill-advised as his stock-market speculations, both symptoms of a deeply insecure existence which at the same time craved security. Petitions to his publishers, and even to relatives, remain a constant feature of Stifter's correspondence. The fact that, in contrast to much of bourgeois narrative literature, money plays almost no part in his work, indicates just how keenly the sense of inadequacy associated with his own impecunity must have affected him.

If we also take into account Stifter's own personal misfortunes [*Unglück*] – his father's fatal accident, his boarding-school education, his unrequited love for Fanny Greipl, his long years of marriage to the almost illiterate Amalie, the early death of his first foster daughter and the suicide of the second, Juliane, who drowned herself in the Danube at the age of eighteen, the frustrations of life as a civil servant, the endless drudgery of his art and the increasingly debilitating effects of his illness – if we take all this into account, then it is by no means illogical that he should in the end have taken his own life at the age of sixty-three. For far too long he had been struggling to maintain a semblance of self-control. The photographs we have of him show an increasingly melancholic and morose character, who to all intents and purposes appears to have systematically destroyed himself emotionally. However, the long overdue pathography of Stifter cannot easily be written, given that up to the last he remained faithful to his affirmatory precepts, scarcely ever expressing anything of his inner nightmares. What we do know, though, is that Stifter – another hunger artist! – mercilessly and systematically ate his way to an early grave via meals of truly grotesque proportions, the description and anticipation of which ultimately take up almost as much space in his correspondence as the enumeration of the increasingly prevalent symptoms of his illness. The exact correlation between his apparently insurmountable compulsive eating and the twelve-year-old's declared intention, on hearing of his father's death, of refusing all food needs no comment here. That Stifter's excessive eating habits indicate a pathological disposition is surely indisputable. What is truly pathological, though, is a pattern of behaviour which, in an attempt at healing, repeatedly turns the knife in the wound in exactly the same place, ritually re-enacting anew the removal or withdrawing of a beloved person or other object of affection. How this is expressed in Stifter's work will be shown in what follows, but first we will attempt to demonstrate, at least in outline, his systematic attempts to transcend his own misfortune [*Unglück*].

In the nineteenth-century novel, conflicts and crises – whether financial, social or psychological in nature – constitute the dynamic centres of the narrative; conflicts and crises which have developed 'over the course of time' become acute, ultimately resulting in a stage of dissolution, be it of social structures or of individual fates. The idea that all this occurs *in the course of time* is a definition of the novel which, in *Der Nachsommer* [*Indian Summer*], Stifter seeks to counteract.[9] Although Stifter refers to *Der Nachsommer* as an 'Erzählung' [story], what we are in fact dealing with here is a utopian blueprint for a model universe located outside of time, in a transcendental realm where everything is in harmony, right down to the very last detail. Since the notion of time is incompatible with that of utopia, in *Der Nachsommer* time, the measure of all things, appears not to pass at all. Tellingly, Stifter solves the problem this creates for him as narrator by having his characters progress from one mealtime to the next. Statements such as 'After taking afternoon tea . . . After breakfast . . . After we had parted in the dining room . . .'[ii] etc., which occur with symptomatic frequency, help us to make it through the essentially identical days. The suspension of time corresponds to the painstakingly executed need for spatialization which is such a striking feature throughout *Der Nachsommer*. From the motionless souls of the protagonists, via the curious predilection for cold, empty interiors, the museum-like aspect of the marble hall and the apparently immutable interior layouts, down to the parcelling up of nature into lots and the repeated invocation of very similar panoramic vistas of distant regions, everything is completely in keeping with the absolute stillness of the spaces which these utopian prospects regularly evoke – which naturally goes some way to explaining the slightly paranoid atmosphere of this extremely rationalistic work. Nowhere in *Der Nachsommer* does one encounter a living being that does not have a preordained place in the overall plan of this *orbis pictus*. Any disruptive elements, like the redstart, are ruthlessly eliminated, and in the surrounding landscape there seem to be as few people and animals as in the huge expanse of forest surrounding Hauenstein in Bernhard's *Verstörung* ['Disturbance', translated as *Gargoyles*],[iii] in which the eccentric industrialist, having withdrawn to the Saurau hunting lodge in order to think, has all the animals shot so that they can no longer disturb the silence. Likewise, on the Isle of the Blessed which Stifter creates for the characters of *Der Nachsommer*, life is no longer alive. The ideal of a state of purity can only be conveyed by means of a hermetic style in which the beautiful concept of a homeostatic equilibrium within human relationships, and between man and nature, can be ontologically established once and for all. The specific stylistic artistic equivalent of this programme is the still life, or *nature morte*, which epitomizes Stifter's imagistic mode of representation.

As will be shown in more detail below, the lovingly detailed description of a dead person or thing represents the affective centre of Stifter's imagination. In such description, he finds a means of eluding suffering in and at the hands of time, a suffering perpetuated by the constant and iterative use of the imperfect tense of narrative prose. In this respect, Arno Schmidt's criticism — one shared, with reservations, by Claudio Magris — that, in *Der Nachsommer*, Stifter composed a quietist work corresponding to a darkly reactionary political position, falls short of the mark, inasmuch as Stifter's consciously constructed utopia 'is as far removed from an affirmation of what exists as its helpless form is from the latter's actual sublimation [*Aufhebung*]'.[10] Seen in this light, it makes little sense to equate Stifter's prose idyll with a resigned or conservative escapism, the more so when one considers that *Der Nachsommer* leaves not only so-called reality, but also the aims and methods of the utopian genre, far behind. Here, it is not only a question of establishing the best of all possible constitutions of society, as a counterpoint to its actual state of corruption; rather, and far more radically, the aim is a release from the uncanny nature [*Unheimlichkeit*] of time itself. Although this has scarcely been recognized to date, Stifter's images of a calm domestic idyll bear undeniably eschatological traits. The prose of *Der Nachsommer* reads like a catalogue of the Last Things, since everything in it appears under the aspect of death — or, as the case may be, of eternity.

Critics have variously commented on the apocalyptic dimension in Stifter's work, the abrupt turns of terror and the sudden irruption of monstrous and unfathomable events. Without warning, everything goes dark; the sun disappears; a dark abyss or terrible chasm opens up; or a lightning bolt strikes from a clear blue sky. Scenarios like these, with their specific atmospheric detail invoking an indifferent destructive force — in one might say almost heretical contrast to Stifter's ultramontane consciousness — are part of the traditional arsenal of nineteenth-century prose literature. It is telling, though, that Stifter elevates this extreme unpredictability — for example, of the weather — to a general principle, as illustrated in the unearthly pyrotechnics of the stories *Der Condor* [*The Condor*] and *Abdias*, which, within the framework of an affirmative narrative tradition stretched almost to breaking point, present a positively antinomian view of the world.

However, it is not solely the view of an indifferent world order — presented in such radical form in literature for the first time – which is characteristic of Stifter's position; no less significant is his attempt – with the lightest of colours, gradually resolving into a bright monochrome, indeed to an absolute whiteness – to bring about, so to speak in the opposite direction, a dematerialization of the world.[11] *Der Nachsommer* is the vision of a secularized heaven, and as such is one of the rare examples in literature of a sustained symbolic representation of an eschatological vision which has no need of the Apocalypse. Since it is easier by far to instil fear than joy, even in theology the convincing representation of heaven has always been the most difficult of undertakings. And in bourgeois literature in particular, representations of the celestial beauty of the soul inevitably tend to hover on the verge of kitsch. Stifter avoids this danger, since he neither makes a doctrine of his colour theory nor allows it to descend to the level of the merely ornamental. The touches of colour which he inserts, with the utmost circumspection and rigour, into the black and white calligraphy of his prose are the abstract equivalents of an extremely subjective emotionality which could only ever be expressed directly in a new life.

Possibly Stifter's endeavours to immortalize beauty are most readily grasped in his descriptions of nature. In the image of the landscape, inviting us to enter, the boundaries between objective reality and subjective imagination become blurred, and nature is no longer merely that which surrounds us, in all its utter strangeness, but rather life on a larger scale, analogous to our own.

> Far and wide the beautiful countryside spread out before me. Not only did I see, at noon and evening, the blue and ever bluer swathes of the great forest outlined against the sky – in the morning and at midnight I saw hills, and slopes,

and plains, and fields, and meadows, and villages, and the silver mirrors of ponds stretching away in the haze, as far as where the city of Prague in all its loveliness might lie.[12]

The poetic transformation of nature in the eye of the beholder conveys a concept of landscape in which civilization painlessly accommodates itself with that which it dominates. Via the lyrical gradations of the receding bands of blue and ever bluer ranges of hills, we come to the Elysian fields of a distant city which is as good as identified with the heavenly Jerusalem. What remains problematic, though, about such intimations of eternity, is that nature can only ever appear as 'beautiful' when seen from the viewpoint of civilization. Descriptions of nature – including literary ones – only came about with the commercial exploitation of the natural world, and there is something to be said for the idea that Stifter learned the art of landscape painting in prose from authors such as Cooper, Sealsfield and Irving, perhaps also from Alexander von Humboldt – authors in whose work, in terms of the history of ideas, the aesthetic representation of topography could already be seen in the context of colonialism. Stifter, of course, was anything but an expansionist. He sought to make himself at home in the narrowest of local spheres, and paradoxically it is precisely this limitation which allows him to confer on the technique of the description of nature – which for his predecessors was a largely unselfconscious and positivistic enterprise – a decisive moral aspect. Stifter was already aware that the identification of the beauty of nature represents the first step not only towards its redemption, but also towards its expropriation. The whole of the Fichtau, the epitome of a place embedded in nature, was once 'nothing but woods', as the landlord in the story *Prokopus* remarks. But now, says one of the guests, everything is changing, the woods are retreating and 'will have to retreat still further'.[13]

Nowhere in bourgeois literature before Stifter is there to be found a comparable scepticism with regard to the expansion of civilization. We can only speculate as to the reasons for this scepticism. Apart from his insight – astonishing for the time – into the functional relationship between natural and economic history, which, though demonstrated mostly by anachronistic examples, is easily a match for Marxian analysis, on a deeper psychological level Stifter's attitude to nature was probably governed by the 'feeling' that it is a crime even to gaze upon her. On the one hand, because the body of nature lying spread out before one evokes the unconscious body of a woman – one of the covert topoi of bourgeois descriptions of nature,[14] as a later pencil sketch by Stifter makes abundantly clear: an almost completely blank page with only the hint of the curved outline of a wood shaded in, one of those 'dark places' which the author also recalls in the autobiographical sketch about his earliest childhood.[15] On the other hand, because the eye – the original organ of possession and assimilation[16] – is of particular significance in Stifter's extremely visual work. As I have indicated above, for the compulsive eater Stifter, the assimilation and digestion of nature presented a moral and psychological dilemma with which he wrestled unsuccessfully throughout his life. Gaston Bachelard[iv] has referred to digestion – the source of our most avaricious desires – as the most potent form of realism.[17] There is no doubt that his conclusion that realists are good eaters is completely appropriate to Stifter's own way of life.

The fact that Stifter could lament mankind's encroachments

upon nature may be what redeemed him. To what extent his fears, fed by his pathological disposition, also touched an objective raw nerve is something we can only begin to measure today, now that the disappearance of nature in and around us appears irrevocable. Stifter's wooded landscapes are emblematic not only as documents of sentimental descriptions of nature, but as examples – going far beyond the state of scientific knowledge in his day – of a diagnostic insight into the entropic tendency of all natural systems. In *Die Mappe meines Urgroßvaters* [*My Great-Grandfather's Portfolio*], Ursula recalls in truly epic sentences what she has heard the doctor say: 'Everything is vanishing in the world, the birds in the air and the fish in the water. [. . .] When I was a girl,' she continues, 'the Glöckelbergau was teeming with lapwings and the Hinterhammerbach with crayfish, and now there is only the odd feather in the meadow and maybe one crayfish in the stream. No longer do you hear weeping in the air above the Kehrau on St Barbara's night, and you can no longer see your cloak beneath the chariot of stars;[v] at most a will-o'-the-wisp glimmers over the marshes, or the merman sits by the Moldau.'[18]

If, in the light of this philosophical lament at the dwindling substance and diversity of organic life, Stifter's major stories have come to appear as conservative and conservationist treatises, this is less an example of a politically reactionary attitude than of a Paracelsian *engagement*, opposed to the mere measuring, quantifying and exploitation of nature. In *Die Mappe meines Urgroßvaters* – although too late for the age of high capitalism – Stifter set out a practical guide for a mode of existence in which mankind and nature have equal rights. Together, the doctor and the Colonel work to protect nature in the interests of society. On the boulder-strewn hillside a wood is to be planted for future generations. 'As the trees grow, needles will fall to the ground and produce soil, and in time a beautiful, delightful and useful pinewood will stand on the hill.'[19] The balance set out here between aesthetic and economic criteria is one which, for Stifter too, was a genuinely imperilled state. That beauty does not pay is certainly a concept he will have been familiar with. Even for him, Thal ob Pirling lay in the distant past – how much more distant, then, for us.

How little trust Stifter may have placed in his hopes for a peaceful reproduction of life can also be seen in the fact that the goal of his desires and longings tended, ultimately, towards the inorganic. The true horizon of Stifter's landscapes is always the high mountain regions which can be seen at the furthest edge of the picture 'as if floating in a faint haze',[20] the region where – as Georg Simmel noted in his essay 'The Alps' – an 'unhistorical' realm begins 'where just ice and snow, but no green, no valley, no pulse of life exists', and where 'the associations with the human fate, which comes into being and passes away, are broken off, associations which in some way or another accompany all other landscapes.'[21] In the brilliant white transcendence of this realm, which illuminates all of Stifter's natural panoramas, we begin to sense that – as Simmel also says – 'life at its most intensive is redeemed by what no longer can be contained by its form.'[22]

In accordance with bourgeois literary convention, the image of nature in Stifter's work is directly related to his portrayal of female characters. Stifter's reverence for untouched nature finds a parallel not only in the predilection for child characters in his work, but also, even more clearly, in his evident preoccupation with the state of virginity and its violation. Bourgeois morality and bourgeois *pruderie* are not of themselves sufficient to explain his interest in the subject of virginity. Rather, the strikingly morbid aspect of Stifter's love stories indicates an imagination directly opposed to bourgeois morality, held in check by a complex set of rules of avoidance and denial. The internalization within the individual psyche of the taboo regarding forbidden erotic desires is – as can be seen in the 'classic cases' of [J. M. R.] Lenz and Hölderlin – part of an aetiology of pathological structures, where however the subjective development of inner deviance always has an objective correlative on a societal level.[23] In Stifter's case, as in that of Lenz or Hölderlin, this objective correlative was his employment as a private tutor, with all its contradictory dynamics of attraction and untouchability. Stifter reconciled the limitations imposed by his inferior social status with his sense of self by elevating the virginity and childlike innocence of the – for him – untouchable young ladies to the lodestar of his unacknowledged desires – which, however, only had the effect of strengthening still further the erotic attachment to the forbidden beings.

It is well known that a pronounced pedagogic talent often goes hand in hand with repressed paedophiliac desires. This, no doubt, will also have been true of Stifter, who appears to have been, or aspired to be, what is known as a 'begnadeter Lehrer' (gifted teacher). It is in the nature of this problematic issue that Stifter was unable to give explicit form to it. And yet he continually seems to be approaching it. The story *Der Hochwald* [*The High Forest*] describes Ronald's obsessive love for the child Clarissa, a love whose hidden violence and venality is not diminished by the passage of time. Stifter was, as we know, not exactly an author given to passionate love scenes. It is, I would suggest, therefore all the more remarkable that his rare display of passion should find expression precisely in the passage in which Roland declares his love for the child Clarissa.

> It is true, in the beginning it was merely the unusual strength and fullness welling up in the heart of the child that attracted me, so that I tentatively, testingly approached her, drew the child's lips to me – but a soul, deep, wild, grand and poetic as my own, grew towards me from the child, so that I started back, but now threw myself at her in a tempest, nameless, inseparable, exchanging fire with fire, bliss with bliss. – Woman! You were a child then, but your child lips thrilled me more than, later, any pleasure in the world, they burned inextinguishably into my soul – I threw away a kingdom for these child's lips . . . – and now here I am . . . asking for nothing more in the whole world than for these lips again![24]

As the story unfolds, it becomes clear that the lovers, who really did fall in love 'in the blink of an eye', are, despite all their best intentions to renounce and reform, not really able to recant. 'Be the child again', Roland pleads, 'who once made me so happy – it's true, isn't it, Clarissa, you still love me? . . . oh my shy, my ardent child.'[24] If one looks closely at what Stifter is actually writing here, the whole story, including its natural setting, becomes an insistent parable of virginity and violation. There is constant talk of impenetrability, of thrusting forwards into the interior, of penetrating deep into the mountain, an ever more difficult pressing onwards, deeper and deeper into the valley.[25] The misfortune [*Unglück*] and ruin that the story relates on the surface level has its origin in the past, in a love which violates social taboos; such love, indeed, is the source of the unhappiness [*Unglück*] of all Stifter's characters: their misfortune [*Unglück*] *is* love itself.

It is probably due to the need to avoid the destructive turbulence of a passion which he could justify neither to society nor to himself that Stifter goes to such lengths to neutralize the image of the beautiful young woman in his work. Natalie, in *Der Nachsommer*, is described thus: 'She also had a veil around her hat, which she had also thrown back. Beneath the hat brown curls peeped out: her features were smooth and fine – she was still a girl. Beneath her brow were large dark eyes, her mouth was lovely and ineffably kind, she appeared to me entirely beautiful.'[26] The two daughters of a neighbouring family are, strangely enough, very similar in appearance:

> She had brown hair, like Natalie. Her hair was rich and arranged becomingly around her brow. Her eyes were big and brown with a gentle look. Her cheeks were fine and smooth, her mouth extremely soft and gracious . . . The younger girl . . . likewise had brown hair, although somewhat lighter than her sister's, her hair was just as abundant and, if possible, even more beautifully arranged. Her brow stood in sharp clear relief from her hair, from beneath it gazed two blue eyes, not as large as her sister's brown eyes, but even more unaffected, kind and true.[26]

These two vignettes, cut according to the same pattern, make it clear that in describing female beauty Stifter kept a tight rein on his imagination. Unsurprisingly, in his stories relations between lovers tend to progress along the socially sanctioned paths of courtship, betrothal, engagement and marriage. Ideally, though, the actual wedding and the associated dismal consequences are best avoided, and the bride, like Margarita in *Die Mappe meines Urgroßvaters* [*My Great-Grandfather's Portfolio*], installed – like a saintly statue of herself – in a chamber designed for this express purpose. In order to understand how much Stifter may have feared the crossing of the threshold, we need only examine the function of the costumes in which Stifter's female characters appear on the narrative stage. The faces of the beloved women are – as the example of Natalie shows – only sketchily executed; by contrast, the author has all the more eyes for what they are wearing. Gundel Mattenklott has shown that Stifter's favourite female characters mostly go about in clothes which must have appeared unfashionable, if not old-fashioned, even at the time. These dresses are all plain and of a simple cut, in black or white, ash-grey, violet, dark green or brown, always of a single colour, regardless of the occasion on which they are worn. By creating such an old-fashioned collection, Stifter is consciously opposing what Simmel called the right to infidelity propagated by all fashion,[27] but at the same time he involuntarily reveals the specific propensities of his erotic imagination. In Benjamin's *Passagen-Werk* [*Arcades Project*] the section on fashion ('*Mode*') contains the following comment:

> Each generation experiences the fashions of the one immediately preceding it as the most radical anti-aphrodisiac imaginable. In this judgement it is not so far off the mark as might be supposed. Every fashion is to some extent a bitter satire on love; in every fashion, perversities are suggested by the most ruthless means. Every fashion stands in opposition to the organic. Every fashion couples the living

body to the inorganic world. To the living, fashion defends the rights of the corpse. The fetishism that succumbs to the sex appeal of the inorganic is its vital nerve.[28]

Benjamin's hypotheses offer a precise insight into Stifter's erotic strategy – including its hidden objectives. Inscribed in almost all the female characters – with whom the author feels an affinity – are the ciphers of the fetishism identified by Benjamin. 'She had again been very beautiful', we read in the story *Das alte Siegel* [*The Ancient Seal*], 'and very noble in the slim, delicate dress of dark green silk with the small folds at the breast. It was, like an enigma to him, that the splendour of those limbs could have been released from the mysterious cloud of clothing, that she might perhaps one day be his.'[29] The small folds at the breast – very noble! – but not the breast itself. As yet, if we may trust the confusion of tenses in these sentences, the splendour of these limbs has not yet been released from the 'mysterious' cloud of clothing. How this will come to pass is an 'enigma', positioned ungrammatically between two commas. Will she still be the same woman as the one who now wears these arousingly lovely garments? 'She loved above all to wear silk,' the narrator continues, and this introduces a description in which the secret objects of fetishistic desire seem as good as revealed to the reader.

> Every dress was closed at the neck. Then there was, as mentioned before, that wondrous head with its great gleaming eyes. Her sense of cleanliness also extended to her person; for her hair, which framed her face as its sole ornament, was simply arranged and kept as immaculate as may seldom be found. Also her hands, and that small portion of her arm

which might show, were pure and lovely. She never wore gloves, never a ring on her finger, no bracelet upon a wrist when her lovely arm looked out from a wide sleeve, and not a single piece of jewellery on her entire body. From beneath the long hem of her dress, as is often found with the upper classes, the tip of a very small foot peeped out.[29]

The line where the dress is fastened at the neck; the hands and the portion of arm which could sometimes be glimpsed; the tip of the tiny foot which peeps out 'from beneath the long hem of her dress'[vi] – it is these points of transition between body and garment which arouse the fetishistic imagination. The demarcations, the golden ratio with which the fetishistic gaze segments the female body, are the source of lust and pain and – according to the principle that only when dissected will nature yield up her secrets – lead, ultimately, to the anatomy theatre, or to pornography.

Now it is, as Freud noted, natural that 'a certain degree of fetishism is [. . .] habitually present in normal life,[vii] especially in those stages of it in which the normal sexual aim seems unattainable, or its fulfilment prevented.'[30] According to this theory, the fetishistic tendency only becomes pathological when the fulfilment of the sexual goal proves, by comparison with the previously imagined bliss, to be a bitter disappointment. This is precisely the case in the story *Das alte Siegel*. 'One evening,' we read a few paragraphs later, 'having stayed rather too long and walking home late at night under a turbulent, thundery sky – something screamed within him: "This is not love!"'[31] The reader may picture for him- or herself what is meant by 'too long'. The storm clouds, at any rate, indicate that the crucial taboo has been broken; for the fetishist, after all, the fulfilment of love is the most desperate fate that can befall him. Hugo, with whom the narrator identifies, does not visit for two or three days after this, and when, on the fourth day, he returns, he finds the house empty and abandoned. Let us recall the passage in which Hugo's dismay at the sight of the empty interior of the house by the linden tree, stripped of all decoration, is depicted in allegorical terms. 'He had found dust and refuse on the stairs; the air from the open sky blew through the rooms in which he now stood, for the windows were open and the walls along which furniture, the marble table, the mirror and other things had been ranged now stood bare.'[31] The key word in this picture of an illusion destroyed is 'bare' [*nackt*], the opposite of all clothing. Nothing remains of that which inspired Hugo's fantasies. The furnishings have vanished, and with them the object of his erotic desires. The bleakest prospect for a fetishist, as Karl Kraus wrote, is having to make do with the whole woman. For Stifter, this whole woman was his wife Amalie, who, as soon as they were halfway able to afford it, would parade around the streets of Linz decked out according to the dubious tastes of the lesser bourgeoisie, a caricature of the love of beautiful clothes which had for all time bound poor Stifter to the unattainable young girls from the upper classes.

Where, in spite of the whole grammar of taboos, the social ritual of love is confirmed in marriage and a family life established, things do not on the whole end well in Stifter's work. Stories like *Die Narrenburg* [*The Castle of Fools*] and *Prokopus* afford an insight into the pathological reciprocity of love and coldness [*Liebe und Lieblosigkeit*] which appears to constitute the holy state of matrimony. The disturbances arising from the almost incalculable strangeness between people who live together is nowhere emphasized or dramatized.

The slow process of corrosion takes place in silence. The bridal procession where Prokopus leads Gertraud – also still a child at the time of the marriage – to his home at Rothenstein moves through the natural surroundings as if in farewell, and even the day of the ceremony itself ends on an ominous note. Still innocent, the two newlyweds are sitting on the balcony looking out into the surrounding countryside. Then, the narrative continues, 'husband and wife arose and entered the room like two blessed shy lovers.' The threshold has been crossed. The very next paragraph therefore begins with a metaphor of death: 'The dark door closed behind them.' The lovers are now, so to speak, no longer part of nature, 'isolated' by sturdy oaken planks 'from the peace, sanctity and silence of the night outside'.[32]

From now on their life will grow every day more wordless, until finally their unhappiness [*Unglück*] appears as irrevocable a state as otherwise in literature only love can be. What is striking about the *Prokopus* story is the radical and understated way unhappiness is a consequence, not of the betrayal of love – as is the case in *Die Narrenburg* – but of love itself. Only in Thomas Bernhard's *Das Kalkwerk* [*The Lime Works*] – in which the story of a love once imagined is in actuality that of its destruction – has marriage, as a social house of correction, since been described with comparable relentless harshness. The ghastly torments in which Konrad and his crippled wife have ritualized their behaviour towards each other are manifestations not of hate, but of love. The prosaic nature of such *malheur* confronts the bourgeois discourse of love – as true as it is deceptive, and still current today – with a significant corrective, one which, in laying bare the impossibility of a continual renewal of intimacy, presents, by contrast with the earlier ideal, a truly appalling degree of estrangement.

In Stifter's work, the only men who are, in their own peculiar way, happy – that is to say inconsolable in a bearable way – are those who, like Risach in *Der Nachsommer*, have either not married at all or who, like the Colonel in *Die Mappe meines Urgroßvaters*, have, through an (un)happy accident [*Un-Glücksfall*], lost their wives. After long years of active service, the Colonel takes as his wife the 'very young niece' of two elderly folk on whom he was billeted years before. Her picture – in actual fact that of a child – had made an indelible impression on him. 'After the wedding,' the Colonel recalls, 'I lifted her into my carriage . . . and drove her to my house almost without stopping.'[33] The relationship between the Colonel and the naïve child, who at first sits in the parlour like a stranger, still wearing her hat, is that of a teacher and his model pupil. In the fifth year of their marriage, soon after the birth of their daughter Margarita, the young woman loses her life. The scene of the accident stands out from the rest of the narrative like a dream sequence. On one of their many walks in the mountains, the Colonel and his wife, who accompanies him everywhere, have to cross a deep ravine on a narrow wooden footbridge with no railings.[viii] The Colonel takes up the narrative:

> I stepped first on to the log with my rough shoes, holding the stick in my left hand. My wife followed, holding on to the stick with her left hand while in her right arm she held the little dog. Then came the woodsman, likewise holding the end of the stick in his left hand. As we continued the abyss yawned ever deeper beneath us. I could hear his footsteps with his hobnailed boots, but not hers. When we were still a little way from the end I heard him say quietly, 'sit down'.

I felt how the stick in my hand grew lighter. I turned around, and saw only him. A terrible thought came to me. But I knew nothing else. My feet ceased to feel the ground beneath me. The fir trees swayed like the candles on a chandelier, and after that I knew nothing more.[34]

Not until the next morning is it possible to descend into the ravine. There the Colonel finds – strange dissociation – 'a heap of light clothes and under them the broken limbs'. The dog has survived, but has gone mad overnight, and the Colonel is obliged to have it shot before he can approach the body. There follows a moment of intimacy almost unique in Stifter's work. 'I bent over her,' the Colonel says, 'her face was cold, I tore open her dress, her shoulder was cold and her bosom cold as ice. O Sir, you cannot fathom,' he says to the Doctor, 'you cannot yet know, how it is when the wife of your heart is still wearing the clothes which you that very morning helped her choose and is now dead and can do nothing more than simply, in all innocence, ask you to bury her.'[35] Only when he looks on the dead woman does the Colonel fully grasp his love, knows for sure that *this* daughter truly loved him, just as King Lear, whose tragedy is often cited in *Der Nachsommer*, only receives his answer from Cordelia in death. In a gesture of loving tenderness – *Pray thee undo this button!*[ix] – melancholy at long last overcomes the coldness of its heart. This is the moment of true feeling, when one heavy in spirit[x] realizes what it is he has killed.

Like all of Stifter's idealized images of women, here too this portrait of a dead woman, intended for eternal remembrance, is a muse of celibacy. The premature death of the young wife results in the restitution of a celibate existence, such as is shown repeatedly in Stifter's work. A bachelor's and a widower's existence seem to have equal status. For the characters of the Colonel and the young doctor, the loss of their respective wives is the precondition for a truly active life. Their single state represents the positive contrast to the frustrations and tensions of marriage. Stifter, though, despite describing the problems relating to this dichotomy on many occasions, never identifies it in terms of his own personal misfortune [*Unglück*] in the way that Kafka later does. 'Celibacy and suicide are on similar levels of understanding,' it says in the third *Octavheft* [Octavo Notebook], 'suicide and a martyr's death not at all, perhaps marriage and a martyr's death.'[36] It is clear that the problem here outlined by Kafka was of central importance for Stifter also. It is equally clear that the particular difficulties of their respective lives could not have been resolved by, in the one case, marriage, and in the other the restitution of a celibate state. Kafka knew this: it does not however appear to have been clear to Stifter. For this reason Kafka never portrayed marriage as such a calm and peaceful state as that described in Stifter's detailed depictions of the lives of solitary men. Stifter thus – at least subconsciously – pinned his hopes on a celibate way of life.

Perhaps it is for this reason that the dreamlike death of the Colonel's wife has about it something of a wishful death. However, there is, as the saying goes, no such thing. In keeping with this, Amalie Stifter outlived her husband, who was only able to realize his desire for celibacy by taking his own life.

The Horror of Love

On Schnitzler's *Traumnovelle* [*Dream Story*]

> Tuer le temps . . . Quand le Bourgeois s'amuse, on entre dans l'éternité. Les amusements du Bourgeois sont comme la mort.[i]
>
> Léon Bloy

More than anything else, the literature of the bourgeois era is concerned with the theme of love and its entanglements. In a discourse stretching back centuries, the mutual attraction of the sexes is circumscribed with such intensity and insistence that it almost appears that, but for the permutations and idealizations of love, the literary imagination would have nothing whatsoever to sustain it. Literature and love, then, are to a large extent concurrent and overlapping spheres. For this reason, as the idea of love – in which lust and pain are framed in a reciprocally parasitic relationship – is developed in and through writing both to and for others, its historical context is increasingly lost to view.

In the literature of the classical period, love becomes an absolute; no doubts can be admitted as to the truth of this secular metaphysics. The merry-go-round of passions is prescribed both as a necessary precondition for the development of the individual character and as the means of deliverance from a life in isolation. Since, in the same period, bourgeois society is being formed according to the principles of utilitarianism, self-interest and indifference to the fate of the other, tragedy and despair become the appropriate expressions of a doctrine of salvation constructed around the personal experience of happiness in love. The idea of love, as Gert Mattenklott has shown in connection with Rousseau's epistolary novel,[1] is based on the separation of bodies. Even in the realist novel of the nineteenth century, the paradoxical nature of this constellation appears only in exceptional cases as a critical opposition to an ideology operating with all manner of complicated strategies of delusion and self-delusion. As a general rule, the irreconcilability of the ideal of love and the reality of life becomes proof positive of the authenticity of emotion. Only now, in retrospect, can we begin to acquire insight into the dialectics of a counter movement in which an emotion which is certainly more than a mere illusion becomes less credible the more it is talked about.

Schnitzler's literary oeuvre came into being at the very point at which the bourgeois concept of love was beginning to enter the phase of dissolution. The enduring fascination of his work lies in the way it describes – with regret, but without pathos – the calamities occasioned by an ideal which has become an *idée fixe*, and thereby does far more justice to actual social and psychological states than the works of many of his contemporaries, which continue to contribute to the hypostatization of love. There are, though, reasons to question the theory that the ideal of monogamous love is in decline in the closing stages of the bourgeois era. The discourse on love has hardly ever been more wide-ranging than at the *fin de siècle*, extending into ever more remote and symbolic areas of the erotic.[2] The models of love propagated in the poetry, prose and drama of the time are joined by psychology, sociology, philosophy and the mythology of the sexes; it is superfluous to cite the relevant authorities here. Via the distribution of goods – as Benjamin's *Passagen-Werk* [*Arcades Project*] demonstrates in countless examples – a diffuse eroticism reaches into all areas of life, and it is only in this silent usurpation that the historical evolution of love is finally complete.

As Niklas Luhmann points out, the ideal of wordless intimacy has its origins in a continual process of verbalization; and Foucault elucidated the fundamental ambivalence in the discourse of love, which not only fosters its emancipation, via the literary elaboration of emotions, but at one and the same time subjects it to closer societal control through the registering of pastoral, psychological, juridical and psychiatric interests.[3] This ever greater dichotomy in the historical development of our concept of love is the reason for the increasingly noticeable scepticism in literature towards the idea of love itself. In the works of the high bourgeois era, this scepticism can, admittedly, only be deduced via analyses of a seismological degree of sensitivity.[4] Even Baudelaire is still working on the pathos and elevation of love, conflating its epiphany with its dying flame, his belief with his agnosticism. Likewise, the *fin de siècle* expresses its misgivings about love only implicitly, deploying the most extravagant of means to revive an ideal already afflicted with consumption. And even Karl Kraus, who thought there was more satisfaction to be had from masturbation than from the physical presence of the women to whom he was so deeply attracted, still pronounces the statement 'die Liebe, quand même' ['Love, after all'].[5]

Only with Schnitzler — and this, over and above his portrayals of contemporary mores, is the particular significance of his oeuvre — does scepticism towards love's habitual arrangements finally start to become explicit. Schnitzler's diaries and letters reveal that, as far as his own attitude to affairs of the heart and matters of marriage is concerned, he remained firmly within the bounds of social convention, often uncritically reflecting conventional patriarchal attitudes. In his work, however, he goes far beyond the bourgeois horizon of expectation. The ironic and melancholic structure of his literary investigations of *Liebesleid* [the sorrow of love] is characterized by a detachment in every way equal to that of clinical case studies. There is much to suggest that, as a scientist, Freud was at first not entirely comfortable with Schnitzler's literary perspicacity — indeed it was a long time before Freud saw his way to sending Schnitzler a sign of his appreciation and admiration.[6] One reason for the unspoken difficulty in their relationship was no doubt the fact that Schnitzler — by contrast with, for example, Hofmannsthal — no longer makes any attempt to redeem the idea of love, but rather — in similar fashion to Freud — presents what amounts to a critique of the whole phenomenon.

Foucault identifies four specific figures in this critique of eroticism, which developed in the bourgeois era as a corrective to the increasingly popular dissemination of the idea of love. The hysterical woman, the masturbating child, the Malthusian couple and the perverse adult constitute the focal points of scientific interest in the regulation of sexuality. Schnitzler shares this interest, thus apparently aligning himself with those forces in society who set less store by the subversive potential of true love than in establishing a canon of erotic reason. Unlike the scientific critique of the idea of absolute love, which ultimately serves conventional, even repressive, ends, Schnitzler's decidedly nuanced critique of the ideal of love also repeatedly crosses over into a critique of society itself.

The Malthusian couple, locked together in reciprocal exploitation – to whom Hofmannsthal erects one last monument, albeit on a very subtle level, in his capacity as marriage broker between Helene Altenwyl and Kari Bühl – is, in Schnitzler's texts, almost completely discredited as a model of idealized or normal erotic behaviour. Like Manet's portraits of couples, whose averted gaze suggests their irrevocable inner distance from each other, so too, in Schnitzler's portraits of marriage, the spouses each live in a completely separate world. Indeed, the married state itself becomes a paradigm for 'the vast domain'[ii] – the huge distances which open up, in the society we have created, between one person and the next. The socialization of reproductive behaviour in the convention of marriage would thus seem to have reached saturation point, yet the system is still perpetuated, and children trained to present their darker desires to themselves in the proper light. While the educational regulation of childhood sexuality – which, in an all-out campaign against onanism lasting almost two centuries, has led to the most grotesque efflorescences of regulatory rationale[7] – has, since the turn of the century, given way to isolated rearguard actions and skirmishes, this is perhaps only because in the meantime more effective methods have been found to divert the attention of the child away from its own body and towards the quasi-magical presence of another.

In the opening paragraph of *Traumnovelle* [*Dream Story*], Albertine and Fridolin are listening to their daughter at bedtime reading aloud an important little moral from a story no doubt designed expressly for the pious edification of young girls. 'Twenty-four brown slaves rowed the splendid galley that would bring Prince Amgiad to the Caliph's palace. But the Prince, wrapped in his purple cloak, lay alone on the deck beneath the deep blue, star-spangled night sky, and his gaze—'.[8] The evocative last sentence, after which the child involuntarily breaks off, focuses her attention entirely on the prince, and just as the moment when the gaze of this fairytale character falls upon her, her eyes close and she falls into the unconsciousness of sleep. The male gaze causes even a child to lower her eyelids. The text does not allow us to follow her into the dream world which she now enters, but it does allow us access to the dream worlds of her parents, which are explored as the story unfolds. There, it transpires that our true dreams do not correspond to the objects of beauty which we pursue in waking hours, but are, rather, filled with a terrifying urge to perversion in which, through violence, beauty is corrupted to ugliness. In the *Traumnovelle*, Schnitzler was evidently making a concerted attempt to uncover the reasons and mechanisms underlying perversion. Chronicler of love's disease that he was, though, it is telling that Schnitzler was otherwise at pains to sidestep the theme of perversity. Given that the *Traumnovelle* cannot readily be classified either as pornographic heresy or as its opposite, the psychiatric documentation of perversion, the significance that so-called erotic aberrations held for Schnitzler will clearly require careful examination.

Among the many different adaptations of sex, the progressive identification of the female body with hysteria is clearly central. In a process which began in the early modern period, and which is almost perceived as natural or biological, Woman has been qualified – and at the same time disqualified – as a wholly sexual being. In the centuries-old persecution and torture meted out to witches as miscegenations of femininity, hysteria – most likely the panicked reaction of the male to a woman who meets his gaze – was projected not only on to the bodies of the victims, but on to all female bodies, where – adopted and internalized by those affected – it manifested itself, in greater or lesser attacks and susceptibilities, up until the end of the last century as *the* classic form of female mental disturbance. In the works of Charcot, Breuer and Freud, hysteria became the starting point for all their later psychological investigations. That this 'illness' could so often be 'cured' by means of hypnotism – that is to say by means of the male gaze and the male voice – is a particularly ironic aspect of the development of psychoanalysis. As a doctor, Schnitzler too had some notable successes with hypnotic treatments. As his father's assistant in the laryngological department of the general hospital, he repeatedly encountered cases of hysterical hoarseness and functional aphonia which proved susceptible to hypnotic treatment, and it is no surprise that actresses and female singers appear to be disproportionately represented among them. Excessive demands on the vocal cords, though, scarcely suffice as an explanation of this phenomenon. Rather, the profession of *actrice*, newly created in bourgeois society, forms an exact correlative to the classification of woman as hysterical. In the declamatory pathos of the great female tragedians, particularly in the literally breathtaking style of arias cultivated in the nineteenth century, hysterical exaltation is inscribed on to, or indeed into, the body of a woman as the precise equivalent of her lack of a voice in all other matters. The heartrending outbursts of such exemplary bourgeois heroines as Aida, Mimi, Manon, Madame Butterfly, Norma, Lucia and Ariadne, the somnambulists and women without shadows, surely deserve to be investigated from this point of view.

Significantly, the myth of female passion thus dramatically

articulated on stage scarcely features at all in Schnitzler's texts. In both his plays and his prose works, Schnitzler is, rather, concerned with how the hysterical perception of woman affects women in an actual social context, and with the hopeless silent suffering of domestic hysteria. In the second chapter of *Traumnovelle*, the doctor, Fridolin, is called out late at night to the bedside of a patient, the Hofrat [Court Counsellor], who has been ill for a long time. The scene which follows in the apartment in the Schreyvogelgasse is instructive in a number of ways. In the past, three grams of morphine had usually helped the Hofrat over an attack. This time, however, when the doctor arrives, he is already dead, an emaciated body lying there motionless, his brow in shadow, 'gaunt, wrinkled, the high forehead, the full short white beard, the strikingly ugly ears with their white hairs'.[9] At the foot of the bed sits his daughter Marianne, 'her arms hanging limply from her sides as if in utter exhaustion'.[9] The encounter between her and the doctor is dominated by the sinister presence of the dead father. Fridolin experiences a rush of sympathy for the pale girl, 'who though still young had for months, for years, been losing her bloom in the course of heavy household chores, tiring care and nocturnal vigils'.[9]

In his writings, Freud repeatedly notes that caring for sick family members is a contributing factor in the aetiology of hysteria.[10] The daughter, bound to the sick father, exemplifies a classic case of the pathological double-bind situation, and her freedom is still curtailed by the father even in death. Under the circumstances, it is entirely logical that she should be moved to a tearful declaration of love for the doctor beside the deathbed of the tyrannical head of household. Not only has Fridolin supported Marianne during her father's long illness; he also represents the authority who will certify the death which has been anticipated with such unacknowledged longing. As such, to Marianne's unconscious perception, he appears as her deliverer, and perhaps as complicit with her in a plot to do away with the father, since to the unconscious mind, as Freud notes, even someone who has died a natural death is a murdered man.[11] Thus it is all too readily understandable, and Fridolin 'had always known' 'that she was in love with him, or imagined that she was'.[12] The term hysteria as a possible diagnosis suggests itself to him when, slipping from the armchair, she prostrates herself at his feet, flinging her arms around his knees and pressing her face against them. At the same time, however, his conscience pricks him. He glances over at her father's body and wonders whether in fact he only appears to be dead and can hear everything – a not entirely rational speculation for a doctor. At this moment, too, Fridolin remembers a novel he had read years ago 'in which a very young man, almost a boy, had been seduced, or rather raped, at his mother's deathbed by her best friend'.[12] Displaced on to a dream, this far-fetched recollection is the masculine counterpart to the hysterical conduct of poor Marianne: an imagined act of blasphemous transgression scarcely likely to occur to the female imagination, even in the state in which Marianne finds herself. Nonetheless, the image suddenly occurring to Fridolin – although far more extreme than Marianne's hopes for love – is more readily compatible with the existing order, as represented by the dead body of the patriarch. Occasional excesses are more manageable than undying love. Thus Fridolin is able to leave the apartment, while Marianne remains behind, abandoned – as it must appear to her – by Fridolin to the mercy of her fiancé Dr Roediger, a precise historian in a dark grey overcoat with galoshes and umbrella, whose timely appearance helps to avoid further embarrassing scenes. The unspoken agreement between the two men – they 'nodded to one another with greater familiarity than was warranted by their actual relationship'[13] – seals the young woman's fate, while at the same time pinpointing the true source of her hysteria. As we take a last look at the fiancés sitting holding hands at the bedside of the dead father, it dawns on us that the hysterical symptoms of female longing for love are not so much an inherent part of the female constitution as symptomatic manifestations of a life circumscribed by the masculine wielding of power.

In the episode about the Court Counsellor's daughter in the Schreyvogelgasse, hysteria is described from a viewpoint similar to the studies of Freud. And yet Schnitzler's narrative presentation, allowing a series of insights into the social dynamics inherent in the hysterical disposition, has certain advantages over Freud's analyses, not least a greater degree of empathy with the psychological state of a woman who, measured against an abstract norm, appears deranged. This is particularly apparent in the idealized images of masculinity as objects of female escapist longing which Schnitzler inscribes, almost as quotations, into his portraits of women.

It is significant for the internal structure, if not for the plot, of the *Traumnovelle* that the Court Counsellor's daughter has a long-lost brother who is 'now living abroad somewhere'.[14] In Marianne's bedroom hangs a picture he had painted at the age of fifteen. 'It showed an officer galloping down a hill.'[14] A little further on in the text it occurs again as 'the picture of an officer in white uniform, charging with sabre drawn down a hill towards an unseen enemy. It was mounted in a narrow gilt frame and the effect was no more impressive than that of a modest lithograph.'[15] The Court Counsellor never set any store by his son's naïve artwork, had always acted as if he could not see it, but for Marianne it evidently has a similar fetishistic value as the picture of the lady in furs for Gregor Samsa. In both cases we have the image of a sibling, at one and the same time highly eroticized and taboo, a clear example of the fact that the greatest desire is also always the most inadmissible.

In *Traumnovelle*, this curious memento is mainly important for the way it is reflected in Albertine's amorous adventure, which remains solely in the realm of pure potential. At the beginning of the story, she asks her husband 'if he remembered a young man the previous summer on the Danish coast who had been sitting with two officers at the table next to them one evening, and who, on receiving a telegram during the meal, had promptly taken a hasty leave of his [. . .] friends'.[16] The mysterious stranger, whom Albertine encounters again as he is hurriedly mounting the steps of the hotel, yellow suitcase in hand, and for whom she was prepared to give up everything – you, our child, the future, as she says – remains a completely undeveloped figure.

All we know about him is that he sits at the officers' table, and that he receives a telegram with an apparently important message. This, admittedly, is enough to distinguish him as the representative of a chivalric ideal that a man from the bourgeoisie, and especially a husband, cannot begin to live up to: the ideal image is *hors concours*. In similarly absolute fashion, in [Kleist's] *Die Marquise von O.*, the Count in his uniform appears to the Marquise of O. at the moment of utmost distress as an angel from heaven. In his behavioural studies, Otto König[iii] has shown the astonishing extent to which the uniform of a fighting man is designed to emphasize masculine attributes, from the contrasting colours and cut of the tunic, through the heightening of the figure by means of plumed helmets and epaulettes, to eye-catching features such as badges of rank and ornamental sword pommels. This fits in well with our argument, inasmuch as the women of the bourgeoisie portrayed by Schnitzler to all appearances still bear deep within them the ideal image of the man in uniform.

Bourgeois society is, according to its own precepts, incompatible with promiscuity. That, as a society administered primarily by men, it nonetheless allowed the latter access to it, no longer merits specific comment.[17] Nor, indeed, does the fact that male promiscuity found a halfway legitimate sphere of activity among the respective lower social classes. Less obvious, though, is the way female erotic fantasies and desires are, by contrast, directed at the respective higher classes, thus confirming the established order in the same way as the hypocrisy of the menfolk. In what follows I aim to demonstrate how, in this regard especially, Schnitzler has written a piece of cultural history.

It is a striking fact that the erotic model of the chevalier or nobleman, the object of the bourgeois woman's fantasies, was, as a rule, no longer in any sense attainable, given that he himself belonged to a dying breed, or else – as the case of Leutnant Gustl demonstrates – was now a mere empty uniform, a shadow of his former self. Possibly for this reason, too, the gentlemen at the secret society ball in their white, yellow, blue and red courtiers' costumes, engaging with their naked female partners in a choreographed erotic ritual, appear as mere abstractions. The text in this passage lacks that realistic quality otherwise so characteristic of Schnitzler's work. Rather, we are here in a realm of pure fiction, as indicated by the circumstantial pornographic elements in these passages, as will be discussed below. The erotic ideal of masculinity on to which the bourgeois woman projects her desires is a creature consigned to irrelevance by history. This is true both in the evolutionary genetic sense, inasmuch as the image of the chevalier belongs in the past, to the literal *ancien régime*, and in the sense of the personal development of the male individual, in which the often fondly remembered period of military service – even K. reminisces about this in *The Castle* – appears in retrospect as a time of permissiveness and heroic freedom. It is the aura, then, of the man in uniform which turns women's heads. 'She had fallen in love with him . . . in his uniform,' Eibenschütz, the Inspector of Weights and Measures, reflects bitterly in Joseph Roth's story *Das falsche Gewicht* [*Weights and Measures*], and he knows that 'after she had seen and possessed him on many a night, naked and without uniform',[18] there is nothing left of this love.

As surrogates for, and last dubious representatives of, the chivalric ideal, we encounter elsewhere in Schnitzler's work various *flâneur* types such as Anatol, who, on account of their social and financial independence, still retain something of the romance of the knights errant of old, although they cannot disguise the inauthenticity of their existence, being armed only with a walking cane, which in actual fact is not much more impressive than Dr Roediger's umbrella. Thus the duels fought on the margins of Schnitzler's work by bourgeois opponents have, as in Chekhov, a rather theatrical air of farce about them. Fridolin, though, when jostled on his nocturnal wanderings by a member of a student duelling society, does not accept the challenge. For him, it is no longer worth it. '[A duel!] And perhaps an arm wound into the bargain, all because of a stupid incident like that. And then be professionally incapacitated for a few weeks? Or lose an eye?'[19] That of course would be the worst thing. But nor does avoiding the threat of castration present a way out of the dilemma, since it is precisely the one-eyed heroes, the hussars with their black eyepatches or the monocled drawing-room heroes and lounge lizards who are endowed with the most piercing male gaze. What is actually at stake here is the ability to give satisfaction, something fundamentally lacking in the man from the bourgeoisie. This is illustrated in the extended dream which Albertine relates to her husband. She describes seeing Fridolin hurrying from shop to shop, buying her the most gorgeous things to be had anywhere – clothes, linen, shoes, jewellery – all objects of his own fetishistic desires. He places them all in a small yellow leather case, without however ever managing to fill it completely. At the same time there appears in the dream, framed in an idealized wooded landscape, the young Dane to whom, as we know, the mysterious bag actually belongs. Again and again he emerges from the forest, again and again he disappears back into it. 'This was repeated', says Albertine, 'two, three, or perhaps a hundred times.'[20] This dream of fulfilment is an area where the bourgeois hero is scarcely likely to be able to hold his own. For this reason, he on the one hand devotes his libidinal energies to the daily routine effort of work, and on the other externalizes them in extramarital affairs which, as we see from Fridolin's nocturnal escapades, he conceives of as an adventure in which he too may stare death in the face.

The foregoing comments on the lack of satisfaction – in both senses – underlying the constant preoccupation in Schnitzler's work with erotic ideals and objects of desire are at odds with the erotic understanding between Albertine and Fridolin emphasized at the start of *Traumnovelle*. Returning home from the masked ball after a swift coach ride through the snowy winter's night, they sink into one other's arms 'with an ardour they had not experienced for quite some time'.[21] As the starting point for a story first and foremost concerned with the centrifugal forces of love, this may appear somewhat paradoxical, unless that is one takes into account the insight – only acknowledged by psychoanalysis, tellingly enough, at a relatively late stage – 'that in genital sexuality, even in the most favourable cases, there always remains a residue of dissatisfaction'.[22] It is this residue which feeds the needs which are brought to the marketplace of prostitution. The practice of prostitution in all its diverse forms – to which Schnitzler paid greater and more sophisticated critical attention than any of his contemporaries – represents, in the bourgeois era, the counterpart to the monogamous model prescribed by society. The ever more ruthless involvement of women in the production and distribution of manufactured goods, starting in the era of high capitalism, goes hand in hand with the spread of prostitution, the extent of which can today perhaps only be gauged by readers of the key sociological studies of bourgeois subculture.[23] In literature, however, prostitution – which, as Benjamin's *Arcades Project* shows, penetrated even the furthest recesses of metropolitan life – was by and large excluded. Even Naturalism's interest in *la bête humaine* did little to alter this. Within the literary canon, the extent to which the love for a prostitute – the more obvious urges aside – would become an 'apotheosis of empathy with the commodity'[24] is only really fully explored in the work of Schnitzler, where the variegated spectrum of love is displayed in all its doings and dealings, and something like a taxonomy of the whole fauna of femininity appears to be explicitly inscribed in the texts. From marital fidelity, harmless flirtation, casual affairs and tragic dramas of adultery, via the occasional prostitution of domestic servants, the temporarily kept seamstresses, milliners, *soubrettes* and ballet dancers, down to the professional services of the population of streetwalkers and brothel dwellers regulated by the police: almost all those with a part to play in love's marketplace are represented here.

Those availing themselves of this incessant activity are almost exclusively the men of the bourgeoisie; and it is to Schnitzler's credit that his works hold this to account, so that, taken together, they add up to a kind of verdict on this one-sided state of affairs. In this context, Schnitzler's autobiography *Jugend in Wien* [*My Youth in Vienna*] takes on the character of a confession of his own amorous dalliances, whereas his literary works perhaps represent a quest for purification. In any case, when it comes to discussing his own *amours*, it is notable that the empathy Schnitzler shows in his work for his female characters takes on a rather cynical edge in his autobiography.

Jugend in Wien contains the portrait, composed with considerable social-historical precision, of a young woman from the lower classes of whom Schnitzler was fond. The author relates how Jeanette had been dismissed from her job in a 'needlework salon where she was earning twenty gulden a month for fatiguing work from eight to one and three to seven, because of heart symptoms, blood in her sputum, headaches and backaches' and now was 'embroidering and crocheting at home and selling her work to various shops, but was finding it very difficult to get the money coming to her, and sometimes never did get it'.[25] Her family background is oppressive in the extreme, there is talk of doctors' visits and dire financial straits – altogether a very different picture from the carefree nature which Schnitzler's young male protagonists, such as Fritz and Theodor in *Liebelei* [*Dalliance*],[iv] are pleased to associate with their girlfriends from the outskirts of Vienna. On Jeanette's side, the correspondence is filled with assurances of love and fidelity, even though her lover has made up his mind never to marry her and suspects that these charming declarations are accompanied by 'quite a few other experiences'.[25] Despite a considerable degree of sincerity, Schnitzler never quite succeeds in setting aside his bourgeois *froideur*. This 'harmless' tone is maintained in the face of all Jeanette's unequivocal statements, and the author basks in the convenient illusion of a 'more natural' love than would be possible with someone of his own class. The piercing diagnostic gaze of the doctor has no power to gainsay the dominant bourgeois ideology to which he too is subject, and which, in the figure of the 'süßes Mädel' [sweet young thing] – combining poverty and cleanliness with petit-bourgeois modesty – invented for itself a convenient alibi for the often truly desperate situation of young women of the working classes.

In order to justify associating with girls who can – in one form or another – be bought, the bourgeois *flâneur* is always conscious of the fact that his amorous adventures involve a not inconsiderable risk to life and limb; indeed that, in a kind of heroic trial of courage, in lust he is literally flirting with death. Looking back on his youthful experiences, Fridolin – who, yielding to Albertine's jealous curiosity, has told her something of his past – can feel like a hero who has finally arrived in a safe harbour after being exposed to great peril. How unpredictable the rewards of love can prove for the errant husband becomes clear when Fridolin follows a seventeen-year-old streetwalker to her room, where his behaviour towards her is reserved in the extreme. 'You're afraid,' says Mizzi, and then to herself, 'almost inaudibly, gazing straight ahead, "What a pity!"'[26] 'These last words', the text continues, 'sent a warm current surging through his blood. He went over to her and attempted to embrace her, reassuring her that she inspired complete confidence in him, and indeed this was no more than the truth. He drew her to him and started to make love to her as he might to an ordinary girl or woman that he loved. She resisted, and feeling ashamed he eventually desisted.'[26] Not only Mizzi's evident affection for him, but also the implicit reproach in her words that — understandably enough, as she reassures him — he lacks the courage to sleep with her; all this makes her — half child, half woman — a *point d'honneur*, an ephemeral beloved. If in the end he escapes unscathed after all, this is due less to his own circumspection than to the modesty of the barely adolescent prostitute, who ceases to respond to his advances and thus saves him from the disease whose symptoms — as we later learn — appear on her body the very next day.

The symbolism of death, everywhere latent and manifest in Schnitzler's work, is emblematic of a praxis of love operating somewhere between legitimacy and illegitimacy, in which the sons of the bourgeoisie are initiated into manhood via a kind of game of chance. The spectre of syphilis plays an even more central role in Schnitzler's youthful memoirs than in his literary works, as for example when he describes how his father — for educational purposes — warns him, with drastic insistence, of the consequences of infection. 'In the end', it says, 'he took me into his study and told me to leaf through three huge yellow Kaposi atlases on syphilis and diseases of the skin.'[27] One is tempted to say that this scene reprises one from 600 years earlier, in which Heinrich von Melk reveals the ghastly contents of the sepulchre as the dark side of courtly love. The *memento mori* of the Kaposi volumes is intended to remind the son of the biblical dictum that what may appear fair on the outside is within nothing but bones and putrefaction. All the more readily understandable, then, is the desire for health and for the 'clean' girls from the lower-middle classes, on whom Schnitzler's gentlemen are particularly fond of lavishing their affections. These girls embody a guarantee of a certain degree of sexual hygiene and protection against the dangers of infection, forever rearing its ugly head even among Schnitzler's close acquaintances. With regard to a friend from his youth, Schnitzler recalls, 'The following day my brother took him into his hospital to perform surgery for an ailment which was the sad result of one of his past love adventures, and six months later he died in an insane asylum, without my ever having seen him again.'[28]

Precisely because medicine was more or less powerless against syphilis, in the mind of the author and writer-doctor, the latter takes on the guise of divine retribution for the unlawful promiscuity of society. The disease moves among us, and, as with death, we do not know whom it will strike next. The horror of it justifies in advance the amoral behaviour of the lover, since in the very pursuit of his goal he is exposing himself to the risk of retribution. The gradual process of deterioration, over years or even decades, which makes of the elegant cavalier a babbling paralytic – the high stakes involved were sufficient to assuage any qualms of conscience, since one can sin all the better when one knows the forfeit. As far as the odds of survival are concerned, as a doctor Schnitzler had, in such circumstances, certain advantages over the usual male competition, as the following episode from *Jugend in Wien* shows:

> Thus it happened, on a November afternoon, shortly after the termination of my year of military service that, with Richard, I accompanied a very pretty chorus girl from the Wiednertheater to her apartment, where we decided to draw lots for the favor of the young lady who was undecided rather than demure. [. . .] But since she had told me the name of her lover, a Hungarian aristocrat, and his doctor's indiscretion had previously informed me as to the condition of his health, and when, with my arm around her neck, I by

chance touched a gland which according to my medical knowledge felt highly suspicious, I nobly waived the prize I had won and left it to my friend.[29]

The casual cynicism with which not so much a warning as the venereal disease itself is passed on is part of a system in which self-interest takes precedence over every other concern. Like the Joker or 'Black Peter' in the pack, the disease is pushed from one player to another, a continuous process that determines the true exchange rate of love, creating a round dance [*Reigen*] which makes Schnitzler's eponymous drama look like child's play by comparison – unless, that is, one sees it as a dance of death.

Syphilis, then, functions as a kind of shibboleth, its name never spoken aloud, but continually passed from hand to hand. Anyone who knows its whereabouts at any given moment can count himself among the true adepts.

Perhaps based on such cynical experience, the profound scepticism in Schnitzler's work regarding love's claims to be an absolute ideal may be read as a critique of a social order in which the fulfilment of love is no longer commensurate with the hopes invested in it. Schnitzler repeatedly demonstrates how the structure of reciprocal expectations on the part of the lovers, the tendency to over-interpretation which characterizes the development of a relationship, is also what hastens its end. The unions entered upon are no match for their own temporality, and are soon dissolved again. Niklas Luhmann, whose arguments I follow here, has shown how this process of corrosion happens faster than can be accounted for by the natural passing of beauty and all those things which inspire the imagination of the lovers. 'By laying claim to time, love destroys itself.'[30] What remains are the rules of the game, the attempt to replace the ideal of eternal love with the most frequent and varied range of experience possible. Once the idea of the uniqueness and singularity of love is relinquished, a pattern emerges in which change and identity become one and the same, and which, in consequence, ultimately converges with the plot structure of pornography and the description of a transgressive act.

When, after hours of aimlessly wandering the deserted nocturnal streets, Fridolin 'at last, with a resolute stride, as though he had reached a long-sought goal'[31] enters a modest coffee house, he crosses the threshold to a different realm from that sanctioned by society. If, until now, his experiences have played out within, or at least on the margins of, legality, he now arrives at a decisive frontier. From the table opposite, he sees a pair of eyes staring fixedly at him. They belong to Nachtigall [= nightingale], a former fellow student who has now advanced to the dubious position of coffeehouse pianist, and who, odd bird that he is, is destined to become Fridolin's psychopompus who will lead him, coat-tails flapping, to the closed society where 'things never start before two o'clock.'[32] In what follows, Schnitzler unfolds a tale whose accoutrements suggest to the reader that this is a somewhat less innocuous masked ball than the one from which Fridolin and Albertine returned the day before. Already a closed carriage awaits in front of the coffee house, a motionless coachman on the box, dressed all in black and wearing a top hat. This vehicle puts Fridolin in mind of a hearse, and the store room of Gibisier's outfitter's establishment, where he still needs to procure a costume, has a definite whiff of *pompes funèbres* about it – silk, satin, perfume, dust and dry flowers. 'Have you any particular preference, Sir? *Louis Quatorze*? *Directoire*? Old Germanic?'[33] Gibisier asks Fridolin, just as the proverbial actress says to the Bishop. The monk's habit and the black mask Fridolin

56

selects; the ensuing drive through the unnaturally warm night; the city floating in the haze below, shimmering with a thousand lights; the garden gate in front of which they finally halt, beyond which the road seems to descend into a deep ravine; the liveried servants in grey masks, and the password 'Denmark' Nachtigall has given him – all this suggests an entry into a world excluded by society, where the utmost profanity is cloaked in the atmosphere of a sacred rite. Hearing the sounds of a harmonium and the softly swelling melody of an old Italian sacred tune, Fridolin imagines he has strayed into a gathering of some kind of religious sect. Standing in the dark, he sees, in the dazzling light of the room opposite, a group of women standing motionless, 'each with a dark veil covering her head, brow and neck, and a black lace mask over her face, but otherwise completely naked'.[34] His eyes rove hungrily 'from sensuous to slender figures, and from budding figures to figures in glorious full bloom; and the fact that each of these naked beauties still remained a mystery, and that from behind the masks large eyes as unfathomable as riddles sparkled at him, transformed his indescribably strong urge to watch into an almost intolerable torment of desire.'[34]

At this point in the story, where, according to its own inner logic, it should tip over into pornography, Schnitzler stages an abrupt volte-face by setting up a romantic encounter, commensurate with a more elevated genre, between Fridolin and one of the ladies so confounding his senses. From the instant their eyes meet, they are aware this is a momentous encounter, thereby revoking the tendency to erotic extremism thus far inscribed in the text. Even in this outlandish house, then, there is no uninhibited acting out of male dreams and desires. The colourfully costumed chevaliers, whom Fridolin believes could be from the nobility or even the Court, are celebrating an apparently purely masochistic ritual, in that, standing in full costume opposite the naked women, their voyeuristic gaze is whipped to a climax of lust, only for their sexual urges, torments and restraint, as truly catholic knights of love, to be prolonged and suspended in a collective dance of armoured and defenceless bodies. The text does not make it clear how exactly Fridolin comes to arouse the suspicions of the camarilla of men. Possibly he commits a faux pas and is for that reason interrogated. The transgression of which he becomes culpable through his mere appearance in these circles cannot, at any rate, be redeemed by his offer to give satisfaction in a duel. As a member of the bourgeoisie, he is in any case unable to give satisfaction, and furthermore, as one of the courtiers makes clear, the question here is one not of satisfaction but of expiation. Thus it seems as if he himself is about to become the sacrificial victim. What form this violent action is to take, however, does not become clear, since at the crucial moment Fridolin's ideal woman steps forward, this time dressed as a nun, and volunteers to ransom him. Before Fridolin is ejected from the house, he hears how she offers herself up to the courtiers, crying 'Here I am, at your disposal – all of you!'[35] What is meant by that is left to the imagination both of the dishonoured member of the bourgeoisie and of the reader, who can picture a mass rape played out behind the scenes of the text. Unlike in Albertine's dream, though, it is not the *man* who is led, hands bound behind him, into a castle courtyard where he is to be whipped until the blood runs down in rivulets; here, the warning example of the destruction of beauty takes the form of violence against a *woman*.

The social background of the woman who voluntarily sacrifices herself, though of great significance for the text, is not immediately apparent. Her whole demeanour indicates that she is anything other than a common prostitute. This is also confirmed by Nachtigall, when he corrects Fridolin's original supposition that they were perhaps headed to an orgy with naked females with the remark: 'Don't call them females, Fridolin . . . you've never seen such women.'[36] The term 'Weiber' [translated here as 'women'], for once not used in any pejorative sense, is more or less a guarantee of the quality of the women involved in the ritual. However, later in the story it transpires that Baroness Dubieski, who – as Fridolin learns the next day from the newspaper – has taken poison in a fashionable hotel in the centre of the city, and whom he immediately suspects is *his* woman from the night before, was in fact not a baroness at all, since no such family of that name existed – or not, at least, among the nobility. If we also remember that, within the existing social hierarchy, female promiscuity on the whole occurs in an upward direction, one may assume that Fridolin experienced the – for him – shattering surge of love for this woman less on account of the specific circumstances of the encounter than because he had, completely in accordance with the societal rules, recognized her as an equal. Love, as administered by society, is not least an expression of class solidarity; in Schnitzler's work, this is repeatedly shown to be one of the determining factors in the lived reality of an apparently unconditional idea.

The epilogue to Fridolin's dreamlike excursion takes us to the mortuary of the Vienna General Hospital. After seeing the report of the Baroness's attempted suicide in the newspaper, Fridolin immediately decides to follow his hunch regarding the identity of the young lady, described as remarkably beautiful. 'At the time they had discovered her, she was still alive. And, after all, there was no reason to assume they had not rescued her in time. In any event, dead or alive, he was going to find her. He was going to see her – come hell or high water – whether she were alive or dead. He simply had to see her.'[37] When, in the course of his investigations, Fridolin discovers that Baroness Dubieski has died in the second in-patients' clinic at five in the afternoon without regaining consciousness, he realizes that he had imagined the face of the dead woman, the only part of which he had seen being her – now lifeless – eyes, as having the features of his wife. From this apparent coincidence, which, characteristically, Schnitzler presents almost casually, and yet which is entirely deliberate, one may deduce that the image of the ideal woman which the man from the bourgeoisie bears within him is a woman faithful unto death, who may be bought by him alone. And it is precisely this ideal image that then lies before him in the Institute of Pathology and Anatomy. There, it is another man with a bird's name, Dr Adler [= eagle], who admits Fridolin to the final mystery of love, whose secret lies in the attraction to a dead woman.

An ashen face with half-closed lids stared back at him. The jaw hung open loosely, the thin, raised upper lip left the bluish gums and a row of white teeth exposed . . . Unconsciously Fridolin bent lower, as if the intensity of his gaze might wrest an answer from those rigid features. And yet at the same time he was conscious that even if it were *her* face, *her* eyes, the same eyes that yesterday had gazed into his ablaze with life, he could never know for certain – and perhaps didn't even want to know. Gently he laid the head back against the slab, and let his gaze follow the torch-light over the dead body. Was it her body? That wonderful, blooming body that yesterday had tortured him with longing? He looked at the yellowish, wrinkled neck, noticed the two small girlish, yet slightly sagging breasts, between which the breastbone stood out under the pale skin with gruesome clarity, as if the process of decay already had set in; followed the contours of her lower body, noticing the way the well-formed thighs spread out impassively from the shadowy regions that had lost their mystery and meaning; and observed the slight outward curve of the knees, the sharp outline of the shin bones and the slender feet with toes turned inwards. One after the other these features receded once more into the gloom, as the beam from the torch swiftly retraced its path, and, trembling slightly, came to rest on the face again. Almost as if driven by some unseen power, Fridolin touched the woman's brow, cheeks, arms and shoulders with both hands; then he intertwined his fingers with the dead woman's as if to fondle them, and, stiff as they were, they seemed to be attempting to move and to take hold of his; indeed, he thought he could detect a faint and distant gleam in the eyes beneath those half-closed lids, trying to make contact with his own; and, as if drawn on by some enchantment, he bent down over her.[38]

The gaze of the surviving lover seeking his lost love is identical with the scientific dissecting gaze of the doctor concerned with knowledge at any price, yet it is also filled with a necrophiliac *désir*. And in the necrophiliac *désir* which Schnitzler imputes to his fictional colleague – as did Flaubert, also from a doctor's family, in the case of the country doctor Charles Bovary – the dark side of the bourgeois idea of love is revealed as 'a desire to look suffused by horror',[39] a voyeuristic desire that knows it can only be indulged without inhibition in the contemplation of a lifeless object.

A Venetian Cryptogram

Hofmannsthal's *Andreas*

Ich weiß nicht, was es für ein Sprung in meiner Natur ist.

I do not know what kind of rift runs through my being.

Hugo von Hofmannsthal

From the outset, the programme of bourgeois culture has always entailed a stringent repression, in the consciousness of both writer and reader, of any interest in erotic objects. For the literary imagination, however, in a kind of paradoxical but tacit understanding, the exploration of the forbidden increasingly becomes the central source of inspiration. Only once the erotic had become taboo could there emerge, in the French literature of the nineteenth century, under the patronage of the divine Marquis [de Sade], the compulsion for explicitness which opens up the wide field of the most diverse obsessions. From Chateaubriand, via Baudelaire and Flaubert, down to Huysmans, there emerges, against the background of bourgeois orthodoxy, a heretical science whose claim to fortune is the seeking out and describing of precisely that which is taboo, putting into practice de Sade's theory of excess.

Something similar occurs in nineteenth-century literature in German, albeit in far more muted imagery. Thus, for example, one reason behind the singularly fascinating appeal of Stifter's prose is a tendency to perversity, of which neither author nor readers were aware at the time. It is only at the turn of the century, when, in France, the obsession with eroticism is already entering its byzantine phase, that – triggered by the delayed reception of the relevant French texts – the boundaries of the bourgeois art of narrative fiction begin to be broken in the German-speaking world. In this context, it is by now superfluous to emphasize the importance of the Wiener Moderne [Viennese Modern Age]. Not only in its theoretical preoccupation with all the diverse modalities of love, but also in practice, as Nike Wagner has shown in her excellent book on Kraus, 'promiscuity and wife-swapping were all part of the erotic customs' of the era.[1]

There can be no doubt that Hofmannsthal was part of the circle of the Wiener Moderne. However, he owed his special position within it – already acknowledged by his contemporaries – not only to the outstanding quality of his oeuvre, but also to the fact that he was affected less directly, if no less profoundly, than others by the rampant erotic fever of the time. At any rate, he took no part in the complex web of personal entanglements which – regardless of all their other differences – connected the leading men of the literary and cultural world, from Kraus, Schnitzler and Loos down to Altenberg, Mahler, Rilke, Blei and Albert Kiehtreiber alias Paris Gütersloh, with, in varying permutations, the pan-erotic muses Alma Mahler-Werfel, Lou Andreas-Salomé, Gina Kraus, Bessie Bruce and the sisters Wiesenthal and Sandrock.

What is less clear, however, is whether Hofmannsthal's old-fashioned erotic modesty can be explained by the fact that — as his outward way of life and his literary *traitements* of the idea of love would seem to suggest — he was a representative of a strictly monogamous type who, from the point of view of societal norms, had brought his years of sentimental education to a successful conclusion. Extensive clues as to how difficult Hofmannsthal's erotic inclinations, and attempts at satisfying them, actually were may be found in *Andreas*, his project for a novel which tellingly remained fragmentary, and which, equally tellingly, literary scholarship has come nowhere near to understanding.

Fritz Martini was of the opinion that Hofmannsthal planned his text as a 'book on the education [*Bildung*] of a person to a complete and rounded character', emphasizing at the same time, however, that the hero's intended progress 'can only be vaguely deciphered from the mass of notes in the *Nachlass*'. Martini's thoughts on the meaning of the *Andreas* project therefore also remain exceedingly vague. There is talk of 'orders in which being-human and being-world could be experienced as an inner, lasting unity leading to the Ur-images of being' and more such hollow phrasings of this ilk.[2] Not even Alewyn's far more authoritative essay,[1] concentrating as it does exclusively on the dual figure of Maria/Mariquita and its underlying psychiatric sources, succeeds in shedding light on the meaning of the *Andreas* fragment. This is probably in large measure due to the fact that, like Martini, he starts from the syncretic concept of *Bildung* — the acquisition and mediation of knowledge — whereas Hofmannsthal has, it seems to me, structured *Andreas* as an exploration of those centrifugal forces of his life and ours which, alien and rebarbative, result not in a beautifully rounded education, but rather in deformation and destruction. The extreme erotic tendencies inscribed in the *Andreas* fragment obstruct the formation of identity; their object is the confusion and dissolution of the protagonist, and as such they run counter to the integrative model of the *Bildungsroman*. Indeed, one of Hofmannsthal's earliest notes, dating from 1907, sees Andreas confronted immediately upon his arrival in Venice with a troupe of actors, and thus with a milieu in which identities, even gender identities, change according to the scenario in which one finds oneself. It is not, then, as Martini claimed, the lofty aims of its concept of *Bildung* which condemned the novel to a fragmentary existence so much as the fact that Hofmannsthal, in mapping out his erotic *âventiure*, soon found himself in rather deeper waters than he was perhaps comfortable with.

Hofmannsthal started work on *Andreas* when he himself was approaching the age of forty. The fortieth year was – as it says in one of the notes – one he believed to be an *annus mirabilis*,[3] in which the gambler arrives at the precarious turning point where he has nothing more to gain and everything to lose.[4] In the secondary character of the Maltese, Hofmannsthal attempted to leave a memorial to his own panic, 'the complete collapse of the man of forty' who can no longer expect any 'redeeming revelations'.[5] The principal motivation of the story Hofmannsthal relates here is not the realization of a synthesis incorporating even the most outlandish elements, but rather the fear of disintegration, exacerbated by hypochondria. In order to investigate the aetiology of the pathological state thus outlined, Hofmannsthal invented the character of Andreas; the description of a kind of Grand Tour which takes the young man out of his habitual social milieu and places him in the extreme artificiality of Venetian decadence serves to examine a specific form of constitutional instability, a marked predisposition to empathy at the expense of an ego deficiency which permits Andreas – to his own horror – to forsake the everyday world and enter into a symbiotic relationship with those elements which are, for him, the strangest and most abstruse. It is precisely this weakness of the ego [*Ich*] which is a prerequisite both for pathological states and for any creative achievement. And this incomplete development of the ego is also what prevents Andreas from overcoming his earlier experiences, so that over and over again he finds himself obliged to 'pass through all the confused and false situations of his life as a child and boy', with all its 'painful confusion'.[6]

As early as 1896, in his study on the aetiology of hysteria, Freud pointed out that the prototypical hysterical reactions – sobbing fits, outbursts of despair, melodramatic suicide attempts – are not to be ascribed to the minor incidental insults which act as triggers, but are a proportional reaction to serious slights experienced in childhood, repeatedly remembered and never overcome.[7] The lasting effects of unresolved experience are reawakened in Andreas, whenever he is faced with any challenges, particularly those of a sexual nature, as a feeling of absolute powerlessness. A note from 1912 ascribes to the mysterious figure of the Maltese, alongside the gloss 'Dero Hochunvermögen' ['His Impotenceship'], a 'fury of impotence'[8] – a hysterical fit, then, the literary potential of which Baudelaire was already beginning to speculate on in *L'Art romantique*: 'L'hystérie! Pourquoi ce mystère physiologique ne ferait-il pas le fond . . . d'une œuvre littéraire, ce mystère . . . qui, s'exprimant dans les femmes par la sensation d'une boule ascendante et asphyxiante . . . se traduit chez les hommes nerveux par toutes les impuissances et aussi par l'aptitude à tous les excès.'[9ii]

Hofmannthal's *Andreas* presents us with the oeuvre Baudelaire might well have been imagining, not just with regard to 'impuissance' but also in the 'aptitude à tous les excès'. Walter Benjamin, who copied out this passage for his *Passagen-Werk* [*Arcades Project*], referred to impotence as 'the bitter cup of male sexuality'.[10] For a person steeped in literature such as Hofmannsthal, this road of suffering [*Passionsweg*][iii] leads to pornography. And in the final analysis, *Andreas* is conceived as a pornographic *étude* on the highest level of art, and is thus the absolute opposite to the concept of the *Bildungsroman*. And it had, too, to remain a fragment, for Hofmannsthal's 'sense of decorum'[iv] did not allow him to become fully conscious of what was really at issue here. Rather, an evidently highly effective inner authority arranges things in such a way that the monogamous ideal Hofmannsthal represented so steadfastly in his own life is affirmed, in the novel, in the projected marriage between Andreas and Romana. However, this ideal was perhaps not quite as firmly grounded as Hofmannsthal may have liked to believe. It is not only his own pronounced narcissistic tendencies which lend support to this idea. A diary entry of Schnitzler's from 1892 notes that Loris[v] had remarked that he 'sometimes senses a theoretical fear that no desire for women will awaken in me . . . what is more, your works make me afraid of Woman'.[11] This *horreur des femmes*, which, notwithstanding his marriage to Gerty Schlesinger, probably never quite left Hofmannsthal, is of course one of the central motifs of the literature of decadence. One need only think of poor Swinburne, for whom Rossetti – just to make matters worse – prescribed an athletic circus artiste for therapeutic purposes. That the terrifying image of the Medusa-like woman must have had a part to play in Hofmannsthal's fantasies is suggested, for example, by a photograph showing Anna Bahr-Mildenburg as Clytemnestra in a 1909 production of *Elektra* by the Vienna Hofoper [Court Opera]: a statuesque matron with a slight squint, armed with a staff and hung about the eyes with metallic ornaments, evidently in full possession of her powers, and capable of striking terror into any sensitive male soul.[12]

One of the more developed sections of *Andreas* consists of a dream sequence in which the young hero, who has after all set out in order to learn what fear feels like, takes part in a hunt before the day is over:

> he was the best shot; whenever he fired something fell. The lovely Countess was at his side as he fired, her eyes playing with him as he with the life of the wild creatures. Suddenly they are alone. Walls a fathom thick, in deadly silence, he is appalled to find that she is no longer a countess, but a woman . . . nothing gallant or honourable about it, nor any beauty either, but a frenzy, a murdering in the dark . . . [He] felt that he had pulled up his horse, and at the same moment his servant's nag stumbled. The man cursed and swore, as if the rider ahead were not his master, but a man he had fed swine with all his life. Andreas let it pass. He felt a great lassitude, the broad valley looked endless under the sagging clouds. He wished it were all over, that he were older and had children of his own, and that it was his son who was riding to Venice, but a different man from him, a fine fellow, a man and nothing but a man . . .[13]

In its whole conception, this passage, in which the encounter with the young Countess abruptly pivots into a terrifying feeling of impotence, betrays a longing as unfulfilled as it is ambivalent for a different kind of masculinity, one which has nothing to do with procreation and yet can still bring sons into the world who are fine fellows, upstanding men and nothing but men.

In what sphere of experience this dream might be realized is something about which Andreas has, so it seems, no idea. Just as he has a horror of women, so too he is afraid of what he will have to risk in Venice. When he arrives in the early hours, the first person he meets is, significantly, a masked gentleman who turns out to be a gambling man whose passion for the game has cost him even the clothes off his back. As this stranger approaches him with an obliging gesture, his coat gapes open at the front, and Andreas sees that beneath it he wears only a shirt; his stockings are sagging at the knees, and his shoes have no buckles. The thought that the stranger is now aware that Andreas has seen him in this strange state of *déshabillé* makes Andreas 'hot with shame, so that he too, unthinkingly, threw his travelling cloak open'.[14]

It is not immediately apparent whether Hofmannsthal was aware of what kind of encounter he was describing here. According to the psychology of gambling, what underlies compulsive gambling is, ultimately, a bisexual ideal, 'which the narcissist finds within himself; the compromise between man and woman, active and passive, sadism and masochism, and finally the incomplete choice between genital and anal libido, which is what is at stake for the gambler in the familiar symbolic colours of *rouge et noir*'.[15] This, then, is the gamble upon which Hofmannsthal embarked in *Andreas*, not knowing where it might lead him and how it might turn out. It does, though, seem as if for him the threat arising from a homosexual encounter was possibly even more terrifying than the fear of being engulfed by a woman. The servant Gotthelff, who is so persistent in his advances in the Schwert [Sword Inn] in Villach that Andreas has no choice but to cede to his demands to take him on as a servant, is the protagonist of a sexual nightmare, where the younger man knows that his role is that of victim. Homosexual rape and murder appear as chimeras on the horizon. Hofmannsthal's later notes contain the entry 'cf. Winkelmann's murder'.[16] Archangeli, who did away with the German scholar in Trieste, was probably one of Gotthelff's fraternity. 'Thank your Maker', Finazzer says to Andreas, after Gotthelff has made good his escape, 'that He has preserved you from spending a night in the woods with a runaway murderer.'[17]

There is much to be said for the idea that the reason Hofmannsthal was able to develop the Gotthelff scenes – which otherwise appear somewhat incidental – in such vivid detail can be put down to the fact that his first experiences of the wider world were as a *Wunderkind*, the object of male adulation. In 1892, Schnitzler wrote in a letter to Herzl about the young Hofmannsthal: 'We will hear a lot more of this curious eighteen-year-old. If you find the opening lines of *Anatol* "good enough to kiss", then I must warn you of the improper thoughts which might arise from the enjoyment of his other pieces.'[18] The innuendo revealed in these lines, and in the atmosphere of the male world paying court to him, must surely have got under the skin of the young Hofmannsthal, who was scarcely more than a boy at the time. On the one hand, this led to a dependence on the cultivation of platonic male friendships, often expressed in positively passionate terms in his correspondence with like-minded souls, such as Eberhard von Bodenhausen: 'Your words, your feelings . . . the touch of your hand – how alone we are, and how wonderful that we have each other.'[19] On the other it led to the rebuttal of Stefan George's desire for a closer collaboration. Werner Volke was one of the first to suggest that Hofmannsthal's nervousness and awkward embarrassment are nowhere as clearly apparent as in his letters to George.[20] It is thus hardly surprising that, in one of the notes for the novel, one finally comes across the explicit comment: 'Malteser = St. G.' ['The Maltese = St(efan) G(eorge)'].[21] The Maltese gentleman who takes Andreas under his wing in Venice soon confesses to him – according to one of the earliest notes – that 'he has never touched a woman. Andreas replies in like manner. The Maltese congratulates him.'[22]

Just as Hofmannsthal was unsure how to react to Stefan George, so too Andreas is unsure what to make of the fateful character of the Maltese gentleman, the embodiment of a type familiar from Romantic literature, a character of 'mysterious origin, but conjectured to be exalted, traces of burnt-out passions, suspicion of ghastly guilt, melancholy habits, pale face, unforgettable eyes'.[23] The suspicion arises that this forty-year-old ghost, as one of the notes says, 'could not have lived' and for that reason 'needs to come to life again in the other'.[24] The vampiric aspect of this constellation, however, reveals not only Hofmannsthal's almost instinctive revulsion towards Stefan George, but also his own relationship – since the forty-year-old Maltese also stands for Hofmannsthal – to the youth Andreas he himself once was. The narcissistic aspect of this very particular constellation is epitomized in the curious note imagining a youth 'dessen Leib sich durch den Harnisch durchbewegte' ['whose body moved through his armour'].[25] The conjunction of Andreas and the Maltese thus stands not only under the sign of the fear of sexual violation by an older man – which Hofmannsthal apostrophizes *inter alia* by reference to Baron Charlus[vi] – but also for the desire to be able to bring into the world a younger man from within the armour of a forty-year-old body. This is glossed, in one of the later notes, in the hope ascribed to the Maltese that 'Andreas might become his "son without a mother".'[26] And the imagined possibility of self-conception must be understood as a reflection of the act of poetic creation, whose true domain, as the Maltese says with regard to Ariosto, is the Impossible.[27]

By contrast with the Maltese Knight, the young Ferschengelder is still in the early stages of his emotional journey [*Passion*]. His *formation* into the homosexual or narcissistic type is by no means a foregone conclusion. What makes him appear so attractive to all he encounters on his journey is his pure erotic potential, which also serves as a foil for the author's own retrospective dreams. For Andreas, a heterosexual relationship is still something to be aspired to; indeed, it seems, if one may believe the initial outline of the plot, to be the true goal of his journey. Romana, the serving maid at the Finazzerhof, awakens in him that blessed desire for the feminine which in our culture is promoted as the only legitimate expression of eroticism. Naturally, here too not everything is as simple as it initially appears. The affection of the two young people for each other, their excursions together into the surrounding countryside, even Andreas's attempt to sneak into Romana's room at night – when, however, he chooses the wrong door and so finds in the bed only an ancient housekeeper with long straggling white hair – all this is harmless enough. But it is precisely in the innocent experimentations of children, as Freud repeatedly emphasizes, that the basis for all our perversions is laid down. Hofmannsthal's text takes account of this in his description of what psychoanalysis calls vicarious scenarios.

In the evening, when the goats return home, Romana – in

what is obviously a well-rehearsed routine – quickly lies down on the ground, and at once a goat is standing over her 'to let her drink, and struggled to stay there till she had sucked'.[28] Andreas is a fascinated witness to this scene, and when Romana then straight away leads him to her room and swings her long slim legs swiftly on to the bed, Andreas, leaning over her, sees that she is lying 'under him as she had lain under the goat'.[29] In his interpretations of so-called perverse attitudes, Freud notes that it is usually said that someone has *become* perverse, when really it would be more accurate to say they have *remained* perverse. From this, one may extrapolate that mankind's erotic utopia consists in the possibility of remaining perverse in all innocence. However, for Andreas this possibility has already passed. Scarcely has he leaned over Romana than the wind bangs the door, and he feels as if 'a leaden-grey face had peered in'.[29]

The fact that Andreas and Romana are like brother and sister to each other also fits the theme of forbidden love. Andreas marvels to hear her 'tell him everything, as frankly as if he were her brother.'[30] The Finazzers are an ancient family of yeomen, for whom love is a family affair. Raiding eagles' nests and marrying beautiful women, that was her grandfather's thing, Romana explains. He'd done that four times, and 'as each died took a still handsomer one, and every time a kinswoman, for he said there was nothing like Finazzer blood'.[31] Romana's parents, too, are like brother and sister, and Romana says that is just how she wants to live with her future husband, 'she would not have it any other way.'[31] Throughout nineteenth-century literature, the theme of love between brother and sister is of central importance, both as a cipher for an erotic utopia and as a warning example of the ultimate irrevocable transgression. In the image of a feudalistic golden age so dear to Hofmannsthal's heart, there is contained every kind of forbidden erotic pleasure – the bliss that Chateaubriand recalls with an exile's regret, when, in *Atala*, he writes of the 'marriages des premiers-nés des hommes, ces unions ineffables, alors que la soeur était l'épouse du frère, que l'amour et l'amitié fraternelle se confondaient dans le même coeur et que la pureté de l'une augmentait les délices de l'autre'.[32vii]

The warm glow of such familial closeness goes hand in hand with the horrors of decadence, death and dying. Six of Romana's siblings, 'the innocent boys Egydius, Achaz and Romauld Finazzer, the innocent girl Sabina, and the innocent twins Mansuet and Liberata',[33] are already dead and buried. The opposite of their heavenly home are the torments of hell, a subject in which Romana is well versed. She shows Andreas a thick book in which these are all pictured, 'the tortures of the damned arranged under the seven deadly sins, all engraved on copper'.[34] By this point, the reader is readily able to deduce the implicit association in the text between the Lives of the Saints and pornography, whose respective antinomic structures stem from the same inspiration, even if in the one case the background is gold-coloured and in the other black.

This duality is in keeping with the image of the feminine which Hofmannsthal outlines in the dual figure of Maria/Mariquita, in whom purity and lasciviousness continually alternate as in a picture puzzle. Andreas encounters this character, comprising two Spanish women plotting against each other, soon after his arrival in Venice. Maria, or M_1, is a character who is hysterical in the extreme. She suffers, as Hofmannsthal notes, from a vague lassitude and 'has a terrible knowledge of things. She is a widow. Her husband was cruel.' Furthermore it states that she has had a relationship 'with a grand Belgian–Bohemian gentleman',[35] probably the worst fate that can befall a woman. The possibilities of dying a martyr's death and petrifying in aristocratic *morgue* are, as it says in a note, equal aspects of her nature. She always wears fingerless gloves, and strives for purification, for immolation of the heart, and represents the glorification of the mortification of the flesh.[36] Like Hérodias and Salammbô, she grows less by the day, waiting for a 'chose inconnue'. This nameless dream is embodied in Mariquita, the other woman whom Maria has repressed in and out of herself to the extent that she exists in the world as a completely separate being. The name Mariquita, which is in itself already suggestive of a pornographic scenario, indirectly links *Andreas* to Lewis's notorious tale *The Monk* (1796) by way of Prosper Mérimée's persiflage *Une Femme est un diable*, in which a certain Mariquita gives a comic twist to Matilda's seduction of the monk Ambrosio.[37] Mariquita, at any rate, represents the woman who is available in every part of her body. Everything about her is unique – 'knee, hip, smile'[38] – whereas Maria can only surrender herself as a whole, with her astral body consisting of thoughts, fears and aspirations.[39] However, Maria is unable to obtain release for her thwarted passion, since her desires are suppressed with redoubled effort when, praying, she is reminded of one of Mariquita's most intense positions, and when she, as it says in the text, feels her coming into her. 'Those are', Mariquita says, 'my nastiest moments. Then I hate her as the man in Hell must hate God.'[40] The excruciating dividedness of a woman driven by the longing for release from the prison of her own body takes on, for Andreas, a paradoxical aspect, since *he* feels happy in Maria's presence, whereas Mariquita makes him feel dark and frenzied – and – as a note confirms – 'afterwards ill-tempered'.[40] He is, however, captivated by both of them – and they are linked superficially 'by a small asthmatic King Charles spaniel, Fidèle by name',[41] who, save on one occasion, is kept hidden in Maria's house.

Alewyn admits that he does not know what to do with the dog, nor with the many other dogs who go about their business in *Andreas*.[42] If the renowned baroque specialist had taken the trouble to read Benjamin's book on *The Origin of German Tragic Drama* [*Ursprung des deutschen Trauerspiels*], he might perhaps have realized that this dog, with its telling name Fidèle, is none other than the incarnation of an ancient symbol for the melancholic masculine soul, which, in its faithful devotion to the image of woman, jealously seeks the pain of passion[viii] – and what is it that causes pain, if not cruelty. The most extreme perversion of the decadent imagination is that it seeks to hammer out the relief of beauty by martyring the object of its adulation. Cruelty is also the name of Andreas's original sin, as we may deduce from his darkest childhood memory, that terrible episode in the text when, as a twelve-year-old boy, with his heel he breaks the back of the little stray dog, most devoted of creatures, which had attached himself to him. Andreas does not know whether he has actually committed this crime against nature, or whether it just keeps surfacing in his consciousness as a figment of the imagination. What he does know is that he has within him the capacity to be cruelly violent. Thus the dog at the Finazzerhof poisoned by Gotthelff, which at the end 'was standing in the full moonlight, its head strangely drawn to one side, and in this posture [was] turning round and round on itself',[43] serves as a reminder of the guilt which humans ceaselessly pass down to one another at the destruction of nature – including their own. When Andreas, in despair, later throws himself to the ground on the spot where the Finazzer dog is buried, it dawns on him that he has something in common with the dead dog, and also with Gotthelff, who was to blame for the creature's death.

This 'something', which Andreas cannot quite pin down, but which he knows is what makes the world go round, is an interest in cruelty, the other side of the suffering of melancholy. For *cruauté* is the mechanism by which *Passion* – in the sense of suffering, passion as desire, and compassion – is forcibly extracted from a state of profound apathy. In the state of *appassionnement*, uncontrolled desire for the opposite sex steers inexorably towards that insane paroxysm illustrated in the text by the perverse anecdote about the Duke of Camposagrado who, in a fit of rage and jealousy, devours a rare bird sent to his mistress by a Jewish admirer the previous day. The brothers Goncourt, who knew about these things, define the phenomenon of passion as a state of corruption. 'La passion des choses ne vient pas de la bonté ou de la beauté pure de ces choses, elle vient surtout de leur corruption. On aimera follement une femme, pour sa putinerie, pour la méchanceté de son esprit, pour la voyoucratie de sa tête, de son cœur, de ses sens; on aura le goût déréglé d'une mangeaille pour son odeur avancée et qui pue. Au fond, ce que fait l'appassionnement: c'est le *faisandage* des êtres et des choses.'[44][ix]

The source of this inclination [*Neigung*] which finds satisfaction only in corruption is, however, not revealed here either. A dream in which Andreas is spared none of the terrible encounters with the ghosts of his childhood directly associates cruelty – that which seeks to corrupt and destroy – with those things before which one recoils in horror. In the dream, Andreas feels the gaze of his first catechist on him, a man he had feared as a child like no other, and feels how 'the dreaded little podgy hand'[45] grabs hold of him. From this panic there surfaces the image of a cat with a doglike face, which he believes he killed as a child, remembering how it took a long time to die, and now, after all these years, is still not dead. The moment of homosexual abuse of the child is the decisive trigger for the emergence of a cruelty which kills the thing it loves, since only the most drastic encounter with the body of the opposite sex is now capable of arousing the sexuality so abruptly stifled. Tellingly, this dream begins with Andreas pursuing the fleeing Romana. When he wakes up – at this point he is at the Finazzerhof – he feels like someone who has been awakened by the executioner's knock. It is as if 'he had committed some dreadful deed and now it was all coming to light.'[46] The most terrible screams are echoing through the house. Thinking it might be Romana, his blood freezes in his veins. But then he says to himself that even if she were being martyred, she would be incapable of producing such sounds. The screams are coming from a maidservant, whom Gotthelff has gagged and bound naked to a bedpost and abused. Around her, everything is smouldering and burning. An image, it seems, from the book depicting the torments of hell. If Romana, watching horrified in the background, were the victim, we would have before us an illustration from the *vita sanctorum*, which would not, however, alter the substance of the events described. The primary mover of the narrative remains the *delectatio morosa*, which, since it is an innocent woman being broken on the wheel, here acquires that specific exaltation [*Überhöhung*] which it takes on in de Sade's *Justine*. Baudelaire, that keen pupil of the Marquis, was of the opinion that it is nature 'qui pousse l'homme à tuer son semblable, à le manger, à le séquestrer, à le torturer'.[47x]

In order to explore the heretical world view testified to in such a statement, Hofmannsthal created the figure of Andreas.

Nowhere else does he venture so far into the depths of his imagination as here. One of the notes made after the autumn of 1913 concerns the affair with the inconsolable widow whom Andreas meets on his way to Venice. 'He puts himself in the place of the wretched murderess,' it states there, 'Romana in the place of the man. He is morbid enough to imagine the murder. All his mania of self-abasement converges on this point; he pictures to himself all that he has destroyed in Romana: – he does not let her die completely, but live on, a joyless spirit – only by this is the richness of her life revealed to him – he feels at one with her as never before, he begins to perceive the sense in life – he is happy.'[48] In the imagined representation of sadistic omnipotence and the dissolution made visible in the person of the executed woman, there also dissolves the mania of self-abasement [*Kleinheitswahn*], and with it the otherwise all-pervasive feeling of impotence.

It is not immediately clear how much further into the territory of *littérature maudite* Hofmannsthal might have penetrated had he – scarcely imaginable under the circumstances – actually completed *Andreas*. At any rate, he was not short of inspiration for an appropriate Venetian setting, along the lines of the *piombi* in *Casanova*[xi] and Piranesi's *Carceri*. As an architectural backdrop for another episode, not specified further, he indicates the 'torture chamber from *l'homme qui rit*'.[48][xii] It is hard to avoid the impression that, during the long years Hofmannsthal devoted to the *Andreas* project, it is precisely the layer of the text associated with such localities which comes ever closer to the surface, almost completely displacing the concept of a *Bildungsroman* to which the author – apparently as a kind of penitence – remains so stubbornly attached. Possibly Hofmannsthal allowed himself to succumb to the fascination of the perverse to such an extent because, for him, it represented a whole new field of knowledge – not least about himself – which would otherwise have remained inaccessible to him. The pornographic urge is famously also an *exacerbatio cerebri*, a desire for the hidden fruit of knowledge for the sake of pure knowledge itself. And the truth, if indeed one wishes to know it, is, as Flaubert says, nowhere 'plus clairement visible que dans les belles expositions de la misère humaine'.[49xiii] It is, then, first and foremost, all about knowledge. It is no coincidence that, in Venice, Andreas almost comes to grief on a tomato [known in Austria as a 'paradise apple']. About knowledge, and about the mystery of art, which, in this ultramontane project for a novel – in which we may discern, as Flaubert does in de Sade's work, the last gasp of Catholicism – is revealed more clearly and unreservedly than in any other work of Hofmannthal's. For the joy of art is a forbidden one. Here a childhood memory of Andreas's may serve as a truly heart-rending example. Many years ago, so the passage in question begins, in the manner of a fairytale,

> when he was ten or twelve years old, he had two friends who lived in the Blue Freihaus in the Wieden, on the same staircase in that fourth courtyard where the 'regular theatre' was housed in a barn. He remembered how wonderful it was to be visiting them towards evening, and to see the scenery carried out, a canvas with a magic garden, a bit of a tavern inside, the murmur of the crowd, the candle-snuffers, the *manoletti* sellers. More poignant than all the rest, the confused hum of the instruments tuning up – to this day the memory brought a pang. The floor of the stage was uneven, the curtain too short in places: between the lights the feet

of Moors or lions . . . once [. . .] a sky-blue shoe, embroidered with tinsel. The sky-blue shoe was more wonderful than all the rest. Later, a being stood there with the shoe on – it belonged to her, was one with her blue and silver gown; she was a princess, dangers surrounded her, dark forms, flaming torches, an enchanted wood closed round her, voices sounded from the branches, monkeys came rolling fruit along from which lovely children sprang, shining. The princess sang, Harlequin was at her side, yet far, far away from her. All that was beautiful, but it was not the two-edged sword which had pierced his soul, from tenderest delight and unutterable longing to tears, awe and ecstasy, when the blue shoe stood empty beneath the curtain.[50]

Apart from the rapturous surge of emotions which the fetishist experiences at the sight of the object of desire, and which is perhaps described nowhere so perfectly as here, this passage evokes the unexpected epiphany of images, whose force Baudelaire acknowledges with the exclamation 'Les images, ma grande, ma primitive passion.'[51][xiv] The poetic image, the incunabulum of the creative imagination, operates at the limits of what we can apprehend. It is profoundly appropriate to the fetishistic tendency, which conceals the libido precisely where no one would think of looking for it. Only in such images is it possible – in the most painful way imaginable – to see restored the joy [*Glück*] of those better times from which we believe we have lapsed. 'Nessun maggior dolor' [no greater suffering] – as Hofmannsthal also noted for his *Andreas* novel – 'che ricordarsi del tempo felice – nella miseria.'[52][xv]

The Undiscover'd Country

The Death Motif in Kafka's *Castle*

> And in the end, or almost, to be abroad alone, by unknown ways, in the gathering of the night, with a stick. It was a stout stick, he used it to thrust himself onward, or as a defence, when the time came, against dogs and marauders. Yes, night was gathering, but the man was innocent, greatly innocent, he had nothing to fear, though he went in fear, he had nothing to fear, there was nothing they could do to him, or very little.
>
> S. Beckett, Molloy

The smooth surface of Kafka's work has remained an enigma in spite of what his interpreters have managed to dredge from its depths. It has preserved its integrity against the advances of criticism. What it conveys is the infinitely sombre gaze of the five-year-old boy who, dressed in a sailor suit and with a shiny black walking stick and a straw hat in his hand, was dragged into the gloomy exoticism of a photographer's studio in Prague. Critics have singularly failed to come to terms with this gaze, they have overlooked the yearning, fearful images of death which pervade Kafka's work and which impart that melancholy whose onset was as early as it was persistent. Sickness unto death, unless purged by suicide, has always been suspect in the eyes of society. It is therefore ignored, and instead one strives to wrest some positive meaning from Kafka's work – if necessary, in the spirit of the existentialist volte-face whereby freedom emerges from the very absurdity of an endeavour. Such interpretations have been attempted in defiance of the obvious fact that Kafka felt constrained to hide any happiness he may have experienced like a physical deformity. It would mean a form of absolution for society if one could place a positive interpretation on K.'s desire for death, since it was society that instilled this grim, deep-seated desire in him in the first place and death – at least according to common supposition – is only a cipher for salvation.

Towards the end of the story K. converses with the landlady of the Herrenhof. '"Didn't you once learn tailoring?" the landlady asked. "No, never," K. said. "What actually is it you are?" "Land Surveyor." "What *is* that?" K. explained, the explanation made her yawn. "You're not telling the truth. Why won't you tell the truth?" "You don't tell the truth either."'[1A] He is not a surveyor then, he does not have anything with him to substantiate his claim, he is merely a wanderer, a figure who first appears with a 'minute rucksack' and a 'knotty stick'.[2] Psychoanalysis designates the image of a journey or a hike as a symbol of death, and Adorno describes the scenario of Schubert's two great song cycles as follows: 'They link up with poems in which again and again the images of death present themselves to the man who wanders among them as diminutively as Schubert in the Dreimäderlhaus. A stream, a mill and a dark desolate wintry landscape stretching away in the twilight of mock suns, timeless, as in a dream – these are the hallmarks of the setting of Schubert's songs, with dried flowers for their mournful ornament.'³ Brown Bohemian earth, where at the end of the Middle Ages another German poet had once talked with death,⁴ also surrounds the Castle, as the pictures edited by Klaus Wagenbach show, and Kafka deliberately avoided introducing the brighter green of organic nature into his landscape as a source of comfort. The ground is covered in frost and snow, a still life, a *nature morte* which precludes any hope of regeneration; this is reinforced by Pepi's statement that winter is long in these parts, so prolonged that in her recollection spring and summer appear to last barely more than two days, 'and even on those days, even during the most beautiful day, even then sometimes snow falls.'⁵ K. complains often enough that it is difficult to make any progress across this landscape. Aggravated by the monotony, the wanderer who tries to cross it always retraces his own tracks. 'The eccentric structure of this landscape, where each point is equidistant from the centre, is revealed to the wanderer who traverses it without making any headway: every development is its own perfect antithesis, the first step is as close to death as the last, and the dissociated points of the landscape are visited in a circle, without it ever being left behind. For Schubert's themes wander just like the miller or the lover abandoned in winter by his mistress. They have no history but are merely viewed from different angles. The only change is a change of light.'⁶ There can seldom have been a more apposite description of the way in which the avowedly unmusical Kafka circles about the geometric location of his yearning than in these lines of Adorno's on the structure of Schubert's work. The debate about K.'s 'development' suddenly seems egregious, for at the point where in the first section of the book he crosses the wooden bridge over the stream and invades the territory of the Castle he is like 'those wretched souls who travel hither and thither but have no history'.⁷ᴮ The busyness in the *paysage mort*, all the to-ing and fro-ing of coaches and litigants, and every attempt to attain some goal in the domain of death bear the marks of immense futility. So too folklore tells us that in that undiscover'd country one takes three steps forward and three steps back.⁸ In the Berliner Ensemble production of *Mother Courage* the heroine marched against a revolving stage through the devastated lands of the Empire with no hope of ever changing her situation. K. too, the first time he tries to press on into the Castle, experiences a paralysis of the will to proceed imposed by some external force. 'At last he tore himself away from the obsession of the street and escaped into a small side-lane, where the snow was still deeper and the exertion of lifting one's feet clear was fatiguing; he broke into a sweat, suddenly came to a stop, and could not go on.'⁹ Kierkegaard describes the humerous [sic] equivalent of a progression directed against its own teleology in a passage devoted to the old Friedrichstädter Theatre in Berlin and a comedian called Beckmann.

> He can not only go, he can come and go at the same time. That's something quite different, to come and go simultaneously, and through this genial accomplishment he can improvise the whole physical setting and can not only represent a wandering journeyman but also come-and-go like one. We see it all, looking up from the dust of the highway towards a welcoming village and hearing its quiet sounds, glimpsing the very path which skirts the village pond where one turns off by the smithy – and there we see Beckmann approaching with his small haversack, his stick in his hand, carefree and cheerful. He can come-and-go followed by urchins whom one cannot in fact see.¹⁰ᶜ

Adorno cites this passage in an essay on Chaplin. But Chaplin of whom we are reminded by the adventures of Karl Rossmann and by many photographs of Kafka himself — Chaplin who became hopelessly entangled in his own hastiness — was the hero of a modern entertainment which Kafka described to Janouch as 'the magic lantern of a neglected youth',[11D] and all his life the neglect of youth appeared to him like a premature death.

We learn only very little about the Castle itself, the imaginary centre of the landscape of death. However, the figures that emerge from it in the course of the story allow us to draw certain conclusions about its nature. There is first of all Schwarzer who wakens the weary K. from his unauthorized sleep. The name draws attention to the colour[i] that seems to be dominant in the Castle; its inhabitants, like the assistants, wear close-fitting black clothes as a sort of uniform. Yet the assistants themselves in spite of their sometimes importunate liveliness, do not appear properly alive. When Artur returns to the Castle in order to lodge a complaint about his master, the latter realizes for the first time what he finds so repugnant about Jeremias, the assistant who remains behind — it is 'this flesh which sometimes gave one the impression of not being properly alive'.[12E] And shortly afterwards the appearance of Jeremias confirms his uncanny suspicion:

> As he stood there, his hair rumpled, and his thin beard lank as if dripping with wet, his eyes painfully beseeching and wide with reproach, his sallow cheeks flushed, but yet flaccid, his naked legs trembling so violently with cold that the long fringes of the wrap quivered as well, he was like a patient who had escaped from hospital, and whose appearance could only suggest one thought, that of getting him back in bed again.[13]

The tousled hair, the soaking beard, the eyes held open only with difficulty, the loose flesh – it is as if Jeremias were already in a state of decomposition, a corpse escaped from the grave. After all, 'bed' and 'sleep' often stand for the abode and condition of the dead, in this and other literature. When Frieda lets K. peep through the spy-hole into Klamm's room, the latter is sitting completely immobile at his table. The only sign of life is a cigar smoking in his motionless hand and the glint of the pince-nez which hides his eyes – the most vital part of a man. Immediately afterwards K. wonders if Klamm is disturbed by the rowdiness of the servants. '"No," said Frieda, "he's asleep." "Asleep?" cried K. "But when I peeped in he was awake and sitting at the desk." "He always sits like that," said Frieda, "he was sleeping when you saw him. Would I have let you look in if he hadn't been asleep? That's how he sleeps, the gentlemen do sleep a great deal . . ."'[14] Sleep is the brother of death and is assiduously cultivated by the inhabitants of the Castle. When they leave their bureaux to attend a hearing, they prefer to do it at night and even then they like to settle themselves in bed like Bürgel, that image of a regressive existence to which K. so fervently longs to return. Bürgel spends a large part of his time in bed, he deals with his correspondence in bed and interrogates plaintiffs from his bed. Unlike other officials Bürgel is plagued by insomnia. K. too is a restless spirit. This may be why Bürgel is willing and able to indicate a way out for K. Yet K., overcome by irresistible weariness, forfeits the chance of revelation, like the character in a Yiddish story who sleeps through the Day of Judgement. Sortini too, whom K. encounters only through Olga's story, is a harbinger of death. He is not one of those officials bloated with age, like Klamm, or one of those with childlike faces, like Bürgel: his features are rather different.

Olga describes him as a small, weak, thoughtful person, and goes on, 'and one thing about him struck all the people who noticed him at all, the way his forehead was furrowed; all the furrows – and there were plenty of them although he's certainly not more than forty – were spread fanwise over his forehead, running towards the root of his nose. I've never seen anything like it.'[15] A physiognomy such as Olga describes here reminds one readily of a mummy distorted by a shrinking process. However, it is not only this which makes the haggard Sortini an envoy of death, but also the scene where with legs stiffened by his sedentary occupation he leaps across the shaft of the fire engine to approach Amalia who is decked out like a bride. Politzer recognizes the fire service party where Sortini meets Amalia as a *sacre du printemps*[ii] but he omits to point out the affinity between the archetype of this ritual and that of death, even though the death symbolism surrounding the sacrificial feast of the maidservants can be shown to be a literary *topos*. Adrian Leverkühn, for instance, is oppressed at the wedding of his sister by the fact that 'the white shroud of virginity, the satin slippers of the dead'[16] are used. Amalia is prepared for the firemen's festival in precisely the same manner. The 'dress was specially fine', Olga recalls, 'a white blouse foaming high in front with one row of lace after the other, our mother had taken every bit of her lace for it'.[17] Olga then describes the necklace of Bohemian garnets and reports her father as saying, 'To-day, mark my words, Amalia will find a husband.'[18] But Amalia rejects Sortini's advances, is alarmed by the ghastly character of the spring rites and the absence of any conciliatory aspect which she may have hoped for in her more obscure presentiments. There are no tokens of any luxuriant scenery promising carefree procreation; of the requisites of the vernal season we glimpse only the bare date, 3 July; and the centrepiece of the feast is a mechanical monster in the shape of the fire engine. For this reason Amalia refuses the next day to obey Sortini's summons which reaches her, according to Olga, in the form of a pornographic document drafted in copperplate handwriting. For this reason too she brings down execration upon her family. Henceforth her father trudges each day up to the Castle entrance or to that of the cemetery, in order to draw the inhabitants' attention to himself and the sad lot of his family as they drive past in their carriages.

> In his best suit, which soon becomes his only suit, off he goes every morning from the house with our best wishes. He takes with him a small Fire Brigade badge, which he has really no business to keep, to stick in his coat once he's out of the village . . . Not far from the Castle entrance there's a market garden, belonging to a man called Bertuch who sells vegetables to the Castle, and there on the narrow stone ledge at the foot of the garden fence father took up his post.[19]

The best suit, soon to be the only one he will have left, the blessing of his family, the small medal, the market garden, the name of the gardener and the narrow stone ledge, all this recalls – if one translates the surreal fantasy images back into rational concepts – funerals and graveyards. The fact that shortly afterwards his wife follows the father on his excursions again adds to this picture of the death of the old couple. When Olga reports, 'We often went out to them, to take them food, or merely to visit them, or to try to persuade them to come back home,'[20] here too the empirical equivalent is a visit to the cemetery and the graveside, the leaving of food for the wandering souls, still perpetuated by the sprinkling of holy water. Indeed the attempt to persuade the departed to return home is an archaic residue which had a great impact on Döblin when during a journey to Poland he visited the Jewish cemetery on the eve of the Day of Atonement.[21] At home, however, the parents have left behind their stiff and helpless bodies which Amalia dresses and undresses, puts to bed and feeds, very much like Nag and Nell in *Endgame*.

When K. tries to reach the Castle, as he twice does at the beginning of his stay in the village, images of home well up involuntarily in his mind's eye. On the occasion of his first attempt, which ends with the regeneration scene in Lasemann's house, he is struck by the similarity between the Castle and the small town where he grew up, and he wonders whether it would not have been better to return home again instead of pressing onwards towards the Castle. The second time he believes himself to be approaching the Castle, arm in arm with Barnabas, again a memory of home is conjured up.

> They went on, but K. did not know whither, he could discern nothing, not even whether they had already passed the church or not. The effort which it cost him merely to keep going made him lose control of his thoughts. Instead of remaining fixed on their goal they strayed. Memories of his home kept recurring and filled his mind. There, too, a church stood in the marketplace, partly surrounded by an old graveyard which was again surrounded by a high wall. Very few boys had managed to climb that wall, and for some time K., too, had failed. It was not curiosity which had urged them on. The graveyard had been no mystery to them. They had often entered it through a small wicket-gate, it

was only the smooth high wall that they had wanted to conquer. But one morning – the empty, quiet marketplace had been flooded with sunshine, when had K. ever seen it like that either before or since? – he had succeeded in climbing it with astonishing ease; at a place where he had already slipped down many a time he had clambered with a small flag between his teeth right to the top at the first attempt. Stones were still rattling down under his feet, but he was at the top. He stuck the flag in, it flew in the wind, he looked down and round about him, over his shoulder, too, at the crosses mouldering in the ground, nobody was greater than he at that place and that moment.[22]

Just as death has always been considered the second home of mankind, so images of his first home flit through K.'s imagination on his way to the Castle. Moreover Adorno reminds us that Schubert too, 'in the cycle revolving around the words "All my dreams are ended", uses the name of "inn" only for the graveyard'.[23] The precise significance of such a notion can be seen from K.'s clear memory of climbing the wall. What a crude psychology is so quick to interpret as an unambiguous orgastic symbol, in view of the ramming home of the flag and its taut fabric – a symbol that conveys the conquering of death by the power of life – is in fact anything but unambiguous even in K.'s mind. On the contrary, the brief moment of triumph when to the boy looking over his shoulder the crosses seem to sink into the ground is treated as the expression of a short-lived surrender to personal happiness. The cemetery exists just as before and then the teacher, a representative of realism, arrives and with a mere glance brings down the whole house of cards. A more appropriate tool to help us understand this episode and the context in which it appears would be Freud's theory, developed in his later years, of the identity of the life and the death wish. Freud regarded both as conservative, inasmuch as both were concerned to escape from a state of spiritual and physical individuation and to enter that condition of painlessness which is beyond the birth trauma. Kafka considers this combination to be at once comforting and hopeless in those passages where K. and Frieda try to lose themselves in one another. We should not, of course, overlook the significant but remote moment when, shortly after his arrival, K. experienced in Frieda's arms the joy of a timeless alienation from himself; yet this mirror of salvation is shattered by the description not long afterwards of their futile endeavour to recreate this *unitas unitatis*.

> There they lay, but not in the forgetfulness of the previous night. She was seeking and he was seeking, they raged and contorted their faces and bored their heads into each other's bosoms in the urgency of seeking something, and their embraces and their tossing limbs did not avail to make them forget, but only reminded them of what they sought; like dogs desperately tearing up the ground they tore at each other's bodies, and often, helplessly baffled, in a final effort to attain happiness they nuzzled and tongued each other's face. Sheer weariness stilled them at last and brought them gratitude to each other. Then the maids came in. 'Look how they are lying there,' said one, and sympathetically cast a coverlet over them.[24]

As so often with Kafka, a single isolated gesture at the end of a description seems to sum up its whole meaning. A sheet is spread over the twisted bodies who have died in love. It is well known that all the women characters in Kafka's novels remain tied to a stage of evolution that preceded the emergence of human life. There is, for example, the bloated Brunelda in *America*, or Fräulein Bürstner, or Leni who has a bind of web between the middle and the fourth finger of her right hand as a token of her origins in some prehistoric swamp; and Frieda too, described as an etiolated creature who shuns the light, belongs to this group, as does Pepi who has risen from the chthonic depths of the Brückenhof, and Gardena, vegetating in her bed like a carnivorous plant. Walter Benjamin saw early on that these creatures belonged to a stage 'which Bachofen calls the hetaeric'.[25iii] Its manifestation is that of self-forgetful life, and thus also of death. Just as the rotational correspondences of 'hetaera esmeralda' haunt the compositions of Adrian Leverkühn after his exposure to the sting of death in the prostitute's embrace, so too Kafka's novels are permeated by the sombreness of a world where the dark forces of matriarchal figures unsex their male partners. These matriarchal figures, however, stand at the gates of hell, for as Berthold von Regensburg tells us hell lies at the heart of earth's steamy swamps.[26] Such is the terrible ambivalence which cripples the power of life in Kafka's work. The death wish of love has its pendant in the message which K. believes he hears in the tolling of a bell, when Gerstäcker drives him back to the Brückenhof on his sleigh after the first fruitless expedition. 'The Castle above them, which K. had hoped to reach that very day, was already beginning to grow dark, and retreated again into the distance. But as if to give him a parting sign till their next encounter a bell began to ring merrily up there, a bell which for at least a second made his heart palpitate for its tone was menacing, too, as if it threatened him with the fulfilment of his vague desire.'[27] As the promise is transformed into a threat of death, the tolling soon dies away, to be replaced by a less ambiguous sound, 'by a feeble monotonous little tinkle which . . . certainly harmonized better with the slow-going journey, with the wretched-looking yet inexorable driver'.[27]

In the context of this argument, it would seem appropriate to explore the messianic traits which Kafka, more modest but also more serious than any of his contemporaries, bestows on his alter ego K. The limits of his messianic vision correspond to the great scepticism with which Kafka regarded the possibility of transcending the human predicament. Admittedly, since K. refuses to disclose to the village secretary Momus details of his identity and thus evades the regular admittance procedure into the realm of the dead, it could be argued he intends to invade the Castle as a living person and annul death's anathema on life. But all the other messianic hopes are imputed to him by others rather than being his o[w]n pretensions, and are therefore an example of those projections held to be the basis of human religion. K. initially represents a hope of this kind for Barnabas's family, a hope which even Olga fears towards the end of her tale is perhaps only an 'illusion',[28] for this family has always awaited the day when 'someone in the long procession of visitors would arrive and put a stop to it all and make everything swing the other way again'.[29] But to bring the process to a halt, to dissipate the mythic power that reproduces itself in an eternal recurrence by forcing it to reverse its direction – this does not lie in K.'s power any more than in that of the young observer in Kafka's story *In the Gallery*. Like him, K. is dazzled and disoriented by the surface events, is himself drawn into the spectacle and thereby becomes guilty of complicity. 'Then,' Olga says, 'we should have lost you, and I confess that you now mean almost more to me than Barnabas's service in the Castle.'[30] For Pepi too, the maid who lives in a damp cellar, K. represents the epiphany of a better life. 'At that time', we read, 'she had loved K. as she had never loved anyone before; month after month she had been down there in her tiny dark room, prepared to spend years there, or, if the worst came to the worst, to spend her whole life here, ignored by everyone, and now suddenly K. had appeared, a hero, a rescuer of maidens in distress, and had opened up the way upstairs for her.'[31] The outcome of these hopes is familiar. After a short respite behind the bar Pepi has to return to the world from which she came, and it looks as if K. goes with her, after losing Frieda and his job as a caretaker. The saviour cannot come up to the great expectations held of him and sinks to the level of those who on his arrival looked up to him in hope. In this connection the episode with Hans Brunswick takes on a curious ambivalence. K. mentions to him that at home he used to be called '"The Bitter Herb" on account of his healing powers'.[32] The 'bitter herb' can stand for gentle Hippocratic healing or be a symbol of death. The doctor is a secularized messiah who expels sickness from the suffering body but he is also the accomplice of death. This ambiguity, present at an early stage in Kafka's work, can be seen in the child's attitude to the stranger. The optimistic energy of the child – for 'nobody is more eager to change things than a child'[33F] – tries to overcome K.'s ambivalence, and out of the contradiction there arises in him:

> the belief that though for the moment K. was wretched and looked down on, yet in an almost unimaginable and distant future he would excel everybody. And it was just this

absurdly distant future and the glorious developments which were to lead up to it that attracted Hans; that was why he was willing to accept K. even in his present state. The peculiar childish-grown-up acuteness of this wish consisted in the fact that Hans looked on K. as on a younger brother whose future would reach further than his own, the future of a very little boy.[34]

Hans's desires, themselves conditional, do not inspire K. to any messianic gesture; rather they arouse 'new hopes in him, improbable, he admitted, completely groundless even, but all the same not to be put out of his mind'.[35] Thus all hope remains circular and in the end it is no more than a 'misunderstanding', as Bruno Schulz, Kafka's Polish translator, put it.[36G] Yet the messianic ideal is imputed to K. once again. Towards the end of the novel he finds himself by mistake in Bürgel's room on his way to an interrogation and there falls into a heavy sleep while the secretary imparts to him vital information that will lead him out of his dilemma. As though under some kind of compulsion Bürgel explains to the sleeping K. the threat which at that very moment he poses to the totality of the system. 'It is a situation', Bürgel elaborates, 'in which it very soon becomes impossible to refuse to do a favour. To put it precisely, one is desperate; to put it still more precisely, one is very happy. Desperate, for the defenceless position in which one sits here waiting for the applicant to utter his plea and knowing that once it is uttered one must grant it, even if, at least insofar as one has oneself a general view of the situation, it positively tears the official organization to shreds: this is, the worst thing that can happen to one in the fulfilment of one's duties.'[37] This is the promise of apocalyptic destruction, but the potential messiah has fallen asleep from weariness – in other words, has succumbed to the brother of death – and he does not hear the summons directed at him. At precisely the point when he draws closest to his own salvation and to the salvation he could offer to the rest of the world, he is also furthest away from it, because of the eccentric structure of Kafka's world. At precisely the moment when his spirit is called, K. is asleep. Bürgel's words, which from the outset K. hears only as a distant murmur, fail to rouse him to a new life but rather lull him into a sleep from which there will not readily be an awakening. '"Clatter, mill, clatter on and on," he thought, "you clatter just for me."'[38] In falling prey to the temptation of sleep and thus offending against Pascal's metaphysical commandment 'Thou shalt sleep no more,' K. averts the danger which an individual such as he represents for the Castle. Though this may be inevitable, it also conveys the crazy irony of all human endeavour to escape from the limitations of one's own existence. 'One's physical energies last only to a certain limit,' explains a Mephistophelian Bürgel. 'Who can help the fact that precisely this limit is significant in other ways too? No, nobody can help it. That is how the world itself corrects the deviations in its course and maintains the balance. This is indeed an excellent, time and again unimaginably excellent arrangement, even if in other respects dismal and cheerless.'[39] However, the latent messianic mission to invade the realm of the dead as a living saviour can be interpreted in another way, if one equates the realm of the dead with the place where one's forefathers are assembled. This search for a buried ancestral tradition is represented by one of those insignificant gestures which seem to offer a key to the Kafka enigma.

> . . . the support of the arm above was no longer sufficient; involuntarily K. provided himself with new support by planting his right hand firmly against the quilt, whereby he accidentally took hold of Bürgel's foot, which happened to be sticking up under the quilt.[40]

This surrealist detail is a memory of orthodox Judaism, in which one sought to ensure a lasting contact with the departed by touching the feet of the corpse. Kafka has this gesture in mind at another point when he writes:

> In Hebrew my name is Amschel, like my mother's maternal grandfather, whom my mother, who was six years old when he died, can remember as a very pious and learned man with a long, white beard. She remembers how she had to take hold of the toes of the corpse and ask forgiveness for any offence she may have committed against her grandfather.[41]

Klaus Wagenbach has moreover demonstrated the topographical similarity between Kafka's Castle and that of the village Wossek, from where his father's family originated. K.'s attempt to penetrate the rambling wings of this castle may then be interpreted as an effort to re-enter the spiritual traditions of his forefathers. Kafka often regretted how remote they seemed to him, alienated as he was by the process of assimilation. 'I am as far as I know the most typical Western Jew among them,' he writes in a letter to Milena, 'this means, expressed with exaggeration, that not one calm second is granted me, nothing is granted me, everything has to be earned, not only the present and the future, but the past too – something after all which perhaps every human being has inherited, this too must be earned, it is perhaps the hardest work.'[42] Small wonder if at the conclusion of the novel (which cannot be too distant from the point where the extant fragment tapers off) K. would, according to Max Brod, have died of exhaustion; small wonder indeed if he has to pay with his life to achieve proximity with his ancestors.

There are other images of death in the landscape surrounding Kafka's Castle. Folklore teaches us that the inn is an ancient symbol of the underworld. It is the place where the dead assemble before descending into hell, and in legend the devil's tavern is the last stage on the journey of the dead. Like the Brückenhof it stands on the border of the other world.[43H] Even the architecture of the Herrenhof has something of a subterranean atmosphere, above all when the servant leads K. across the yard and

> then into the entry and through the low, somewhat downward-sloping passage . . . The servant put out his lantern, for here it was brilliant with electric light. Everything was on a small scale, but elegantly finished. The space was utilized to the best advantage. The passage was just high enough for one to walk without bending one's head. Along both sides the doors almost touched each other. The walls did not quite reach to the ceiling, probably for reasons of ventilation, for here in the low cellar-like passage the tiny rooms could hardly have windows.[44]

And then the noise is described, a chaos of sound, of dictating and conversing voices, the clink of glasses and the blows of a hammer – a cacophony which may well have appeared as the most appropriate image of hell to a Kafka notoriously sensitive to noise. The fact that coaches are used for travelling about similarly fits into the landscape of death, as does the telephone, that mystagogic instrument to which Proust and Benjamin paid such eloquent tribute.[45] It is from the telephone that K. hears the same eleusinian humming which many of us remember from childhood walks beside the telegraph wires and which made a peculiarly melancholy impression. But the clearest evidence that the administrative apparatus of the Castle is occupied with the endless cataloguing of the dead comes from the claim that despite of [sic] all confusion and contradictions nobody can slip through the official net.[46] What strikes us as the most disconsolate aspect of this sphere of death is the fact that even here, just as in life, the powerful and the helpless are separated, that (again in accordance with folklore) the village people dwell together in one room beneath the earth, while the gentlemen occupy a castle as in their previous existence.[47] Finally a particularly valid argument for K.'s proximity to death when he enters the village is proffered by Ronald Gray's book on the *Castle*. In his interpretation of the last scene of the novel fragment, Gray does not, admittedly, arrange the death symbols which he discusses into the kind of pattern described above; in his view K. encounters death here almost by accident: it appears as a reflection of a narrative convention rather than a long since anticipated event. The landlady of the Herrenhof talks in this passage about her strange old-fashioned and overcrowded wardrobe, about dresses reminiscent of the *pompes funèbres* to whose dusty vulgarity K. has taken exception. 'If the dresses', Gray writes, 'are the disguises which the hostess is accustomed to wear when she announces to men the moment of their death, a good deal falls into place.'[48] The landlady as Mistress World, as a barmaid in an inn belonging to the devil, occurs in a poem by Walter von der Vogelweide, and Rilke in his elegy dedicated to travelling acrobats pays homage to the very same allegorical persona as Kafka when he recalls the place 'where the modiste Madame Lamort / winds and binds the restless ways of the world, / those endless ribbons, to ever-new / creations of bow, frill, flower, cockade and fruit, / all falsely coloured, to deck / the cheap winter-hats of Fate'.[49] It is, then, safe to assume that Gray is correct in his interpretation of this last scene and after all that has been said, it is manifest that the Kafka fragment could scarcely have found a more precise ending; here the fragmentary character of the novel transcends itself. This ending is appositely summarized in Gray's commentary as follows:

> The Charon-like figure of Gerstäcker already has K. by the sleeve, to carry him away on his flat, seatless sledge. On the preceding page the hostess seemed to be giving him instructions about K.'s destination. And now the hostess concludes with the possibly ambiguous remark: 'Tomorrow I shall be getting a new dress; perhaps I shall send for you.'[50]

That K. has attained the end of his natural course can only be regarded as a source of comfort and salvation if one compares it with the alternative that might have befallen him: to remain an eternal 'stranger and pilgrim' on earth as in the legend of Ahasver, the Wandering Jew. And to avoid this fate, K. seeks out the land of death of his own accord, for as he says in rejecting Frieda's dream of emigrating to Spain or the South of France, 'What could have enticed me to this desolate country except the wish to stay here?'[51] The yearning for peace which in K.'s world only death itself can provide, and the fear of being unable to die (like the hero of Kafka's *Gracchus the Huntsman*),[iv] the fear of a perpetual habitation in the no-man's land between man and thing – that yearning, that fear must be reckoned the ultimate motive for K.'s journey to the village whose name we never learn.[v] Yet this village is at once the place where Jean-Paul [sic] causes the souls who have reached it to sigh, 'At last we are in the courtyard of eternity and but one more death and we shall see God.'[52]

Summa Scientiae

Systems and System Critique in Elias Canetti

> As men abound in copiousness of language, so they become more wise, or more mad than ordinary.
>
> Thomas Hobbes, *Leviathan*

In his *Aufzeichnungen* [*Notebooks*], Canetti repeatedly laments the fact that history is written from the point of view of the stronger, and that historians associate themselves with power, inasmuch as they tacitly presuppose the latter to be axiomatic, the means and quite possibly the end goal of all social development. In provocative and polemic opposition to the world view of historical science, which views the principle of power as both normative and natural, Canetti is concerned in his work with a pathography of power and violence. In common with many leading authors of the modern age, from Jarry and Kafka to Beckett, Genet and Bernhard, he describes the processes of power as a closed system which, in order to sustain itself, continually demands the sacrifice of those outside it.

Power [*Macht*], for Canetti, is not an objective fact but an arbitrary concept, a product of the subjective imagination, representing a world at one remove that can only – tautologically – assert itself as reality through the exercise of force or violence [*Gewalt*]. In his case studies of Muhammed Tughlak, the Sultan of Delhi, and of the *Senatspräsident* [Senate Judge] Daniel Paul Schreber, Canetti demonstrates the structural congruence between systems of power and those of madness. Whereas the academic discipline of history generally tends to downplay the instances where, through the exercise of violence, madness has become history, reinforcing the terror of power by uncritically registering the *res gestae*, Canetti recognizes, in what becomes history by means of violence, an intensified form of paranoid expression.[i] He elucidates the fundamental affinity between *Machtpolitik* (the politics of power) and paranoia using the case of the *Senatspräsident* from Dresden, whose system of madness [*Wahnsystem*] includes characteristic elements both of Wilhelmine ideology and of the threat of violence inherent within it.

Schreber's system is based on an acute fear about his position, a kind of one-man *Wacht am Rhein* [Watch on the Rhine][ii] demanding pre-emptive measures to repel each and every hostile foreign plot and conspiracy. This pre-emptive strategy consists of attracting the attention of the legions of enemies by provocative and conspicuous behaviour, so that the paranoiac – like Germany, a lone giant beleaguered from all sides – can assimilate into his own system the teeming masses bent on his destruction. Thus in his imagination the paranoid subject increases in size and substance, expanding into all those areas in which he has, by means of incorporation, decimated the hordes of his enemies. The Wilhelmine dream of dominion finds its true reflection in Schreber's expansionism, laying claim in equal measure to both time and space. In the end nothing shall remain but the *Senatspräsident*, or the German 'essence' [*das deutsche Wesen*]. Many other elements of German Reich ideology are also reflected in Schreber's system, such as the anti-Catholicism of the *Kulturkampf* [struggle between Church and state], a pronounced Slavophobia, and the increasing virulence of political anti-Semitism. Long processions of obsessively imagined groups of enemies take up residence in the mind of the paranoiac, where they are put to death and, as dead souls, become trophies of power, until such time as the 'ideal' ruler is 'the only man left alive, standing in an immense field of corpses'.[1]

This extreme vision is the point where the chaotic heterogeneity of paranoid — or as it may be ideological — systems meets its opposite, their radical need for calm and order. Seen in this light, the *Denkwürdigkeiten eines Nervenkranken* [*Memoirs of My Nervous Illness*][iii] documents, as few other works can, the continuity of German ideology from the still relatively naïve dream of Empire down to the most extreme consequences of fascist violence. The delusions of the paranoiac subject and the claim to power both have a symbiotic relationship with the ideology of the times, obsessively anticipating the end.[2] Canetti's essay on the architectural fantasy world that Speer designed for Hitler describes how, in the imagination of the paranoiac, 'both desires, construction and destruction, are actually present, adjacent and operative.'[3] Speer's plans, which nowhere take account of the social dimension of life, are the stage set for a dead age; they represent the triumph of ideology ossified in a monumental panorama. The longing for total order has no need of life. Rather, as Canetti notes,[4] its instinct is a murderous one. The Reich as a desert, and the dwelling place as a mausoleum in which the creator of order can rest for eternity, in a pose of his own choosing and in absolute safety – these are, as it turns out, the ultimate models to which the paranoid imagination aspires. Thus Hitler was fascinated by the pyramids, the perpetuation of power in stone, and by the irreversibility of death, in which the paranoid subject is emotionally invested, since death – as the Castle administrators in Kafka's novel know – represents the most arbitrary, and at the same time the most perfect, system of all.

The paranoid ruler's systematic division of the world into fields of death is also continually practised, on a smaller scale, in the organization of daily life. The 'rigour of disciplines'[5] – of which Canetti has a low opinion – punishes any violation of frontiers, forcing reality to conform to its systematic categories. Whatever does not fit is cut off. 'Nothing is meant to live where it is not allowed. Order is a small, self-created desert.'[6] This extends, as we all know, into the psychopathology of everyday life. 'A man feels poor without such a desert-realm, in which he has the right to choke everything in a blind rage.'[6] Anyone able to extend their system of order, anyone who has mastered their subject, can lay claim to power and authority. This is shown most clearly in disciplines where an openly regulatory capacity is inherent in their function. Foucault's *Histoire de la Folie* [*History of Insanity*][iv] gives a comprehensive view of the subjugation of madness through the system of official psychiatry, whose advocates, as Canetti notes in *Die Blendung* [*Auto-da-Fé*], advocate their theories with the obstinacy of the insane.[7]

The categorical voices of such administrators of order are omnipresent, and, as Canetti's novel demonstrates, usurp the consciousness and language of the average citizen. Therese complains: 'Everything for the children, these days. Nobody is strict any more. Cheeky they are: you wouldn't credit it. Playing at their lessons and going for walks with teacher . . . Whoever heard of such a thing in my time? Let 'em do a job of work.'[8] And the caretaker knows even better: 'Shave their heads in prison, they do; cut 'em off would be more like it. A burden on the taxpayer . . . The bleeding State pays. I'll wipe the vermin out. The cat's at home now. The mice can keep in the holes.'[9] The tone of command, the death threat, is unmistakable. The system is all. Anyone who does not conform is pursued by the voices of the authorities. For *Senatspräsident* Schreber, there is no escaping their clutches. 'What are you thinking of now?' he is asked. If he himself remains silent, the voices answer for him: 'You should be thinking of the Order of the Universe.' 'Both questions and commands' – thus Canetti on these inquisitorial tactics – 'were an infringement of his personal freedom. Both are familiar means to power and he, as a judge, had made frequent use of them.' – 'The ways in which Schreber was tried', Canetti continues,

> were varied and inventive. First he was interrogated; then various thoughts were dictated to him; then, from his own words and sentences, a further catechism was constructed. His every thought was controlled, not one was allowed to pass unnoticed; every word he used was examined to determine exactly what it meant to him. His lack of privacy in relation to the voices was complete; everything was searched, everything brought into the light. He was the objective of a power which insisted on being omniscient.[10]

This reads like a precise description of the treatment to which Handke's *Kaspar* is subjected.[v] The voices represent reason, order, clarity and cleanliness, and demand unquestioning conformity to the system. Those who fail to conform feel themselves persecuted, completely surrounded by rules and prohibitions. 'The whole world is one monstrous jurisprudence. The whole world is a prison!'[vi] says a so-called madman in one of Bernhard's stories.[11] He should know. The prison is a panoptic building. The warder in the tower always has the inmates in view without ever having to move from the spot. The ingenious prison architecture symbolizes, over and above its controlling function, the system of order and surveillance. Nothing disturbs the hunted so much as unremitting observation. 'He sees eyes everywhere', Canetti writes, 'and all round him; they are interested only in him and their interest is menacing in the extreme.'[12] Kafka's *Trial* contains an astonishingly frequent incidence of verbs such as look, see, being seen, looking up, looking at, looking round, observing, being looked at, following with one's eyes, and more of that ilk. Josef K. knows he is exposed on all sides. The eye of God has multiplied. The eye of the Law sends its agents out into the streets, and in the totalitarian regime whose dawn Kafka witnessed, everyone is called upon to keep watch on their fellow citizens. The system of power is thus a matter not just of hierarchical organization, but also of contiguity. It extends its tentacles downwards, conquering the base, and extends its reach laterally, so that ultimately there is no escape.

Once surrounded by the omnipresent administrators and higher authorities of society, the reserve of nature is closed to us also; it becomes foreign, a theatre one may enter only in utopia. The system of nature, too, is now no longer that of a beautiful paradigm of order, such as Stifter tried to recreate. It is already contaminated by the madness of society, insofar as this madness does not itself originate in a Nature in which everything merely coldly coexists, and where the actual functional connection consists solely in one part continually being eaten by another.

Canetti's hostility towards death originates in his consternation at the insanity of the natural system. 'Ever since I saw a human stomach,' he notes, 'nine-tenths of a human stomach, within less than two hours after it was cut out, I know even less why we eat. It looked just like the pieces of meat that people roast in their kitchens, it was even the size of an ordinary schnitzel. Why does like come to like? Why the circuitous route? Why must meat incessantly go through the bowels of other meat? Why must this in particular be the condition of our life?'[13] The fear which rises to the surface here relates to the fact that human beings are, 'in accordance with the purpose of their own biological constitution, themselves predestined to be eaten'.[14] This pathological apprehension, as it might appear to some, is probably felt only by those affected, who can see themselves in the position of the hunted. For them, the natural process of procreation, love, is an illusionary consolation, since – as in the image by Blake[vii] – everything takes place inside an all-encompassing digestive system. For Canetti, then, the prerequisite for a humane form of progress would mean resisting the functional context of power as well as the metabolism of nature. 'The eating man has less and less compassion, and finally none. A man who wouldn't have to eat [. . .] – that would be the highest moral experiment conceivable.'[15] Kafka, of course, had similar thoughts, and Canetti's utopian hypotheses, too, set their sights not on reform but on redemption.

Seen from this viewpoint, it is scarcely surprising that Canetti has only limited faith in what art can accomplish. The egocentrism of the artist beavering away at his own construction[viii] is, for him, a suspect activity which leads to yet further proliferation of systems. In the course of the development of bourgeois society, the culture of the novel as a whole created its own body of laws, and at the time when Canetti was working on *Die Blendung* [*Auto-da-Fé*] attained one last apogee in the grandiose novelistic plans of the brothers Mann, of Broch, Musil, Arnold Zweig, Döblin et al. Canetti himself for a time cherished the most ambitious notions of writing a kind of eccentric *Comédie humaine*. The fact that he more or less gave up literature for good after the warning lesson of *Die Blendung* can no doubt also be ascribed to his suspicion that the hieratic ordering system of aesthetics corresponds to that of the ruling powers. 'Every work is a rape, through its sheer mass. One ought to find different and purer ways of expressing oneself.'[16] What Canetti particularly objects to about the products of art and so-called *belles lettres*[ix] is their tendency to distance themselves from reality. 'In novels you always found the same thing,' it says in *Die Blendung*.[17] The invariability of art is an indication that it is its own closed system, which, like that of power, projects the fear of its own entropy on to imagined affirmative or destructive endings. The inherently autistic inner logic of systems ultimately calls for an act of violence. Already in the great symphonies one hears, in the final notes, the desire for destruction. In the twentieth century, the bourgeois artist surrenders completely to the myth of apocalypse and, another pyromaniac, consigns his own world to the flames. As a novelist, Canetti is no exception. That he then gave up writing novels seems to me to indicate that he no longer wished to be bound by their systematic order, no longer felt able to reconcile the aporia of an art oscillating between creativity and destructive vision.

The more art clings to its own stereotype, the more it loses the ability to imagine a different world, and the less it is capable of this, the more sceptical Canetti becomes towards it. His creative energy is directed towards a speculative alternate existence, in which the conditions of life would be completely different. 'As of a certain age it would be nice to grow smaller again from year to year and go backwards over the same steps that we once so proudly climbed.' What might not be possible in such a world? 'The oldest kings would be the shortest; there would only be very tiny popes; the bishops would look down on cardinals, the cardinals on the pope. No child could wish to become something great. History, because of its age, would lose significance; we would feel as if the events of three hundred years ago had taken place among insect-like creatures, and the past would have the good fortune to be overlooked.'[18x]

Models of this kind, worlds in which people love only from a distance, and such and similar constructions, recur over and over again in Canetti's work. Sketches like these are where he is most at home. But he takes care to avoid executing his utopias according to a fixed plan, recognizing in the geometric structure of the unfolding system the labyrinth from which the author will never be able to extricate himself. 'The most difficult thing is finding a hole through which you can slip out of your own work.'[19] In order that his own head does not become a prison, he tries to stick to concrete matters. Abstractions contain the danger of hypostasis. For this reason, he only approves of heuristic constructions. 'I enjoy all systems', Canetti writes, 'if they are perspicuous, like a toy in your hand. If they get complicated, they make me nervous. Too much of the world has come to the wrong place, and how shall I get it out of there again?'[20] Large-scale systems obstruct [*verbauen*] reality in the truest sense of the word, for which reason it is Canetti's declared intention to see to it that his own system 'never fully closes'.²¹ If, then, in opposition to the prevailing trends of power and art, he seeks neither a whole nor an ending, preferring rather a host of new beginnings, this goes some way to explaining the puzzling phenomenon as to why he did not give freer rein to his decidedly satirical temperament, since even the negativity of satirical vision – as Canetti recognized in Swift, Gogol and Kraus, the greatest representatives of the genre – has a tendency to see things in absolute terms. 'The prophet, speaking about the most fearful things, can be anything, but not ridiculous. Thus, the feeling that people have, namely that he in his way embodies the evil he threatens them with and helps to bring about, is not altogether groundless; if they could *force* him to predict something else, perhaps something else might happen.'²²

Few have reflected as thoroughly as Canetti upon the fateful processes of our century – the rise of fascism, the hypertrophic evolution of the apparatuses of power, the murder of the Jews, the scale of atomic annihilation – and like few other writers he had, in the course of his own development, the insight to realize that representations of the end will not suffice. His ideal is not the prophet, but the teacher, whose great good fortune – as one can read in Canetti's comments on the *Analects* of Confucius[xi] – is that learning never ends. Whereas the ruler always remains in one place, the learner is always on a journey. 'Learning has to be an adventure, otherwise it's stillborn. What you learn at a given moment ought to depend on chance meetings, and it ought to continue in that way, from encounter to encounter, a learning in transformations, a learning for fun.'²³[xii] The central activity of the learner, however, is not writing, but reading. 'Lesen, bis die Wimpern vor Müdigkeit leise klingen' ['To read until one's eyelashes gently chime in weariness'].[24][xiii] The knowledge the learner accumulates – as long as the process of learning is not interrupted – is not possession, not education [*Bildung*] and not power; it remains pre-systemic, and is, at most, a function of studying, which is its main concern. For Canetti, learning appears identical with life itself, as it should be. In this, he is part of a long Jewish tradition, in which the ambition of the writer is directed not towards the work which he has created, but to the elucidation of that which is written. The literary form which this illumination takes – one characteristic of Canetti also – is that of the excursus, the commentary and the fragment. It stays true to the objects of contemplation, without devouring them like the pig with the books in the pawnshop.[xiv] For Canetti, there is a crucial difference between the act of reading and the assimilation of knowledge with a view to power. Freedom, for him, is the 'freedom to *let go*, a giving up of power'.[25] The stance alluded to here is that of the sage, who is capable of resisting the temptations of the knowledge he bears within him. 'From day to day, you grasp more, but you are reluctant to *sum up*; as though it could ultimately be possible to express everything in a few sentences on some single day, but then definitively.'[26][xv] The few sentences, uttered at the right time – this, for Canetti, would be the correct response to the compulsion of the system, which madness, and power, and art and science are forever passing down to one other.

Wo die Dunkelheit den Strick zuzieht [Where Darkness Draws Tight the Noose]

Some Marginal Notes on Thomas Bernhard

> Omnes morimur. Es muß gestorben sein. Wer es nicht glauben will, frag Wien in Österreich darum.
>
> Abraham a Santa Clara*[i]

Thomas Bernhard has, in recent years, achieved considerable fame and notoriety not least because of the outrageous statements on history and politics in which he repeatedly indulges, both in his creative work and in his miscellaneous writings. Neither politically committed criticism nor any received notions of artistic indifference can provide a framework within which Bernhard's attitudes would make much sense. Flying in the teeth of progressive and conservative expectations alike, his continuous denunciations of all kinds of social and political phenomena tend to strike the reader as simply scandalous. Only a certain – not

---

* 'Everything dies. Death must be died. If you don't believe it, ask Vienna in Austria about it' (Abraham a Santa Clara, *Merk's Wien*).

uncommon – type of liberal intellectual seems to be capable of approaching Bernhard's works in the spirit in which they were conceived, presumably deciphering their intransigently negative vision as an apologia for their own political indecision. If one uses the less complicated principles of straightforward pragmatism as a criterion, Bernhard comes across as a rather twisted character who takes unwarranted liberties by stubbornly disregarding the fact that the Austrian dream suggested by the sugar-candy scenery of the Zauberspiel tradition has been realized in the 2nd Republic. A benevolent fate has transformed the setting in a most gratifying fashion; the bourgeois dynasty is firmly established; Raimund's Barometermacher Quecksilber has returned as Kaiser Kreisky governing the country from the breakfast table. Strikes, inflation, unemployment and similarly horrifying spectres occur only in the outside world while the proverbial Austrian enjoys the pretty prospect of his ever-improving circumstances. In spite of such evident achievements Bernhard unashamedly proclaims the bankruptcy of the individual, society, the state, civilization and nature. In this the Austrian condition which he describes serves as a paradigm for the madness of the world and Bernhard is at pains to point out that his accusations are not meant merely symbolically. Thus on the occasion of receiving the Austrian State Prize for Literature, he stated with considerable vehemence: 'Natürlich herrschen in diesem Land die fürchterlichsten Zustände, die man sich vorstellen kann, ein unvorstellbarer Schwachsinn kurbelt an unserer Staatsmaschine.'*[1] Although it seems fairly clear what these apodictic judgements are getting

---

* 'Naturally in this country the most appalling conditions imaginable prevail, an unimaginable idiocy is cranking up our state machinery.'

at, it is less clear from what point of view they have been arrived at. Accordingly, in this paper I will try to determine the nature of Bernhard's political, moral and artistic credo. While it is true to say that existing secondary studies have variously touched upon this problem, they have largely remained preoccupied with the rather complex but far less contentious formal aspects of Bernhard's works.

Seen within the spectrum of possible political attitudes Bernhard's invective appears as a heresy which can only manifest itself in completely unchanging antipolitical and antisocial pronouncements. At the heart of this lies an affective structure dating back to the sombre experiences which the author underwent early on in his life. The irregular circumstances of his family in particular and the regulatory powers of society in general clearly have left deep marks on Bernhard's consciousness. It is hardly surprising, therefore, that Bernhard should have felt compelled to produce autobiographical accounts of his formative years. These writings reveal a disconcerting case history and document a growing aversion towards all forms of authority, especially 'gegenüber den Regeln des bürgerlichen Gesellschaftsapparats, der ein menschenverheerender Apparat ist'.*[2] Peter Handke, whose *éducation sentimentale* is analogous to Bernhard's in this respect, identified the origin of his own political solipsism in his early childhood experiences. In the text 'Geborgenheit unter der Schädeldecke' he writes: 'Seit ich mich erinnern kann, ekle ich mich vor der Macht, und dieser Ekel ist nichts moralisches, er ist kreatürlich, eine Eigenschaft jeder einzelnen

---

* '[towards] the rules of the bourgeois social apparatus, an apparatus designed to destroy human beings'.

Körperzelle.'*³ Furthermore, Handke speaks of his 'Unfähigkeit zu einer politischen Existenz', †³ which resulted from this purely emotional antipathy. Handke's aetiological account helps to explain Bernhard's passionately antipolitical and antisocial stance as a constitutional weakness which was presumably reinforced at a later stage by the long-standing Austrian tradition of political agnosticism. Throughout Austrian literature, one finds literary works manifesting acute symptoms of this apolitical disposition, especially during the epoch when the highly ritualized power structure of the Holy Roman Empire was entering its final stage of coma and when 'das wimmelnde Grauen unter dem Stein der Kultur'‡⁴ was becoming apparent. The works of Hofmannsthal, Kraus and Kafka abound with examples of a semi-conscious feeling of nausea engendered by the spectacle of decomposing power. The unsavoury habits of the *Castle* officials whose abstract power thrives parasitically upon the helplessness of the village population; the obscenity of the new regime which, in *The Trial*, emerges from beneath the cadaverous remains of the old legal order; the foul cage in which Prinz Sigismund subsists on the fringes of life; Karl Kraus's campaign against the disreputable practices legitimized by what he saw as the perverted mores of patriarchal society – all this goes to show that the artistic sensibility of the beginning of the twentieth century was inclined to see filth and authority as complementary phenomena.⁵ All the authors referred to here share a profound scepticism towards the doctrines of socialism. Hofmannsthal and Kafka thought that

---

* 'Safety under the skull': 'Ever since I can remember I have been revolted by power, and this revulsion isn't something moral, it's instinctive, physical, a quality inherent in every cell in the body.'

† 'unfittedness for a political existence'.

‡ 'the horror teeming under the stone of culture'.

those in power stood as much in need of redemption as those who were oppressed and it is precisely this symbiotic relationship between authority, order, form and conservatism on the one hand and impotence, disintegration and the potential for sedition on the other which is central to Thomas Bernhard's world view. The text *Verstörung* (published in 1967),* particularly the chapter *Der Fürst*† which deals with the imminent dissolution of the saurausche Herrschaft‡ provides an extensive example of this. In the course of Saurau's paranoid monologue which goes on for more than 100 pages we hear 'daß er den von seinem Vater übernommenen Besitz im Laufe von nur dreißig Jahren mehr als verdoppeln konnte' and this 'entgegen allen Gerüchten . . . der ganzen politischen Entwicklung in Europa, der ganzen Weltentwicklung entgegen'.§[6] The feudal system which has thus developed 'in einem ungeheuren Land- und Forstwirtschaftsanachronismus'¶[7] is now said to be on the point of collapse because of the paranoid visions which increasingly dominate Saurau's ways of thinking. He himself knows 'daß in seinem Gehirn aus einer wunderbaren Ordnung auf einmal ein entsetzliches Chaos geworden ist, ein entsetzliches, ohrenbetäubendes Chaos'.**[8] The text suggests that the progressive disruption of Saurau's mind is ultimately due to the unresolvable contradiction between the idea of a perfectly

---

* 'Disturbance' (translated into English as *Gargoyles*).

† 'The Prince'.

‡ 'Saurau domains'.

§ 'that in the course of only thirty years he had been able to double the property he inherited from his father, contrary to all rumours'; 'contrary to the whole political development in Europe, to the development of the whole world'.

¶ '[in a] tremendous, *anachronistic* agricultural and forest economy'.

** 'that a wonderful orderliness inside my brain had suddenly become a frightful chaos, a frightful deafening chaos'.

ordered feudal environment as this is envisaged, for instance, in Stifter's *Nachsommer** and the sheer power resulting from the accumulation of enormous estates. Saurau's latent desire to rid himself both of the responsibility for his life's work and of the oppressive weight of power through the liquidation of the Hochgobernitz domains is projected into the figure 'seines in England schweigend studierenden Sohnes'.†[9] He claims: 'Mein Sohn wird Hochgobernitz, sobald er es in die Hand bekommt, vernichten.'‡[10] In the following section of the novel Saurau reproduces verbatim a long document that has been composed by his son as an account of the wilful destruction of his inheritance. This document constitutes one of Saurau's many nightmares. It is drawn up by his son in the future, to be precise, eight months after his father's suicide, and Saurau refers to it, because of the disruption of temporal order in his mind, as though it were a piece of historical evidence. The document reveals that the son is preoccupied with questions central to bourgeois and proletarian revolution, especially with the conflict between compassion and terror and his reading includes Schumpeter, Luxemburg, Morus, Zetkin, Kautsky, Babeuf and Turati. Because of a deeply felt revulsion towards active violence and his pronounced political scrupulousness the son is attracted to the idea of translating into practice, through bloodless means, the anarchist hope of an ungoverned life in order to create at least a limited realm within which power has simply ceased to exist.[11] 'Die riesige väterliche Landwirtschaft ist mir immer mehr als ein ins Unendliche hineinwachsender Irrtum

---

* *Indian Summer*.
† '[of his] silently studying son in England'.
‡ 'My son [. . .] will destroy Hochgobernitz as soon as he receives it into his hands.'

erschienen.'*[12] Consequently, upon inheriting the father's vast estates the son decides to leave the 'dreitausendachthundertvierzig Hektar Grund'† — that is, about 10,000 acres — completely unattended. 'Solange ich existiere, wird auf diesen Grundstücken nichts mehr getan, das nützlich sein soll.'‡ And Saurau, who relates all this, comments in total exasperation: 'Nichts mehr, nichts mehr, nichts mehr, nichts mehr.'§[13] However, as I have already pointed out, the son's destructive instinct is by no means alien to the extremely conservative ideas of Saurau himself who thinks of everything below the level of Hochgobernitz as being communist. The son's destructive instinct is rather an extension of Saurau's own desires and entirely consonant with his feudal distrust of the state's sinister machinations against whose 'ruinous' and 'catastrophic' influence he wages a continuous battle. In his heart of hearts Saurau seems to realize that his son's anarchist tendencies are only a more recent version of his own attitudes, long since bypassed by actual political developments. The text's ultimate irony is generated by our knowledge that even the alternative which the son holds up to the hypertrophied power embodied in his father's estates represents, at best, one of the hopes of the past. The message implies that all our political conjectures, no matter how radical they may be, come too late. The classics of Anarchism, the writings of Bakunin and Kropotkin, which are frequently referred to in Bernhard's texts, do not represent a set of political attitudes which would

---

* 'This whole vast ancestral agricultural enterprise has more and more come to seem to me a mistake grown to vast proportions.'
† '3,840 hectares of land'.
‡ 'As long as I exist nothing profitable or useful will ever again be done on these fields.'
§ 'Never again, never again, [. . .], never again, never again'.

make sense under our present circumstances. Rather, they function as an image of the world which is as utopian as the earlier idea of the *ordo pulcher horlogium dei*. It is the unreality of the respective ideals that unites the father and the son. After the father's self-sacrifice, the son will return from abroad to fulfil his work by annihilating it. If, as in the trinitarian scheme of things, the father is not identical with the son, nor the son with the father, then, in Bernhard's novel, their conjunction comes about in the gnostic idea of the guilt which has been handed down from the father to the son. 'Auch meinen Sohn sehe ich, ja, auch meinen abwesenden Sohn . . . insgesamt sehe ich alle als *durch mich*, und mir kommt eine ungeheuere Konstellation, eine, möglicherweise *die* Fürchterlichkeit überhaupt zu Bewußtsein: *ich bin der Vater!*'*[13a] The gnostic vision articulated in this desperate statement is concerned with the increasing darkness in the world and does not hold out any hope for its diminution. The sentence 'Die Welt ist ein stufenweiser Abbau des Lichts'†[14] spoken by the deranged painter Strauch in *Frost* is a central assumption of gnostic philosophizing and negates redemptive as well as secular history. Under the auspices of this mode of thinking the search for truth is always an act of desperation. Kafka's story of the investigations of a dog provides us with an appropriate parable of such a hopeless enterprise. Like the dog, father and son Saurau, and Bernhard, the holy spirit, perceive 'die Fundamente unseres Lebens',‡ they watch 'die Arbeiter beim Bau, bei ihrem finsteren Werk'§ and, like the

---

* 'I also see my son, my absent son . . . see them all together through myself, and a monstrous constellation dawns on me, possibly the one concept that is sheer horror in itself: *I am the father!*'
† 'The world is a progressive dimming of light.'
‡ 'the foundations of our life'.
§ 'the builders at work, at their dark labour'.

dog, they seem to expect that because of their incessant questioning 'alles dies beendigt, zerstört, verlassen wird.'*[15] Within such perspectives the difference between ultra-reactionary feudalism and anarcho-socialist experiments of liberation becomes meaningless, and for this reason the question of Bernhard's political attitude has to be related to wider issues.

The Austrian literary tradition demonstrates that the originators of radical critiques of culture tend to satisfy their emotional needs by taking refuge in the idealizing description of the past, or in notions which imply the unadulterated purity of language or nature. Bernhard's cultural pessimism, which, like that of Kafka, refers to the 'geological' layers of feudal, bourgeois, socialist and totalitarian forms of societal organization, appears so unrelievedly negative not least because the relentless process of decay in the natural world serves as its backdrop. The consoling hope of a return to nature is not shared by Bernhard, since he considers the idea of the humanization of nature and of the naturalization of man encountered in Marx (no less than in Stifter) to be the ideological conjecture of an age which, in reality, has begun to see nature in exclusively instrumental terms. For Bernhard, the concept of nature as it was cultivated by the literature of the nineteenth century is a fiction. Anwalt† Moro, one of the protagonists of the text *Ungenach* who, incidentally, is also kept busy by the dissolution of a vast inheritance, comments on this point as follows: 'Die ganze Menschheit lebt ja schon die längste Zeit vollkommen im Exil, sie hat sich auf die genialste, weil gegen sich selber doch rücksichtsloseste Weise aus der Natur hinauskomplimentiert,

---

* 'all this [will] be abandoned, destroyed, forsaken.'
† Lawyer.

hinausbugsiert . . . und der Naturbegriff, sehen Sie, wie wir ihn immer noch verstehen und wie ihn die Leute, die wir anhören, wie ihn die Zeitungen, die wir aufmachen, die Bücher, Philosophien usf. immer noch auf die absurdeste Weise verstehen und anwenden und praktizieren, existiert ja überhaupt nicht mehr . . . Die Natur existiert gar nicht mehr.'*[16] Bernhard's critique of the humanized conception of nature implies that nature has always been a rather joyless institution which appeared to man as [a] kind of paradise only because society, as Chamfort put it, had made further contributions to 'les malheurs de la nature'. Bernhard's works demonstrate with single-minded persistence that the natural world is as lunatic an affair as human society. If society is unable to free itself from the burden of time and thus bound to accumulate guilt to an ever-increasing degree,[17] then natural life, because it dates back so much further, grants even less breathing space. Thus the inexorable decay of nature is even more unpalatable than the afflictions of society. Although our cities may be ridden with disease, nature scarcely provides the panacea evoked by so many lyrical hymns to country life. The country, in Bernhard's works, is not the healthy resort which Rilke and those who composed in his wake still wished to believe in. On the contrary, the country is the place of unmitigated disaster. 'Speziell hier ist alles morbid,' we read in *Frost*. 'Das Land ist verkommen, heruntergekommen, viel tiefer heruntergekommen als die Stadt!'†[18]

---

* 'The whole of humanity has been living in exile for the longest time, it has excluded itself, bowed out of nature in the most brilliant, most ruthless way, since directed against itself . . . and the concept of nature, you see, as we still understand it and as the people we listen to, the papers we read, the books, philosophies etc. still understand it, in the most absurd way understand and apply and practise it, no longer exists at all . . . Nature no longer exists any more.'

† 'Most particularly here [everything] is diseased . . . the country is degenerate, debased, so much more debased than the city!'

The country displays 'das systematische Absterben'*[19] of nature, its cannibalism and an inevitable process of corruption. The theoretical equivalent of this negative picture is the concept of entropy, the final state of degradation in which there exists neither form nor hierarchy, nor any other kind of differentiation. The account, contained in *Verstörung*, of the dreadful circumstances which govern life in the Fochlermühle† presents us with a microcosm of this desolate view of the world. The narrator's father, a country doctor, describes the miller 'als einen schwerfälligen sechzigjährigen Mann, der unter der Haut *verfaule*, immer auf einem alten Sofa liegt, nicht mehr gehen kann, seine Frau, deren Mundgeruch auf einen rasch fortschreitenden Zersetzungsprozess ihrer Lungenflügel hindeute, habe Wasser in den Füßen. Ein alter fetter Wolfshund gehe zwischen beiden hin und her, von seinem zu ihrem Sofa und wieder zurück. Wären nicht in allen Zimmern frische Äpfel aufgeschüttet, würde man den Geruch der beiden alten Menschen und des Wolfhunds nicht aushalten. Das rechte Bein des Müllers faule schneller als sein linkes, er werde nicht mehr aufstehen können . . . Die Müllerin könne nur die kürzeste Zeit auf ihren Beinen sein, so lägen sich die beiden beinahe immer in ihrem gemeinsamen Zimmer gegenüber und befaßten sich mit ihrem Hund. Der sei, weil er nie aus dem Zimmer hinauskommt, in seiner Verstörung *gefährlich*.'‡[20] Those of Bernhard's characters

---

* '[the] systematic extinction'.

† Fochler mill.

‡ 'as a heavy-set man of sixty who was simply *rotting* beneath the skin; he lay on the old sofa all the time, could no longer walk; and his wife, who to judge by the smell of her mouth was undergoing rapid degeneration of the lobes of her lungs, had water on the legs. A fat old wolfhound ran back and forth between the two, from her sofa to his and back again. Were it not that fresh apples were kept heaped in all the rooms, the smell of the two old people and the wolfhound would be unendurable. The miller's right leg was decaying faster than his left; he would never stand again . . . The miller's wife could stand on her legs only for a few moments at a time. The two of them lay in their room almost all the time

who actually think about the problem react to the disgusting secondary manifestations of this process of entropy by trying to escape into contraction, cataleptic stupor and *rigor mortis*. For example, the painter Strauch in *Frost* wanders off into the snowbound wilderness of the mountains in order to die of cold. In accordance with the sombre philosophies of nature of the Romantic period, freezing to death and petrification are suggested here as a means of redemption. At the same time, however, redemption is preceded by a phase of mental hyperactivity involving ceaseless questioning, speculation, remonstration and general restlessness which can be equated with the author's attempts to find the peace of his mind [sic] in the indefatigable pursuit of his ideas. This state of nervous exaltation may, at the slightest provocation, be converted into mental paralysis. Bernhard's concept of what is the truth corresponds perhaps most closely to the realizations generated by the 'mehr und mehr philosophischen, philosophistischen Vereinsamung des Geistes, in welcher einem', as Saurau explains, 'fortwährend alles bewußt ist, wodurch das Gehirn als solches gar nicht mehr existiert'.*[21] Clearly, this epistemological experiment can never yield any communicable results. The scientific study of the sense of hearing which Konrad seeks to undertake in the almost complete seclusion of the Kalkwerk† cannot, even in the remoteness of this outpost, be developed beyond the apparently endless process of planning. The absolute silence, to Konrad's mind the only true school of hearing, is too frequently disturbed by the

---

and occupied themselves with their dog. The animal, because it never went out of the room, was absolutely *dangerous* in its derangement.'

* 'the more and more philosophical, philosophistic isolation of the mind: the point where everything is continually present in consciousness, where the brain as such no longer exists'.

† Lime works.

interference of sound. Furthermore, the heightening of the sensibility of the experimenting subject is outweighed by increasing difficulties of articulation. It was said of Kaspar Hauser that he was capable of distinguishing between colours in pitch darkness; similarly, Konrad is capable of hearing – even when the eye cannot perceive the slightest ripple on the surface of the Kalkwerk lake – 'die Bewegung der Wasseroberfläche, oder: die Bewegung in der Tiefe des Wassers, Geräusche von Bewegungen in der Wassertiefe'.*[22] The pursuit of this kind of science leads into the area of mysticism and it is not the least of Bernhard's merits that he never succumbs to the temptations which beckon from just beyond the borderline. Like Konrad, he sticks to the task of completing his study without allowing room for metaphysical speculation. And, as is the case with Konrad, this has brought him 'in den Verdacht und in den Verruf absoluter Verrücktheit, ja selbst des Wahnsinns'.†[23] The narrator of Konrad's story quotes Konrad as saying: 'Es wäre natürlich nichts leichter, als einfach wirklich wahnsinnig zu werden, aber die Studie ist mir wichtiger als der Wahnsinn.'‡[23]

The strenuous determination to maintain the structures of rationality in the face of the attractions of madness is characteristic of an intellectual and creative disposition which, among other things, causes Bernhard's work to be an extreme form of satire. The sense – that everything is ultimately quite laughable – which pervades precisely the most gloomy passages of Bernhard's writings derives from the tension between the madness of the

---

* 'the surface of the water moving even when no such motion was perceptible to the eye, or: he could hear the movement in the deeps, the sound of movement in the depths'.

† 'under suspicion and into disrepute as a total madman'.

‡ 'Nothing could be easier, of course, than to go really insane . . . but my task is too important to let myself be deterred by the fear of insanity.'

world and the postulates of rationality. Saurau remarks in *Verstörung* 'daß das Komische oder das Lustige an den Menschen in ihrer Qual am anschaulichsten zum Vorschein (komme)'.*[24] While the reader, because of the material with which he is presented, finds it impossible to give way to the stimulus of laughter, he clearly senses strange sounds of jeering behind the actual setting of the text. The analogy, developed by Benjamin in his famous essay on Karl Kraus, of Rumpelstilzchen secretly performing his frantic dance comes to mind. It illustrates the fate of the demon dwarf whose excentric [sic] temper forces him to keep up his riotous act.[25] The highly strung nature of the satirist which is the source of Bernhard's aggressive energies stems from the fact that ethical rigorism and the pleasure of destruction have no common denominator. Consequently the satirist renews again and again the bond between himself and the objects of his loathing in the passionate recreation of the most insane aspects of natural and societal life, a classic example of the double-bind situation which one encounters in the causal patterns of all so-called mental diseases.[26] It is this connection which frequently acquires for the satirist the reputation that he actually cultivates the conditions he is castigating. This hypothesis certainly fits Swift, Quevedo and Gogol as well as the exponents of the satirical tradition in Austria from Heinrich von Melk, Paracelsus and Abraham a Santa Clara down to Nestroy, Kraus and Canetti. The dictum *ubi cadaver ibi aquilae* is the stigma of all satirical critique the secret core of which consists, according to Benjamin, 'im Verspeisen des Gegners'.†[27] Benjamin writes: 'Der Satiriker ist die Figur, unter

---

* 'that the comic or humorous aspect of people is displayed most vividly in their suffering'.
† 'in the devouring of the adversary'.

welcher der Menschenfresser von der Zivilisation rezipiert wurde. Nicht ohne Pietät erinnert er sich seines Ursprungs und darum ist der Vorschlag, Menschen zu fressen, in den eisernen Bestand seiner Anregungen übergegangen.'*[27] It would be difficult to deny that Bernhard who, with the incisive instruments of his highly sophisticated language, habitually prepares the most unwholesome meals, belongs to the type described here. The moral dilemma with which this kind of author is obliged to cope found expression in the scruples of Karl Kraus, who was driven to ask himself whether, ultimately, the horrors of his age were not just 'das Echo (seines) blutigen Wahnsinns'.†[28] Bernhard is inclined to seek redemption less in the acknowledgement of his own guilt than in the enormity of laughter. There is much to be said for the idea that this tendency is becoming increasingly pronounced in his works. The text 'Enttäuschte Engländer'‡ from the recent book *Der Stimmenimitator*§ may serve as an illustration:[ii]

> Mehrere Engländer, die auf einen Osttiroler Bergführer hereingefallen sind und mit diesem auf die Drei Zinnen gestiegen sind, waren, auf dem höchsten der drei Gipfel angelangt, über das auf diesem Gipfel von der Natur Gebotene derartig enttäuscht gewesen, daß sie den Bergführer, einen Familienvater mit drei Kindern und einer, wie es heißt, tauben Frau, kurzerhand auf dem Gipfel erschlugen. Wie ihnen aber zu Bewußtsein gekommen ist, was sie

---

* 'The satirist is the figure in whom the cannibal was received into civilization. His recollection of his origin is not without filial piety, so that the proposal to eat people has become an essential constituent of his inspiration.'

† 'the echo of [his] bloodstained insanity'.

‡ 'Disappointed Englishmen'.

§ *The Voice Imitator*.

> tatsächlich getan haben, stürzten sie sich nacheinander in die Tiefe. Eine Zeitung in Birmingham hatte daraufhin geschrieben, Birmingham hätte seinen hervorragendsten Zeitungsverleger, seinen außerordentlichsten Bankdirektor und seinen tüchtigsten Leichenbestatter verloren.*[29]

What happens in this episode contradicts all accepted norms of human behaviour and points to a complete reversal of rational order. It makes perfect sense, however, within the confines of the 'ganz und gar karnevalistische System'†[30] as which Saurau in *Verstörung* perceives the world. Michail Bachtin's [= Bakhtin] brilliant essay on 'Carnival and the Carnivalisation of Literature' describes how carnival which, for over one-third of the calendar year was the quasi-legal state of the big cities of the middle ages, was successively repressed during the bourgeois epoch by the notion of a homogeneous culture which sublimated the antinomian function of laughter in the forms of humour, irony and other more refined moods.[30a] The uniform blackness of Bernhard's satire can be seen as the final stage of this development. The laughter which makes itself felt in Bernhard's texts is affected by aphonia and like that of the abstract creature Odradek in Kafka's story *Die Sorge des Hausvaters* 'nur ein Lachen, wie man es ohne Lungen hervorbringen kann'.‡[31] The desire to create a precinct of

---

* 'Several Englishmen who were inveigled by a mountain guide in Eastern Tyrol into climbing the Drei Zinnen with him were so disappointed, after reaching the highest of the three peaks, with what nature had to offer them on the highest peak that then and there they killed the guide, a family man with three children and, it seems, a deaf wife. When, however, they realized what they had actually done, they threw themselves off the peak, one after the other. After this, a newspaper in Birmingham wrote that Birmingham had lost its most outstanding newspaper publisher, its most extraordinary bank director, and its most able undertaker.'

† 'completely and utterly carnivalistic system'.

‡ 'the sort of laughter you can only produce if you have no lungs'.

freedom by releasing pent-up instincts through outbursts of laughter has thus been converted into an entirely private gesture on the part of the author and the reader respectively. The decisive question is perhaps whether the compensatory pleasure derived from the horrors of this world and, more particularly, the *repression* of this pleasure does not, even more directly than the negative phenomena themselves, point to the increasing deficit of natural and social evolution. Using *Gulliver's Travels* as an example George Orwell bases his critical appraisal of the nature of satirical imagination precisely on an examination of the satirist's shortcomings. According to Orwell, Swift's sole aim was to remind man 'that he is weak and ridiculous, and that he stinks'.[32] In an interview with André Müller, Bernhard, whose world picture corresponds to that of Swift in many respects, came up with a rather revealing answer to the question why it was that families with children so disgusted him and whether he really had said that all mothers should have their ears cut off:[iii]

> BERNHARD: Das hab' ich gesagt, weil es ein Irrtum ist, wenn die Leute glauben, sie bringen Kinder zur Welt. Das ist ja ganz billig. Die kriegen ja Erwachsene, keine Kinder. Die gebären einen schwitzenden, scheußlichen, Bauch tragenden Gastwirt oder Massenmörder, den tragen sie aus, keine Kinder. Da sagen die Leute, sie kriegen ein Bauxerl, aber in Wirklichkeit kriegen sie einen 80jährigen Menschen, dem das Wasser überall herausrinnt, der stinkt und blind ist und sich vor Gicht nicht mehr rühren kann, den bringen sie auf die Welt. Aber den sehen sie nicht, damit die Natur sich weiter durchsetzt und der Scheißdreck immer weitergehen kann. Aber mir ist es ja wurscht. Meine Situation kann nur

die eines skurrilen . . . ich möcht' nicht einmal sagen Papageis, weil das schon viel zu großartig wäre, sondern eines kleinen, aufmucksenden Vogerls sein. Das macht halt irgendein Geräusch, und dann verschwindet es wieder und ist weg. Der Wald ist groß, die Finsternis auch. Manchmal ist halt so ein Käuzchen drin, das keine Ruh' gibt. Mehr bin ich nicht. Mehr verlang' ich auch gar nicht zu sein.*[33]

The accusation of megalomaniac tendencies, frequently levelled against Bernhard, is invalidated by the diminutive purpose which Bernhard ascribes to his own writings in the last sentence of this quotation. The suggestive power of paranoia to which all those who went through the school of misanthropy are susceptible is never allowed free reign [sic] in Bernhard's works. Inasmuch as extreme forms of political reaction result almost invariably in paranoiac structures, this observation also provides an argument against those who, like Orwell, believe that the political expression of the satirical temperament is necessarily an obscurantist form of conservatism. This judgement fails to consider the fact that political reactionaries devise paranoiac plans for the sake of their practical application while the satirist escapes from the threat of paranoia through the creation of a work of art. Whether,

---

* 'I said that because it's a mistake if people think they're bringing children into the world. That's far too simple. They're having grown-ups, not children. They give birth to a sweaty, hideous pot-bellied innkeeper or mass murderer, that's what they get, not children. People say they're having a cute little bairn, but in reality they're having an 80-year-old leaking everywhere, blind and stinking, who limps and can't move for gout – that's who they bring into the world. But they don't see that, in order that nature can carry on and the whole crap keeps on going. But I don't give a damn about it. My situation can only be that of an odd little – I don't even want to say parrot, that would be way too grand – of a protesting little bird that just makes some kind of noise and then is gone again. The forest is large and so is the darkness. Sometimes there's one of those odd little owls in there that won't shut up. That's all I am. I don't ask for any more than that.'

in the last resort, the satirist actually does go mad like Swift or whether he remains capable of mustering the determination which is necessary for the defence of his precarious task is perhaps less important than Orwell's in many ways profoundly disturbing insight 'that a world view which only just passes the test of sanity is sufficient to produce a great work of art'.[34iv]

Beneath the Surface

Peter Handke's Story of the Goalkeeper's Anxiety

Unter all diesen seltsamen oder wohl gar unheimlichen Dingen hing im Schiff der Kirche das unschuldige Bildnis eines toten Kindes, eines schönen, etwa fünfjährigen Knaben, der, auf einem mit Spitzen besetzten Kissen ruhend, eine weiße Wasserlilie in seiner kleinen bleichen Hand hielt. Aus dem zarten Antlitz sprach neben dem Grauen des Todes, wie hülfeflehend, noch eine letzte holde Spur des Lebens; ein unwiderstehliches Mitleid befiel mich, wenn ich vor diesem Bilde stand.

Theodor Storm, *Aquis Submersus*

In the nave of the church, among all these curious and mysterious objects, there hung the simple portrait of a dead child. It depicted a lovely boy of about five years, lying on a lace-embroidered pillow, and in one pale hand was clasped a water-lily. In the delicate face was contained not only the awesomeness of death, but also — as if in supplication — one last fair breath of life. An irresistible sense of pity filled me whenever I stood before this picture.

Beneath the Flood, tr. Geoffrey Skelton[i]

Reading case histories compiled according to the accepted models of psychiatric medicine, one is repeatedly struck by how little they can tell us about the point at which the borderline is crossed between normal and pathological behaviour. On this key point, the scientific descriptions of the case in question appear in the main to rely on the accounts of decidedly unreliable narrators, such as family members and other agents of social order and authority. A contributing factor in the patient's misfortune [*Unglück*] – and indeed that of psychiatry – is that the latter is concerned not so much with anamnesis, the patient's own account of his or her illness, as in the classification of symptoms and the recording of the response to treatment or, as the case may be, to hospitalization.

Peter Handke's story of the anxiety states of a certain goalkeeper Bloch, in many ways a classic work of literature, raises the question as to whether the shortcomings of science might not be compensated for by a discipline which, by its very nature, relies on a certain degree of empathy, enabling it not only to diagnose this crossing of the border, but also to identify with it and trace its course. The objective insights into the nature of – among other things – emotional estrangement [*Entfremdung*] which might emerge from such a literary process would surely prove just as worthy of consideration by psychiatry as the latter's own case studies have been for literature, at least since the end of the last century. The reluctance on the part of psychiatry to engage with this in many ways extremely productive attempt at an empathetic description of pathological behaviour may in part be explained by the tendency – found in Döblin, Mann, Broch, Musil and even Bernhard – to depict disturbed mental states in a highly stylized artistic form. However, in contrast to a literary practice which psychiatry – for good reason – regards with suspicion, Peter Handke's text leads not to the cul-de-sac of over-emotive identification, but to an utterly matter-of-fact, indeed dispassionate investigation into the specific forms of schizophrenic flight from reality. Handke, who unlike many authors is prepared to bring not only the much vaunted quality of sensitivity, but also intelligence to bear on the issue, has, in the story in question, created a work which is no less indebted to scientific principles, and does them no less justice, than to those of art.[1]

At no point does the tale of the goalkeeper's flight from the capital to the provincial borderlands convey the uneasy sense that an author who knows exactly what time the next trains leave is here exploiting the fears of a disturbed subject for his own literary ends. By contrast with, for example, Heinar Kipphardt, who, in his novel *März* and its associated film and theatre scripts, has appropriated the life of the Klosterneuburg poet and asylum patient Ernst Herbeck,[2] and who then goes on to explain in the greatest detail the underlying structures and origins of schizophrenia, what Handke offers the reader by way of Bloch's previous history is every bit as sparse as any medical case history. We learn nothing more of Bloch's previous life than that he used to be a well-known goalkeeper, and that up to the point where the story begins he was a construction worker on a building site. Now and again, mention is made of his ex-wife, as well as of a child who, when Bloch telephones, immediately begins to reply with a 'rote sentence',[3] which so irritates Bloch that he immediately hangs up. However, Bloch himself, when he later gets through to his wife, can hardly manage anything more than clichés and idiomatic turns of phrase. 'He'd got cold feet and now he was high and dry,' he says, and tells her she will have to 'give him a hand'.[4]

This ready-made and somehow inherently inhibited mode of communication is the only insight the text gives of Bloch's former life as a private individual. At most, it can be deduced that psychological disintegration is often preceded by social disintegration – whether overt or hidden – but not, however, how it comes to pass that some people of an unstable psychological disposition 'react to non-specific psychological stresses with a "schizophrenic psychosis"'.[5] The missing back story, however, gives a more precise idea of the current inner reality of the afflicted person than could any pseudo-historical reconstructions or authorial omniscience, since an extremely contracted recollection of the past is, in fact, very typical of the cursory autobiographies of diagnosed psychotic schizophrenics. Thus, under the heading 'My Childhood', Ernst Herbeck writes: 'I lived in Stockerau and spoke of a small trivial thing. Then I was thrown out, flew out of the house. My grandmother wept. Then I flew beneath the lake and could go no further. A lady left me. Downfall I found pleasant.'[6] The quasi-staccato, disjointed details, which the poet later known as Alexander provides in these utterances about himself, permit the hypothesis that the origins of schizophrenia should be determined not only by what has happened to the subject, but via the gaps and omissions in their earlier life. Kipphardt's artistic indiscretions, by contrast, perpetuate the rationalistic assumption that the causes of mental breakdown can be apprehended by means of a carefully researched – and, if need be, invented – back story. That Handke refrains from delving into his protagonist's private life for the benefit of his nonetheless very curious readers is not the least merit of his story, which, in focusing on the subdued outbreak of a crisis, suggests that one reason the 'enigma' of schizophrenia has not yet been solved is because there have been so few attempts to portray what happens at the moment the border is crossed. Bloch's protracted, almost slow-motion flight thus documents precisely how, from an ill-defined sense of panic and a series of minute catastrophes, quite unspectacularly and logically there evolves a mode of existence no longer compatible with definitions of normality.

The state of panic in which Bloch is shown at the beginning of the narrative, when on the basis of a highly subjective interpretation of the looks of the workers and foreman he leaves the construction shack and, more through his eccentric behaviour than by design, causes a taxi to stop, is the product of an ever-increasing irritation which, as the text explains, is triggered by everything he sets eyes upon. The need this creates 'to notice as little as possible'[7] is, however, constantly subsumed [*aufgehoben*] in a kind of compulsive urge for perception, such that Bloch 'could hardly bear looking at the magazines but at the same time could not really put down a single one of them before he had leafed through it completely'.[8] Handke frequently comments in his journal from November 1975 to March 1977 on the difficulty of describing an everyday state of panic, and how, in this state, personal obsessive habits 'chase each other'; how 'one constantly has to be bending down wiping grains of dust off the floor; inability to sit still, inwardly'.[9] With a '"feeling" of disgrace and guilt, but with no claim to tragedy', panic is here associated with a form of behaviour concomitant with a continual and diffuse anticipation of pain [*Schmerzbereitschaft*]. The essential ambivalence of all phenomena and possible reactions intensifies the cumulative potential for anxiety. The more distant objects are from the observer, the more obtrusive they become, appearing strange as only things can which one thinks one has seen repeatedly before.[10] It is striking, too, that panic – whose calm and ordered counterpart is everyday routine – only manifests itself as long as the afflicted subject is confined to his own place, his house or home town. The labyrinth of spaces, as exemplified in the social patterns of urban settlement, frustrates the instinct to flee, which is directed outwards to the countryside. The panic resulting from these coexisting and contradictory impulses, the need for flight and the prevention of flight, the gap between inner agitation and the lack of any real progress, is something that Bloch can only overcome through the murder of the girl at the cinema box office.

In the context of the narrative, this murder provides the motivation for a kind of inverted crime story à la Patricia Highsmith, but it is nevertheless at first somewhat disconcerting, not least on account of its studied casualness. What matters here is clearly not the depiction of a crime so much as the phenomenon of a momentary, even accidental, lowering of the threshold of inhibition, identifying the murder – which for Bloch happens as if in a dream – as the one each man commits. Yet even if the unmotivated killing of the cinema cashier seems to have, in the context of the sheer arbitrariness of events and things reflected in Bloch's panic, no more significance than buying grapes on the Naschmarkt – especially cheap at this time of year – nonetheless the 'snapping noise'[11] with which the cashier gives up her life in Bloch's stranglehold signals that the all-pervasive threat, which, in the state of panic, is experienced subjectively but which, viewed objectively, is purely imaginary, has now become real, so that Bloch's flight from the city immediately after the deed does after all demonstrate something like a sense of purpose and inner logic. That this flight leads only to a place near the border, rather than somewhere actually 'outside' [*draußen*], is significant particularly because the flight of a human being – who no longer has any natural enemies – can only ever be a flight from himself or from other representatives of his own species, and thus can only ever be of an illusory nature.

The literal self-reflection expressed in Bloch's flight from one hopeless situation to the next alludes – as does the book's title – to the concept of existentialism, although without the latter's speculative pathos. The fact that Handke never allows his protagonist to become an anti-hero is the first prerequisite for a literary study concerned less with metaphysics than with a concrete phenomenology of the behavioural aspects of anxiety and fear. In this context, the precision with which Handke illustrates the difficulties associated with the use of language is key. Bloch's breakdown first manifests itself in the fact that, for him, language can no longer be taken for granted; he can only use it like a learned idiom in a foreign language. His powers of comprehension are impaired, and he guesses at least as much as he understands, since the order and pattern of language increasingly merge with the background noise of a reality growing ever more distant. The American couple conversing at the breakfast table, the cries and wild noises of the cartoons coming from the cinema, the Greek workman shouting into the receiver in a telephone booth – all these are signs that reality as it is articulated now only reaches Bloch through a kind of distorting filter, in scrambled form and as a confusing interference. The inverted logic of this means that

Bloch asks himself whether the policeman he has called to in greeting across the street has misconstrued his words. The interpretative aspect which thus inexorably becomes associated with every linguistic exchange is symptomatic of a dialectics of subjective estrangement and objective strangeness. Likewise it also 'seems' to Bloch that the saleswoman in the general store does not understand him when he speaks to her in whole sentences. 'Only when he told her word for word the names of the things he wanted did she start to move around again.'[12]

The question of how it comes about that the language of a person bound for a self-centred existence [*Subjektzentrismus*] is no longer 'heard' by the addressee, even when everything is semantically and grammatically correct, is one of the grey areas of psycholinguistics, which still has little revealing to say about how the mother tongue can disintegrate into a foreign language. What is clear, though, is that for the person whose disturbed social behaviour means they have already been floundering in misunderstandings for a long time, language itself becomes another area where they are liable to make a lot of mistakes. To the panicked inner gaze, fixated on the intended signifiers even before any attempt at articulation, the physiognomy of the words begins to shapeshift, so that language appears to take on a life of its own, further intensifying the insecurity of the speaking subject.

In one of his fascinating futurological essays, Stanislaw Lem describes how the communication problems of artificial language machines consist, *inter alia*, of the fact that their definition of existing terms diverges from the semantic norm, so that for example they decode 'Au' ['ow', 'ouch'; but also 'meadow'] as 'sensitive meadow' or 'Schwerhörigkeit' ['hard of hearing'] as 'darkest slavery'.[13ii] The associative interferences which suspend understanding at those points where interpretative behaviour more or less redundantly focuses on something which in fact goes without saying, appear, in the context cited above, as technical defects, the correction of which requires a continual input of reality into language, as well as an ongoing decoding of reality via the key of language [*Sprachschlüssel*] itself. However, what for machines of this kind is a routine correction of their own performance, in the case of human beings spells the onset of despair, where thought becomes a motor activity tending ultimately to silence, finally coming to a standstill in the intuitive insight that the human mind is incapable of distinguishing between getting to grips with something and getting lost in an illusion, because – to quote Lem again – 'language, being a useful tool, is also a self-locking instrument – and at the same time a perfidious one, since it tells nothing about when it becomes a pitfall itself.'[14] Just as someone walking on a sphere or globe can go round in endless circles without ever encountering a border, so too thought 'launched in a specified direction [. . .] encounters no limits and begins to circle in self-mirrorings. In the last century Wittgenstein sensed this' – here we should bear in mind that the context for this passage of Lem's is a critique of the human capacity for language from the advanced standpoint of the language machine GOLEM XIV – 'suspecting that many problems of philosophy are knottings of thought, such as the self-imprisonment and the Gordian knots in language, rather than of the real world.'[14]

Handke, whose analytical precision owes much to the Austrian tradition of *Sprachskepsis* [language scepticism], and to Wittgenstein in particular, demonstrates, by means of the 'pathological' disintegration of his protagonist's capacity for language, that language can never go beyond reality, but can only ever operate within it. If, therefore, linguistic expression can achieve nothing more than a duplication of what exists, the pathological way of seeing, constantly registering everything, even if only in one's head, is, as the following passage shows, nevertheless the most precise mode of perception, and as such is something on which, like the literary transcribing of the world, we have no choice but to rely.

> He saw two farmers shaking hands in a store doorway; their hands were so dry that he heard them rustling. Tractors had left muddy tracks from the dirt paths on the asphalt. He saw an old woman bent over in front of a display window, a finger to her lips. The parking spaces in front of the stores were emptying; the customers who were still arriving came in through the back doors. 'Suds' 'poured over' 'the doorsteps'. 'Featherbeds' 'were lying' 'behind' 'the windowpanes'. The blackboards listing prices were carried back into the stores. 'The chickens' 'pecked at' 'grapes that had been dropped'. The turkeys squatted heavily in the wire cages in the orchards. The salesgirls stood outside the doors and put their hands on their hips. The owner stood inside the dark store, absolutely still behind the scale. 'Lumps of yeast' 'lay' 'on the counter'.[15]

The empathetic writing gaze, seeking to verify, by comparison with reality and each of its components, what language allows it to know, leads – as the above quotation makes clear – to a kind of incantatory recapitulation. The tautological relationship of language and reality, of which, talking to himself, the speaker becomes acutely aware, betrays the fact that all mankind owns of the things that surround him is no more than the echo of his own fictions. The degree of insight into this dilemma may be what determines whether the conversation with oneself fades away into an autistic mumbling or crosses over into the metafiction of a literary text. That there is, however, no fixed boundary between these alternatives is something Stanislaw Lem has illustrated with the example of his anticipated language machine. 'The transitions from "unthinking", "chattering" machines "working purely formally" to "thinking", "speaking" machines showing "insight" occur in smooth stages,'[16] as it says in the introduction to the imaginary five-volume history of Bitic literature published in '2009' by the Presses Universitaires in Paris, and he goes on to describe how, around thirty years previously – towards the end of the 1980s – beginning with the 15th binasty of language computers, it turned out to be a technical necessity that the machines be provided with periods of recovery, in which, 'deprived of programmed directives', they were allowed to lapse into a specific kind of 'mumble' [*lallen*],[iii] which came to be known as 'machine dreams'. The 'bits', units of non-semantic information contained in these dreams, were supposed 'by this method of "shuffling" [*Mischen*] . . . to recover their partially lost efficiency'.[17] The recognition that autistic monologue had a positive part to play in the creative economy of the machines, indeed was the essential prerequisite for their authentic autonomous literary production, here reflects, in the form of an extensive conjecture, the still insufficiently explained relationship between pathological apperception and artistic creation [*Gestaltung*]. Handke's description, as sober as it is empathetic, of the progressive *dérangement* of the goalkeeper Bloch suggests that being deprived of the vital – even for language machines – phases of productive relaxation is a key factor in the aetiology of psychological estrangement, and demonstrates that literature's linguistic capacity and richness [*Sprachvermögen*] is only kept alive by an awareness of the dangers of its loss [*Sprachverlust*].

The symptomology of estrangement Handke develops in this tale of the goalkeeper's anxiety is concerned primarily – over and above the unreliability of reality reflected in language – with the sensory experience of an existence deprived of social contact. The echoing void in which the isolated individual believes himself to be abandoned further amplifies the sounds registered by a sensibility already stretched to breaking point. Bloch's hearing is so sensitive that:

> at times the cards didn't fall but were slammed on the next table, and at the bar the sponge didn't fall but slapped into the sink; and the landlady's daughter, with clogs on her bare feet, didn't walk through the barroom but clattered through the barroom; the wine didn't flow but gurgled into the glasses; and the music didn't play but boomed from the juke box.[18]

The phenomenon of hallucination, which is the symptom of pathological states hardest for a normal understanding to grasp, is rendered comprehensible via the disproportionate reactions of an extreme sensitivity. When Bloch posts the postcards he has written in the postbox, it makes an echoing sound [*hallen*], even though said postbox, as the next sentence assures us, is so tiny that nothing could 'resound' in it.[19] The retrospective rational correction however no longer has any impact on the reality of hallucinatory experience, which in Bloch's case is also manifested in a distorted perception of space: 'The mattress he was lying on had caved in, the wardrobes and bureaus stood far away against the walls, the ceiling overhead was unbearably high.'[20] The eccentric distortion of space corresponds to a slowed-down experience of time, reflected in the unhurried pace and almost Mediterranean feel of the southern Austrian province. The young men standing at the bar, who 'every time they laughed ... took one step backward' and always '[could be seen to] stiffen up just before they all screamed with laughter',[21] and the policeman on the moped who, after Bloch had already caught sight of him in the convex mirror on the bend, then really appeared around the bend, 'sitting up straight on his bike, wearing white gloves, one hand on the handlebars, the other on his stomach',[22] seem to belong to a cast of characters from an age lost to time, whose chronometer is the turnip leaf caught in the spokes of the policeman's bike wheel. The dislocations of space and time ultimately also affect Bloch's perception of his own body. When, having just dropped off to sleep, he woke up again, it seemed to him in the first moment:

> as if he had fallen out of himself. He realized that he lay in a bed. 'Not fit to be moved', thought Bloch. A cancer. He became aware of himself as if he had suddenly degenerated. He did not matter any more. No matter how still he lay, he was one big wriggling and retching; his lying there was so sharply distinct and glaring that he could not escape into even one picture that he might have compared himself with. The way he lay there, he was something lewd, obscene, inappropriate, thoroughly obnoxious. 'Bury it!' thought Bloch. 'Prohibit it, remove it!' He thought he was touching himself unpleasantly but realized that his awareness of himself was so intense that he felt it like a sense of touch all over his body; as though his consciousness, as though his thoughts, had become palpable, aggressive, abusive toward himself.

> Defenceless, incapable of defending himself, he lay there. Nauseatingly his insides turned out; not alien, only repulsively different. It had been a jolt, and with one jolt he had become unnatural, had been torn out of context.[23]

The negative transubstantiation which Bloch undergoes here, his revulsion at his own body which thus also becomes 'untouchable' for others, immediately brings to mind the metamorphosis of Gregor Samsa, which likewise presents a flight into a form of transhuman existence. The sense of revulsion or nausea – a central characteristic of the image of humanity as conceived by existentialist philosophy from Nietzsche to Sartre – marks the point at which the subject is cut loose from the safeguards of civilization and is confronted with his own savage origins, of which sensory over-sensitivity, violent outbursts expressed as sudden explosive motor activity, fearfulness and timidity are all part.[24]

Rudolf Bilz has pointed out that fear, 'even the fear of the most modern person, can only ever flow along the most ancient of pathways',[25] and that schizophrenia should, accordingly, be understood as an exposed state in which the afflicted individual is at the mercy of a palaeo-anthropological state of preparedness [*Erlebnisbereitschaft*]. The 'savage' behaviour which anachronistically asserts itself, regardless of the acquired reactions of civilized existence, Bilz notes, 'is likewise associated with an apparently anachronistic way of relating to and conquering space'.[26] Bloch's apparently aimless wanderings across the landscape arise as much from a need to secure the territory as from the instinct to escape his enemies. The passage which follows illustrates how these as it were biological necessities function as the generative elements of a paranoid state of mind, in which all behaviour is dictated by a response to suspicious circumstances or perceived threats.

> Even though the window was open, it was impossible to see into the customs shed; the room was too dark from the outside. Still, somebody must have seen Bloch from the inside; he understood this because he himself held his breath as he walked past. Was it possible that nobody was in the room even though the window was wide open? Why 'even though'? Was it possible that nobody was in the room because the window was wide open? Bloch looked back: a beer bottle had even been taken off the windowsill so they could have a better look at him. He heard a sound like a bottle rolling under a sofa. On the other hand, it was not likely that the customs shed had a sofa. Only when he had gone farther on did it become clear to him that a radio had been turned on in the room. Bloch went back along the wide curve the street made toward the town. At one point he started to run with relief because the street led back to town so openly and simply.[27]

Bloch's reactions are, on the one hand, an example of how, from the viewpoint of a non-paranoid state of health, the process of estrangement gives rise to pathological episodes; if, on the other hand, one views paranoia as a behavioural throwback to an earlier stage of human development, formed by the needs of a world determined by flight and hunting, such episodes appear as entirely logical, particularly in view of the fact that Bloch really is trying to escape, or at least attempting to reach a place of safety. For this reason, the hunt motif, introduced early on in the text via the image of the circling hawk, is one of the constant layers of meaning in the story. In this context, Bloch realizes 'that he had not been watching the hawk fluttering and diving but the spot in the field for which the bird would presumably head',[28] which seems to suggest that he identifies with the invisible victim, not with the attacker. The other side of this is the lesson the customs officer gives him on the technique of vigilance, so indispensable to his profession:

> 'If you're facing each other . . . it's important to look the other guy in the eyes. Before he starts to run, his eyes show you which direction he'll take. But you've also got to watch his legs at the same time. Which leg is he putting his weight on? The direction that leg is pointing is the direction he'll want to take. But if the other guy wants to fool you and not run in that direction, he'll have to shift his weight just before he takes off, and that takes so much time that you can rush him in the meantime.'[29]

The focused and at the same time multidirectional vigilance the customs officer refers to here is an exact counterpart to Bloch's situation. Bloch is the one constantly under surveillance, and is thus even less able to escape the anticipated arrest – potentially already accomplished – inasmuch as this is already predicated by his profession as goalkeeper. If the players on the field appear as relatively free agents, the figure of the goalkeeper, significant on many levels in the text, could be interpreted as an analogy for what ethnography refers to as the concept of 'subject-centrism' [*Subjektzentrismus*], according to which 'everything which occurs all around is experienced by the subject as if related directly to him, the subject . . . One sits or stands there as if bristling with antennae, reaching out into the sphere of experience . . . The subject is located at the focal point of three-dimensional space, which in this way becomes the space of his own experience [*Erlebnis-Raum*].'[30] In precisely this sense, the goalkeeper is fixed to the spot, and the entire game is directed exclusively at persuading him, in the small space he has at his disposal, to make a 'wrong movement'.[iv] The pathological intensification of such experience, where everything ceaselessly crowds in upon the subject, defines the state of psychosis, the feeling 'of being observed while unable to see the observers'.[31] Since, unlike in the game he knows so well, Bloch can no longer see the hostile hordes bearing down upon him, he can only gaze in panic at an environment which now seems occupied in its entirety by enemy forces. From this perspective, nature is transformed into a series of still lifes, in which everything is separate from everything else in the most intolerable manner. 'Through the door Bloch looked at the apple parings lying on the kitchen table. Under the table there was a bowl heaped full of apples; a few apples had rolled off and were scattered around on the floor. A pair of work pants hung on a nail in the doorframe.'[32]

The photographic images which the subject, aware of the threat to his very being, is compelled to make of the objects and occurrences in his surroundings have, in addition to the security they represent for the disturbed individual, the further significance that the artistic recording of reality, too, can only translate 'life' into the two-dimensionality of the picture or text as *nature morte*. This process of foreshortening, in which life is invariably deprived of life, but what is dead is never brought to life, is a recurring theme in the literature of the nineteenth century. Poe's story 'The Oval Portrait' explores the relationship between artistic likeness and living reality, as does Storm's novella *Aquis Submersus*. In both works, the apparent life of the image, deeply moving to the observer, is intrinsically bound up with the death of the subject represented in the portrait.

The suggestion implicit in the above, that in depicting a pathological world view Handke was ultimately also concerned with a scrupulous examination of his own artistic 'guilty' conscience, and his own distance from 'normal' life, is confirmed by his story in another regard also. Insofar as the text permits identification between narrator and protagonist, this occurs at the point where Bloch's story converges with that of the missing schoolboy. The unfortunate child, who is sometimes described as speech-impaired and sometimes as mute, is only discovered when Bloch's time too is almost up, suggesting the parallel trajectory of their two fates. In contrast to Bloch, though, who, when he sees 'below him in the water the corpse of a child',[33] turns away and returns to the main road without making the connection, the narrator projects his emotions, hitherto kept very strictly under control, on to the image of the schoolboy, which encapsulates the pathogenesis of both his protagonist and himself. As his time on the run comes to an end, Bloch is confronted with the unrealistic image of himself on a wanted poster, put together according to the descriptions of others, but is incapable of making the connection between the appearance of this outlandish portrait and the premature death of the schoolboy. The sentence 'The paper carried only a school picture of the boy because he had never been photographed alone'[34] is uttered by the narrator. In it is articulated the insight that the development of goalkeeper Bloch's pathological state goes back to pre-existing handicaps of a social nature, and that his own art only goes beyond the pathological inasmuch as it opens up, for both author and readers, an understanding of the wretched and utter hopelessness of such circumstances.

The story of estrangement presented in Handke's tale is, ultimately, identical both with Bloch's – wordless – and the author's – articulated – search for the devastation which marked their respective childhoods. Bloch's ephemeral fame as a goalkeeper, which may for a time have helped him to overcome the difficulties of memory, would thus come to stand in for Peter Handke's fame as a writer. The unfortunate schoolboy, though, who stands behind both of them, is the cipher for a consciousness which, as Handke noted in his journal, has to contend with the thought 'of belonging to a lower class, of being an upstart without a background'.[35] The pathography of the protagonist and the biography of the narrator thus converge in what, from the point of view of societal normality, appears as the illegitimate nature of both illness and art, which, each in their different way, recall the destruction that is wrought in the lives of children.

A Small Traverse

The Poetry of Ernst Herbeck

Kunst heißt, das Leben mit Präzision verfehlen.
Art means missing life with precision.

Nicolas Born[i]

In Grönland wird der 1. Mai im Iglu gefeiert.
In Greenland the 1st of May is celebrated in an igloo.

Ernst Herbeck

The poetic texts created in the last twenty years by Ernst Herbeck — better known by his chosen pseudonym Alexander — who has spent most of his life in the Landesanstalt für Psychiatrie in Klosterneuburg, Lower Austria,[1] are characterized by their immediately striking imaginative power and by symptoms of language decay. This combination makes Alexander's texts difficult terrain for critics, so that those elements more accessible to the sympathetic imagination tend to be given precedence over the enigmatic language of signs and symbols of incoherent utterances. Such a limited reconstruction of the 'meaning' of Alexander's texts can, though, only be justified insofar as it retains an awareness that its attempts at explanation are no less flawed than the lyric excursions it discusses, since what corresponds to the lack of clarity in the original text is not the lucidity of the psychological or interpretative system, but rather the lack of understanding, also perpetuated in the latter, which is one of the causes of the author's illness. Out of respect for its own logic, academic exegesis is inclined to disregard anything that might disrupt its scheme, a tendency all the more readily indulged in the case of Alexander, given that neither he nor his writings conform to the usual literary norms. However, it must be remembered that even canonical literature – the work of Kafka, for example – contains 'blind spots' which utterly defy interpretation. The resultant awareness of one's own inadequacies would, in many ways, be the most appropriate starting point for a study of Alexander's 'condition-related art' [*zustandsgebundene Kunst*].[ii]

In addition, it is important to bear in mind that the extreme sensibility evident in Alexander's talent for poetic combinations, as shown in such extraordinarily empathetic lines as 'Der Rabe führt die Frommen an' ['The raven leads the pious on'] or 'Die Treue ist des Hundes Rast' ['Loyalty is the dog's rest'],[2] has its origins in the same process as that which also gives rise to the disintegration of language. If a high degree of psychotic arousal leads to language decay [*Sprachzerfall*], in a more moderate form this state is likewise a prerequisite for a synthesis of images which far exceeds – in a positive sense – our expectations of language. It is Alexander's personal misfortune [*Unglück*] that he does not have at his disposal the means of achieving the inner equilibrium necessary for a more measured literary production on his own initiative. Apart from that, however, his 'condition-related' art is essentially not that different from the work of regular poets, whose productivity is likewise conditioned by a specific emotional state of arousal. This essay will, therefore, attempt to understand Alexander's texts, in all their apparent incoherence [*Ungereimtheit*], as the utterances of someone who is, essentially, normal; it thus consciously distances itself from an attitude, still prevalent today, which takes delight in eccentricity at the expense of those afflicted by it.[3] 'For histrionic or fanatical stress on the mysterious side of the mysterious takes us no further,' Benjamin writes in his essay on surrealism; 'we penetrate the mystery only to the degree that we recognize it in the everyday world.'[4]

What is often missing in Alexander's texts is not the primary ability to see things in a new light, fundamental to lyric poetry, but rather the latter's secondary system of discursivity which permits us still to number poets among ourselves. The technique of de-scription [*Be-schreibung*] and the progression from there to reflection – as typically cultivated, for example, in the teaching of essay writing in schools – forms the basis of social discourse, but not of the poetic imagination. As a secondary or subordinate phenomenon, discursivity in lyric poetry is by no means indispensable; and if Alexander's poems are lacking in it, this indicates at most a societal rather than an aesthetic shortcoming. From the point of view of art, the opposite of discursivity – namely disintegration – is not a symptom; rather, it is an essential component, a 'site of the most intense vitality'.[5] Not only from an aesthetic but also from a psychological viewpoint, linguistic disorder [*sprachliche Unordnung*] acts as a reservoir of regenerative energy. Freud was of the opinion that the libidinal investment of the verbal idea [*Wortvorstellung*], manifested precisely in words in isolation [*Vereinzelung des Wortes*], is directed at a reconstruction of our lost emotional attachment to objects. '[T]he investment of the word-idea has nothing to do with the act of repression, but instead represents the first of the attempts at recovery or cure that so conspicuously dominate the clinical picture of schizophrenia.'[6] The symptoms of disintegration are therefore, at least potentially, the starting point for a new connection between emotion, word and object. The accumulation of all kinds of disparate material[iii] has the subliminal aim of a return, via a process of condensation and displacement [*Verdichtung und Verschiebung*], from words to things. Statements such as 'Der Regen ist die Traufe zur Natur'[iv] ['Rain is nature down the drain', or more literally 'Rain is the gutter to nature'] or 'Die Dame ohne Unterleib[v] ist die Liebe in Berlin' ['The lady without legs is love in Berlin'],[7] which, their flawed logic notwithstanding, are of considerable suggestive power, arise from just such attempts at reconnection.

According to Piaget's treatment of symbolism, condensation and displacement of the signifiers are 'functional equivalents of generalization and abstraction – the processes of logical conceptual thought'.[8] In unconscious symbolic thought, for which one might also use the term *pensée sauvage*, Piaget sees 'an extension of normal thinking'.[9] This means that, seen from the position of logical thought, no negative conclusions should be drawn as to the legitimacy or otherwise of symbolic constructions. In symbolic thinking, the utilitarian concept of language is an alien, or rather an absent, one; its aim is not a definitive de-scription of reality, but a continued and continuing engagement with it. Even in their completed form, Herbeck's texts illustrate the discrepancy between the experiential act of writing and the meaning of the work of literature. The completed work is primarily directed at the audience, and thus, for the author, no longer embodies what the act of writing meant for him. *Writing* is essential, not literature. The more an author needs to write, the less interest he takes in his work. For Herbeck — who, according to Leo Navratil,[10] does not keep his writings, neither correcting nor evaluating them — writing is more necessary than for other authors, even though he always first has to be prompted to do it. Writing, he traverses his fractured life, making it traceable on the page precisely through his faithful registering of incidental slips and interferences. These 'interferences', often in the form of arbitrary punctuation and interpolations without rhyme or reason, are the objective correlative of Ernst Herbeck's own fragmented life story, and as such, for the author Alexander, at the moment of writing they represent significant signposts in his personal predicament. It is precisely in their openness to apparently nonsensical interjections that his poems remind us that the idea of a preestablished harmony is merely an illusion produced by the completed work, and that, for authentic creativity, the dissociation of meaning is just as important as the construction of it.

Admittedly, for the reader accustomed to linguistic order, the positive function of dissociation only becomes apparent when the interferences and catachrestic displacements result in images in which the discordant material comes together in constellations which, despite their apparent wrongness, somehow approximate to his or her own imagination. In indicating the possibility of a bridge between the concepts of discordance and concordance, Herbeck's texts disprove the theory of the opposition between sense and nonsense, suggesting that there are far more subterranean connections between these two poles than all our book learning can ever dream of.

The only difference between Herbeck's language and that of

sanctioned literature is that Herbeck also includes within his texts the propaedeutic stage of the creative process, namely dissociation as a medium for the invention of new structures. It is, though, precisely this aspect of his texts which makes clear the process by which the 'poetic image' arises. Conventional attempts at explaining this, which cleave either to the concept of irrational inspiration or else to that of rational montage, remain inadequate hypotheses. Konrad Lorenz has pointed out[11] that, in the field of natural history, the origin [*Entstehung*] of new phenomena has never found adequate expression in language; from the point of view of language logic [*sprachlogisch*], terms such as 'creation' [*Schöpfung*] or 'emergence' [*Emergenz*] awaken a false impression of what actually occurs. Lorenz uses the term *fulguratio*, or the 'creative flash', to describe the process by which two independent systems unexpectedly come together, via a kind of short circuit, to create a new connection.[vi] It is precisely this process, characteristic of every instance of genesis – to some extent dependent on the free-floating availability of the potential components, and hence only rarely visible in conventionally ordered literature – which determines even the foreground and appearance of Herbeck's texts. Sentences like 'Es geht bergup in jedes Tal'[vii] ['You walk uphill into every valley'] or 'Von hier in die Waldheimat Peter Roseggers in den Weltkrieg' ['From here to the woodland home of Peter Rosegger to the world war'][12] indicate how, via the 'false' track, one may yet approach true insight.

The creative act is one subject to a high degree of manipulation by art – and by verbal art in particular. Such manipulation ranges from the creation of an environment conducive to inspiration to the deliberate elimination of unproductive elements. The seemingly spontaneous semblance of beauty for its own sake which is characteristic of the work of art is, paradoxically, the result of the very deliberate arrangement of the component parts. Even if Herbeck is capable of this manipulation only to a limited degree, his sense is all the keener of the fundamental aporia of art it expresses; an art whose mythologemes, seen from an evolutionary point of view, appear – precisely on account of their presumptive meaningfulness – as a kind of confidence trick. In his illuminating anthropological studies on the origins of the earliest mythologemes, Rudolf Bilz discusses the corrective subject-serving interpretations which allow us to calibrate and compensate for the discrepancy in meaning between our perception of self and the environment, which in a crisis situation may admittedly result in a stabilization that increases our odds of survival, but which also means that, 'by comparison with the animal world, naïvely at the mercy of its own repertoire, we are nothing more than *Falschspieler*' [cheats and fraudsters; literally 'false players'].[13] It is precisely the above interpretations which, from the animal viewpoint, must surely create the impression that we have – as Nietzsche said – 'taken leave of our sound animal common sense'.[14]

By contrast with projective and discursive mythologemes such as God, the Hereafter, Freedom and Justice, with which we console ourselves for our existential inadequacy, the poetic image could almost be defined as a memory of an earlier phase of evolution, in which such inventions were not necessary. Herbeck's statement 'Die Poesie lernt man vom Tiere aus, das sich im Wald befindet' ['Poetry is learnt from the animal in the woods'][15] outlines this hypothesis with marvellous precision. For a poet capable of the requisite empathy for such a poetic learning process, the whole performance of art must appear a fairly ridiculous affair. Herbeck's mistrust of the mendacious business of art is perfectly encapsulated in the phrase 'Es werden die Künstler wie Semmeln gebacken. Preis 6gr.' ['They turn out artists like bread rolls. Price 6 Groschen'].[16] By comparison with the difficult emotional predicament of someone as exposed as Herbeck, art – and Herbeck does not except his own – stands accused of having nothing to offer but cheap thrills. Even though Herbeck repeatedly invokes art's deceptive tendencies, ironically he himself is prepared – for example for visitors interested in his texts – to adopt the pose of an artist. He carries his book around with him in his jacket pocket, leafs through it casually, says, too, that writing takes a lot of time, which – given that he mostly dashes it off quickly – does not quite correspond to the facts, being true only in a profounder sense. Talking to the poet Alexander, the 'Propheten des Mittelalters' ['prophet of the middle ages'] 'der es ermöglicht Gottes Vers zu ebnen' ['who makes it possible to smooth out God's verse'],[17] one has the clear impression that he has mastered this role with an actor's ease, so that it appears to go hand in hand with an almost humorous attitude. The obliging performance Herbeck is prepared to give as a poet contains, both in its gestures and in the qualitative discrepancy between his symbiotically experienced poetry and the mimetic and merely imitative, an implicit criticism of the inauthenticity of the artistic way of life and of the work of art. Behind the artist Alexander, who, rather like Chaplin in the famous department-store scene, showing us how easy roller-skating is while teetering on the brink of an abyss, the long-term patient Herbeck, who has far graver things to deal with, is actually making a bid for our attention.

Some of the arguments outlined above regarding the origins of Herbeck's texts might seem to suggest that their author has no need of technique, and that the images arise exclusively from arbitrary syntheses. Such a conclusion, though, reducing the role of the writer to a mere intermediary, falls wide of the mark, since it overlooks a crucial aspect of the specific quality of Herbeck's poetic output. It must be remembered that he tends, on the whole, to stay very close to the topic suggested to him, organizing the disparate material which comes to hand according to the topic in question. This 'combination model' is perhaps best described by the term *bricolage* used by Lévi-Strauss in his analysis of mythical thought. Lévi-Strauss defines the *bricoleur* as someone who 'works with his hands and uses devious means compared to those of a craftsman'.[18] This method, drawing on very varied but at the same time often inappropriate means, is also evident in Herbeck's word combinations [*Wortverbindungen*], where the connections between individual components often seem hand-made rather than logical. The fact that, in schizophrenia, more ancient forms of human expression resurface further justifies the use of the anthropological term *bricolage* in a study on 'condition-related' art. Lévi-Strauss is at pains to emphasize in his argument that the – by comparison with the scientific repertoire – relatively primitive means of mythical thought in no way implies that it is any less complex than scientific description.

The same argument applies when considering the relationship of 'condition-related' texts to those generally accepted as literature, since in the case of psychotic utterances, too, what counts is not the relative impoverishment of the product, but the incidental nature of the means, which as a general rule have only a provisional relationship to the intended project. Lévi-Strauss explains that the *bricoleur* constantly replenishes his unsystematically accumulated materials with 'the remains of previous constructions or deconstructions'.[19] Similarly, the tendency to absolute *disponibilité* [availability] is one of the central criteria of the process of 'condition-related' writing, whose finished products still retain an air of something only partially assembled – or disassembled. If art in the conventional sense aims to transcend its material, Herbeck's texts are to be understood as an ongoing dialogue with language, a dialogue whose evolution is largely determined by the contingency of reality. Great art is always oriented towards eternal values – a position outside of time – and is therefore constrained to draw on lasting, precious or imposing material for its subject matter. By contrast, the work of the *bricoleur*, comprising remains and debris from the 'fossilized evidence of the history of an individual or a society',[20] lives *in* and for time and for the moment of its making; it is a functional object, which, having only a heuristic purpose, already bears within itself the destruction to come.

In this regard, Herbeck's texts fulfil in exemplary manner the criteria for *littérature mineure* postulated by Deleuze and Guattari in their studies on Kafka. 'Minor literature' is written *against* culture, not for it; its material poverty is a sign of lack, but also of independence. Accordingly, Herbeck's marginalia on existing texts by famous poets illustrate his propensity for subverting works of high culture. An elaborate Rilke poem with the typical lyric set pieces of the early twentieth century – summer afternoon, view through a window, piano music, park, scent of jasmine etc. – is, once Herbeck has first painstakingly made a more or less accurate copy, soon stripped back to its bare essentials: 'Das Klavier stand schräg zum / Fenster und die Musik war I. Klasse' ['The piano was at an angle to the / window and the music was I. class']; and a three-stanza lake poem by C. F. Meyer is reduced, in his transcription, to 'Tiefblauer Himmel – Zwei Segel' ['Deep blue sky – two sails'].[21] *Démontages* [deconstructions] of this kind are eminently typical of Herbeck's practice as a writer, whereby a work which already exists in complete form is reworked and over-written until the answer turns into a question, and the image becomes an enigma.

This process reveals that, like palimpsests, Herbeck's texts owe their specific effect to the use they make of the narrow spaces between the prescribed lines of another text. The shifts and displacements at the hand of the *bricoleur* in the structure of the words and sentences are the medium for the lyric description of the world, whose art lies less in deciphering reality – including that of language – than in encoding it. The 'mytho-poetical nature of "bricolage"'[22] cited by Lévi-Strauss resists all concepts and accepted precepts and sets its sights on signs and wonders. For this reason, in Herbeck's language, 'Die Freundschaft' ['Friendship'], for example, is not merely an abstract concept but – as the text 'An die Freunde, die hier in der Anstalt sind' ['To the friends who are here in the institution'] shows – 'ein marinäres Bekennungswort. Von Schiff zu / Schiff – von Kapitän zu Kapitän' ['a marinerly signalling. From ship to / ship – from captain to captain'].[23] The as it were passing beauty of these lines is utterly inconceivable without the tangible physical presence of the author in the placing of the words. Where the artist rises above his work, the *bricoleur* renounces all authority and dwells – in the many senses that the German preposition allows – 'unter der Sprache' [under, beneath, amid language].

It is entirely conceivable that, in the long run, it is only by means of such a symbiotic connection with language, and the associated 'intensified experience of significance',[24] that literary art can avoid erosion and calcification. What we tend to think of as a phenomenon marginal to our culture would thus be of central importance, especially in the face of our increasingly digitalized need for expression. As Rudolf Bilz explains,[25] at an early stage of human history, when, due to an evolutionary leap, the species had entered a danger zone, subject-centric and fantastical associations and hallucinations served as tools for survival. Applied to the present situation, in which technical progress is already teleologically oriented towards catastrophe, this means that the tendency to symbolization and physiognomization which characterizes the language of schizophrenics – diametrically opposed to the language of administration [*verwaltete Sprache*] – is better able to define where our hope lies than conventionally ordered discourse. Naturally, something of this hope is also at work in established culture. However, the more that culture, like science before it, is itself drawn into the sphere of administration [*Verwaltung*], the greater the potential significance of minor literature – as whose ambassador we should understand Ernst Herbeck.

The impulse to keep trying out new combinations of heterogeneous elements, according to the formula 'a + b leuchten im Klee' ['a + b glow in the clover'][26] is the vehicle for articulating the constantly fluctuating world view of psychosis, in which perceptions of space and time appear distorted. Inasmuch as Herbeck makes only incidental reference to his own personal history and that of contemporary society in his texts, it is easy for critics to fall into the trap of idealizing their ahistorical quality at the expense of what could, in fact, offer a possible insight into the historicity of mental disturbance. The timeless and visionary components of psychotic utterance often suggest the misleading conclusion that the malfunctioning of memory [*Gedächtnis*] is the same as an absence of memories [*Erinnerungslosigkeit*]. Herbeck's texts, however, attest to the fact that memories [*Erinnerung*] are fundamental to his view of himself. Again and again, in his various accounts of his life, he tries to put in order the few facts available about his existence. Date of birth, place of birth, mother and father, school, taking a job, internment — that is pretty much all he has to work with. It seems that it is less the lack of memories than the paucity of experience which creates an ahistorical impression. If Herbeck sometimes intersperses the accounts of his life with false or fictitious details, this is not because he is unable to remember, but because his memories are distorted by the experimental imagining of a different life. An example of this may be found in the 'Brief an meine Frau' ['Letter to my Wife'], which he signs as Alexander H. Ltn. d. R. Lds. Sch. Bataillon 327. Stand Retz i Hausruck:

> Es war im Winter 1945. Rußland. Der Krieg
> i. S. R. änderte sich seinem Ende zu. Stalin-
> grad. betrübt ging es der Heimat zu. – Viele kamen
> nicht mehr mit zurück – In Ehre verblieben sie draussen. –
> Meine Liebe Grete, was denkst Du darüber, wirst
> Du Dich etwas zusammennehmen, freuen! Oder
> hast Du Dich mit einem anderen verheiratet!
> inzwischen: röm. Kath. Rythus und so.? Na ja und
> nennst Du mich wieder einen Dyno. SS-Mann! – – –
> Ich weiß nicht mehr weiter! Alexander, verbleibe ich
> hiermit, und herzl. Grüße Alexander! Servus!![27]

[It was in the winter of 1945. Russia. The war / i. S. R. was changing to its end. Stalin- / grad. Saddened we headed homeward. — Many did not come / back with us. — Honourably they remained. – / My Love Grete, what do you think about it, will / you take hold of yourself, be glad! Or / have you married someone else! / meanwhile: rom. Cathl. rites etc.? Oh well and / you call me a Dyno. SS-man again! – – – / I don't know what else to say! Alexander, I remain / yours truly and best greetings Alexander! Adieu!!]

The story of Ernst Herbeck, who, even though – as will be shown in what follows – the image of woman is central to his fantasies, was never able to marry – this story of his very personal catastrophe is just as present in his letter from the front as the historical lunacy of war. The way the individual gets caught up in the haphazard course of history – 'Der Krieg i. S. R. änderte sich seinem Ende zu' ['The war / i. S. R. was changing to its end'] here becomes tangible in a similar way to Alexander Kluge's description of the Battle of Stalingrad, in which the complexity of the organizational construction of a historical disaster [*Unglück*] is identified as the reason for the apparent irrationality of our individual and collective fate. The catastrophes staged by history, as it were off its own bat, no longer find an exact correlation in the rational agency of the bourgeois *Bildungsroman*, but in the individual devastation wrought by history.

A curious commentary on the inextricable enmeshing of the private life of the individual with that of the collective may be found in a text by Herbeck which, under the title 'Wörter, die mir einfallen' ['Words that occur to me'], recites a long sequence of names.[28] After two dozen weird and wonderful names such as Hubano, Herodek, Birsenpichler or Weichenpuchfink, suddenly Herbeck makes an appearance between Heidl, Heidt and Nurmannshöfer, and Lehár and Schiller find themselves next to Hitler and Hirt. Adolf comes after Mann and

Muhm. There is a Hirsch Allein [Stag Alone], an Österreicher [Austrian] and an Ernst Heldentum [Ernest Heroism], Meidaneg and Schuschnigg[viii] follow Dau, Dangl, Berger and Huber, and towards the end there is also an Ich [I] between Ignaz and Riederer. The impression this people's assembly of names conveys is that fascism is a family affair, which may just as easily develop into individual illness as, on the level of history, escalate into the fiasco of world war. Ernst Jandl's fantastically obscene poem about the *Anschluß*, 'wien: heldenplatz',

>wien: heldenplatz<, wo
der glanze heldenplatz zirka
versaggerte in maschenhaftem männchenmeere
drunter auch frauen die ans maskelknie
zu heften heftig sich versuchten, hoffensdick[29]

[Heldenplatz Vienna where
the whole and glory heroes' square circa
went weak at the knees all massed up in the mannekin sea
among them women too who hurled themselves heavily
at the muscle-masculknees, bellies fat with hope]

describes the connection between the repressed eroticism of the nuclear family and the political high spirits anticipating the violence to come. A similarly ambivalent feeling of connectedness is articulated in Herbeck's text. Listed one after another, as in a Register of Deaths, the surnames already prefigure the unholy national collective to come. The irruptive presence of the I [*Ich*] Ernst Heldentum in the context of the mass of all the Austrians representing the force of history acts as a footnote to Nietzsche's famous hypothesis that when it comes to groups, peoples and ages, madness is the norm, but in the case of the individual, it is by contrast rather rare.[ix] In a text with the title 'Ein Erlebnis' ['An Experience'], Herbeck recalls the day of the *Anschluß*:

> Das war 25. September 1938
> Es war der Einmarsch Hi-
> tlers nach Österreich nach
> Wien. Wir fuhren mit
> einem Laster hinein und
> sahen Hitler und die beg-
> eisterte Wienerstadt.
> Reichskanzler Ad. Hitler
> hielt eine Rede in der Er
> sagte: Wir, die Deutschen und
> ich werden den Wienern und
> Österreichern helfen und
> Euch Arbeit verschaffen. Es
> war das Erlebnis meines
> Lebens.[30]

[That was 25. September 1938 / It was Hi- / tler marching into Austria into / Vienna. We travelled in / on a truck and / saw Hitler and the enth- / usiastic Vienna city. / Reichs- kanzler Ad. Hitler / gave a speech in which He / said: We, the Germans and / I will help the Viennese and / Austrians and / find work for you. It / was the experience of my / life.]

That Ernst Herbeck, unlike Herr Karl,[x] did not succeed in travelling further on the juggernaut of history and making the continually necessary concessions is, over and above his psychological frailty, also a testament to his personal integrity. The outbreak of illness, which also always represents a breaking out of history, is the opposite of the accommodations demanded by society; however, it does not, as Ernst Herbeck well knew, result in independence from historical events. Rather, the curious way in which he sometimes associates himself with the figure of Hitler alludes to the suspicion that the destruction of his personal life at the end of the war is directly related to the preceding ravages of history. Adolf, Herbeck writes,

> ist ein Werwolfname Name, und
> heißt ERNYst HITL'ER und will
> machen das er fortkommt weil
> er keine Freude Hat am Dasein
> und immer nicht eingesperrt
> bleiben will. Sein Name richtig ist
> Amadeus Mayer er Trinkt mehr
> und ißt mehr weil er Appetit hat.
> er will das gericht verlassen fort
> und wandern in die Stadt.[31]

[is a werewolf-name name, and / is called ERNYst HITL'ER and wants / to see that he gets away because / he Has no pleasure in existence / and doesn't always want to stay / locked up. His name really is / Amadeus Mayer he Drinks more / and eats more because he is hungry. / he wants to leave away from court / and walk into the City.]

The bearer of the werewolf name Adolf is actually called ERNYst, not very different from Ernst Herbeck, born with a cleft palate

[*Wolfsrachen* = wolf throat], whose other name, Alexander, finds an echo in Amadeus Mayer. The connection made here between Alexander, Ernst and Adolf signifies that the rather misshapen little man who was responsible for all the history is identical with the one who suffers at its hands. The symbiotic relationship between power and powerlessness, which Kafka too explores repeatedly, shows that Ernst Herbeck has a thoroughly critical grasp of what the role of *his* story is within history. The truth of his insight is in no way diminished by the relatively hermetic form he gives it.

The combinatory art of the *bricoleur*, creating diagrammatic word-relations between the life of the soul and the history unfolding above our heads, is also the technique by which Herbeck creates lyrical compositions of a beauty seldom found in literature. As a representative example of the singular aesthetic quality of many of his texts, the poem 'Blau' ('Blue') may be cited here:

> Die Rote Farbe.
> Die Gelbe Farbe.
> Die Dunkelgrüne
> Der Himmel ELLENO
> Der Patentender
> Das Sockerl, Das Schiff.
> Der Regenbogen.
> Das Meer
> Die Auenblätter
> Das Wasser
> Die Blattnarbe
> Der Schlüßesl (R) ('r.')
> Die Schloß + Das Schloß.

Blue[xi]

The Red Color.
The Yellow Color.
The Dark Green
The Sky ELLENO
The Patentender
The Pedestal, The Ship.
The Rainbow.
The Sea
The Shoreleaves
The Water
The Leaf Vein
The Kleyf (R) "r."
The Locks + The Lock.[32]

The title word 'Blue', together with the first two lines, evokes a kaleidoscopic magical world of colours, which gradually sinks into the dark green, rising later in more muted tones as a rainbow. The more hermetic terms which follow – the sky ELLENO, whose capital letters seem to flame against the horizon,[xii] and the mysterious tiny figure of the 'Patentender', reminiscent partly of a stag, partly of an official[xiii] – these word images open out a vista on to a faraway world, in which even perfectly simple words like sea and water take on a poetic life of their own. The combination principle at work here functions differently from that of subordination and precedence demanded by the regimen of ideas that otherwise prevails in literature. There are no secondary words: each is equidistant from the imaginary centre, which is why the few adjectives are consistently written with an initial capital letter like nouns.[xiv] The equal quality of every note in relation to the centre of the composition, which Schoenberg demanded as the alternative to the hierarchies of polyphony and homophony, is in this text realized more effectively than in many an example of concrete poetry. While concrete poetry is often characterized by a certain academic dryness, in Herbeck's poem every word is surrounded by its own particular aura. The language thus reanimated becomes the many-tongued expression of an unfulfilled longing, on whose waves the poet sails along happily for a while aboard one of his favourite metaphors, the ship. The last lines create out of 'Auenblättern' ['meadow / shore leaves'] and 'Blattnarben' ['leaf scars'] a sukkoth [in German *Laubhüttenfest*][xv] to the memory of a lost life in nature. The mysterious 'Schlüßesl (R) "r."' is the key which opens up, for Herbeck's creative imagination, the labyrinthine home of a letter in which one can live as undisturbed as in the eponymous villa of Paul Klee.[xvi] 'Die Schloß + Das Schloß', further obstructed (b/locked) by the wrong definite article,[xvii] sets a final flourish under a written image which shows that, as with K.'s experiences in *Das Schloß* [*The Castle*], the goal of our desires is nothing other than the blue emptiness at the centre of the concentric circles we are forever drawing. Though composed entirely of incongruities, the aesthetic coherence of the poem, immediately apparent to the reader, is evidence enough that Herbeck's texts, too, operate with the classic subjects of lyric poetry. The beauty of nature, the astonishment – experienced as a long-drawn-out pain – that despite everything it still exists, is an underlying theme in most of Herbeck's texts. To this anguished astonishment are added the sorrows of first love, never overcome, which also forms part of the traditional repertoire of lyric poetry. Herbeck however goes beyond the latter, reimagining the image of the 'ferne Geliebte', or distant beloved, as an unapproachable woman towards whom he harbours distinctly ambivalent feelings:

> Die Dame ißt nicht.
> Und deshalb geht sie spazieren.
> Eine Dame macht harte Späße.
> Eine Dame sieht wie ein Marienkäfer aus.
> Eine Dame huscht wie ein Fasan.
> Eine Dame geht allein herum.
> Eine Dame spricht viel.[33]

[The lady does not eat. / And therefore she goes for a walk. / A lady makes hard jokes / A lady looks like a ladybird. / A lady flits like a pheasant. / A lady walks around alone. / A lady talks a lot.]

A literally ungraspable coldness and hardness are associated with the figure of the lady, who, as another poem of Herbeck's elaborates, is identical with the moon – who was once the siren in the wood ['die Sirene im Wald einst war'] and now rides in the sky as a lady's mouth ['als der Mund einer Dame am Himmel steht'].[34] The image of the lady, like the picture of Venus in furs in Gregor Samsa's room, is that of the sister, who at one and the same time arouses erotic longing and renders it illegitimate. Faced with the desolate fact that the lady was therefore 'ein schöner Mond und nichts im Knie der Dame [war]'[34] ['a beautiful moon and nothing in the lady's knee'], all that is left for the unhappy victim of unrequited love is to retreat into a life of celibacy. Deleuze and Guattari recognized in Kafka's writings on bachelor existence the expression of a desire which goes far beyond incestuous longing in both extent and intensity. The bachelor is 'the deterritorialized, the one who has neither "centre" nor "any great complex of possessions": "[H]e has only as much ground as his two feet take up, only as much of a hold as his two hands encompass, so much the less, therefore, than the trapeze artist in a variety show, who still has a safety net hung up for him below." His trips are not those of the bourgeois on an ocean liner, "with much effect, roundabout", but the schizo-voyage, "on a few planks of wood that even bump against and submerge each other".'[35] 'The highest desire', as expressed in the precarious life of the bachelor, 'desires both to be alone and to be connected to all the machines of desire.'[36] Since living such a paradox is essentially impossible, the bachelor must grow continually smaller in successive metamorphoses. For this reason, Herbeck's maxims and reflections also include the sentence 'Je größer das Leid / desto kleiner der Dichter' – 'The greater the suffering, / the smaller the poet'.[37]

If one assumes that sensitivity to pain diminishes in proportion to increasing aggression, then the state of resignation in which Herbeck has persisted for many years would represent the outward sign of his extreme sensibility, and he himself, as someone continuously subjected to pain of various kinds, a poet of the most diminutive stature. The mythology of fairytales furnishes many examples of the correlation between the experience of suffering and the dream of becoming smaller. Thus it is not surprising that the figure of the dwarf [*Zwerg*], who turns up several times in his poems – including once as a rather deformed 'Zwergck'[38] – should come to represent, for Herbeck, a kind of secret self-portrait:

Wer der Sonne sich gelüstet
steiget auf den Berg.
Und atmet streng allein
die Luft ein wie ein Zwerg.[39]

[Whoever longs to see the sun / must up the mountain climb / and up there like a dwarf / breathes in the air alone.]

The Man with the Overcoat

Gerhard Roth's *Winterreise*

Mein Herz ist wie erstorben
kalt schaut ihr Bild darin.

Wilhelm Müller, *Die Winterreise*

It seems my heart is frozen
Her face etched on the ice

tr. Barry Mitchell[1]

When it gets dark, the schoolteacher Nagl enjoys sitting alone in the empty classroom. He likes 'the washed green blackboard, the sharpened pieces of chalk, the sponge, and the stiff dried washcloth'.[1] It is the last day of the year. Outside, on the frozen fishponds, the children are skating. A most evocative scene. The reader is not disinclined to identify with the atmosphere of melancholy. He understands the schoolteacher, his affection for the children, who must learn so much to so little avail, understands why, when he thinks about them later, he has a lump in his throat. It is probably the discrepancy between their innocence and his own anxiety which has often made Nagl think of 'vanishing in Pompeii or plunging into Vesuvius'.[2]

As Nagl then spends time in his room looking at photographs of volcanic activity, sulphurous efflorescences, white-hot lava flows, violet ash deposits and other pathological natural phenomena, we could be forgiven for thinking that he is destined for a stay in hell. Certainly, in normal life, the clock is ticking: 'The silver peasant watch with the eggshell-colored face and the tiny decorated golden hands, which he had inherited from his grandfather, lay on the table, on the newspaper, where he had left it that morning after winding it. He took the watch in his hand, it was cold, he held it to his ear and let it tick.'[3] The sound of time, of the passing hours. The last brings death, as a Catholic saying has it. Perhaps the best thing, Nagl thinks, would be 'to entrust oneself to life the way one entrusts oneself to death, even if the nearness to life means a nearness to the terrors of life'.[4] Unfortunately, though, this sentence already proclaims, a little too loudly, the programme of the story; otherwise, up to this point the opening is beautiful, unsettling and consoling at one and the same time. We see that it marks a transition from what has been to what is yet to come. The hero of the novel pauses for a while on the bridge, holding his breath and gazing up into the seeming emptiness, before taking the decisive step into the fictions which await him on the other side.

Leaving the narrow confines of one's home country, associated as it is with a border crossing in a psychological as well as a literal sense, is a central theme in recent Austrian literature. For the narrator, the decision to remove his protagonist from his own history and let him fend for himself abroad imposes crucial limitations. The solitary departure, the conscious renunciation of familiar surroundings, entails a loss of substance which, as far as language is concerned, has to be translated into a prose which operates with all the more finely calibrated forms of description. What is lost in the way of realistic detail must be compensated for by a correspondingly increased precision of observation, and by the invention of linguistic means capable of translating such precision into words. Handke, in his tale of the goalkeeper's anxiety, set a precedent which is hard to equal, and his more recent texts also systematically concern themselves with a dematerialization of the objects of narration, striving for a literary autonomy which entails the narrator – despite his all-pervasive presence in the work – learning to remove himself and his own fears from the text. Roth, who – as well as *Winterreise* – in his books *Ein neuer Morgen* [*A New Morning*] and *Der Stille Ozean* [*The Ocean of Silence*][ii] presents similarly ambitious narrative models, has, it seems to me, not yet succeeded in finding the requisite formal – that is to say linguistic – concentration with which to counter the tendency to dissipation inherent in such projects. The concept of fiction with little in the way of plot, reducing the usual narrative props and scene-setting to a bare minimum, can only be realized in the *abstract*, on the reflective level of a new metaphysics – even if the latter is never explicitly articulated. Kafka opened up the possibilities of an as it were abstinent prose, inscribing into his stories a transcendental potential which is both inexhaustible and utterly heuristic. If, within the text, such potential does not succeed in functioning indirectly as a secret meaning, in order to move the plot forward the author is obliged to resort to conventional mechanisms and devices, and such devices inevitably tend to hamper even the most well-disposed of readers in the suspension of their disbelief.

Towards the end of a passage in which Nagl is reflecting on episodes from his grandfather's life, the text abruptly veers away from this train of thought with the words: 'How strange it was for Nagl to sit here on the Tiber and think about the life stories of dead people.'[5] This explicit summing up of the protagonist's emotions only serves further to disconcert the reader, who, like it or not, for some time now has been all too obviously confronted with the alternation of identities between author–narrator–protagonist, a sequence whose vertiginous and abrupt transitions should in fact be productive in and of themselves. Whereas Handke's best passages go far beyond the conventional process of narration, relying only on the most precarious faith in the meaning of the words and the art of language, Roth's prose, no doubt in spite of his best intentions, continues to fall back on obsolete forms of depiction and narrative. Although Roth's aim – as indeed some of his most successful images demonstrate – is to craft a prose which, by means of the arrangement of words [*Wortsatz*] alone, is literally intended to present the reader with a new way of seeing, he generally allows neither himself nor us sufficient time to linger over the objects and sights which merit further contemplation.

In his novel *Ein neuer Morgen* [*A New Morning*], Roth rationalizes the way in which he integrates the surrounding environment into his prose by making the central character a photographer working on a book about New York, who therefore has a reason for constantly taking pictures of the city and its inhabitants. One episode in the novel sees Roth – uncharacteristically – reflecting on the problematics of his own technique of illustration:

> When the Jewish shopkeeper noticed Weininger looking at the shop, he reached into the back and encouragingly held

up a bundle of ties, and Weininger reached for his camera, whereupon the Jew hunched his shoulders and disappeared into the shop. Cautiously he peered through the door, and when Weininger made no move to take a photograph, he re-emerged, and Weininger photographed him just as he was raising his hand to cover his face. When Weininger looked at the developed image later he saw that the Jew was smiling. It was an indulgent, human smile, which Weininger liked a lot.[6]

The picture, 'developed' here in more than one sense through the narrator's commentary, gives us an idea of what is missing in Roth's images – which usually just follow one after another – namely, time for closer consideration and reflection, which even the author himself does not take. Roth's dilemma as a narrator is that, because of the way his texts are constructed, they have a tendency to read like film scripts. The sketchy, paratactic sequence of the slices of life perceived by the narrator corresponds to the 'shots' prescribed for the camera down the left-hand column of the storyboard.

This lack of insistence on the meaning of what is described moreover has the effect that Roth constantly has to resort to stock phrases in order to show his characters' processes of perception and reflection. Typical of this are openings such as 'He sat there thinking and watching . . .',[7] followed by the images purportedly registered by the protagonist. The controlling hand of the author at work is all too obvious here. Set pieces such as 'Nagl felt that . . .', 'Pompei seemed to him like . . .', 'Nagl recalled . . .', 'it seemed to him as if . . .', 'It was as if . . .',[8] which appear in the text with conspicuous frequency, reveal all too clearly that the invented characters' thought processes, and the prose conveying them, are nothing more than a façade. It is telling, too, that whenever the narrator wishes to bring Nagl back to the memories of his grandfather, he feels the need to insert a deliberate phrase to mark the transition. Thus we read: 'He was riding there [on the train to Venice] and thinking about his grandfather,' or 'Once again, Nagl thought of his grandfather.'[9] Demoted in this manner to a mere intermediary between author and reader, Roth's protagonist only rarely comes into his own. In general, though, the author's usurping of his protagonist's consciousness is also transferred to the reader, who – slightly irritated – once again finds himself obliged to look at whatever it is that Roth has researched and written up by way of local colour in New York, Venice or Styria.

Since the narrative deficiencies in Roth's prose make themselves felt relatively frequently, they gradually coalesce within the text into an unintentional system, with the effect of restricting both the narrator's and reader's freedom of imagination. In *Winterreise*, this negative collusion between author and protagonist is reinforced by a further narrative device, namely the almost schematic 'interpolation' of set pieces from the pattern book of the pornographic canon. The pornographic text is calculated to entrap the reader, on whose voyeuristic inclinations it depends. To what extent the reader's passive desire corresponds to the exhibitionist fantasies of the author must remain a matter for speculation; nor should it be overlooked that this dynamic of confession and complicity is one of the basic underlying structures of narrative literature, forming the crux of each and every narrative. On the other hand, though, our stories only go above and beyond the rendezvous of the more dubious genres to the extent to which they succeed in establishing themselves as a self-sufficient model between the imagination of the author and that of the reader. The *nouveau roman* has shown that crime fiction, once liberated from the usual narrow definitions of thriller and mystery solving, can be used as a template and encoding device [*Rätselraster*] for the construction and development of literary fiction; Roth himself attempted something similar in his novel *Ein neuer Morgen. Winterreise*, though – and this is no doubt ultimately the particular significance of this text – calls into question whether analogous effects can be achieved via a pornographic narrative, and indeed whether pornography can be reconciled with the precepts of narrative prose at all.

> No sooner had Nagl closed the door behind him than Anna knelt in front of him and opened his pants. He unbuttoned her blouse, took out her breasts, reached between her legs, fingered her vaginal lips and clitoris, and inserted his penis into her. While making love, he lay down on the bed and watched his cock vanish in her and come out again. 'Go slower,' he whispered. She was breathless, and he turned her around and stuck his cock in her behind. He pressed her to his body, she screamed, wept, but suddenly went silent and began gasping. Then they lay mutely side by side.[10]

Scenes such as this show that the artificial foreshortening of imagined reality, with which all forms of prose have to operate, in the case of the pornographic text – which, as the least sentimental form of fiction, can never get to the point fast enough – may easily acquire an air of unintentional humour. The amount of explicit detail simply does not fit the pace and evident omissions in the act described. Roth's reader is further disconcerted by the uneven register, oscillating between the crude terminology of pornography and a rather more elevated and at times embarrassingly conventional diction, which can, perhaps, be attributed to the author's own half-heartedness. The somehow false equivalence between 'Glied' ['member', here translated as penis] and 'Schwanz' ['cock'] or the jarring formulation 'while making love' ['während sie sich liebten'] are typical examples of the stylistic faux pas to which Roth succumbs in the pornographic passages in his text.

Nor do the pornographic passages appear to be integrated within the wider context of the narrative. The rather obvious attempts at imagistic association with volcanic craters and the dark depths of the universe misfire, since a fundamental characteristic of pornographic texts is that they suspend everything which has been read previously. Thus pornography's abrupt technique of exposition reflects the difficulty, for the reader – following breathlessly and yet repeatedly asking dumb questions – of finding a way out of the wondrous abyss the text has lured him into, back on to the level of so-called art. The denouements to the pornographic intermezzi that Roth inserts into the text every few pages thus always have a rather embarrassed and apologetic air about them:

> Then they lay mutely side by side. He again remembered everything that had happened to them, his feeling of shame and despair, his loneliness and the powerful sense of absurdity that had accompanied him. Previously he hadn't reflected much.[10]

Following on from the extremely graphic description of the previous scene, these rather lacklustre reflections on the part of the protagonist make scarcely any impression. For one thing, we know that any decent pornographic text should really just go on and on – and for another because, like silent film comedies, pornography perceives characters purely from the outside, in a behaviouristic sense,[11] and for this reason the attempted transition to an interior monologue seems like a miscalculation on the part of the author.

A further problematic aspect of pornographic texts, which by their very nature can only have their own projections in mind, is the image of women they present. John Berger has shown that the representation of the naked female body always presupposes a male viewer – whether within the picture (with characteristic recurring motifs, such as *The Judgement of Paris* or *Susannah Bathing*) or outside it (Titian's *Venus of Urbino* or Manet's *Olympia* being prime examples); and even where male characters, like Bacchus, are included in the picture as *active* erotic figures, the gaze of the central female 'object' is usually directed outwards, towards a presumed male observer.[12] In precisely the same fashion, the conventions of the pornographic text demand a *male* reader whose gaze occupies the voyeuristic perspective implicit in the construct of the whole.

The pornographic passages in Roth's *Winterreise*, in which the gaze of the reader is harnessed to that of the protagonist, often fit this model all too well. 'In the morning,' the narrator relates, 'Anna pushed back the blanket and took his penis in her mouth. *He pretended* to be asleep, he was still tired, but it was fun lying in bed, *squinting his eyes,* and watching Anna excitedly sucking on his penis.'[13] The obviously voyeuristic content of this scene reflects – as it were in reverse – the ideal male fantasy, familiar from conventional erotic literature, of the woman feigning sleep who, full of passion, suspending any desires of her own, observes through half-closed eyelids the experiments performed upon her by the technicians and mechanics of love. Only the sleeping, unconscious, comatose – or, not to put too fine a point upon it, dead – woman is truly in accord with masculine desires.[14] The fact that Roth has reversed the roles in this necrophiliac arrangement does little to dispel the suggestion that male fantasy finds its ideal complement in a lifeless female figure, given that, even with the roles reversed, the scene in no way corresponds to a comparable ideal of female desire.

Just as the negative implications of the nude in painting – which quite literally surrenders the woman to the male gaze – can only be transcended where a woman is perceived through her own agency [*Intentionalität*], so too, in literature, male fantasies can only be given a more nuanced direction via an empathetic portrayal of female characters. Indeed, the rise of the novel in England and France was closely linked to the psychological emancipation of a female audience. The narrative development and transmission of the concept of feminine sensibility, from Richardson, via the English women writers of the nineteenth century, down to Flaubert's *Madame Bovary*, Tolstoy's *Anna Karenina* and Fontane's *Effi Briest* – this protracted literary process circumscribed with the greatest precision the erotic trials and tribulations threatening to engulf any female character who allowed herself to give free rein to her emotions. The form this took was that of symbolic representation, implication and suggestion, a concealing of what was meant beneath the cadences and ornaments of prose – a process, then, which granted the reading woman the same freedom of imagination as that of the male reader. The fact that Proust transposed his homosexual desires on to the female character of Albertine was, in the end, done less in the interests of decorum than for the more telling reason that only in this way was it possible to incorporate the psychological acuity which literature had developed in its explorations of the feminine psyche. The marked sense of tact in [Proust's] *Recherche* is first and foremost of an aesthetic, rather than societal, nature. And only by means of aesthetic tact can the destructive dialectics of Eros and civilization be transcended.

In contrast to these artistic exercises in sublimation, following the naturalism of Zola, and in the wake of Lawrence and Joyce, the last few decades in particular have seen the emergence in the novel of an erotic *vérisme*, less concerned with psychological superstructure than with the actual processes of sexuality. This counter-movement increasingly made use of explicit borrowings from the underground scenarios and vocabulary of pornography, looked down on by the official bourgeois system; not without justification, it perceived itself as a revolutionary gesture, and it was often interpreted as a badge of the avant-garde. No amount of radicalization of female desires and ideals could hope to counter the decidedly masculine perspective thus established. Beatrice Faust, in her study on *Women, Sex and Pornography*,[15] argues convincingly that there is no such thing as female pornography, in the sense here understood, and that the images which are a source of such incessant fascination to the male imagination arouse in a female audience at most casual interest, and more often merely a feeling of ennui.[16] Rather, Beatrice Faust takes the view that romantic fiction, à la Barbara Cartland – now produced on an industrial scale – is the true female pornography.[17] Such novels, however – dealing as they do with the elaborate entanglements of True Love – were, paradoxically, not ripe for reassimilation into the ranks of serious literature, not least for the reason that they were never, either in a legal or in a social sense, seen as taboo, and therefore also did not violate any taboos. However, this by no means allows us to conclude that pornographic passages, as conventionally understood, are necessarily any more compatible with prose committed to verbal artistry than those of a sentimental–erotic variety.

As a general rule – and Roth's *Winterreise* is no exception here – these pornographic interludes, in a prose which claims its content to be of a groundbreakingly radical nature, remain formally conventional and underdeveloped, since their medium, the technical jargon of pornography, notwithstanding the apparently infinite variety and dynamics of human sexuality, remains for purely physiological reasons incapable of going beyond the really rather restricted range of gestures, acts and accoutrements available in this sphere.[18] In the end, once the code has been cracked, all that is left is for the plot to proceed according to the binary logic of 'Löcher und Schwänze' ['holes and pricks']. In order to live up to its own ambitions, then, the pornographic text must needs have recourse to ever more convoluted choreographic arrangements, and, like minor symphonic works, to a virtuosic orchestration with a whole repertoire of the most diverse instruments. In *Winterreise*, too, there is no lack of such props, as for example tables, chairs, bidets, bathtubs, umbrellas, widow's veils, cigars, bottles and suchlike. In addition, it is in the nature of pornographic texts to assume a stupendous potency on the part of the protagonists, who – since for them the world and the 'myth of work' no longer exists[19] – now have to work through a no less rigid programme with each other. In all of this, the woman is no less yoked into the 'production process' than on the factory production line. In any case, the deciding factor is the performance-oriented masculine perspective. Where a text unhesitatingly adopts this perspective, the reader cannot help but view the prototypical woman from the same angle as *he* – author, narrator, protagonist and hence a whole series of men – has always viewed *her*. Like the system of work, the system of pornography does not allow for any differences between man and woman. The woman reacts and functions without further ado, exactly as the man imagines, becoming a fixed component of his fantasy according to a model reduced purely to action and largely independent of language. This is probably why Nagl sometimes thinks that Anna 'senses what he senses', has 'similar thoughts'[20] to him; and her unstinting willingness to cooperate only serves to emphasize to the reader her identical attitude. In accordance with the inner logic of the text, the woman who accompanies the schoolteacher Nagl on his journey to colder climes is equipped only with the barest minimum of individual traits. It is enough that she has a first name and a young, pretty face. Anything else would be superfluous. By contrast to Nagl, whose thoughts often turn to his grandfather, she has no need to think about her grandmother, and when finally our hero, with whose anxiety and despair the text is alone concerned, sets off for Alaska, she can just take the train home.

Roth's attempt to represent the wordless relations between two people, the opposing forces of attraction and strangeness, through the chagrins of sexuality alone, is not of itself invalid. What proves to be irreconcilable, though, is the desperate absolutism of the pornographic world view with the generally anodyne mode of narration of *Winterreise*. Pornography which is serious in its intentions must completely renounce the outside world, know nothing but its heretical passion for the word made flesh. Genet's rhapsodies, or Georges Bataille's *Story of the Eye*, testify that pornography as an art form can only come into being in the airless space of total obsession; only by magnifying its own potential into the realm of the surreal is it able to encompass the pathos and tragedy of a species which has taken leave of its own sound animal common sense – and in its most precise expression, pornography does indeed describe the debacle, in terms of natural history, of a species emphatically not concerned with procreation, but solely with 'pure' knowledge. Whether this intention becomes apparent in a given text depends on the stylistic means deployed. By comparison with the glacial humour with which Bataille removes his voracious offending eye, or the high lyric register which permits Genet amid the most ruthless explicitness solemnly to distance himself from the merely obscene, the pornographic *études* of *Winterreise* would scarcely be likely to hold their own.

In continually returning to the safe ground of the common or garden narrative – putting the dangerous toy, hardly has it been taken out and given a little shake, safely back in the box – the author disrupts the ideal topos of pornography, whose perverse purity as an art form consists precisely in the fact that it is less easily manipulated than the traditional ingredients of narrative prose. If art – even pornographic art – represents a mode of consciousness, then the author of *Winterreise* may perhaps count himself lucky that he lacks the necessary personal qualifications for an immanent transcendence of the genre. At any rate, he cannot be accused of that specific form of monomania able to transform pornography into something more than a bizarre divertissement. 'Pornography', writes Susan Sontag, 'is one of the branches of literature [. . .] aiming at disorientation and psychic dislocation.'[21] If this aim is to be realized, whether in the person of the author or in that of the reader, then it is not sufficient to administer measured doses of pornography as one artistic means among many. Heretical rhetoric is no more able to brook compromise than that which is held sacrosanct. For this reason, the few examples of great pornographic literature, a kind of antinomian exercise, constitute a law unto themselves. A 'very brief introduction'[iii] to pornography would be an absurdity. On the level of art, pornographic discourse can be neither adopted nor learned, nor can it be transmitted in the form of a quotation. As an absolute system, it only comes into its own in the language of pathos, in a diction which opposes the intransigence of reality with its own speculative force. Bakhtin suggested that the language of pathos [*das pathetische Wort*] is always 'the language of the preacher without a pulpit, of the strict judge without power to judge or punish, of the prophet without a mission, the politician without political power, the believer without a church'.[22] Accordingly, the specific pathos of pornography is due to the act of transgression directed against its own powerlessness, in which it reveals – to itself and to us – its own secret, a secret which consists not in sexuality but in death. 'It's towards the gratifications of death, succeeding and surpassing those of eros, that every truly obscene quest tends,' writes Susan Sontag. 'Death is the only end to the odyssey of the pornographic imagination when it becomes systematic.'[23]

The inherent weakness of Roth's *Winterreise* lies in the fact that the prosaic framework of the story prevents the systematic application of the pornographic imagination. Thus the theme of death as the epitome of pornographic discourse in Roth's work cannot be deduced naturally from the pornographic episodes, and has instead to be introduced separately on a different level of the text, as an aspect of the characterization of the protagonist. It is not that Roth is unaware of the affinities between death and pornography; rather, the all too explicit and circumspect manner in which he weaves them into the text is what compromises the credibility of his vision. In the very first pages of *Winterreise*, there is constant talk of death, with a directness which is scarcely convincing. Nor do the sinister figures who cross Nagl's path – as with his precursor Aschenbach at the start of his own Italian journey – exactly conform to the rules of narrative discretion. Precisely because the text of *Winterreise* is presented as a story [*Erzählung*], it is not acceptable for it continually to state its intentions, for it to 'strike' Nagl that religion is 'an artistic handiwork from the hands of death', that the frescoes in the Villa dei Misteri are 'a fata morgana of death'[24] and so on. Were the pornographic passages in *Winterreise* successful in fulfilling the unspoken aims of the genre – to embrace death in the horrors of life – it is unlikely that such obvious signposting would have been necessary.

There can of course be no doubt that Roth's novel is informed by a far-reaching and profound inspiration, which in many ways reflects the latent Levantine melancholy of much of Austrian literature. It is, then, all the more disappointing that Roth repeatedly fails to realize his aims on a formal level, since he does justice neither to the exigencies of the prose style nor to those of pornography. Only towards the end of the novel does he produce an episode of curiously macabre maturity, which gives an idea of how the concept he may have had in mind when he began writing could have been realized with some degree of literary merit. The girl Anna has returned home, and Nagl, alone in Venice, decides to follow a woman who has taken a seat in front of him in a vaporetto. She is wearing sunglasses and a fur coat, and as such appears as the quintessential anonymous and ubiquitous image of her sex. Only when they both alight at the next stop does Nagl get a clearer view of her. 'Her hair was dyed blond and well-groomed, and her hands revealed that she was about fifty years old.'[25] Nagl follows her into a *birreria* and speaks to her. She is any and every woman. He tells her he is an Arctic explorer, talks of volcanoes, ash rain and glaciers. The woman listens. She was once married to an actor. A suitably baroque charade. Then they travel together in silence to the Canale della Guidecca [sic], and from there walk to the spartan room Nagl has rented. Nagl is not allowed to turn on the light, so that now – in contrast to the previous scenes with Anna – he can see nothing, can only touch. 'Her bosom was large and solid and her cunt was hot and wet, but she didn't want him to kiss her. She sat up, panting for air, while Nagl embraced her. She had a marvellous way of tightening her cunt and then loosening it again, and her buttocks were soft and gentle, and her breasts, which Nagl reached for, were heavy. She asked him if he would ever come back to Venice. Nagl said yes.'[26] Finally, without the narrator having to comment explicitly on it, Nagl now has all women in one, death and life, the female sex – as seen from his desolate male viewpoint – in its entirety. When he awakes the next morning, he sees the woman getting dressed in the half-light. 'He promptly saw that her head had grown small because the hair had been squashed. Her false eyelashes were coming off the lids, and her mouth made a noise like false teeth pressing on gums. Nagl remembered that she hadn't let him kiss her. He stared at the ceiling and heard her rummaging in her handbag. After a while, she came toward him, fragrant and made-up.'[26] Restored to her former glory, Frau Welt [Mistress World],[iv] the keeper of that well-known cold inn we all must pass through, leaves her address on the bedside table 'in case he might return'.[v]

This episode, which differs from the pornographic clichés of the scenes with Anna in its consistent representation of a completely unknown woman, shows that the *effet du réel*, indispensable to narrative, depends not on the probability of the events narrated, but on the imaginative possibilities which the text creates by conferring an allegorical meaning on what is described. The encounter with the symbolic figure of the mysterious stranger allows Nagl to emerge, at the end of the story, as a more mysterious man himself. It even helps that the author has had him running around the whole time in a crumpled Burberry. Men in mackintoshes, after all, are always mysterious, as easily shown by the critics who were so sorely exercised by the superfluous, apparently pointless Mr MacIntosh in Joyce's *Ulysses*. A few scholars suppose that MacIntosh is a revenant, doomed to wander the world eternally,[vi] and a reincarnation of James Duffy who, in the story 'A Painful Case', appears as a shadowy figure, the lover of a woman now dead: the embodiment of what Joyce called 'this hated brown Irish paralysis'.[27] If one draws a comparison between the relationship of the Irish literary tradition to the English one and the relationship which, even today, on account of the common language, connects Austrian literature with its German counterpart across the border, then it is not hard to imagine that the malaise which afflicts the schoolteacher Nagl could most exactly be diagnosed as 'that hated brown Austrian paralysis'[vii] – a speculation which could open the way for all manner of further hypotheses.

Light Pictures and Dark

On the Dialectics of Eschatology in Stifter and Handke

> Es hätt' ihn nämlich besonders der *blaue* Streusand ergriffen, in dessen Äther ich die gestirnten Gedanken meines Blättchens gestreuet hatte. Er bat mich geradezu um meine Sandbüchse; 'denn es kann sein', sagt er, 'daß ich noch an jemand schreibe, vielleicht an Gott selber.'
>
> He was particularly taken with the *blue* writing sand in whose ether I had strewn the star-studded thoughts of my note. He positively begged me for my sand caster; 'for it may well be', he says, 'that I may still write to someone, perhaps even to God himself.'
>
> Jean Paul, *Leben Fibels*

On an engraving from the Biedermeier period I acquired a long time ago in a second-hand bookshop in Freiburg, and which has always seemed to me like an illustration of Adalbert Stifter's work, a sunlit prospect of the Mittelgebirge stretches far away into the distance. In the foreground of the picture, though, are four human figures: a wanderer with stick and portmanteau, a woman with furled umbrella, and two further walkers, one of whom is just raising a pocket telescope to his eye. They have a small dog with them too, and all are gazing, leaning slightly forward, into an apparently bottomless chasm which opens up at their feet. As has often been remarked, Stifter's prose frequently leads us to such places. Towards the horizon, the most attractive prospect presents itself to the eye: 'valleys like hazy folds', lakes like 'a small plaque' and the 'regions spread out before me like a [. . .] faint portfolio',[1] a panorama seemingly inspired by a technique of monochrome watercolour washes, using only the lightest of colours applied in the most sparing fashion.[2] At the same time, it often seems to the observer 'as if the world had died out, as if all the hustle and bustle of life were only a dream',[3] and thus in actual fact not alive at all, but dead and gone. The ambivalent emotions this implies towards the beauty of natural, and then also of artistic scenes, is related to the sensation of vertigo, echoing also the author's earliest childhood memories – which consist entirely of abrupt precipices where the ground suddenly seems to give way beneath one's feet.

In a curious autobiographical fragment, in which – rather like, later, in the work of Thomas Bernhard – there is much talk of the anonymous quality of 'terror and annihilation',[4] Stifter evokes the earliest visual impressions of his own life, in an attempt to return to a pre-linguistic phase in which inner and outer worlds are not yet differentiated, but alternate continually in an indistinct sensation of pain. Thus he recalls ominous dark patches, of which only in retrospect can he say 'that these were forests which existed outside myself'.[5] As a contrast to the dark threats to existence this implies, Stifter cites the image of a garden which, as he says, 'from those days remains foremost in my imagination', and which he sees as clearly 'as if painted on porcelain in glowing colours'.[6] From this primeval opposition of form and formlessness, there emerge both Stifter's programme of a transition from the natural world to a realm where life is protected and secured by images of nature, and his quest to progress 'to ever more composed and ordered depictions'[7] which ultimately finds expression in *Der Nachsommer* [*Indian Summer*] in the homeostatic equilibrium of an idealized utopia.

That said, over the effort invested in the careful arranging of natural and artificial objects evident in every line of *Der Nachsommer* there nonetheless hovers the constant fear of a relapse into that state which the author views as his own prehistory, and most probably also that of the bourgeois species as a whole. And it is surely not wrong to assume – bleak though the prospect is – that the ever-increasing amount of artificially achieved order cannot be equated with a progressive overcoming of a fear of lightning, but rather with the anxious anticipation, which goes hand in hand with the structuring of the world, of the irruption of destruction at any given moment. In *Der Nachsommer*, this is expressed metaphorically in the largely unexplored region behind and beneath the light-filled surface of the work, which 'upon closer examination' turns out to be an immense expanse of forest with scattered charcoal workings where 'whole trains of the blackened carts with their blackened carters plied the dark highway' and where the author, prisoner of his own origins, can only obtain 'a single room' with 'just small windows covered in iron gratings' in a dismal forest inn, the Tannwirtshaus [Pine Tree].[8] Passages like these, where, as in the landscape described here, the blackness seeps even into the grass, cast a long shadow over Stifter's artistic intention of increasing light, echoing precisely the degree to which his pre-conscious mind is assailed by that which was repressed with the acquisition of language.

The starting point for this inherently divergent development, in which the unspoken is always sacrificed to what is described, is marked by Stifter in his autobiographical sketch with the symbolic name Schwarzbach;¹ in this passage he recalls how, as a child, sitting on the windowsill looking out of the window, he first believed he understood the way of the world in the repeated naming of this name in all its tautological reaffirmation of reality. 'There's a man going to Schwarzbach, there's a man driving to Schwarzbach, there's a woman going to Schwarzbach, there's a dog going to Schwarzbach, there's a goose going to Schwarzbach.'[9] Hans Blumenberg interprets the ordering, almost legislative function of naming as a characteristic feature of the protohistoric [*frühgeschichtlich*] and mythological world view. Within the individual development of the writer, the verbal gesture of conjuration signifies the hope, glimpsed here for the first time, of escape from the narrow confines of his own existence – which in Stifter's case can be equated with the desire to find a way out of his underprivileged existence in a provincial backwater, and to acquire, by means of writing, a legitimate entry into the idealized world of bourgeois civilization. A similar trait is also evident in the works of Peter Handke, where ghastly individual words like *Mehlschwitze* [roux; literally 'flour-sweat'] and *Ölkrapfen* [fried doughnuts or fritters] and all the fat and grease he is gagging on which for him epitomizes Austria,[10] are signs of a quasi-pathological state which he hopes to escape through writing, but which has a way of catching up with him at odd moments in the form of a sense of illegitimacy, the feeling of 'belonging to a lower class, of being an upstart without a background'.[11] Ceasing to write would mean a relapse into the panic of childhood, whereas the continued invention of the right words contains the prospect of rising above a life burdened with disturbing memories.

From this point of view, it is understandable that any attempt at exorcizing the ghosts inevitably entails their revocation, and that enlightenment – the creation of lighter colours and ultimately the idea of light itself – can be achieved only through precisely measured doses of the onerous material substance of life. This illumination of the world in a lovelier light, which is clearly what Stifter's *Nachsommer* and Handke's *Langsame Heimkehr* [*The Long Way Around*]^ii and *Die Lehre der Sainte-Victoire* [*The Lesson of Mont Sainte-Victoire*] are concerned with, in practice requires a very specific refraction of reality, which, as Goethe suggests in his *Farbenlehre* [*Colour Theory*], is generally connected to particular pathological states. In the didactic part of the *Farbenlehre*, for example, it says that 'hypochondriacs . . . frequently see dark objects, such as threads, hairs, spiders, flies, wasps',[12] which almost reads like a commentary on the hallucinatory episodes which repeatedly interrupt Kaspar's reform into a bourgeois individual. The case of Kaspar also makes clear, however, that any critical understanding of reality which goes beyond mere affirmation is inconceivable without an understanding of how our own subjective *dérangement* affects the representation of objective reality.

In his essay on the colour theories of Goethe and Newton, Werner Heisenberg recalls that for a long time the goal of all natural science was, as far as possible, to describe nature in itself, that is to say how it would be without our intervention and without our observations.[13] A similar intention may be discerned in the paradigmatic depictions of pure nature [*reine Natur*] in key passages of literature of the high bourgeois era, albeit with the qualification that, in the realm of literature, 'pure nature' is a moral, not a physical, category. Pure nature as a literary utopia with the power to convey epiphanies – 'moments of ecstasy' ['*Beseeligungsmomente*'], as Handke notes at the beginning of *Die Lehre der Sainte-Victoire* [*The Lesson of Mont Sainte-Victoire*] – is 'the world of nature and the work of man, one with the help of the other',[14] which is precisely what Stifter, with infinite patience, elaborates in *Der Nachsommer*. If it is true that literature, in its idealizing portrayal of man-made landscapes, has already preempted the integration demanded by modern physics of the observing subject into the field of the objects observed, this is only really the case in those instances where the disturbance which characterizes the inner life of the writing subject is not completely masked by the beautiful depictions of nature. The attempt to establish a connection between the – in places almost over-exposed – texts of Stifter and Handke will thus first have to seek a fuller understanding of those aspects of their utopian compositions which are hidden from the light.

One particularly characteristic feature of Stifter's work, it seems to me, is the fact that – even when showing us the dark sides of his idyllic world view – he scarcely ever attempts to arrive at an explicit psychological understanding of what is responsible for the latent sense of panic beneath his quietist prose. This as it were absent characteristic is responsible for the peculiar two-dimensionality of Stifter's work, which is often animated only by a feeling of ennui. This absence is also probably what gave rise to the manifold speculations about Stifter's inscrutable inner life. Since the beginning of the [twentieth] century, when A. R. Hein put forward the theory of Stifter's suicide, the series of diagnostic speculations has scarcely abated to this day. From a melancholic disposition and a manic-depressive constitution, all the way to alcoholism, we encounter pretty much everything which might remotely occur to the imagination of a medically inclined layperson in such a case. Little of it is still tenable today. The only thing that can be established with any certainty, thanks to the Swiss doctor Hermann Augustin's commendable study on Stifter's illness and death, is that the writer finally succumbed to cirrhosis of the liver, from which he suffered for many years, enduring typical symptoms of auto-intoxication which at times resulted in pre-comatose states. Extreme nausea, feelings of oppression, anxiety attacks, fits of mental confusion and other rather indeterminate conditions: all are symptoms of an illness characterized by a progressive poisoning of the entire organism.

Stifter's malaise, often particularly acute in his later years, was a source of almost hypochondriac interest to him, and he attempted, as we know, to ameliorate his illness – as excruciating as it was ill-defined – with visits to spas and frequent restorative stays in the country. However, he also strenuously avoided allowing himself to become conscious of the source of his *malheur* [*Unglück*], which was clearly to be sought in his positively chronic gluttony. While he is still capable of registering the reactions of his body with scrupulous exactitude, particularly during pre-comatose phases, even then – doctor's orders notwithstanding – he seldom succeeds in restraining his eating mania. His correspondence reveals that, as a starter alone, he would often consume dozens of crayfish, or six or more trout. And the list of what he systematically ingests, even at a time when he often believes himself to be at death's door, is gruesome indeed: 'Ate beef, baked kid, roast chicken, hazel grouse, pigeon, roast veal, ham, liver with onions, roast pork, sardines, paprika chicken, baked lamb and partridge, much beef (dry); noodle soup, some beef and mutton, baked rice, brains with sour beets, potted veal, schnitzel with anchovy sauce, a snack of tea with hazel grouse, a snack of tea with chicken (ample portions), snack of tea with ham, snack with much chicken, thick herb soup with egg and so on.'[15] Although Stifter is aware that his eating habits are responsible for his condition – he notes, for example, 'in the evening rather restless as a result of eating carp, perhaps too much roast pork and herb salad at lunch'[16] – he only seems able to combat his indisposition by fortifying his already stalwart body with yet more copious amounts of food. And if he does, from time to time, decide to exercise a little more dietary restraint, he then immediately complains of the worst hunger pangs, depicted most graphically in his letters, as for example when he says that a modest snack has as it were 'fallen into the bottomless pit'[17] of his stomach, accustomed to abnormal supplies of food. It would seem, too, that writing serves as a means of prolonging the pleasurable anticipation of eating – or, as the case may be, the intensification of appetite – for as long as possible. In a letter of 1861 he writes: 'Then more work on *Witiko* until 9 o'clock, then a whole duck is waiting upon my enjoyment. But I am now so hungry that I think I will eat two.'[18] The only thing which is unclear here is what means more to Stifter: the prospect of the actual consumption of the duck, or the idea, inspired by hunger, that he is already engaged in the act of eating two whole ducks. In either case, in writing he has the possibility not only of forgetting or postponing hunger, but also of intensifying it, thus strategically bridging the gap between one meal and the next in the way best suited to his physical needs.

In this context it is also striking that in *Der Nachsommer*, where everything is supposedly focused on the sublime harmony of art and nature, with much talk of the purity of the air and water on which, ideally, the ethereal creatures of this novel should alone subsist, mealtimes are constantly brought to mind. The book, in which, significantly, time itself scarcely progresses at all, is positively peppered with references such as, for example, 'Next morning after breakfast . . . at midday all the guests gathered again around the table for the meal . . . After the meal several guests departed . . . At dinner the conversation turned to . . . The table was already laid . . . After our afternoon tea . . . After we had taken leave of one another in the dining room', and so on and so forth.[19] While it is true that, out of consideration for the finer feelings of the reading public, the sacrificial beasts delivered to the table are not explicitly named, what does become apparent is that this elaborate description of an idyllic civilization devoted to the idea of purity stands in a sinister relation to the desires of the clown Hanswurst, who announces from the stage of every popular theatre that what he would like to do most of all is to gobble up the whole world. If we further take into account how meagre and meatless the bills of fare of the less privileged sections of society still were in the nineteenth century,[20] then we will not go far wrong in the assumption that the continual ingestion of vast quantities of animal foodstuffs represented, for Stifter — alongside his work on the transfiguration of bourgeois culture — a way of proving his credentials as a member of the better classes of society. From this we might in turn conclude that the hecatombs Stifter sacrificed to the maintenance of his physical and social status continued to rumble on in the form of a guilty conscience.

A central weakness of Stifter's work is that nowhere does it reflect upon this connection, conceiving instead, so to speak for the exoneration of the soul, an image of the world in which the culpable concatenation of all organic life is transcended in the most consummately artistic fashion. However, as will be shown in what follows, the central concern of this world view is the representation of a heavenly existence which rises above the abyss of the natural world. It is a curious feature of such an endeavour, adhering as it does strictly to the guidelines of orthodox vision, that its advocates, from St Thomas [Aquinas] onwards, have all been hearty eaters, while those authors who, as agnostics, believed there was no choice but to despair at the order of the world – here we might first and foremost name the great satirists, from Swift and Lichtenberg to Kraus and Bernhard – all have characteristics which correspond, if not to an ascetic, then at least to a heretical view of human existence.

Nonetheless – as has often been noted, particularly in recent years – Stifter's work also contains passages which express in figurative, but significantly not in discursive, language the heretical notion of a world governed by the principles of evil and of darkness. In the story *Der Condor* [*The Condor*] – which bears the hallmarks of late Romanticism, in particular the wilder fantasies of Jean Paul – after 'the tiresome evening tumult of crowds' has died down, there descends a most 'deathly calm', in which a young painter keeps watch throughout the night so as to observe through his telescope, as dawn breaks, the ascent of a hot air balloon. The latter, 'a large black orb' beneath which 'suspended . . . by invisible threads' hangs a gondola, 'a mere bent card carrying three human lives', becomes a world adrift in a hostile universe, whose passengers, 'even before the blush of dawn',[21] may easily plunge to the ground. The second part of the story describes the balloon journey from the point of view of the balloonists themselves, to whom it appears, in the first light of morning, as if 'the whole balloon was alight' against an indigo-blue sky, while far down below, 'still quite black and indistinguishable', the earth dissolves in darkness.[22] The little spot 'we call home' can soon no longer be made out, 'like vast shadows' the forests 'stretch [. . .] away to the horizon', and the gondola is soon enveloped on all sides in 'white, thin, billowing, moving shrouds'. 'The entire vault of the sky, the lovely blue canopy of our earth had become a black abyss, plunging into the depths without measure or limit.' 'As though in scorn', the stars become visible – 'tiny, impotent, golden pinpoints strewn at random through the void; and lastly the sun, a threatening body, without warmth, without rays, a sharply edged disc of seething, billowing, white-hot metal; that is how it glared out of the chasm with devastating gleam.'[23]

This depiction, a terrifying counterpoint to the idyllic transfiguration of nature, moves, in accordance with its own inherent dynamics, inexorably towards the point from which the universe, seen from the perspective of the heretic, appears as the creation of a madman. In the *Farbenlehre*, Goethe was still of the opinion that the pathological colours reported by the balloonist [Francesco] Zambeccari and his fellow aeronauts – who claimed to have seen, from their highest ascent, the moon and the sun glowing blood-red – were due to their perception being impaired by altitude fever.[24] In the Stifter passage, however, the pathological colouration is ascribed to the objective constitution of the universe, a constitution already subject to entropy, with no distinction between above and below, light and dark, hot and cold, life and death. Small wonder, then, that Stifter, troubled as he was by both the chaotic processes within him and the scientific insights into the terrifying precariousness of the world, should, in a kind of literary autotherapy, have expended such huge effort throughout his life on the depiction of a brighter world. The threat of entropy, which in the *Condor* story has implications far beyond the emotional context of the narrative, is, however, something which never left him.

Probably the most compelling example of this is his much later report from the Bavarian forest, *Aus dem bairischen Walde*, in which he relates the 'natural phenomenon' of a snowstorm lasting 'two and seventy' hours. 'The forms of the landscape' – for Stifter the all-important thing – 'were no longer visible. There was a blur of impenetrable grey and white, light and twilight, day and night, which, constantly moving and swirling wildly about, swallowed up everything, seeming of infinite magnitude, giving birth now to flying strips of white, now to whole white planes, now beams and other forms, and even in the immediate vicinity not the faintest line or contour of any solid entity could be discerned.'[25] Faced with this dissolution of reality, in his panic the narrator can only 'keep on staring out into the chaos'.[26] He himself is in acute danger of physical disintegration. His tongue sticks to his palate, he stops eating, only dissolving a little Liebig's meat extract in warm water and drinking the broth[27] – for someone of Stifter's appetite, a truly eschatological experience. In the dissolution of time and space in the driving snow, the author's own person too dissolves, and yet strangely enough it is in precisely such passages that his narrative presence is most pronounced, far more so than in the idyllic images of an Indian summer with which he sought to assuage his restless anxiety.

The more Stifter focuses his narrative interest on a distillation of the quintessence of beauty, guaranteed by all the rules of art, the less able he is to be present himself in these most beautifully arranged scenes. A prime example is the famous passage in *Der Nachsommer* in which, 'at the touch of a button', Freiherr von Risach opens a concealed door in the wallpaper, affording his guest, who represents the author, a glimpse into the miniature world of the rose room [*Rosenzimmer*], with its cushioned seats and chairs all upholstered in the heavenly colours of rose-pink and pale grey silk, and its window through which 'between the green vaults of the trees . . . the landscape and the mountains'[28] appear framed as in a picture, and thus as part of the interior. Inspired by the idea of aesthetic perfection, this secluded chamber — so perfect that it is almost impossible to imagine living in it — mirrors the interior decor of the bourgeois soul, which somehow is never quite able to make itself at home between the longing for comfort and the desire for immovable order. It is, of course, no coincidence that this room, in which even the character of the narrator himself seems to dissolve in the ethereal colour scheme, should be that of Mathilde, and thus a woman's room.[iii] What happens if one rings the little golden bell resting on the small side table may be left to the gentle reader's imagination.

In such passages, though, it also becomes apparent that the secularization of utopia envisaged by the bourgeois imagination — the attempt to create for oneself a heaven on earth — may easily edge over into the realm of kitsch, an area where the narrator's credibility is no longer guaranteed. It may well be that this insufficiency is what motivates Stifter's need to extend the calm of the domestic interior and household order into the realm outside, to the garden, the landscape and thence to nature itself. Thus the complement to the secular piety [*Weltfrömmigkeit*] of Stifter's protagonists is the measuring, cataloguing and classification of anything and everything in nature which, as something alien or not yet understood, might interfere with the bourgeois notion of an ideal state of equilibrium, represented in the colours of eternity. In Handke's *Langsame Heimkehr* [*The Long Way Around*],[iv] the protagonist — the naturalist Sorger — is likewise striving to move on from the 'hard work' prescribed by the bourgeois ethos to a state of blissful 'exhaustion' in which all spaces are joined together, 'the particular, freshly conquered one with those that had gone before, [forming] a dome encompassing heaven and earth, a sanctuary, which was not only private but also open to others'.[29] However, a concept of art which seeks to transform the private feeling of ecstasy into something which is also of social significance must necessarily exclude and set aside anything incompatible with these lofty and beautiful visions.

Faced with this task, the naturalist Sorger and, through him, the writer Handke take on the characteristics of the prophet who has endured a long spell in the wilderness, in order now to emerge as the herald of a better and more peaceful world. The privileged status to which they thus lay claim is justified in their sympathetic identification with those whose work does not allow them to escape from 'the yellow wilderness'. To be alone in the Arctic landscape and feel the 'desolation of a man who, without faith in the power of forms or rendered incapable of such faith by ignorance, might find himself as in a nightmare confronting this part of the world alone: his horror face to face with the Evil One at the irrevocable end of the world, unable to die of loneliness then and there — since there would no longer be a then and there'.[30] The imagined fear of this less privileged being, conceived here by Sorger in the subjunctive mode, is fixated on the figure of the Evil One [*der Leibhaftige*], the negative principle of all metaphysics, who behind the artistic prospect of utopia merrily continues in his evil ways. Handke acknowledges this malign presence, manifested in fleeting attacks of disturbance, by having Sorger also faithfully record images in which the process of dissolution of forms, the ultimate decay of life occasioned by an incomprehensible power, seems already very far advanced:

> A dead pink salmon had been washed up on the sandy shore, a faint color in the rigid recumbent darkness, over which, strictly separate, lay a pale sky with a colorless moon that seemed to have fallen over backward. The fish, which lay lopsidedly bloated on the sand made muddy by the dew, as though tossed at random into the cold early-morning landscape, seemed to form a companion piece to the bloated mounds enclosed by white wooden fences in the Indian cemetery on the far side of the huts, whose black and gray walls gave no sign of life except for the humming of generators [. . .][31]

In the face of such negative revelations, Sorger is repeatedly assailed by a feeling of faintness, 'mere warmth without blood', and the fear of being not only 'alone in the world, but alone without a world'.[32] He feels as if he has been 'forsaken not only by speech but by the power to make the least sound',[32] and only in the repeated overcoming of this aphasia can he find the way back to his other world view. The therapy which he – like Stifter's protagonists – prescribes for himself consists in copying everything 'line for line – as faithfully as possible, without the schematizations and omissions that had become customary in his science', so that he can claim 'with a clear conscience, if only to himself, to have been there'.[33] The mechanism of artistic production as a means of quieting the conscience referred to here recalls, in a not unproblematic way, the role of photographic reproductions in our understanding of the world. Susan Sontag has pointed out that travel – so characteristic of Handke's protagonists' way of moving through the world – has increasingly become nothing more than a strategy for the accumulation of photographs, which is something to which nations handicapped by a ruthless work ethic – Americans, Germans and Japanese – are particularly prone.[34] The decisive difference, though, between the writer's method and the technique of photography – avid for experience and wary of it in equal measure – is that the act of describing fosters reflection and recollection, whereas photography promotes forgetting. Photographs are mementoes of a disappearing world bent on a process of destruction; painted and written images, by contrast, have a life in the future, as documents of a consciousness which has some interest in the continuation of life.

This positive intention, allowing Sorger and Handke to see themselves as 'Friedensforscher' [peace researchers] rather than – like most photographers – war correspondents, is developed in the texts under discussion as the idea of a genuine feeling of happiness and ecstasy even in the face of terror; a feeling oriented towards a transcendent realm, in which all time and place is suspended [*aufgehoben*], not in the sense of destruction, but in the sense of immortalization. Thus in the endless procession of passers-by in Central Park in New York, Sorger quite suddenly, but completely naturally, sees the likenesses of his own lost loved ones in the crowd. In the new, reconciled life this experience opens up, 'for the length of one lucid moment', Sorger conceives of 'time as a "God" who was "good"'.[35] Every single attribute of the space in which Sorger, filled with this sense of time regained, feels himself truly alive for the first time, appears transfigured in the light of a quasi-theosophical aura; and the coffee shop which the homecoming hero enters seems to him to start to 'glitter along with the tin ashtrays and sugar bowls (which became gold and silver)' like a ballroom,[36] and, filled with the steam from the coffee machine and the music from the radio, appears to him as a heavenly emporium. 'What I am here experiencing', Sorger says to himself, 'must not pass away,'[37] an imperative which Handke's prose reflects, inasmuch as it moves away from the eschatological dynamics of narrative literature towards an image of writing [*Schriftbild*] in which 'the truth of storytelling' is realized as 'clarity'.[38v]

> Sorger spread out his notebooks, each with its special color, on the table. The tabletop became a sort of geological map, with different colors indicating the different geological eras. He was seized with an intense but vague feeling of tenderness: naturally, he wished for 'more light'! He stood motionless, bent over the varicolored pattern, which in places was pale with age, until he himself became a tranquil color among the others. He leafed through the notebooks and saw himself disappearing in the writing; in the story of stories; a story of sun and snow.[39]

In conscious opposition to the apocalyptic tendencies of the here and now, the theological precept of a progressive dispelling of darkness in the history of nature and mankind and beyond becomes a model and guiding principle for the writer's work. A falsification, yes, Sorger knows this himself, but he sees falsification, intentional as it is, not as reproach, but as an idea of salvation, reflected in the comforting vision 'that the history of mankind would soon be ended, harmoniously and without horror',[40] exactly like the art practised here. In the end, following this preordained path to its logical conclusion, Sorger even finds himself going to Sunday mass.

> The faces of the faithful were reflected in the bronze covers of the collection boxes, and in making his contribution

Sorger felt himself to be one of the community of money, while the hands of the ushers, tapping on the railings, made the sound of bakers taking bread out of the oven. The whole world swayed when the bread was transformed into the Lord's body and, *simili modo*, the wine into the Lord's blood.[41]

Simili modo, in similar fashion, one might say, literature too achieves, via a ritual of transubstantiation, the transformation of the flesh and blood of reality into something easily consumed that serves to salve a guilty conscience, which has its seat – as we have seen in the case of Stifter – not so much in the author's heart as in his stomach.

The long-drawn arc, spanning half the world, which Sorger traverses in his slow homecoming is in many ways also reminiscent of the expeditions prescribed by the practice of shamanism to the adepts of a metaphysics that transcends the logic and gravity of earth-bound existence.[42] Shamanism is originally an Arctic phenomenon, one which has been ascribed to the effect of the extreme environment on the unstable nerves of those living in the polar regions. It involves the learning of a technique for attaining a state of ecstasy which allows the candidate, in a trance-like state, to release the soul from the body on journeys through the heavens and the underworld. On his return from the other world on the far side of the highest mountains, the shaman tells of the perils and wonders he has been privy to by virtue of transgressing the limits of mundane human existence. The narrative, as a rule, follows the stages of a dream of flight,[vi] and is furnished with images in which feathered beings often appear as the shaman's spirit guides, for which reason the shaman also adorns himself with feathers and strives to imitate the birds on his journey through the air. It is, then, no coincidence that both *Langsame Heimkehr* and *Die Lehre der Sainte-Victoire* contain emblematic bird figures which hint at a world beyond life on the surface of the earth. 'Not far above me, almost within reach, a crow was gliding on the wind. I saw the characteristic bird yellow of the retracted claws, the golden brown of the wings shimmering in the sun, the blue of the sky.'[43] The idea of weightlessness which is literally pictured in these sentences is, though, something the author is able to experience for real only when, on one of his many plane journeys, he sees the earth spread out beneath him in the apparently undiminished array of colours familiar to the naturalist from the colours on his geological maps. The reader, however, understands that Sorger has for a while at least been in another world entirely when he closes the report of his return to Europe with the words: 'Roaring, the plane burst through the clouds.'[44]

In this context it is also fitting that the author's alter ego, having returned from the Indians, is, in the text which follows *Langsame Heimkehr*, transformed back into his own self,[vii] and that the mode of locomotion should change from flying to walking. The journey described in *Die Lehre der Sainte-Victoire* [*The Lesson of Mont Sainte-Victoire*] is thus less the journey of the initiate into the otherworld [*Jenseits*] than the artist's journey into art. Franz Sternbald[viii] and the narrator of *Der Nachsommer*, both seeking a utopia of art at whose centre creativity and restoration are combined in the idea of the preservation of creation in and through art, are the inspiration for the wanderer Handke on his way to the centre of the world – which he believes he will find at the spot 'where a great artist worked'.[45] It is also true, however, that for the pupil – one of the abiding images Peter Handke has of himself – the masters of bourgeois art appear as the 'teacher[s] of mankind in the here and now',[46] and thus the journey appears as more than merely an aesthetic symbolization of our secular existence. Only through the metaphysical dimensions of the text is it possible to explain why the mountain [Mont Sainte-Victoire] 'attracted' the author 'as nothing in [his] life had ever attracted [him] before'.[47] Seen in this light, the journey on foot becomes a kind of *Pilgrim's Progress*, and the stages along the way those of an imagined history of salvation. The decisive factor, however – as one of the more cryptic comments in Goethe's *Farbenlehre* [*Colour Theory*] would seem to suggest – is not so much the goal the wanderer has in view, but rather the act of walking itself: 'Set out on the road to one goal or another, whether actually or merely in thought: between the goal and the intention there is something that contains both, namely the act, the progression. This progression is as good as the goal: for this will certainly be reached, if the decision is firm and the conditions adequate; and yet this progression can only ever be called intentional, because the walker can always just as easily be paralysed before the last step as before the first.'[48]

In this ominous reference to the ever-immanent threat of paralysis is contained what, in the end, forms the sole justification of the intrinsically hubristic attempt on the part of the wanderer to enter an essentially sacred realm; even in the most ancient stories, salvation depends upon a fearless overcoming of the utmost danger and peril, a danger represented in *Die Lehre der Sainte-Victoire* in the chapter 'Der Sprung des Wolfs' ['Wolf's Leap'], where Handke describes the terrifying encounter with 'his' dog. This creature is to be found in the grounds of a barracks belonging to the Foreign Legion, paved in concrete and surrounded by a high barbed-wire fence. Its body is motley-coloured, streaked with yellow; its head and its face however are deepest black. In the confrontation with this unspeakably hideous creature, in which he recognizes his own first and worst enemy, the wanderer literally takes leave of his senses. If we understand the terrible hound as the traditional symbol of saturnine melancholy, then it becomes apparent that the narrator, on his journey into the light, gazes down through the purple flesh of the beast's maw on the fear and depression which lies buried deep within his own soul. Similarly, in the first canto of the *Divina Commedia*, the wanderer, halfway up his ascent of the *dilettoso monte*, finds lying in wait a she-wolf [*lupa*] whose gaze turns him pale with fear: 'drob ich vor Furcht erschauert, daß ich die Höh nicht hoffte zu erreichen: ch'io perdei la speranza dell'altezza' ['so much discouragement / by terror of her aspect that perforce / I forfeited all hope of the ascent'].[49] How to avoid the clutches of this creature, which lets none pass unmolested, is something Dante discovers by entrusting himself to his guide and master Virgil,[ix] who from now on will lead him through the eternal depths. A similar arrangement pertains in *Die Lehre der Sainte-Victoire*, whose text traces the line drawn by Cézanne from the dark pictures of horror[x] to the representation of light through the medium of colour. Cézanne, too, Handke recalls, began by painting images of horror, and in the Jeu de Paume he realizes that in Cézanne's still lifes everything seems to be on an inclined plane, and that the pears, peaches, apples and onions, the vases, bowls and bottles are painted 'as though these things were the last of their kind'.[50]

The transition from this apocalyptic perspective to that lighter concept of the last days, so striking in the paintings of Mont Sainte-Victoire, is not only the longest but also the shortest way, just as the step from grief to consolation is not only the greatest but also the smallest. Only a consciousness which has learned not to surrender completely to the conjuration of catastrophe — and Handke has repeatedly emphasized that the evocation of horror is not in itself enough – only to such a consciousness will there appear, through 'a vaulted gateway leading into the distance', and in 'the bright colours of the sky', the 'slopes of Mont Sainte-Victoire',[51] whose rock face, as he writes later, extends to the horizon like an unbroken bright white band.[52] The bright white band marks the way to a plateau, from which the wanderer can just make out to the north-east, gleaming in the farthest distance, the snowfields of the Alps – '"really pure white"',[53] as he notes with amazement in quotation marks. Now absolutely pure white is, according to one of Lichtenberg's aphorisms, something very few people have ever seen,[54] and it is also the colour – if it can be termed such – of which Wittgenstein claims that it 'does away with darkness' ['die Dunkelheit aufhebt'].[55] The theological and theosophical connotations of these ideas are of the most far-reaching significance, going back to colour symbolism in the Scriptures.[56] They are the incidental results of the hope for redemption from the guilt-ridden conditions of life, a hope fleetingly realized in art, in the creation of images which allow author and reader to enter almost bodily into the nature of all things, which yet remains forever strange to us.

Handke exemplifies this in the closing passages of *Die Lehre der Sainte-Victoire*, beginning with the description of Jakob von Ruisdael's painting *Der große Wald* [*The Great Forest*] in the Kunsthistorisches Museum in Vienna. At this point it becomes clear that the narrator's journey on foot represents not so much the journey itself as a kind of composition in which, for the narrator, the world coalesces into images in which it is possible to dwell for a while. The artistic image of the 'great forest' is overlaid, in the course of the text, by a real forest close to the village of Morzg near Salzburg. On the way through this real forest, the wanderer disappears into his imagination in the same manner as the legendary Chinese painter into the landscape he has just painted. There is, too, an important connection here to Stifter, who also liked to give his pictures symbolic titles. At the end of his journal on his paintings, in which he set down the exact time spent on painting down to the last minute, the last entry just before his death consists of the sentence, repeated twenty-three times over, 'An der Ruhe gemalt' ['painted Peace'].[57] The painting in question depicts a lake with a snow-capped mountain peak rising behind it, and, like the wanderer's progress through the wood near Morzg, the observer has the sense of a silent transition into another state of being. The quality of restraint at work in pictures and prose of this kind is the expression of a state of mind concerned, if not with obliteration [*Auslöschen*], then at least with exhalation, fitting for that no-man's land conceived of by art situated between life and death, and rising above all earthly concerns; a no-man's land in which the wanderer comes to an isolated former 'keeper's house', where 'in the evening, one of its windows glows with an almost imperceptible inner light and muffled singing can be heard from within.'[58] From this outpost of eternity, the road leads to a cemetery with an inn in front of it, from which now and then drunks are ejected, remaining in front of the door for a while singing defiantly before suddenly falling silent and departing. Through this region, already halfway to the hereafter, there move 'slow funeral procession[s]' where 'bells toll, and for a moment a stranger walking behind the coffin becomes a friend or a relative.'[59]

The parable of this curious scene, where it is unclear whether it is viewed from the perspective of the stranger or of the deceased, is also embodied by Hebel in his character Kannitverstan,[xi] adrift in a strange country; it draws us inexorably on into the heart of the text. On the far side of a sunken path there begins a 'night-black thicket' where a 'black hole tempts one to enter'.[60] The faces of the village children at play, 'strangely separated from their bodies, like the faces of saints in old pictures',[61] appear here and there out of the darkness, as well as a lone runner, out of breath, 'the skin of his face, mask replacing mask, changing from dead to alive and back at every step';[62] lost souls all, who, as Benjamin wrote, wander restlessly but have no history.[63] From the brow of the hill which the protagonist eventually reaches, the dialect spoken by the people walking far down below 'sounds like all the languages in the world rolled into one',[64] that lingua franca of those no longer separated from one another by the boundaries of time and space. The path comes to an end at a pond, at the edge of which, rocking gently, a raft hammered together from doors awaits. In the gathering dusk, which tempts the wanderer now standing on the shore to cross over, the latter, mindful of the lessons which preceded his last expedition, instead fixes his attention on a woodpile, 'the only brightness against a darkening background'.[65] He gazes at it 'until nothing remains but colors'.[65] 'Ach, when I really gaze into the colours,' Jean Paul writes, 'which God has given to the dark world and for which He always employs His sun: why, then I feel as if I have already died and gone to heaven.'[66] This is not so much a wish for death as a reversible simulation of dying. '[U]ntil nothing remains but colors . . . Exhale. Looked at in a certain way – extreme immersion and extreme attention – the interstices in the wood darken, and something starts spinning in the pile. At first it looks like a cross-section of malachite. Then the numbers of color charts appear. Then night falls on it and then it is day again.'[67]

PART TWO

Strange Homeland

Essays on Austrian Literature

Foreword

The present collection of essays is the result of my continued preoccupation with a tradition of writing which means a great deal to me. These essays, though, aim to shed light on a different context from the studies published in the same series five years ago as *Die Beschreibung des Unglücks*.* Whereas that volume was more preoccupied with the psychological factors which govern writing, the present collection is concerned more with the social determinants of the literary world view, although naturally the one can never be completely separated from the other. Work on this project was supported by various grants from the Bundesministerium für Wissenschaft und Forschung, the University of East Anglia and the British Academy, whose support I gladly acknowledge here.

W. G. Sebald
Norwich, Norfolk
January 1990

---

* Part One of the present volume.

Introduction

The singular, often traumatic, evolution of Austria[i] – from the vastness of the Habsburg Empire to a diminutive Alpine republic, and thence via the *Ständestaat* [Corporate State] and the *Anschluß* [annexation] by the fateful Großdeutschland [Greater Germany], to its refounding in the years after the war – means that concepts such as *Heimat*, *Provinz*, *Grenzland*, *Ausland*, *Fremde* and *Exil* [home/land, provinces, borderland, abroad, foreignness and exile] occupy a strikingly prominent position in Austrian literature of the nineteenth and twentieth centuries. There is room for the view that the preoccupation with the idea of *Heimat* is – despite all the irruptions of history – one of the constant features of that otherwise rather indefinable entity which is Austrian literature, even if, given the sheer diversity of ethnic and political denominations involved, the idea of what *Heimat* once was, is or could be, is even today so volatile as to render a systematic survey of the terrain all but impossible. At most – and this study attempts no more than this – it may be possible to examine, on a case-by-case basis, the particular viewpoints from which *Heimat* is represented in the works of each of the authors discussed. I am, of course, abundantly aware that such a method must necessarily omit as much as – indeed far more than – it can include. For this reason, much of what could have been discussed under the title of this book does not feature here; nevertheless, I hope that the inevitable incompleteness is redeemed by insights which might, perhaps, not have become apparent in a more systematic survey which placed less emphasis on the quality of the texts involved.

The concept of *Heimat* is a relatively recent one. The more difficult it became to remain in the home country, with individuals and entire social groups finding themselves forced to turn their back on their country of origin and to emigrate, the greater the currency the term *Heimat* acquired. Thus, as is often the case, the concept stands in an inverse relationship to that to which it refers: the more *Heimat* is talked about, the less it exists in reality. The New World, which first makes an appearance in the German-speaking world in Sealsfield's exotic depictions of landscape, makes clear, in its vertiginous vastness, that nothing can ever make up for the loss of one's homeland. But even at home – as might be demonstrated anywhere in the works of Stifter – it is clear that mankind's relationship to its original home is fractured from the very moment it becomes a theme in literature. Stifter's protagonists, even as they move through a region they know like the back of their hand, are still strangers and foreigners within it; convinced, like the children in *Bergkristall* [*Rock Crystal*] that they are on the right path, they have been heading in the wrong direction for the longest time, and the ancestral home, which in the story *Der Hochwald* [*The High Forest*] always stood out against the jagged blue line of the horizon, is, the next time the telescope is raised, nothing but a smoking ruin. Those who attempted to reclaim Stifter as a *Heimatschriftsteller* [local or provincial writer] overlooked the extent to which, for him, the *Heimat* had already become *unheimlich*: a strange, uncanny, even inhospitable place. A great chill pervades everything, both between people and in nature – which they have now suddenly come to perceive as 'other'. Large swathes of Stifter's work – written at the time of the emergence of high capitalism – read like the story of a second expulsion. The fact that, despite his obvious relevance, Stifter is not considered here is chiefly due to the fact that I have discussed his world view in previous articles and wished to avoid undue repetition.[1]

By no means the least important reason for the prominence of the theme of *Heimat* in nineteenth- and twentieth-century Austrian literature is the fact that, for writers of Jewish provenance, it was of paramount importance during the whole period of assimilation and westward migration [*Westwanderung*]. As the writings of Leopold Kompert and Karl Emil Franzos show, at the latest from the mid-nineteenth century onwards, for those who had left the confines of the ghetto the question presented itself as to whether, arriving in Vienna, they had finally come home, or whether they had in fact forsaken their one true *Heimat*, the *shtetl*. In this respect, the nineteenth-century German-language tales from the ghetto are full of ambivalence; nor does the literature of the *fin de siècle* offer any solutions. What becomes ever more apparent, from Schnitzler and Altenberg to Broch and Roth, is a complex illusionism, fully conscious of its own untenability, which, while still developing the idea of a home country [*Heimatland*], was at one and the same time a rehearsal for exile.

Even if members of the Jewish diaspora always tended to identify with their host country, their attachment to Austria was still a singular phenomenon. Theodor Herzl famously revelled for a while in the vision of Vienna as a New Jerusalem, and he would – had such a thing been feasible – happily have led the whole Jewish population of Vienna to be baptized in the Stefansdom

[St Stephen's Cathedral] as a means of ushering in a Jewish–Christian utopian state. Had this extravagant plan for reconciliation – which Herzl intended to submit to the Pope – come to pass, it would have resulted, so to speak, in the transformation of Austria into the Holy Land. The realization of this dream of a new apostolic empire of Jewish–German nations [*deutsch-jüdischer Nation*] was however – setting aside for a moment any practical political considerations – doomed to failure from the outset, not least because it was essentially a product of the very anti-Semitism which it sought to eradicate. Considering what preceded it, the idea of Zionism which Herzl soon went on to disseminate appears a positively pragmatic compromise between a romantic utopian scenario and the actual political circumstances of the time. Remarkably, the wishful thinking characteristic of the early days of Zionism – not confined to Herzl – in no way impinged upon the critical perspicacity of contemporary Jewish–Austrian authors. This is true not only of Karl Kraus – probably one of the first to see 'das österreichische Antlitz' ['the Austrian face'][ii] as an allegory of terror – but equally so of writers such as [Peter] Altenberg and Joseph Roth, both of whom have, on occasion, been accused of glorifying or sentimentalizing Austria. In the works of Jewish–Austrian authors, criticism and loyalty are extremely finely balanced, and one would not be far wrong in seeing in this balancing act one of the mainsprings of inspiration for Austrian literature during its most productive phase. This yearning for synthesis remained more or less unchanged right up to the comatose phase of the First Republic. The attachment to Austria held strong, even after the latter's dubious mutation into a Christian *Ständestaat*. No one described this earlier and more exactly than Franz Kafka in the story of the

Barnabas family in the *Castle* — a paradigmatic tale of exile in which the oppressed, too, remain in thrall to the regime. By contrast, [Hermann] Broch — who in his *Bergroman* or 'mountain novel' had a similar aim in view — became so deeply enmeshed in the mythologization of the *Heimat* that he scarcely even noticed that his right to remain in it had already been revoked.

The ideological appropriation of *Heimat* which gained the upper hand in Austria in the 1930s would ultimately lead to its destruction. *Heimat* — as Gerhard Roth once put it in an interview — now signified a condition in which everyone and everything is appropriated by everyone and everything else.[2] What was being contrived at the time was the abolition of all dissent or nuance, with narrow-mindedness elevated to a universal principle, and betrayal the new public morality. *Holzwegliteratur* [backwoods literature] played a central part in this complete reversal of values, which also included the perversion of the concept of *Heimat*. So thoroughgoing was this process that for a long time any recuperation of the term in 'serious' literature appeared completely out of the question. Names such as Weinheber and Waggerl[iii] will suffice to demonstrate the idea of *Heimat* which persisted until well into the 1960s. Only with the work of the Wiener Gruppe, with [H. C.] Artmann's dialect 'gedichta r aus bradnsee' [poems from bradnsee],[iv] and later, in a wider context, the now legendary 'Graz breakaway',[v] could anything like a reconstitution of *Heimat* within the framework of an ideologically uncompromised literature take place.

For an author like Jean Améry — who, as he himself says, never managed to get over the loss of his homeland — this development came several decisive years too late. It is, however, hardly surprising that the process of rehabilitation should have been a very gradual one. It took a new generation, and a substantial number of books – equally committed both ethically and aesthetically – to offset and outweigh the legacy of fascism. Such books have been and continue to be written. Their *raison d'être* lies in their accounts of all that was false and intolerable about the *Heimat* in which the contemporary generation of writers came of age. The conspicuous, one might say ethno-poetic, interest in the deep-seated damage wrought by the lingering effects of everyday fascism on a provincial and rural population, a large proportion of whose lower classes were barely politically literate – this interest, for the new generation of Austrian writers, a disproportionate number of whom came from this same damaged milieu, suggested a means of overcoming their own nameless status. As representatives of the radical critique of the false *Heimat* in contemporary Austrian literature, these authors, not a few of whom are in fundamental opposition to their social milieu, are themselves potential exiles liable to find themselves without a *Heimat*. This is reflected just as much in the attitude of Thomas Bernhard – held by many to be paranoid – as in the fears and anxieties documented by Peter Handke. It is, evidently, still not easy to feel at home in Austria, especially when, as has happened all too often in recent years, the uncanny and unwelcoming aspects of this homeland – the *Unheimlichkeit der Heimat* – are brought to mind more often than one might wish by the resurgence of diverse revenants and spectres of the past.

Beyond that, what becomes apparent in the important works of recent Austrian literature, from Thomas Bernhard via Peter Handke, Gerhard Roth and Peter Rosei to Christoph Ransmayr, with their anxious and apprehensive registering of changes in the light, the landscape and the weather, is the gradually dawning realization of the wholesale disintegration and destruction of humankind's natural home. If the restoration of the social *Heimat* was something which – by virtue of the right words – still lay within the bounds of possibility, it now seems increasingly doubtful whether such artistry can suffice to save that which we should, above all else, learn to grasp is our one true home.

Views from the New World

On Charles Sealsfield

> Farewell, my native land!
> Farewell trees!
>
> *The Indian Chief*

The work of Karl Postl, alias Charles Sealsfield, born in 1793 in Poppitz [now Popice] in Bohemian Moravia, was, in the 1840s, considered by liberal critics to be the pinnacle of prose writing in German.[1] The grand scale of his national and supranational novels [*National- und Weltromane*] seemed positively to exemplify the high point of the age. Perhaps because of his direct association with the expansionist spirit of the times, though, Sealsfield's work did not conform to the normative criteria of the school of realism which emerged in the following decades, and – like so much else which was a product of the *Vormärz*[i] – was forgotten, or at least fell out of favour. His relegation from the canon of 'serious' literature persists to this day. Not that there has been any shortage of attempts at recuperation, but since these were in the main politically motivated, they generally proved something of a liability when it came to Sealsfield's literary rehabilitation. Thus, during the First Austrian Republic,[ii] Sealsfield was on the one hand hailed as a freethinking *Volksschriftsteller* [popular writer/writer of the people], while on the other hand 'the pronounced Germanism' ['der ausgeprägte Germanismus'][2] of his work also accorded with the ideology of the ever more rightward-leaning *Deutschösterreichertum* [German–Austrianness]. In the Großdeutsches Reich [Greater German Reich] that followed, much was made of an author whose ethnopsychological and geopolitical excursuses appeared to an ethnographer such as Josef Nadler as models of true epic art.[3] It is no surprise, then, that the foundations of Sealsfield scholarship should have been laid during the Third Reich. Eduard Castle's biography of Sealsfield, based on extensive research, was completed as early as 1944, but could no longer be published at the end of the war. Its publication in 1952 also had a political dimension, given the then recent emphasis on German– or Austro-American affinities. All of this was, as noted above, scarcely advantageous to Sealsfield's work. It continued to be virtually inaccessible, available only in more or less bowdlerized individual editions for younger readers. The facsimile reprint edition of Sealsfield's collected works which began to appear in the early 1970s[4] is mainly confined to specialist libraries. It is, therefore, unsurprising that his works have not found a wider readership. What is more surprising is that, with a few exceptions,[5] literary scholarship also seems wary of engaging with Sealsfield[iii] – an omission which may well be due to the fact that the literary works of the renegade priest from the Austrian provinces in many ways reproduced the contradictions of the era of high capitalism in unadulterated form. These contradictions are – as will be shown in what follows – of both an ethical and an aesthetic nature. So glaring are they that Sealsfield's works, even now, remain hard to classify, given that the business of descriptive classification is ill-equipped to deal with irreconcilable opposites. Only a determinedly critical approach, then, will be able to begin to answer the as yet unresolved question as to whether Sealsfield was a decent chap or a charlatan, a genius or a mere scribbler.

Karl Postl was thirty years old when he left Austria in 1823. What moved him to this step can no longer be established with any certainty. At the age of fifteen, Postl had been admitted as a convent student to the *Kreuzherrenstift* [Seminary of the Order of the Knights of the Cross] in Prague. Five years later, he entered the order as a novice. After three further years he was ordained as a priest, and shortly thereafter he had risen to be the youngest ever Secretary to the Order, which brought with it considerable responsibility in business affairs. There is, then, everything to suggest that Postl derived a certain satisfaction from this career, one by no means straightforward for a wine grower's son. During his travels on the business of the Order, he came into contact with local princes – an aspect of his work which was probably of no small significance for someone who had always had a taste for connections in high places. In order to live up to his social aspirations, he took up English, French, riding and the piano. All the available biographical information shows him, even in later years, to have been someone interested chiefly in his own advancement. It seems, therefore, improbable that the ambitious young cleric, who most likely already had his eye on the post of Grand Master General, would have casually put at risk his excellent prospects in favour of an insecure and unsettled existence. Friedrich Sengle is surely right when he suggests that Postl's precipitate departure for America cannot be explained on the basis of his individual psychology alone, for example as a rebellion against the rule of celibacy, or against the discipline of the Order; rather, as Sengle suggests, it is likely to be a direct result of the Restoration of 1819–20.[6] For Postl, the forced retirement of his theologically liberal mentor Bolzano will have been a sign that, in the growing climate of illiberalism, his own stock too was sinking – an assumption probably confirmed when, furnished with a recommendation from one of his benefactors,[7] but without the knowledge of his superiors, he travelled to Vienna in the summer of 1823 for an audience with Graf Franz Josef Saurau[iv] in the hope of an appointment to the *Studienhofkommission* at the Court. It is not impossible that this interview with Saurau – one of the most feared exponents of the reactionary movement of the day – was what finally convinced Postl that he would not be able to realize his ambitions in Austria. In any case, the circumstances under which he left his homeland gave rise to the rumour that he had been an unreservedly free-thinking, not to say revolutionary, spirit who could no longer bear to remain in Austria – whereas in actual fact he was probably merely unable to accommodate himself to an ultra-reactionary regime. Either way, his situation was now precarious in the extreme. A return to the Order, after his highly irregular departure, would almost certainly have meant a demotion, and since a renegade cleric in the Austria of the time had no legal status, Postl had no choice but to leave for good. His escape route took him, that same summer, via Stuttgart, Zurich and Le Havre to New Orleans,[8] while in Vienna a description of him 'zur womöglichen Zustandebringung Postls' [for the arrest of Postl] was circulated to all district authorities, *Kur* inspectors and chiefs of police in the German provinces, because, as a memorandum of 27 June 1823 of the *Polizeihofstelle* [Court Police Headquarters] to Graf Kolowrat states, 'the flight of the priest and secretary of the Order of the Cross of the Red Star in Prague, Carl Postl . . . made a most unpleasant impression in this present place':[9] a rather ominous remark, which suggests that Postl was wise to make good his escape.

One of the characteristics of Sealsfield as a writer is the fact that he nowhere expresses anything of the emotions Karl Postl may have felt when leaving his homeland, nor indeed when he first caught a glimpse of the continent of America. But for someone who, up to the age of thirty, had barely ventured outside the confines of Bohemia and Moravia, the desolate wilderness of the Mississippi delta must, as for the banished lovers at the end of Prévost's *Manon Lescaut*, have made an impression of overwhelming bleakness – a thesis which certain passages in Sealsfield's novels would seem to support. In the first chapter of *Das Cajütenbuch* [*The Cabin Book*] – in a passage which will be returned to later – the Mississippi delta is described as 'grausenerregend'[10] ['horrifying'], and the beginning of the seventh chapter of Sealsfield's first novel, *The Indian Chief* – first published in English – also conjures up this impression. 'The endless waste of waters rolling towards the gulf' – such a bleak, grey prospect must truly have appeared to Postl as the gates of exile. 'No habitation of man,' the text continues, 'no herb, no bird is to be seen. The wind, sighing mournfully through the cane, the hoarse cry of the pilot, or the hissing of the steam-boat, are the only sounds that interrupt the oppressive dreariness.'[11] It remains unclear whether such passages give an indication of Karl Postl's state of mind in the late summer of 1823, just as his first American voyage, ending in 1826, offers almost no clues about the person of Karl Postl himself. Although Postl's first book, *Die Vereinigten Staaten von Amerika*

[*The United States of America*],[12] demonstrates an impressively detailed topographical and ethnographic knowledge, the studiously factual text bears hardly any trace of the disorienting sense of strangeness which Postl must have experienced on his grand tour — mostly undertaken on the steamboats which plied the Mississippi and Ohio rivers — from New Orleans to Kittaning in Pennsylvania. The fact that Postl, now in possession of a passport issued in Louisiana under the name of Charles Sealsfield, returned to Europe in the summer of 1826 may be taken as a sign that he was unable to establish himself in America — either economically or emotionally. This may also be seen in his more or less desperate efforts to come to some kind of renewed understanding with the *Heimat* he had abandoned.

One of the most astonishing volte-faces in Postl's biography is the letter which he — a former secretary to the Order, indirectly at least driven into exile by the reactionary politics of the Austrian Restoration — wrote in August 1826 to Chancellor Metternich, then residing at Schloss Johannisberg on the Rhine, offering him his services as a counter-revolutionary agent.[13] This letter, written in rather uneven and at times incorrect English,[14] refers to seditious uprisings in Hungary, allegedly masterminded by the English, about which the undersigned claims to be in a position to furnish further information. That nothing should have come of this proposal, since in this whole ill-fated episode Postl evidently cut an all-too-amateurish figure,[15] is less significant than the attempt it represented on the part of the émigré to reopen negotiations with Austria, even at the expense of completely disregarding any and all defensible principles. It can hardly be denied that this business casts a long shadow over the republicanism which Sealsfield himself later always emphasized. The unseemly haste with which the outwardly progressive man of letters set about selling his political soul already seems to anticipate the *trahison des clercs* – that very widespread, though barely investigated, phenomenon in bourgeois literature, motivated not least by the fear of loss of livelihood and *déclassement*. There are, in Postl's further life and works, many indications that he still harboured a deep-seated longing for an association with power. Even in his later years in Switzerland, when his writings had already accumulated for him a considerable fortune, he still liked to vaunt his important political connections with Jackson's party in the United States of America. From time to time he would also let slip that his true place was not in literature but in the White House,[16] a piece of wishful thinking which Sealsfield may have ended up believing himself, even though the letter he addressed to the Secretary of State in the White House, offering his services as a European agent, never produced any discernible results. In this letter, Sealsfield explains that he is about to depart for Europe, and from there, where he is in contact with leading figures, and has access to the most important circles in Vienna and Berlin, he would be willing to furnish 'more detailed hints about the hidden motives and political movements than even a well-paid ambassador'.[17]

These somewhat dubious ambitions on Postl's part are also in keeping with the fact that, for a while at least, he occupied a semi-official position in the service of the House of Bonaparte. In 1829 and 1830 he edited the *Cour[r]ier des [É]tats-Unis* in New York, acquired after the July Revolution by the former King Joseph of Spain [and Naples] – then resident in New Jersey under the name of Count Survillier[s] – as an organ for Bonapartist interests. After his move to Switzerland, Postl was in close contact with Queen Hortense and Prince Louis Napoléon, who at the time were in

Arenenberg awaiting a more favourable turn of events. How far he was actually privy to the machinations of the Bonapartists cannot however, as Castle notes, be determined with any certainty.[18] What does, though, become clear from these episodes is that Postl's relationship with power was a decidedly ambivalent one, whether on account of his own character or because of the *déformation professionelle* incurred during his time as an ambitious young cleric. Straightforward distinctions are in any case impossible, since, even during the *Vormärz*, liberal ideology and reactionary political practices did not necessarily rule each other out.

A few months after Cotta's publication of the two volumes of *Die Vereinigten Staaten von Nordamerika* [*The United States of North America*] in Stuttgart, Sealsfield's work *Austria As It Is* appeared in English[v] in London in December 1827;[19] not until 1919 was a German-language version published in Vienna. In the Preface, the author identifies himself as 'a native of the Austrian Empire; who, after an absence of five years, has revisited his country',[20] thereby implying that everything that follows has the status of an authentic report. In reality, Postl had not been in Austria in 1826, and thus his observations draw less on contemporary events than on memory. He was aided and abetted in this not very grave act of deception by the system of the Holy Alliance, intent on preserving the greatest possible degree of stasis, and effectively thwarting any kind of development. Sealsfield's main motivation for writing *Austria As It Is* was probably an attempt to remedy his dire financial situation.[21] An attack on the 'shocking despotism' in Austria, to which the Preface refers, was by no means the author's primary aim. What prompted such utterances was less his own political views, or any personal resentment, than the fact that – as the French translation of 1828 already notes – Sealsfield was writing with the predilections of his English readers in mind. For this reason, Sealsfield's much vaunted liberal convictions only surface somewhat sporadically in this work. All in all it is a mixed bag of journalistic reportage, steering a more or less entertaining course between picturesque travel description and political pamphlet.

The description of the journey Sealsfield claims to have made from Le Havre to Vienna, via Frankfurt, Dresden and Prague, is, initially, cursory in the extreme. For example, regarding the stretch between Frankfurt and Leipzig we learn only that '[The country,] if we except the Fichtel mountains and a dozen small residences of Saxon princes, is of little interest.'[22] The text only becomes more detailed when Sealsfield comes to describe the provinces of Bohemia and Moravia – one might almost say as a lost paradise. The evocation of 'beautiful Bohemia, with its infinite variety of ruins, castles, towns, villages', many of which lie 'buried, as it were, under forests of fruit trees'[23] seem to have unleashed waves of nostalgia [*Heimweh*] in Sealsfield – who is nonetheless at pains not to let his feelings show. However, his homesickness surfaces via a certain effusiveness in the phrasing: 'The road from Teplitz to Carlsbad leads through an expanse of wheat fields,[vi] forty miles in length, without the least interruption';[24] the estates of the princes are easily equal to those of the English aristocracy; St Vitus cathedral[vii] is 'the prettiest Gothic church on the Continent',[25] and the environs of Znojmo [Zuarya], Postl's actual home town, 'almost an uninterrupted vineyard, softly rising and descending on the eminences',[26] appear as the very epitome of idyllic longing. There are 'orchard[s] or . . . wheat fields in the lower grounds',[26] the villages are prosperous, and no one need emigrate from here, unlike the German peasants 'wander[ing] to the coasts of Holland to seek a new fatherland'.[27][viii] There is even a description of a typical house of one of these 'cultivators of the grape' with a 'small garden before the house with green or painted railings' and, as if that were not enough, in the best room, on a table covered with a Tyrolean carpet, two bottles and a number of glasses stand ready,[28] exactly as if at any moment the prodigal son were about to walk in through the door. The sentiments that Postl was at such moments concealing, perhaps even from Sealsfield, will of course not have been apparent to his English readers; the description of affairs in Vienna, by contrast, is likely to have been of the utmost interest. It is in this context that Sealsfield's extremely critical portrait of Metternich should be seen – the very same Metternich to whom he had so piously offered his services by letter only a few months before. A number of anecdotes illustrate Metternich's scheming nature, concluding with the remark that, while as a diplomat he has no equal, as a statesman he is 'very indifferent'.[29] The portrait of Kaiser Franz himself makes clear how it is precisely this ruler's 'plainness of manner' [*Biederkeit*] and bonhomie [*Leutseligkeit*] which are among his most dangerous attributes, since the apparently affable gentleman in his 'shabby capotte' is perfectly capable of sending you, before you know it, 'in the plainest way into the dungeons of Munkatsch, Komom or Spielberg'.[30] In his notes on the Kaiser's obscurantist system of government, on the ramifications of the Secret Police, of which, as he writes, '[i]t is impossible to form an adequate idea,'[31] and on the vampiric bureaucratic reach of the state, Sealsfield demonstrates a perspicacity which could have been a match for the most critical minds of the day, had he himself not been so susceptible to the temptations of power.

If Postl's relationship to the reactionary politics of the post-Napoleonic era was an ambivalent one, his position vis-à-vis the revolutionary movements of the *Vormärz* and the events of 1848 was no less so. For someone who, with hindsight, claimed to have 'championed the cause of Republicanism all his life',[32] the strange conservatism which Postl exhibits in the mid-1840s is not exactly a badge of political consistency. At a time when such distinguished protagonists of the revolutionary movement as Herwegh, Herzen and Bakunin were all in Zurich, Postl was at pains to distance himself from the 'Züricher Zustände' [Zurich affairs] which clearly disconcerted him.[33] And when the 1848 Revolution finally breaks out, he, like Metternich, considers it not to have its origins in the *Volk* [people], but rather to be the result of a weak and indulgent domestic policy. But where the situation in Vienna is concerned he does not stint on caustic criticism. 'These Viennese and Viennese students', he writes to Erhard on 1 June,[34] 'seem to be afflicted by revolutionary sunstrokes every few weeks. The Viennese couldn't go about things any more stupidly. They are systematically dismantling the state — are so obviously playing into the hands of the French and Russians — and are so evidently ruining the future of their city, that, if a *deus ex machina* in the form of some strong-minded minister or general doesn't soon appear on the scene and have a few hundred of them shot to blazes, in a short time the powerful empire of Austria will and must become a mere shadow of its former self.'[35][ix] In Castle's view, Sealsfield's comment is evidence of his political far-sightedness, since, as he notes, 'following the populist rabble-rousing of 6 October, incited by foreign emissaries', in which, Castle continues, Latour, the Minister for War, was a 'blood sacrifice', there was in fact discovered in Windischgrätz[x] the strong-minded General 'who, after taking Vienna on 31 October, had a few hundred shot to blazes'.[36] It is possible that Sealsfield's somewhat unnuanced attitude to the events of the

Year of Revolutions was, like Grillparzer's, coloured by his early education in the principles of enlightened absolutism, particularly in the Josephinian tradition. The distaste which 'the dissolution of the organically organized *Volk* into vulgar mobs'[37] evoked in him – as in Grillparzer – could then be seen merely as a sign of his being out of step with the times, and thus at least excusable. On the other hand, though, Postl's commentary on the closing phases of the Vienna uprising is an early example of the newly emerging bourgeois Age of Reason, with its peculiar ability to anticipate and condone the most extreme expressions of counter-revolutionary terror as all being part of the logic of the unfolding course of history. A further aspect of this new age of reason was the way interest in political independence was increasingly displaced by concerns about money and material possessions. In this respect, Sealsfield is no exception. In the decade between 1835 and 1845, his novels commanded good fees and he was thus, like many of his contemporaries, in a position to console himself regarding the loss of political hopes – which were perhaps not so sadly missed after all – by investing in shares in the railway and suchlike concrete values whose progress could be measured on a daily basis.

Yet the question as to whether, and how far, an author like Sealsfield was able to resist the current of the *Zeitgeist* cannot be determined on the basis of his conscious and explicitly stated views alone. The ideological infrastructure of his work, which is not really susceptible to conscious manipulation, is as a general rule a more reliable yardstick, as may be shown by Sealsfield's treatment of the subject of 'race', a theme in many ways central to his novels. There is no getting around the fact that, in principle, Sealsfield thought slavery a good thing. In support of this view – with which he often provoked reactions of utter horror in

Switzerland – he would advance a whole gamut of sound humanitarian and economic reasons, for example that the Negroes [sic], because of their high market value, on the whole enjoyed more considerate treatment than the white hired hands.[38] This as one might say pragmatic view becomes, in the description of a patriarchal idyll near the end of the *Cajütenbuch*, almost ideological. 'The negro village', the text states,

> was another charming feature in this southern picture. It consisted of two rows of huts, each with a China tree before the door, in whose double colors each lay as if imbedded. The greater part of them had little galleries, after the fashion of the master's house, on which here and there sat the patriarchs of the black colony smoking their 'bacca, while the old women, babbling to them and to each other, cleaned vegetables or performed some other light work.

'In the north', Sealsfield goes on to explain on the following page, 'one has no conception of the love and tenderness with which our blacks cling to their masters and mistresses, and these again to their dependents. It is, indeed, the most affectionate band that, at the present day, unites masters and dependents, for it is interwoven in their nature from childhood.'[39]

The sentimental patriarchalism Sealsfield cultivates here is a secular version of the strategy for the salvation of Black souls familiar from Chateaubriand's *Atala* and Beecher Stowe's *Uncle Tom's Cabin*. While the dead Indian girl Atala – whose cheeks, as Chateaubriand emphasizes, are suffused with a wondrous pallor[40] – appears as an allegory of virginity,[41] Uncle Tom, in his dying moments after his fatal beating, utters the memorable phrase 'O, Mas'r George! What a thing 't is to be a Christian!'[42][xi] In the one case as in the other, the deathbed scene, culmination of a lifetime's suffering, is intended to represent the 'triomphe du Christianisme sur la vie sauvage'.[43] The life of poor Atala, who, out of a 'natural' Christian impulse, has saved the narrator, Chactas, from a martyr's death at the stake, in this context resembles a pilgrimage which leads the noble savage out of the depths of the forests and up a high mountain to the dwellings of the Christian hermit. On this difficult path, the lovers Chactas and Atala are preceded by the hermit's faithful dog 'en portant au bout d'un baton la laterne éteinte',[44] a most singular detail which, looking back on this touching tableau, so moving to the bourgeois heart, seems to me to represent something like the extinguished eternal light, or the quenched lamp of Reason. It is, after all, precisely the touching sentimentality of these stories of conversion that leaves a bad taste, and is ultimately used to justify what is visited upon the Blacks and Indians in the name of the expansion of civilization.

Sealsfield's first literary work, *The Indian Chief or Tokeah and the White Rose*,[xii] features a similar Christian-inspired constellation. The white girl who grew up with the Oconees, the White Rose of the title, ultimately – to the readers' satisfaction – returns to civilized society, and, what is more, without any major sacrifice being demanded, whereas Canadah, the actual daughter of her foster father, the chieftain Tokeah, can only resolve the conflict between her loyalty to her Indian origins and her love for her white sister by becoming a martyr. Despite this key episode, of central importance to the plot, the Christian model of redemption is by no means typical of Sealsfield's treatment of the fate of the Indians, since the novel also contains passages in which the author – unlike the vast majority of his contemporaries — paints an empathetic picture of what banishment and persecution meant for the Indians themselves. Thus Tokeah's lament, with its biblical echoes, goes well beyond the usual stereotypes of 'Indian language' encountered in literature from James Fenimore Cooper up to and including Karl May. Tokeah relates how, after the Whites had overrun their land and become as numerous as the buffalo in the hunting grounds of the Cumanchees, his brethren had risen up and been 'broken and struck down'. And he continues: 'Their white bones . . . are now covered with earth, and their blood is no longer to be seen. Their lands are no more their own, the canoes of the white men paddle on their rivers, their horses run on broad roads through the country, their traders have overrun it . . . Tokeah has seen the holy ground, and the burnt villages of his people.'[45]

The affective moment of identification which allows Sealsfield to express the innermost thoughts of the chief of the Oconees is, it seems to me, the experience of exile, which, at the end of his life, Tokeah articulates one last time in a kind of eulogy for the lost world of his ancestors. He was, he says, born as the chief of a mighty people and the master of the boundless forests. Now, though, he stands like a fugitive at the final frontier. Like an outcast he now wanders in the wilderness, and seven summers have passed since he turned his back on the land where his forefathers dwelt[46] — approximately the same amount of time as had passed between Postl's own flight from Austria and his setting down these lines. The emotional connection between narrator and protagonist is there for all to see.

If, during the course of his later literary career, Sealsfield really had become an advocate for the Indian people, whose numbers continued to be decimated with unprecedented ruthlessness, he would have attained a unique position in nineteenth-century literature. As a committed son of the Josephinian Enlightenment, and as both a political and private agent of the dawning age of high capitalism, he is, however, convinced of the inherent logic of the historical tragedy unfolding before his eyes. Since what is happening is perceived as necessary and inevitable, ethical and moral questions simply do not arise. Darwin predicted that 'At some future period, not very distant as measured by centuries' – how drastically this remark underestimates the speed of development! – 'the civilized races of man will almost certainly exterminate and replace throughout the world the savage races.'[47] This prediction, anticipating without any sense of outrage the coming extermination, is the product of a system of ideas which, as Sternberger noted, made it possible to ignore the 'spectacle of a vast battlefield strewn with corpses', replacing the manifest 'senselessness of universal annihilation' with the presumptive '"sense" in the formation of ever more perfect surviving species'.[48] In accordance with this model, Sealsfield – who, in one passage in *The Indian Chief*, ascribes the 'melancholy' look in the eyes of the Indians to their awareness of the '[deep-felt] superiority of their [White] oppressors'[49]– had no doubt as to the 'higher sense' of the extermination of the 'savages'. In a characteristic late nineteenth-century commentary, Gottschall, also without the slightest qualm, describes Sealsfield's contradictory attitude towards the fate of the Indians thus: 'The elegy for a doomed race finds the most moving expression in this by nature dull and sullen people; the lament of the simple feelings for nature and *Heimat* chimes with the lament which the necessary inevitability governing the history of the peoples [*Völkergeschichte*] imposes upon thoughtful observation.'[50] Whether the thoughtful observer really was 'filled with mourning for the irredeemable victims of the *Weltgeist*',[51] though, must remain doubtful, since this mourning tends to be mentioned in the same breath as the 'triumph of the progressive spirit'.[52] The devastating consequences of such ambivalence, which even today essentially characterizes the inwardly moralistic, outwardly amoral bourgeois way of thinking, can be discerned at several points in Castle's biography. According to Castle, Sealsfield — in contrast to Cooper, who used the Indians merely as local colour — accurately sums up the 'race problem': 'the inevitable retreat, though brought about by means of cumulative injustice, of the redskins before the Whites, the retreat of the primitive legitimate owners of the land before the intruders possessed of a higher degree of civilization, and of a superior system of state organization'.[53] If one considers that, in all probability, Castle set down these lines about the absolute necessity of extermination in Vienna in 1944, at a time when the annihilation of the Jewish people was well under way, one may truly grasp something of the workings of the so-called *Weltgeist*. Castle also offers an explanation as to why Sealsfield, despite his evident sympathy for the Indians, is still able to take the view that their extermination is inevitable. The reason, as Castle, here in absolute agreement with Sealsfield, notes, is their inability to adapt and their reluctance to assimilate and allow themselves to be civilized.[54] Since, however, tolerance is only extended to those who demonstrate themselves capable of bourgeois improvement, the Indians, who epitomize the threatening 'Other', must needs be eradicated. That, though, does not mean that they cannot first be 'registered' by the ethnographic gaze, which is interested in nothing more keenly than a species on the brink of extinction. The 'softly lit tableaux' of Indian life which so struck Gottschall about Sealsfield's works[55] are examples of that technique of 'literary photography which was invented long before the chemical process',[56] which not only seeks to capture, one last time, the endangered object, but in the process often identifies it as such for the first time.

Sealsfield's racism, in no way unusual but, rather, entirely typical of its time, is also demonstrated in the way he classifies people and nations in a hierarchical system according to their alleged viability and potential for future survival. On the lowest rung of all are the true savages and uncivilized tribes, then come the semi-domesticated Negroes [sic] and Creoles, and then, not far above them, the Mexicans. Colonel Morse, who occupies the position of narrator in *Das Cajütenbuch* [*The Cabin Book*], describes them as 'dwarfish, spindle-legged fellows . . . with tremendous whiskers, beards, and mustache, and a habit of knitting their brows', scarcely taller 'than our American boys of twelve or fourteen'; inferior figures, then, 'all of whom' – thus Morse – 'I could have put to flight with my riding-whip'.[57] The Spaniards, with their olive complexions, also get short shrift from Sealsfield; the French, too, are already on the way down, and the English are in the process of betraying their glorious past in favour of a shabby self-interest. The highest rank in this taxonomy of psychological and physiological national characteristics is occupied by the Germans, in other words the Americans of Germanic origin. Sengle has noted that, for Sealsfield, the Germans in the Habsburg state represent, not just any people, but the chosen bearers of a Holy Empire.[58] In common with many proponents of the contemporary *Germanismus* [Germanism], Sealsfield was convinced that the hour of *Deutschtum* [Teutonism] had finally come. It is thus scarcely surprising that some really rather bizarre speculations became associated with the references to the new doctrine of salvation everywhere manifest in his work. In the *Vorlesungen über die moderne Literatur der Deutschen* [*Lectures on the Modern Literature of the German People*], for example, published in Sealsfield's lifetime, the Sealsfield admirer Dr Alexander Jung alludes to the theory that the works of the great unknown author Sealsfield 'can be ascribed to a school of educated Germans who are scattered in the worldwide diaspora [*Weltzerstreuung*] – albeit in the tragic sense of the word – so that it was precisely this school of diasporic Teutons [*Germaniden*] who composed the works of Sealsfield that so astonish the world'.[59] Following the waves of emigration from Germany from the nineteenth century onwards, the idea of a Germanic diaspora of the highest calling went hand in hand with the idea of America as the new *Heimat*. In Kürnberger's novel *Der Amerikamüde* [*The Man Tired of America*], the schoolteacher Benthal, a veteran of the Hambach Festival,[xiii] explains how, in the course of the great migration, the oppressed German people, initially despised in America also, will come to be the chosen people charged in future with the world mission – in the elaboration of which fantasy he draws an analogy between the German and the Jewish peoples. The Germans are, he maintains, still objects of contempt, and, like the Jews, threatened not only by persecution but also by a tendency to self-destruction – in which, however, they will not succeed, because 'they always spring up again alive from the ground to which they sank lifeless.' At present, they are a mere 'ragged collection of people who are by no means yet a nation', but – thus Benthal – in them is being forged, 'as in a tenfold fire, the conviction that there is only one God, and the Germans are his chosen people!'[60] While Kürnberger does not necessarily endorse Benthal's opinions, Sealsfield takes his philosophy absolutely seriously. Already in Switzerland in the 1840s he freely confides to Zschokke his view that 'America [is] the citadel which guards the harbour, in whose bosom the riches of the whole world may lie safely at anchor,'[61] and that there, in America, lies 'the focus where the beams unite and whence they radiate';[61] America is thus the promised land of the Germans let down by their own history. Such trains of thought would come to determine the *Weltbild* [world view] of reactionary republicanism, whose outlines are already visible in Sealsfield's work. Europe is threatened by an increasing Asianization, but America will shine in the light of freedom, science and art.[62]

Texas, *God's Own Country*, was the territory where the doctrine of German–Anglo-Saxon superiority became the cornerstone of a political praxis as ruthless as it was self-righteous[63] – a territory, as it says in the preface to the *Cajütenbuch*, where 'the German race has once again, through the foundation of a new Anglo-American state on Mexican soil, prevailed at the expense of the mixed Latin one.'[64] One of the most dubious aspects of the reactionary tendencies in the *Cajütenbuch* is perhaps the narrator's comment – with the evident approval of Sealsfield – that the Texas Revolution, among other things, gave to men 'banished from the States on account of murder' the opportunity to '[bear] their burden like men, willing to repent it like men, to make up for it against the Mexicans'.[65] The description of the decisive battle, where 'in less than ten minutes [. . .] nearly eight hundred of the enemy were shot, struck, and knocked down',[66] is a convincing illustration of the doctrine subscribed to by Sealsfield that 'States and kingdoms [are] founded . . . by open brute force on the field of battle.'[67] This is justified by the sophistic argument that 'the right of the stronger, with all its wrong, brings in its train much good.'[68] By way of example, Sealsfield cites the way '[t]he seizing by force of the wilderness of Massachusetts and Virginia has laid the foundation for one of the greatest states of modern times.'[69]

Political expansionism appears, if one twists the argument a little, as merely one instrument in a far more fundamental confrontation between mankind and nature. Ultimately, the frontier ideology came about through the implementation of organized human violence against nature. While untouched nature is still praised here and there in Sealsfield's work as an immaculate divine world untainted by sinful human hand, the secret power of his much vaunted descriptions of nature does not rely on such rather conventional formulations for its effect. Sealsfield apprehends Nature as the quintessential Other, something which must be broken if one is not to be broken by it. The antagonistic relationship between man and nature, the full force of whose destructive potential was only really unleashed with the onset of the capitalist market economy, is exemplified in a well-known passage in the *Cajütenbuch* in which the narrator very nearly loses his life among the boundless beauty of the Jacinto prairies. This passage is immediately preceded by a description of the brute force used to break in wild horses in Texas. 'When the animal is caught', it says,

> [h]is eyes are bound; a frightful bit, more than a pound in weight, is placed in his mouth; and then he is mounted by a rider with spurs six inches in length on his feet, and is forced into a swift gallop. If he attempts to rear, a single [. . .] pull at this bit is quite sufficient to tear his mouth in pieces, and make the blood stream in torrents. I have seen

horses' teeth broken like matches by this barbarous bit. The poor animal winces, groans, from anguish and pain, but in vain; and thus wincing and groaning, he is fiercely spurred and ridden until he is ready to drop. Then, for the first time, he is allowed a quarter of an hour to breathe, after which he is brought back the same distance. If he sinks or breaks down during the ride, he is driven away or knocked down as useless; but, in a contrary case, he is marked with a burning iron, and dismissed loose on the prairie. From henceforth there is no particular difficulty in taking him. The wildness of the horse is quite tamed, but in its place is formed violence and malice, of which it is difficult to conceive any idea.[70]

There can be few passages which better demonstrate the relationship between man and nature in the first half of the nineteenth century. Within the narrative, it has the function of providing the motivation for Colonel Morse's headlong pursuit into the prairie. One of the most malicious of the beasts has thrown him, and in his rage he leaps on to another horse to chase after it, with never a second thought for the fact that, with the prairie extending seventy miles in all directions, without a single landmark he is as good as lost. This truly wide field[xiv] is all the more dangerous in that its beauty entices one to venture ever deeper into it. Morse sees around him nothing but a carpet of flowers, 'the most variegated carpet of flowers – red, yellow, blue, and violet' that he has ever seen, 'millions of the most beautiful prairie roses, tuberoses, dahlias, and China-asters', an extraordinary magnificence 'which appeared in the distance like rainbow upon rainbow extending over the horizon'.[71] Yet the feeling Morse experiences at this sight is not one of joy but 'akin to the most painful anxiety',[72] for he has in fact stumbled into one of nature's traps, 'a real Eden . . . having this in common with Paradise – that in it one is easily misled'.[73] Seduced and intoxicated by nature, even the most experienced and upstanding of men may stray from the right path, riding around in circles like madmen until they drop exhausted from the saddle. [August von] Platen's famous lines 'Wer die Schönheit angeschaut mit Augen, ist dem Tode schon anheimgegeben' ['He who gazes upon beauty / is already rendered unto death'] would be a fitting motto for this constellation, in which the misogynistic reflex of a male-dominated world [*Männerwelt*] governed by violence is projected on to a nature which – like Woman – is perceived as hostile. Put slightly differently, one might also say of nineteenth-century man, whose prototype Sealsfield in many respects represents, that as he becomes progressively – and ever more rapidly – integrated into society, nature increasingly becomes a foreign country, a place of exile. If, then, he needs to be redeemed from something, it is from nature, and, as if that were not enough, nature too has to be saved from itself, 'redeemed', as a singular turn of phrase in *The Indian Chief* has it, 'from luxuriant wildness'.[74] For the expansionist mindset, the redemption of nature can only be effected by the use of violence. Only through violence [*Gewalt*] does chaos become order; and this transposition legitimizes the use of violence as a quasi-divine act of creation. At the beginning of the *Cajütenbuch* is a description of Galveston Bay, already cited above. Beyond this bay, the land is so flat that it only appears 'like a line stretching out into the sea' and 'disappears behind the lightest wave; the waving grass resembles the waves of the equally green coastwater; so that it really requires a sharp eye to discern the one from the other.'[75] Even once ashore, one has the impression of still being on the open sea. Nowhere is there any boundary, 'neither tree nor hill, neither house nor farm'.[xv] It is like the world at the beginning of creation, where land and water are not yet divided. Whoever arrives here believes it his mission to complete the apparently incomplete work by making the strange familiar, if needs be by violent means. The significance of Sealsfield's novels, and in particular of their descriptions of nature, lies not so much in the detail and accuracy of representation – such as it is – repeatedly noted by contemporary and later critics, as in the fact that, in common with the burgeoning genre of travel literature, they offer up the most remote and untouched regions to the imagination of the European reading public. Sealsfield's descriptions of nature arose at precisely that critical juncture at which nature finally ceased to be the natural home of mankind. The ever more elaborate depictions of precisely this provocative beauty and untouchability could be identified – in very similar manner to what Foucault did for the discourse on sexuality – as the means of its subjugation and extirpation.

Postl, the *déraciné par excellence*, blown hither and thither by the times, left Switzerland once more for the United States in 1853, less with the intention of spending the rest of his days in his first adoptive *Heimat* or of collecting material for further literary works than out of a concern for his capital, largely invested in American shares, which on account of the turbulent political situation were subject to extreme fluctuations in value. In 1858, disillusioned with the changes in the Union, he returned to Switzerland, bought a house in the vicinity of Solothurn and began to wait for the end. The gathering storm clouds of the American Civil War only served to heighten Postl's fears regarding his investments, already acute, to the point of a positively feverish fear of poverty,[76] and the Austrian defeats in northern Italy also appeared to contribute to his increasingly depressive state of mind – all of which would seem to suggest a continuing emotional attachment to the *Heimat* so long ago forsaken. If Postl did not once return to Austria from Switzerland, this was – as Max Brod noted in his book on the Prager Kreis [Prague Circle] – most likely due to the fact that 'an Austrian cleric who had sworn a vow of poverty was, according to Austrian law, not able dispose of his assets by will.'[77] Thus Postl was forced to choose between definitively taking leave of his mother country and – were his identity to be discovered – the possible transfer of his monetary assets to the now vehemently loathed Catholic Church. Nor – as various recollections from the Solothurn years show – were his domestic arrangements such as would have made life easier for a man of almost seventy. In his later years, Postl twice attempted to come by a wife. First, he attempted to court a young girl in Stein am Rhein who sold cigars in her father's shop; then, during his final stay in New York, the widow of a German banker. Castle proffers a few insights into Postl's idiosyncratic mode of courtship, a mixture of exaggerated promises, attempts at blackmail, open threats and curses.[78] It is hardly surprising, then, that he should have emerged from these farcical episodes a bachelor, finally having to make do with a Swiss housekeeper who was clearly capable of responding to his importunities with equal incivility.

The fact that Postl steadfastly remained incognito to the very end was – the reasons identified by Brod aside – probably also due to the fact that, during the long years of exile, he had become an abstraction even to himself, and beyond the cipher 'Charles Sealsfield – der Große Unbekannte' ['Charles Sealsfield – The

Great Unknown'], no longer had a clear idea of who he really was. After his death, little by way of personal possessions was found in his house: no letters, no manuscripts, scarcely even any books. There exists only a single photograph of him, taken by a Solothurn photographer in 1863. It shows a rather square head – Lower Austrian, not Slavic, as Castle is at pains to point out.[79] His expression is at once animated and embittered. The most striking feature is the huge protruding left ear, a literally enormous defect which must have caused Postl a great deal of grief during his lifetime. We know that, in his last years, peering over the edge of the newspaper in the Solothurn museum, Postl was wont to give vent to misanthropic observations, and on one occasion made the comment 'Beware all those whom God has marked.'[80] The possibility cannot be ruled out that he included himself in this number, and that he restricted his existence in this way out of a kind of self-hatred. Either way, his actual, as well as his moral, physiognomy remains ill-defined, a fact which naturally also gave rise to all manner of speculation after his death. For example, in his *Erinnerungen an Sealsfield*[81] [*Recollections of Sealsfield*], the Hungarian writer Kertbeny, to whom Postl disclosed a few things in the course of conversations in Solothurn, started the rumour that Sealsfield was an Austrian Jew. On this, Gottschall commented that Kertbeny's motives were completely untenable. This far-fetched hypothesis is, however, not without a certain logic, inasmuch as it finally and irrevocably made an exile of Karl Postl.

Westwards – Eastwards:

Aporia of German-Language Tales from the Ghetto

> Das Grauen bildet den durchweg unbemerkten Untergrund der Rührung, die sich am Genre labt.
>
> Dolf Sternberger, *Panorama oder Ansichten vom 19. Jahrhundert*

> Horror is the unnoticed undertow of the compassion which feasts on genre . . .
>
> Dolf Sternberger, *Panorama of the Nineteenth Century*[i]

In the Crown Lands [*Kronländer*] of the Austrian monarchy, the slow pace of economic development meant that the bourgeois emancipation of the Jews inaugurated by the Edicts of Tolerance made only very gradual progress. During the *Vormärz*, and even after 1848, reforms that had already been enshrined in law, such as the right to acquire land, were variously suspended or curtailed.[1] Despite such setbacks, and even though full legal equality for the Jews was not achieved until 1897,[ii] during these decades, generally characterized by a liberal optimism, many changes came about, both in material conditions and in attitudes that for centuries had remained virtually untouched by the vicissitudes of history. In particular, the right to free movement – even before the great wave of westward migration began in the eastern provinces of the Reich – meant that, in the Bohemian lands in particular, something like an internal migration took place as the Jewish population moved from rural communities into the towns and cities; a development which broke with generations of settled residence in one place, and which was a major factor in the emergence – motivated by the émigré's last backward glance – of something like a Jewish *Heimatliteratur* in German. This genre, some aspects of which will be examined below, is – as could scarcely be otherwise – marked by profound ambivalences. The longing for the new bourgeois home also contains a nostalgic regret for the world left behind, and a certain uneasy sense that the opening of the ghetto – for so long the only abode possible – would now begin to pave the way for a new diaspora.

One of the first exponents of the new genre was Leopold Kompert,[iii] born in 1822 into a Jewish family who had been resident in Münchengrätz [Mnichovo Hradiště] in Bohemia for well over a century. Like his brothers, Kompert was obliged to leave his home when barely more than a child, since his father's small business was unable to support the whole family. Via Prague and Budapest, he arrived in Vienna, where, thanks to an extensive, albeit rather mediocre body of writing, over the years he achieved a not insignificant status in this culturally rather insignificant era. Kompert, like most of the representatives of the progressive party at the time, was inclined towards a German nationalist view, reflected also in his long years of tireless activity in the *Schillerstiftung* [Schiller Foundation]. However, Kompert's literary importance lies not so much in the pieces he wrote in accordance with this political stance – often somewhat schematic, both ideologically and formally – as in his early sketches and stories from the ghetto, which were first published as a loose series from 1849 onwards and later appeared in numerous collections. Kompert brings to these stories the feeling which may have motivated him to start writing in the first place, namely the painful attachment to something one knows to be already irretrievably lost. His sketches from the ghetto are thus not intended for the entertainment or edification of those back home, to whom the literary portrayal of their lives would have meant little; rather, they are written for those already so far away from the ghetto that a memento of their humble origins had an important sentimental value – for which reason the sketches and stories initially appeared as small prose vignettes in the *Jahrbuch für Israeliten* [*Israelite Yearbook*], a decidedly bourgeois institution, as indeed the title makes clear.

That Kompert's sketches had another purpose besides the reverential recollection of the lost *Heimat* is indicated by the explanations of Jewish customs and expressions embedded in the texts, explanations which would have been superfluous even for Jews already far from home. The intended audience of these annotations is the non-Jewish bourgeoisie, whose image of Jewish life – generally informed by rather far-fetched and prejudiced notions – these quasi-ethnographic texts are intended to correct. The nineteenth century had, as is well known, an almost insatiable desire for the strange and the exotic, appealing and appalling at one and the same time. In this context, the so-called ethnographic tale is chiefly of interest because, in assiduously depicting what is 'characteristic', it engages in a rather suspect mediation between, on the one hand, scientific study, and on the other crass caricature. Kompert's tales of the ghetto are no exception here, although doubtless the question of whether 'the amalgamation of the Jews with the people among whom they live can and should be accomplished'[2] was one that continued to preoccupy him to the end of his life.

The difficult conflicting feelings encountered by the Jewish writer returning to the world of an almost forgotten Jewish way of life, in order to file reports to his bourgeois readership, are clearly demonstrated in Kompert's story *Der Dorfgeher* [*The Peddler*], in which Emanuel, who had years ago left his home town to study in Vienna, returns incognito as a Sabbath guest [*Sabbatgast*] to his parents' house, where he catches a glimpse of his own past in the person of his younger brother. Emanuel undertakes this in many respects cruel experiment because he wants to give his bourgeoise fiancée, Klara, as lifelike an account as possible of his origins, perhaps in order to show her – for whom culture and civilization are a birthright – what she means to him, the Jewish pretender [*Aspirant*]. Seen from Vienna, the ghetto had come to seem to Emanuel a dark and distant place,[3] but on his return, as Kompert notes, reflecting on his own position, he finds himself 'so confused by the conflict in his soul that he often forgot that this man was his father. Instead, he saw a stranger with a mysterious essence he had to examine and penetrate to prepare interesting comments for his Clara.'[4] The dubious process by which the secrets of the once familiar, now strange, face are to be extracted is, for Kompert, indicative of an attitude oscillating between affection and aversion, a dilemma he himself was unable to reconcile. While there is a desire truly to return home, and 'for memory . . . to sound all the bells of childhood', there is at the same time also a curious aversion, such as for example when the 'disorderliness, [. . .] the complete independence with which those assembled were crying out their prayers' in the synagogue, 'offends' Emanuel's 'soul'.[5] The soul is, as we now know, the seat of bourgeois reason and orderliness, and thus it is only with considerable effort that Emanuel manages to justify to himself and Klara the uninhibited nature of Jewish religious practice, 'this breathless, unmelodious bawling and pagoda-like bending and bowing down'.[6]

As a counterpoint to the representation of certain atavistic aspects of Jewish life, marked by a distinct aversion, the tales from the ghetto also contain numerous transfigurations of Jewish family life of a decidedly sentimental nature, especially in the scenes where the family is gathered around the table on the Sabbath. What is important here is not, as one might initially expect, the holiness of the Sabbath, but rather the way the family gathers together on this day. Clearly it is those aspects of Jewish custom most readily reconcilable with the bourgeois notion of order which, in retrospect, appear as if surrounded by a golden aura. For an author like Kompert, there was doubtless also the complication that those aspects of Jewish life most compatible with the bourgeois ideal were of less interest, ethnographically speaking, than the less readily comprehensible and apparently more eccentric forms of orthodox Judaism and life in the ghetto. The fascination is exerted by the 'exotic' aspects, an example of an otherness on the brink of disappearance which is generally perceived as negative by the observer. Kompert's story *Die Kinder des Randars* [*The Randar's Children*] tells how Moschele, who has grown up in a Christian village as the son of a Jewish innkeeper and, now at grammar school living in a rented room in the Bunzlau ghetto, regards his present surroundings as being as stuffy as the grave.

The peace of his home village appears to him like the island of the blessed, when, returning from a visit home, he is once again confronted with 'this constant restlessness, this shouting, bargaining and haggling . . . The false notes in this hurly-burly of the ghetto were terrible to his ears. Even the wildest noise in his father's inn was less unpleasant. "These people", he said to himself, "are certainly not drunk, and yet sometimes it seems that way." At such times a sense of deep anxiety would overcome him.'[7]

In such passages concerned with 'ethnographic objectivity', the reflex of a pre-existing vocabulary of aversion spontaneously gains the upper hand. The 'realistic' snapshots of the obscure inhabitants of the ghetto all look the same. Susan Sontag has described photography as the modern counterpart of artificial ruins. Every photograph, she claims, in the same way as the artificial ruins of the Romantic age, is suggestive of the past.[8] This persuasive analogy is just as true of photography as of the literary genre sketches which anticipate it. In the process of depiction, the world of the ghetto is already consigned to the past, even before its dissolution has properly got under way.

Just as the social reality of the ghetto disappears into the remembered images – whether painted in dark or bright colours – so too the vision of the future *Heimat* Jerusalem comes, in Kompert's tales, to epitomize complete irreality. At the aforementioned Randar's inn, there occasionally appears, at ever greater intervals, a *schnorrer* who many years ago had set out from the Wilna ghetto and who, without ever getting further than the Bohemian villages, each time claims Jerusalem is the goal of his never-ending journey. This Polish *luftmensch*, who left Wilna the day after his wedding still in his wedding clothes,[9] within the story occupies the role of a quaint eccentric, amiable but obsolete. No one now pays the slightest attention to his enthusiastic tales of the wonderful city shimmering in the distance – no one, that is, apart from the boy Moschele, who, having solemnly taken leave of his parents, sets off one morning with Mendel across the fields outside the village in the direction of Jerusalem. Only when they have gone quite some way and Moschele shows no signs of turning back does Reb Mendel send him home. 'Do you really think', Mendel says, 'that I can take you to Jerusalem? You need to be a lot older before that happens. But for now don't break my heart, Moschele, go home! Your father and mother will be worried about you.'[10] Kompert supplies a moving comment to this farewell scene, which leaves Moschele equally disappointed and relieved: 'Children often have a wonderful instinct which tells them where their blissful folly ends; they sense from the note that blows down their house of cards when it is time to stop wishing. Even more wonderful is the docility and mute heroism when they are left standing amid the ruins of their happiness.'[11] Abandoning a happiness no one has ever seen, the imaginary *Heimat*, the boy turns around and sets off back home. When he reaches the village he has left only a short while before, he is seized by a great sadness, like one who has returned from far, far away. What Kompert describes, in these comforting lines, as a wonderful instinct, the ability to give up one's dreams and to forsake happiness, is, in fact, nothing other than the no less wonderful efficacy of bourgeois reason, imbibed at an early age, which we can recognize by its fruits of docility and mute heroism.

This scene of Kompert's seems to me particularly significant not least because a very similar scene recurs in one of Franz Kafka's earliest prose works, entitled *Kinder auf der Landstraße* [*Children on the Country Road*]. Here too, at the centre of the story there is a young boy who, almost submerged in his rural surroundings, dreams of the far-off mountains, or even just the air above him. It is a summer evening, and some of his friends entice him to leave the house at a late hour for an adventure on the country road. From a bridge over a rushing stream, with the water dashing against the stones below, tirelessly, as if night were not fast approaching, out of the corners of their eyes they catch sight of a train emerging from behind a clump of trees. 'All the carriages were lit up and no doubt the windows were down'[12] – an image which holds the promise of a great journey. Moved by all this, the young hero – still scarcely more than a child – leaves his friends behind. He goes back the way he has come, but turns off and makes for that city in the south of which it is said in the village that the people who live there never sleep. Kafka's story does not give any clues to the outcome of this departure. Only this much is certain, that the boy searching for the city in the south wants to block out the gathering shadows of the night in a different way from just going to sleep like the rest of the world. As far as Moschele is concerned, though, we know that after the transformation effected by his bourgeois education he takes the German name Moritz and 'as a doctor in a quiet ghetto in Bohemia heals sick bodies and souls'.[13] The reference to the sick souls is probably meant to suggest that, for Moritz, taking the so-called light of reason to the darkness of so-called superstition counts as part of his duties as a doctor, a view which Kafka could surely no longer have wholeheartedly shared.

The gloomy world of the ghetto, in which, since the middle ages, the Jews 'were obliged to learn the art of existing and living without land or property, without house and home, without rights and freedom, without light and air',[14] is, as we see in the example from Kompert, ultimately transformed, under the benign influence of bourgeois reason, into a peaceful idyll, evidently no longer disturbed by intolerable noise and false notes. This quietening, too, is a sign of dissolution. It is notable that some thirty years later, in Max Hermann Friedländer's memoir, *Tiferet Jisrael*, from which the last quotation is taken, the ethnographic portrayals of the inner lives of the Jews can only be described in the past tense. By the year of its publication, these descriptions clearly were no longer current. They document an identity, or rather an otherness, already on the point of vanishing, if indeed it had not already vanished, although it still persisted in the eastern provinces of the Reich, where the same process would take place a generation later. Thus in the stories of Karl Emil Franzos, collected and published in 1877 under the title *Die Juden von Barnow* [*The Jews of Barnow*], the ghetto still appears as a remote, outcast part of the town extending into the 'unhealthy marshes near the river. It is always dark and gloomy there, however brightly the sun may shine, and dark pestiferous vapours infect the air, although the meadows beyond may be full of flowers.'[15] As in Kompert's tale, the dispelling of the gloom which surrounds the dwellings of exile is primarily evoked in the depiction of the Sabbath rituals, which fill 'the dismal irregularly built houses of the Ghetto . . . [with] thousands of candles, and thousands of happy faces. The Sabbath has begun in the hearts of these people and in their rooms, a common and usual occurrence, and yet a mysterious and blessed influence that drives away all that is poor and mean in everyday life. To-day, every hovel is lighted up, and every heart made glad.'[16] The sentimental tone in which the light and reflections of the Sabbath candles are described and which, in comparable Yiddish texts, nowhere appears in such glowing homiletic terms, gives an idea of how distant from the object of his description the author has already become, concerned less now with the empathetic evocation of a thousand-year-old ritual than with the secular miracle of the Enlightenment. For this reason, too, the mysterious revelation which takes place on the Sabbath is compared to an 'everyday natural event', like the day which has already dawned in the west, and before which in the east, as Franzos notes with some displeasure, unfortunately no one yet raises his hat.[17iv] The theological image of the lightening of the darkness thus becomes a metaphor for the dawn of the bourgeois era, which views itself as the Sabbath of human history.

One might conclude from this that Franzos's stories, many of which are openly didactic, are intended for the inhabitants of the ghetto who, dwelling in the darkness of ignorance, are most in need of enlightenment. However, Franzos expressly states that he wrote them 'for the Western reader',[18] which is to say not only for their spiritual edification, but also as a warning against any attacks of regressive sentimentality which might befall them. Franzos may be said to have been all the more successful in this last aim in as much as his often drastically negative depictions are the more convincing for being portrayed against a generally balanced background, which makes a point of showing – often in a most impressive fashion – the bravery, generosity and truth-loving nature of the Jewish people. What is more, while very modest about his accomplishments as a short-story writer, as an ethnographer Franzos demands that his words be taken at face value.[19v] Thus when he takes the Jewish (or Christian) reader from the West by the hand and leads them through 'the sea of mud in the small town', and shows them 'the stuffy houses with their kaftan-wearing, dirt-encrusted inhabitants', in whose 'angular faces are etched ascetic zealotry or cunning avarice',[20] this depiction, with its phraseology bordering on prejudice, will have been read, coming as it does from such a reliable ethnographer [*Kulturschilderer*], as an unvarnished report of the facts. In his short stories, Franzos reserves particularly harsh criticism for everything he perceives as the obduracy of orthodox religion; his castigation of the representatives of the Hasidic tradition is positively spiteful, presenting their 'worshipful company' to his readers as hunched over their large tomes, rocking back and forth and muttering under their breath as they read, or else 'discussing the things of the world in strident tones'; or even, as is inevitable in such 'breeding grounds of idleness', reaching for the brandy bottle.[21] With such deliberately pejorative depictions, Franzos believes himself to be a trailblazer of Enlightenment, a determined opponent of 'the most zealous enemies of light' and the 'most fanatical supporters of the old dark faith'.[22]

That great treasure house of experience and wisdom, the Hasidic tradition, which Martin Buber would later introduce to an unsuspecting Western readership, by 1870 was, on account of his ideological position, no longer accessible to Franzos. Nevertheless, he remains committed to the Jewish passion for learning, even if its orthodox, or rather Hasidic, variants seem to him only to further the cause of obscurantism. Again and again Franzos invokes how an 'unquenchable longing for knowledge'[23] provides the impetus to leave the ghetto. The learning of German – the medium for the acquisition of knowledge – and the relinquishing, at least in public, of Yiddish, which Franzos regards as a perverted jargon – gives access to the letter writer [*Briefsteller*] as well as to the general Austrian statute books, and thus paves the way for the transition from small-scale retail to true commerce. However, the passion for learning is at its most notable when it comes not only to practical knowledge, but to the assimilation of Western, that is to say German, *Geisteskultur* [intellectual culture]. Anything that comes to hand is voraciously consumed – 'Heine's *Reisebilder*, Klopstock's *Messiade*, *Kaiser Joseph* by Louise Mühlbach, the new Pitaval, Eichendorf's [sic] poems and the novels of Paul de Kock'. 'She read them all,' we learn of Esther, the daughter of the Shylock of Barnow, 'devouring them much as a hungry wolf does a lamb. She read them in the shop whenever her father's back was turned, and [then] at night.'[24] In this manner, by reading and studying, and spurred on by the ambition sanctioned by the Jewish tradition of overtaking one's teacher as soon as possible, the dedicated pupils are in a very short time able to attain the level of education of the average European – a process described by Kafka in the *Bericht an eine Akademie* [*Report to an Academy*].

In this process of transition to the other culture, driven by a ruthless urge for learning, a special place is occupied by the life and works of Friedrich Schiller. In his sketch *Schiller in Barnow*, Franzos relates the story of Aaron Tulpenblüh, a poor tailor's son from Brody who, starting from great poverty and deprivation, has 'studied his way up' to the point where, at the age of thirty, he is in a position to return to his home town as a doctor. Melanie Feiglstock, beside whom he is soon standing under the wedding canopy, requests as a wedding gift a small private library – Schiller, Börne, Heine – and also that Aaron should henceforth call himself Arthur. Both wishes are granted. However, Melanie soon has no time to read anything apart from the *Illustrierte Frauenzeitschrift* and the *Neue Freie Presse*. Arthur, on the other hand, in one of his few leisure hours, takes down a volume of Schiller from the shelf and immediately becomes engrossed. Soon he feels 'like a short-sighted man who, by putting on a pair of spectacles, can find beauty and life in the very things that seemed dead and hideous to the naked eye. And truly, what splendid things he perceived; he saw the stream of enthusiasm flowing, the roses of love flowering, and the shady bower of a proud and noble philosophy arching overhead.'[25] The emotional and intellectual world of German idealism as the sukkah, a leafy bower[vi] in whose shade one could imagine oneself finally to have arrived home after the long journey through the desert: a truly moving image in view of the ingratitude with which such trust was shortly to be rewarded. The extent of the as it were festive, even solemn identification on the part of the Jews with the ideals of German *Bildung*, as represented by Schiller, is also shown years later in a charming vignette in one of Leopold von Sacher-Masoch's tales from *Jewish Life*.[26] There we read of a poor bookbinder, Simcha Kalimann, whose whole passion is books and learning and who, on catching sight in the house of a well-off customer of the picture of Schiller in Karlsbad riding on a donkey, bursts into tears. This intense emotional identification with the trailblazer of idealism and its values is, however, not only due to the fact that Schiller's writings embodied a solemn and fervent promise of freedom and justice – by comparison with which the Austrian literature of the time had little to offer – but was rather due also to the fact that the Jews in the Austrian provinces had no way of knowing about the political realities of the *Vormärz* and the years after 1848 in Germany, whereas they naturally had a very clear idea of the uncertainties of the 'constantly fluctuating system' that surrounded them, the 'brutal Belcredi regime' which determined the political climate after 1848, as well as the fact that 'justice in Galicia . . . lay largely in inert and corrupt hands.'[27] As a consequence, as Franzos summarizes in a piece on reactionary Austrian politics,[28] 'most of us' – by which he means the generation of 1848 and their disciples – 'have remained good Germans.'[29] That such declarations of loyalty made the already complicated social and psychological position of assimilated Jews yet more confusing goes almost without saying.

It is hardly surprising that stories on the subject of leaving the ghetto and entering the world of the bourgeoisie should place particular emphasis on the ideas of love and the realities of marriage. For Franzos, the starting point is the Jewish custom of marriage 'without mutual attraction', which he deplores in the strongest terms, and which, for example in the tale *Das höhere Gesetz* ['The Higher Law', translated as *Chane*], he contrasts with the 'natural emotion' of love. At the centre of this story, shot through with finely nuanced feelings of resignation, is Chane, a young Jewish woman who – although very fond of Nathan, the man to whom she is married – is, as the saying goes, passionately in love with Negrusz, the district judge living in the same house. Having learned to read and write German in order to help out in the shop, and thus in a position, from her place behind the counter, to catch a glimpse of the enticing world of the bourgeoisie, Chane sees in the judge – who is completely above reproach – the very embodiment of all her indistinct longings. The story follows the pattern familiar from so many bourgeois love stories and dramas which show how even class barriers are no obstacle to true love, and where the lovers always find each other in the end – even if only in death. The fact that, in Franzos's story, the barriers to be overcome are not those between the bourgeoisie and the nobility, but those between Jewish and Christian middle-class citizens, makes little difference to the scenario. In both cases we see the emancipation of emotions, the public baring of the soul of someone who until shortly before no one had imagined even had a soul at all. Much of the early bourgeois literature on love is intended as a demonstration of the bourgeois capacity for love and suffering, a model which proved eminently useful as Jews gradually entered the world of bourgeois sensibility. Nor is it a coincidence that, when it comes to the singular spiritual and emotional growth which is at issue here, the model chosen to demonstrate this higher sensibility is invariably a woman. For it is, according to the 'natural law' of love, only women who are capable of achieving social advancement or assimilation through love; men can only gain entry to bourgeois society by demonstrating that they have the money and possessions commensurate with their aspirations. Seen from this angle, the transplanting of the bourgeois soul into the (female) Jewish breast, as advocated by Franzos, is perhaps after all a little dubious. To be more precise, the price the Jewish woman has to pay, over and above the assiduous cultivation of fine feelings, is that of her body, which, as can be seen in almost all of Franzos's stories, has to comply with clearly defined expectations, and, in an oft-repeated formulation, must be 'of slender yet voluptuous build'.[30]

The attentive reader may also be oddly struck by the fact that the huge effort which Franzos expends on the idea of love in the story of Chane Silberstein is not quite borne out in the course of the tale itself. The description of the marriage between Chane and Nathan, contracted 'without affection', seems to radiate, involuntarily it seems to me, far more warmth than what appears to be a rather chilly married relationship once Chane, having completed her emotional apprenticeship, appears at the side of her district judge as the bourgeoise Christine von Negrusz. Thus the true hero of the story is not so much Herr von Negrusz, with his aura of noble pallor, but the businessman Nathan, who, as high-minded as his famous namesake,[vii] without resentment releases poor Chane, no longer mistress of her feelings, from the marriage – an act of self-denial of which Nathan only becomes capable when he thinks back to his reading of Schiller's poems. Calling this to mind, Nathan comes to realize the true meaning of bourgeois love – namely renunciation [*Entsagung*].

The social advancement possible for female Jewish characters through the transaction of love is, as indicated above, not usually applicable to male Jewish protagonists. David Blum, in the story *Das Christusbild* [*The Picture of Christ*], left the ghetto as a young man and has advanced in society to the point where, almost a decade later and now called Friedrich Reimann, he occupies a position as doctor at the spa in Baden-Baden. The love which develops between him and a countess who is also spending time in Baden-Baden comes to grief when, after Friedrich has confessed to her the secret of his origins, Jadwiga cannot bring herself to elevate her Jewish friend to her own social status. Thereupon Friedrich Reimann travels further afield, to France, England and America, until at last he realizes that everything he has experienced is pointing back 'in the direction of home' in the 'midst of those people' whom he, the son of the rabbi destined to be their teacher, had left twelve years previously.[31] Returned from 'Americum', as they say in the ghetto, he puts aside his Western attire, dons traditional garb once more and devotes himself to caring for the sick and gathering herbs in the immediate vicinity of his place of birth. This story, though, also contains indications that Franzos's optimistic belief in progress was not entirely straightforward, sometimes giving way to another mood in which it is not the German bourgeoisie but the plains of

Podolia, long since left behind, which appear as the true *Heimat*. There is much in the story of David Blum which anticipates Kafka's *Castle*, where K., the Land Surveyor — like Blum a herbalist — returns to a place which is as strange as it is familiar. The return to the *Heimat*, however — as the tone of deep resignation in both texts makes clear — is a metaphor for death. The *Heimat* is the 'good place'. And the 'good place' is the Jewish cemetery, where 'the blue sky smiles down upon the little field with its fresh green grass and sweet-scented flowers.'[32] Kompert already laments the fact that the Jews have so little feeling for nature, a trait which Lucien Goldmann ascribes to the centuries-long exclusion of the Jewish people from the rural world.[33] Never — thus Franzos on this subject — does it 'occur [. . .] to the Eastern Jew to plant trees or sow annuals . . . only between the graves does the fresh green grass grow, only over the dead does the scent of flowers waft.'[34] For this reason, too, the natural congregation of the homecomer is in truth that of the dead. In rehearsal for this ending, unable to endure either the society of the ghetto or the machinery of assimilation, David seeks the company of the sick. Seen from this perspective, the secular history of his people again becomes the biblical *historia calamitatum* whose chronicles can be studied in the Jewish cemetery, where, as Franzos notes, a remarkable number of graves are inscribed with the same year of death, for example the one in which 'a Czartoryski hunted the Jews because there was so little game left in the neighbourhood'.[35] Inscribed in the chronicle of the cemetery are also the three terrible summers in which 'the wrath of God — the cholera — raged throughout the great plain. Grass makes more resistance against the scythe than these people did, in their narrow pestiferous streets.'[36] What is most noticeable about the cemetery in Barnow, however, is the disproportionately large number of graves for such a small community; none of them, as Franzos notes by way of explanation, is ever removed, since 'whoever has been given a resting place and headstone here, retains both, even the poorest, for ever.'[37] The inflections at the end of this quotation are as it were the syncopations of a scale of emotion which allows the author to give way to his repressed longings for home. The Jewish cemetery in Barnow, where even the most lowly has a right to dwell for all eternity, is situated on a hill from which one has a view in all directions.

> From thence one can see ten ponds, hard by which some villages are situated, whose houses, roofed with brown thatch, resemble collections of bee-hives; and finally, at the foot of the hill is the town, which has a very respectable appearance from there, although, in reality, it is neither more or less than a wretchedly dirty hole. One is able to breathe more freely when enjoying such an extensive view, such a wide horizon line. For to east, north and south the only limit is the sky, and on grey days the same is the case to the west. But when the air is clear and bright, one can see what looks like a curiously shaped blue-grey bank of cloud on the horizon. On seeing it for the first time one is inclined to believe that a storm is brewing there. But the cloud neither increases nor decreases in size, and though its outline may seem to shift now and then, it stands fast for ever – it is the Carpathian range of mountains . . .[38]

Franzos, who otherwise almost never attempts landscape descriptions, here, from his vantage point in the cemetery of Barnow, evokes the image of a rural *Heimat*, which all those who live in the ugly town at the foot of the hill, or those who were obliged to emigrate to the far-off cities of the West, would surely have been glad to call their own.

The twenty-six short tales of *Jewish Life* [*Jüdisches Leben*] which Leopold von Sacher-Masoch published in Mannheim in 1892 are, like the stories of Kompert and Franzos, intended for a Western readership. This copiously illustrated volume found a wide circulation as a kind of *Hausbuch* [house book or compendium] for the bourgeois Jewish family, not merely in German-speaking Central Europe but also, under the title *Contes Juifs*, in France. Leopold von Sacher-Masoch, who during his lifetime acquired a rather one-sided renown on account of his erotic fantasies about the lady in furs, and who was in actual fact an extremely bizarre and motley character, continuously gave rise to the most extravagant speculations about his person. His family tree, as he explains in an autobiographical sketch,[39] goes back to one Don Mathias Sacher, who in 1547 fought in the Battle of Mühlberg as a cavalry captain under Charles V. The Sacher family is then documented in Bohemia and, later, in the eastern provinces of the Empire in Lemberg [Lviv], where Leopold was born on 27 January 1836 – Mozart's birthday, as his autobiographical notes inform us. The curriculum vitae of this descendant of the Spanish–Austrian knight, which there is no space to go into further here, is quixotic in the extreme. With the image of his ideal woman in his head, Sacher-Masoch travels widely, turning up in Austria, Germany, Italy and France before retiring in the custody of his noble lady wife Hulda von Sacher-Masoch in a village in Upper Hesse. His unusual persona was so at odds with the late bourgeois order of things that, as he says himself, he was not only thought to be a

German, Austrian, Spaniard and Frenchman but also 'a Jew, a Hungarian, a Bohemian and even a woman'.[40] These wild conjectures were, no doubt, correct to the extent that Sacher-Masoch, in an age sinking into the most narrow-minded chauvinism, had an affinity for all peoples, but especially the Jewish one.

Sacher-Masoch's Jewish stories are written at a time when political anti-Semitism was rapidly gaining currency in Berlin and Vienna, and as such represent a consciously unfashionable *hommage*. However, Sacher-Masoch's identification with the Jewish people is probably motivated less by his own internationalism than by memories of his distant *Heimat* in Galicia, which he had in common with many of the Jews now living in the West. A specific impulse for his attachment to the Jewish people may also stem from the early impressions the young Leopold gained when accompanying his grandfather, Dr Franz Masoch – the first Christian doctor to visit Jewish patients in their homes – on visits to the Lviv ghetto; for the grandson, these excursions into another world, hand in hand with the doctor revered like a prophet, must have revealed a great deal of love and affection, thus preparing the ground for his own later empathy for and interest in the Jewish people and their fate.[41] Each of Sacher-Masoch's tales from *Jewish Life* takes place in a different country. From Palestine via Turkey and Russia, and thence to Poland, Rumania, Hungary and Germany, we come to Sweden and Denmark, Holland and England, to Italy, France and Switzerland. Since the tales are intended for the diaspora spreading gradually westwards, where '[for many] the old Jewish life is today merely a poetic memory like that of the Ghetto,'[42] they take the form partly of devotional objects, partly of literary confirmation texts, reassuring the bourgeois Jews of the West that they perhaps have more right to feel at home where they are living now than back in their former *Heimat*. Here too, then, the ambivalence is all-pervasive.

In his contemporary commentary on the tales from *Jewish Life*, Wilhelm Goldmann [sic = Goldbaum][viii] praises the freedom with which Sacher-Masoch places his colours, and the way his texts succeed in opening up the most wonderful vistas and landscapes. Indeed, this particular facility – despite the propensity for repeatedly trotting out gleaming golden ears of corn, boulder-strewn mountains, ancient pines and suchlike set pieces[43] – was, from the very start of his career, one of the unmistakable hallmarks of his prose. Ferdinand Kürnberger was so impressed by this aspect of Sacher-Masoch's earliest stories[44] that he compared them to the work of Turgenev, 'the Shakespeare of the sketch'.[45] However, the speculations that follow make clear how little the idea of an ecumenical community of peoples, by which Sacher-Masoch set such store, was compatible with the nationalist German expansionism of his literary champion. 'How would it be', Kürnberger writes, full of enthusiasm,

> if instead of the Great Russian Turgenev we had a Little Russian, that is to say someone from East Galicia, that is to say an Austrian, that is to say a German? How would it be if in this Austria, which has thus far failed so miserably to realize its vocation as a German nation, if at this time, when the different Austrian nationalities are in open rebellion against all that is German, a Slav-born writer from the banks of the Pruth were to send an excellent German *Novelle* to the banks of the Main and Neckar . . . if German literature conquered new easterly latitudes . . . annexing fresh new *Naturvölker* [indigenous peoples].[46]

An ominous way of thinking, to say the least, and yet one that sets out in the clearest possible terms what is happening at the time. For even a tale from the ghetto, written in German, becomes part of the vision of a process of Germanization, which, in the course of the bourgeois century – and to the chagrin of the increasingly numerous adherents of geopolitics – was so far from becoming a political reality in the east of Europe that a few generations later it was implemented by violent means.

In his commentary, Wilhelm Goldbaum further notes that, notwithstanding Sacher-Masoch's undoubted talent for creating rounded and lifelike characters, his hand is less sure when it comes to 'drawing the occupants of the Galician ghettos from life'.[47] It is easy, Goldbaum says, for the lines to become blurred, resulting in sentimental portraits and – albeit unintentionally – not a few 'caricatures'. However, the author's hand is unsteady not because, as Goldbaum writes, unlike the other composers of ghetto tales such as Kompert, Bernstein and Mosenthal, he is not himself Jewish – and hence at a greater remove from the subjects of his stories – but rather because the dichotomy of sentimental representation and caricature is an inherent weakness of the genre. Sacher-Masoch cannot quite be exonerated from the charge of sentimentality, since, even though he sometimes succeeds in capturing something approximating to the authentic voice of the people [*Volkston*], his stories for the Jewish *Hausfreund* [family friend][ix] are generally rather more didactic than is compatible with the rules of art. As far as caricatures are concerned, though, Sacher-Masoch is far less prone to these than even Kompert or Franzos. Only the illustrations, all contributed by Jewish artists, and which, so Sacher-Masoch hoped, would give the text a truly 'warm expression of life',[48] reveal the darker side of the sentimental genre, that fateful moment where it lapses into caricature. These illustrations make use of pretty much all the stylistic stock-in-trades available at the end of the nineteenth century: romantic night scenes, Biedermeier interiors by lamplight, rustic realism, *Gartenlaube*-style vignettes,^x images after the manner of the Nazarenes and Art Nouveau. The one constant element in the many heterogeneous images is the contrast between the beautiful young Jewish women and the old men with their goatee beards who, beneath that bourgeois symbol, the top hat, display a grinning monkey-face.[49] The beautiful young women of course represent the lost *Heimat*, but the ugly old men stand for the fear that, despite all one's best efforts, one is still not nearly bourgeois enough.

A generation later, just before the destruction of the Eastern Jewish world and the extermination of its inhabitants by the ranks of the German armies, going about the business of murder with true petty-bourgeois thoroughness, the novelist Joseph Roth — who, like Dr Aaron Tulpenblüh, hailed from Brody — takes a last look back at his Galician *Heimat*. In his story *Das falsche Gewicht* ['The False Weight', translated as *Weights and Measures*], published a few years before the *Anschluß*, Roth — who in the two brief decades of his writing career had seen any pragmatic political hopes dashed, one after another, and could now only believe in pure illusion — paints a picture of a country which since time immemorial has been slipping with incredible slowness ever further into oblivion. The outlines of the objects and characters in this text, set down in the simplest words, are of such clarity, the shadings and colours of a calm and impassive nature where scarcely anything stirs so wonderful, that their like is only glimpsed in those dreams of flight where one sometimes catches sight of regions long forgotten or never seen spread out beneath one in the most beautiful and vertiginous manner. On the very first page of the story – beginning, like a fairytale, with the words 'Es war einmal' ['Once upon a time'], Roth achieves, apparently without the slightest effort, a degree of concreteness seldom found in narrative literature. We see the Inspector of Weights and Measures, Anselm Eibenschütz, driving about in the region of Zlotogrod in a swift golden yellow gig drawn by a grey horse[xi] which, though blind in the left eye, is otherwise a stately beast from the stables of the civil authorities. Next to Eibenschütz sits the sergeant of gendarmerie Wenzel Slama, whose sad story is already familiar from *The Radetzky March*. 'On his sand-coloured helmet glittered the golden spike and the imperial double eagle. Between his knees projected his rifle with fixed bayonet atop. The Inspector held reins and whip.'[50] So it goes along, and already we can almost guess how it will end. Eibenschütz, originally from the small Moravian town of Nikolsburg [Mikulov], has, after serving many years in the army, ended up, along with his wife – whom, like many a retired non-commissioned officer, he had married who can say whether by mistake, for reasons of loneliness or for love – in this strangely empty countryside on the far side of which, as the story ultimately makes clear, begin the vast reaches of eternity. Things are set in motion when the Inspector is one day informed that his wife Regina, who spends her evenings sitting in the lamplight 'diligent, spiteful and embittered in her humility', working 'with two terrifying menacing needles' a 'dangerous poison green' piece of knitting – Eibenschütz's fate![51] – is deceiving him with the clerk Josef Nowak. A case of adultery, then, like so many before it in the literature of the bourgeois era, from Flaubert to Tolstoy and Fontane. Except that this aspect of the story here merits hardly a mention. Against the dissolution of the bourgeois dream of love in the realist literature of the nineteenth century, which is still largely rooted in the ideology of love, Roth sets the story of a male passion breaking all the bounds of convention. The focus and flashpoint of the passion which seizes the now solitary, and perhaps always solitary, Eibenschütz is the Bessarabian Gypsy woman Euphemia, who keeps house, or rather holds court, at the border tavern, a place from whence the road leads either to heaven or down into the underworld. As soon as she appears at the top of the stairs, Euphemia fixes her deep blue eyes on the Inspector. She is wearing a dress which is 'a kind of living, magic tent', which 'seemed to turn a soft, gentle cartwheel on each tread of the stairs',[52] the narrow shoes appearing beneath it. All this exerts on Eibenschütz, who believes he recognizes in Euphemia the first and only woman, a force he is neither willing nor able to resist. As the obedient servant of this miraculous being he – the Inspector whose job it is to check weights and measures – is soon helping Euphemia out behind the counter, serving customers. And finally he lies like a wretched animal in front of the threshold to her room. It is, however, not the case that Eibenschütz's humiliation at the hands of a woman shows the latter in a bad light. On the contrary, we gradually come to understand that once, in a different time, a set of rules held sway different from those of men – a regime in which the menfolk humbly shared a woman, as Eibenschütz does with the chestnut-roaster Sameschkin, who regularly stays at Euphemia's house in the winter months. Although at first Eibenschütz sees Sameschkin as a rival, in time he comes to know and understand him and begins 'to love him, as one loves a brother'.[53]

In the far-off land which Roth imagines, men's claims to power and possession dissolve of their own accord, love's exchanges are less exclusive, and in other transactions, too, in this Galician *Heimat*, things are not weighed and measured against each other, and little is bought and sold; instead, much is given, and even more forgiven. The pitiful commodities from the budget of our emotions, of which so much was made in bourgeois literature, seem, in the world Roth tells us about here, hardly worth the trouble of a regulated market economy. This is epitomized in the tiny shop run by Mendel Singer, which Eibenschütz and the gendarme Piotrak order to be closed for a few months following an inspection. This last official act leaves Eibenschütz with the feeling of having committed a great injustice, for the Singers' business – far removed from any rational commercial enterprise, consisting as it does only of a few onions, dried figs, nutmeg and raisins of dubious condition – was merely one component, almost negligible, of a completely different mode of life: the life of learning, to which Mendel Singer, crouched between the beds in the narrow room behind the shop, devotes himself day and night. Mendel Singer's studies, which are concerned not so much with carving a better way in this world as with, at most, a good way of leaving it, become, at the end of Roth's story, the measure by which it is shown that the Inspector, already humiliated by his passion, still has something to learn. When, at the end, a dying man, he is bound to a sledge and driven through the winter's night, he sees himself transformed into a trader who has so many false weights that the counter cannot hold them all. 'And at any moment the Inspector might come.'[54] And when the Great Inspector arrives, he looks 'a little like the Jew Mendel Singer'.[55] To show that he is saved, the Inspector Singer says to the trader Eibenschütz that all his weights are false and yet still true. The point of this parable of human generosity, springing from a pious hope, is that the so-called progress of civilization and the growth of law and order cause far more injustice and misfortune to be visited upon us than the natural causes of such ills as we in any case are heir to.

It remains to add that the figure of Mendel Singer, described by Roth with such sympathy, indeed reverence, and who administers to Eibenschütz his final lesson,[xii] is in no way reminiscent of those nineteenth-century genre portraits which so often betray their own best intentions. His view of the world of the Eastern Jews is a different one. Nor should it be forgotten that, at the time in question, this world was not merely a nostalgic fantasy on Roth's part, since, despite successive waves of emigration, it did in fact still exist right up until the autumn of 1939. Evidence of this – after its complete and utter destruction – can be found in the photographs which Roman Vishniac took in the ghettos of Eastern Europe at precisely the same time as Roth's recalling of his lost *Heimat*.[56] Among the many profoundly beautiful and melancholy portraits of the men whose faces gaze out at us from Vishniac's pictures is that of the proprietor of a small shop in Teresva in the Ruthenian Carpathians, who stands, hat on head, in front of a narrow shelf bearing all manner of cartons, tins and jars. His eyes are slightly lowered, and from beneath his eyelids he gazes out into a boundless distance, far from the shop in which there is almost nothing to keep him occupied. On the counter, in the foreground at the lower edge of the picture, there stands a simple pair of brass kitchen scales, and on one side or the other there rests the false weight.

In his last book, devoted to the mysteries of photography, Roland Barthes suggests that every photograph inevitably bears within it the sign of a future death.[57] Barthes' surmise is doubly true of this portrait of one of the brethren of Mendel Singer, taken shortly before the German troops marched in, since, while we do not know what became of the owner of this *Kramladen*, we can be almost certain that he met with a violent and untimely death.

Peter Altenberg

Le Paysan de Vienne[i]

In meiner Kindheit die Sonnenaufgänge auf dem Schneeberg,
Kaiserstein. In meinem Alter die Sonnenaufgänge hinter der
Lagune, Lido. Beides blutrot und leuchtender dampfender
Nebel. Dazwischen mein ganzes kompliziertes Leben.

In my childhood the sunrise on the Schneeberg, Kaiserstein. In my old age the sunrise behind the lagoon, Lido.
Both blood-red, glowing, steaming mist. In between my
whole complicated life.

Peter Altenberg, *Der Nachlass*

Even in his own day, Peter Altenberg was seen as the *Stadt-literat* [literary man about town] par excellence, as much a fixture in Vienna as the Graben where he liked to take a stroll, or the Café Central, where he was resident. However, the backdrop and inspiration for his collections of literary vignettes was not so much the Imperial capital as the countryside where he had spent the holiday months – at first endless-seeming, then over all too soon – of his childhood and youth. These regions, repeatedly evoked in the prose pieces of Richard Engländer – who only embarked on his literary career at the age of thirty-six, when by bourgeois standards he was already a failure – form a kind of idealized Austria of the imagination, consisting of little more than the Traunsee and Gmunden, Bad Vöslau, the Semmering and the banks of the Danube upstream from Vienna at Altenberg – the place to which Engländer, in metamorphosing into the author of the same name, pledges eternal loyalty. His sense of identification with this magical second birthplace is so strong that when, towards the end of his life, Altenberg revisits it after a long interval, he falls to wondering whether Altenberg is named after him, or he after it.[1] No matter is the answer he gives himself, for this *unio mystica*, seen from the writer's current position, goes back to a mythical union forged in time immemorial. It is the same sense of distance that Adorno evokes in his monograph on Mahler when he writes 'that in youth infinitely much is apprehended as a promise of life, as anticipated happiness, of which the ageing person recognizes, through memory, that in reality the moments of such promise were life itself. The missed and lost possibility is rescued', Adorno continues, 'by the very late Mahler, by contemplating it through the inverted opera glass of childhood.'[2] It is just this note which is struck when Altenberg evokes, in prose, that enchanted time in which everything might still have been possible. Just as, in Mahler's music, we from time to time hear echoes of a quasi Upper-Austrian slow-motion *Ländler* theme,[3] so too, in Altenberg's prose *études*, over and over again vistas open up affording glimpses of the countryside beyond. All at once the lake is there, milk-blue, the *mare austriacum*,[4] like a *fata morgana*; or Gmunden appears 'with melancholy might', as the almost sixty-year-old Altenberg writes, 'in my darkened soul', Gmunden, the 'idyll of peace', and the counterpoint to the whole 'crazy, ambitious, restless, ridiculous *Weltgetümmel*' – the turbulent business of the world.[5] Altenberg would sometimes ask himself how it came to be that 'after every summer sojourn, he retrospectively felt such a strong sense of home.'[6] The implied answer is that *Heimat*, home, appears all the more as *Heimat* the more distant one has become from it. Thus, with the last look back, Gmunden becomes 'the most home-seeming place in the world';[7] and, moved by loneliness and already overshadowed by the coming end, Altenberg addresses Gmunden, the place itself, directly with the rueful confession 'I now think of you almost as the only home I have ever had';[8] indeed, in summer 1917, in utter desperation, as he writes, he begs 'the authorities for a transfer to my beloved Gmunden'[9] – a petition which resulted in his being referred to the Viennese police.

Heimat, then, remains unattainable not just because of the difficulties arising from the collision of longing with law and order, but also because it represents nothing less than the key to a former life. As Benjamin noted, it has less to do with history than with prehistory, that *vie antérieure* which held such fascination for Baudelaire – with whom Altenberg had not a little in common. 'The wanderer', Baudelaire wrote in a review, 'looks into the tear-veiled distance, and *hysterical tears* well up in his eyes.'[10] Hysterical tears at the sight of the lost country – that is Altenberg's case exactly. Twenty-three summers – as he recollects in his sixtieth year – he has spent in Traunsee.[11] And strangely enough he was also twenty-three when the deep and irreparable rupture occurred between him and the mother whom he loved above all else. The reason for the quarrel was apparently that Altenberg, having first broken off his studies of law and medicine to work briefly as an assistant in the royal Court bookshop

Hühnersdorf & Keil in Stuttgart, had, after resuming his studies in law and passing the first state examination in Graz, come to the conclusion that he was unsuited to a so-called professional life – which insight, to the infinite disappointment of his mother, was confirmed without reservation by a doctor's certificate, citing an oversensitive nervous system. In the two or three years that followed, Altenberg became increasingly estranged from his family, in particular, it seems, from his mother, whom, it has been claimed, he would see again only on her deathbed.[12] In this final separation from his mother we find repeated the pain of separation experienced by the child when his 'wonderful idolized mother went out in the evenings to the theatre or in society'.[13] The fear of being abandoned for ever by the woman most loved is – as countless literary sources attest – of central importance for the emotional development of the bourgeois individual. At all events, Altenberg recalls that his infantile protestations were usually cut short by the *bonne* with the words 'He'll calm down soon enough, *gnädige Frau* . . . just leave quickly – – –.' 'But', Altenberg adds, 'he never did calm down'[14] – a claim unlikely to be exaggerated, since a peaceful night's sleep was something which for Peter Altenberg, even in later life, was almost completely out of the question. However, Altenberg was equally aware of how intimately feelings of deprivation were connected to what made him a writer, since, as he writes, 'When a woman whom one likes, does *not* like one, at least one has the bonus of "sehrende Sehnsucht" – the burning, yearning pain of desire.'[15] Not that he was under any illusion that one could in any sense make a living from such a bonus, conscious as he was of being definitively cast out, not only from his mother's sight, but also from nature, thenceforth obliged to spend by far the greater part of his very restricted life exiled in the desert of the metropolis.

How little Altenberg – hailed from the start by his publishers as a Poet of Vienna – thought of his place of exile has, to date, scarcely been remarked upon. Altenberg in no way shared the belief in progress common to his entrepreneurial contemporaries, as represented by Otto Wagner, who conceived the most grandiose plans for the sanitization, beautification and further extension of the capital. On the contrary, Altenberg claimed there could be no such thing as a beautiful metropolis, and indeed that big cities were the source of all kinds of oppressive insalubriousness.[16] To him, the city meant an endless sea of ill-kept houses,[17] a Babel,[18] a vast unnatural monstrosity.[19] Indeed, there are indications that Altenberg – whom Beer-Hoffmann, in his usual melodramatic manner, called a slave of the asphalt[20] – was familiar with the fear induced by the big city [*Großstadt-Angst*], especially when returning from the country; a surge of panic he could only overcome by plunging into the cold, just as, as a child, he would leap from the diving board into the water.[21] Altenberg is only able to cope with life in the big city, whose reality becomes ever more pressing the more nature comes to resemble a lost paradise, if he is able to move from one oasis to the next without undue delay. Apart from the safe haven of the Café Central, where an accommodating regime has created a sanctuary for him and his like, it is only really in the city parks that Altenberg can relax and be himself. The Stadtgarten [City Park], Botanic Garden, the Volksgarten and the Rathauspark [City Hall Park] – these are the few islands in the sea of houses whose praises he sings time and time again. What he finds particularly touching is the way that, in these public gardens, a small piece of nature is preserved 'in wrought-iron cages',[22] while all around everything has already been turned to stone. Anxious to reduce his own needs to the barest minimum, Altenberg identifies with this captive nature – not only with the outcast world of animals and plants, but also with human nature, which, threatened by itself, only ever shines through in occasional glimpses. One example of this is the story of the 'Hofmeister' ['The Private Tutor'][ii] who, on a visit to the zoo, watches as his charge, Fortunatina, her elbows propped on the wooden railing, gazes for a long time at the lioness behind the bars, as if in anticipation of her own fate.[23] And it is not only animals who are exhibited at the zoo. There is also a West African village with real Negroes [sic] from the Gold Coast. Sir Peter visits them often and is full of sympathy for their lot. One day he finds them all – Akolé, Akóshia and Tíoko – in tears. Only Monambô is not weeping. When Altenberg asks if he is not sad, he replies, 'Sir, I am far from home. I'll cry till I'm back in Africa . . .' ['Ich werde weinen, bis ich wieder in Afrika bin'],[24] which being translated from the Viennese African dialect means that he will only weep when he is back in Africa again. The reason for their general sorrow is the news of the death of a brother back home, which has just reached them in their exile. Sir Peter, however, who understands these things, knows better. 'They are weeping for Africa,' he explains to his young companion, the daughter of a French secretary: 'c'est le mal du pays, the tenderest sickness of our souls.'[25]

The cause of sorrow, then, is homesickness: nostalgia for the lost home in nature, to which the victim of separation longs so ardently to return that he is inclined to imagine it may be found where, according to the dictates of society, it is always assumed to reside, namely in the nature of Woman. For him, she is a 'living art work' of nature – a superlative paradox – that he would like to 'observe, experience and worship'.²⁶ Since, though, the idealized female body in its pure immaculate form appears to him as the fateful eternal recurrence of the identical, his gaze seeks compensation in the apparently truly inexhaustible variety of forms and colours with which fashion contrives to reinvent the natural woman. Straw hats with white violets or sprays of hemlock, dresses of velvet or of rust-coloured moiré silk with a broad knitted dark gold belt, such trappings,²⁷ which arouse the attention of the nature-lover Altenberg, are designed to transform women into specimens of exotic flora which, like a kind of second nature, are intended to replace the real thing, and yet are at the same time evidence of the increasingly radical process of socialization. The ever-growing alienation from the self, as expressed in the pseudo-natural system of fashion investigated by Roland Barthes,[iii] goes hand in hand with an erotic desire which takes its pleasure first and foremost in lifeless objects. In his *Passagenwerk* [*Arcades Project*], Benjamin outlines the transformations of emotional life which occur when a mere object, a souvenir or keepsake, becomes a complement of, or indeed even a substitute for, the experience itself. The consequence – thus Benjamin – is the reduction of the past to a catalogue of lifeless goods in a collection of relics.²⁸ While we can at most speculate about the actual love life of the troubadour Altenberg, there can be no doubt whatsoever about his passion for collecting, of which we have very ample evidence. In three large lacquered cabinets, he carefully preserved a collection, amassed over many years, of 1,500 postcards – images of landscapes, mountains, lakes and flowering meadows. One of the cabinets, as Helga Malmberg states, contained 'only pictures of consummately beautiful women and children. Over and over again,' she relates, 'when he was unable to fall asleep, he would sort and arrange these treasures.'[29] It appears that Altenberg's obsession with images also extended to the walls of his study. Images provided him with emotions, which he then translated into images. Camillo Schäfer writes that if Altenberg was attracted to a woman, he would promptly send her the address of a photographer he had paid to take her picture.[30] Souvenirs were what mattered to him above all else. It would, though, be wrong to assume that there was anything naïve about Altenberg's passion for collecting; in a reply to a questionnaire from the *Internationale Sammlerzeitung* [*International Collector's News*] he considers the matter and comes to the conclusion that '"collecting" means being able to concentrate on something situated outside the sphere of one's own personality, yet something not quite so perilous and thankless as a beloved woman – – –.'[31]

The missing details here stand for the intricate novels Altenberg did not write on this subject. They would have told of a passion which knew how to arrange matters so that its objects of desire were always available and unresisting, of rituals which meant that the lover – notwithstanding the absolute nature of his desire – had no need to get too close to the beloved women in question. A small handkerchief which he clutched in his left hand in order to be able to sleep filled him with 'billions of secret intimacies'.[32] A scrap of bread from the beloved's evening meal, a glass whose rim her lips had touched, hairpins from her hair, pins from her dress – all these were, for him, 'more real' than the presence of the beloved herself.[33] The fetishist is well aware that, in the end, objects are never unfaithful. He can cover the picture of a body with his writing and become a part of it for ever. And the fetishistic imagination is also capable of converting the deceptions of fashion – the means by which nineteenth-century consumer society was beginning to regulate the anarchism of desire – back into the concealed body itself, in a veritable process of transubstantiation. 'The dress', Altenberg comments on what attracts him about his beloved, 'becomes a symbol of her body! The loose pleat in her dress, which hangs a little apart, becomes her body! We can touch her body in the loose fold of her dress. We!'[34] The royal We with which the fetishist here introduces himself is a sign of the omnipotence which his perfect strategy of love affords him. He is secretly in league with the arbiters of good taste. The more varied the accoutrements with which the creators of fashion conjure up the appearance of the natural, the richer the spoils the lover can carry off in his specimen box. It was Baudelaire who wrote, 'J'ai plus de souvenirs que si j'avais mille ans.'[35][iv] Anyone who can pride themselves on such a claim also knows that it is hard to live by souvenirs alone, since they are the measure of the losses that we continually suffer. 'Next to me', writes Altenberg, 'lies my beloved grey felt hat, a little chamois-hunting-Kaiser-hat.[v] It reminds me of everything I have lost. Everything! I bought it in Mürzzuschlag after searching for a long time – it is my Ideal Hat. Now I gaze at it with the profoundest tenderness, as if it still held, in its felted fabric, the dear keen breezes and scents of the Semmering paradise.'[36]

This wonderful homage to a hat was written after Altenberg's return to the city. Here the 'Semmering paradise' shines through once again – though already half unreal, already retreating into the realm of the imagination; yet at the same time, the stylization of the beloved grey felt hat from Mürzzuschlag into a treasured memento is also a kind of farewell, a renunciation of far-off places, such as that which Benjamin identifies as a defining moment in the poetry of Baudelaire.[37] Like Baudelaire, in his later years Altenberg leaves the city only rarely. In any case, travelling is really no longer necessary any more, now that the whole wide world has been brought to the all-encompassing metropolis. In the changing displays of the Viennese panoramas one can, for a small entrance fee, visit the Ampezzo valley and the Vosges mountains, New York, the pyramids of Egypt, the Golden Horn, Florida and Alaska.[38] So long as the native city dweller adopts the mindset [*Habitus*] of a traveller, he can voyage more or less endlessly in his imagination. And if, like Altenberg, he takes this illusionism to the logical conclusion of living in a hotel in his own city, then, on returning to his room at night, he can make notes and sketches just as if he had been on a trip to heaven knows where. Tellingly, Altenberg was also in the habit of placing his nocturnal jottings in a large travel holdall, the contents of which he would once a year hand over to his publisher in Berlin for the further editing and compilation of his excursions and escapades. The travel correspondent doing time in the 'prison "Metropolis"'[39] no doubt yearns to be on the outside, suspects however – not altogether incorrectly – that most travellers cannot begin to hold a candle to him when it comes to the experiences they have brought back from their travels. When, sitting in his usual place in the Graben kiosk, he observes how the waiters greet the guests on their return to the city in the autumn as if they were 'world travellers who have survived many perils',[40] he realizes, watching this performance, that none of these city escapees has ever travelled as far afield as he does every day.

The type of the *flâneur*, to which Peter Altenberg belongs, emerged at a time when it had become possible to explore the world without leaving home. While the traveller is even more than usually subject to the strictures of time and organization, the *flâneur* can legitimize his idleness[41] in the city by keeping an eye on everything happening in it and in the world. His vantage point is far and away the most favourable, and so, like the Viennese *promeneur* Daniel Spitzer,[42] whose reports of his excursions, starting in 1825, appeared every Sunday in *Die Presse* for almost thirty years, the *flâneur* became a kind of oracle, able to give the most reliable information on all the latest events. A commentator on economic, political and social life such as Spitzer naturally found his métier in the ever-expanding field of journalism, an occupation which, as the names of the newspapers (*Observer*, *Observateur*, *Osservatore*) show, had elevated the business of observation to a hallmark of their trade. By contrast, an author like Adalbert Stifter, in his own Vienna walks,[vi] was attempting to sketch something like a physiognomy of the capital. His literal overview, from the spire of the Stefansdom [St Stephen's Cathedral], of the vast sprawling agglomeration of dwellings and the busy doings of the inhabitants, his visit to the catacombs, his reports from the Prater, the Tandelmarkt [Flea Market], the Wiener Stadtpost [Municipal Post Office] and the shop-window displays and advertisements – all this can be seen as an attempt to discover the unknown territory of the *Großstadt* [big city], and to make the manifold wonders of this brave new world accessible to other wanderers. By the time the *flâneur* Altenberg comes on the scene, the vitality of the metropolis was already waning, and his aims were necessarily rather different. His concern is neither journalistic reportage nor epic description. Rather, it appears that his doubts about travel also extended to roaming about the city, which is after all an indispensable quality for the *flâneur*. In his after all rather rambling oeuvre, there are scarcely any indications that he ever ventured beyond the confines of the central 1. Bezirk (First District). And even Gisela von Wysocki's attempt to stylize Altenberg into a committed walker, who claimed 'the extended labyrinth of streets and alleys, streets, courtyards and passages' of the inner city as his domain, is not really very convincing.[43] I can find scant evidence in Altenberg's writings that – as Gisela von Wysocki claims – he was fascinated by the intricate complexities of the city inside the Ringstraße and the dovetailing of the traces of history with present-day reality, allowing himself to be enticed into all manner of detours and diversions. In fact, even in the city centre Altenberg did not perambulate anything like as much as is proper for a *flâneur* worthy of the name, notwithstanding the fact that he valued sturdy footwear just as much as one condemned to eternal wandering. 'For two years now I have had another pair of American lace-up shoes in reserve. This makes me carefree, free and happy.'[44]

Altenberg was able to make *his* observations from his various regular haunts; nor did he have any need to go roaming about the streets in order to peddle his wares. Rather, he pokes fun at those 'peripathetics' who (despite the fact that as a *flâneur* too it is perfectly possible to sit down comfortably somewhere) 'continually wander up and down and back and forth à la Socrates, wearing out their sandals'. 'Of course,' he adds, 'hacks evidently have a need for this performance, since without it the futility of their own miserable existence would quickly be unmasked.'[45] Altenberg insists upon his own sedentariness. By contrast with the figure of the *flâneur*, invisibly adrift in the crowd, he was always extremely exposed, and the few places where he habitually spent his time were anything but secret. The panic-stricken state of immobility which characterized his life is also the reason why the topography of Vienna can be extrapolated from the writings of this Poet of

Vienna only in a metaphysical sense. A *flâneur* for whom, like Baudelaire, his own city 'had long ceased to be home',[46] he depicts neither the inhabitants nor the city itself.[47] This inability-to-be-at-home-in-the-city is also apparent in his continual changes of address. Baudelaire had fourteen different addresses between 1842 and 1858,[48] and Altenberg too, after the break with his family, for the next sixteen years moved constantly, until in 1902 he found more lasting abodes, first in the *Stundenhotel* London, a seedy establishment with a lively turnover of clients, and later in room 33 of the Grabenhotel in the Dorotheengasse. Both writers sought to counter their fear of appearing dispossessed in the eyes of society – Schnitzler after all called Altenberg not only a wonderful poet, but also a *Schubiak* [scoundrel, rogue][49] – by means of their dandyism and eccentricity, which permitted them to keep their public interested while at the same time laying claim to their outsider status. Admittedly, not even this display of self-confidence was quite enough to banish the fear which haunted them. Both were aware of being persecuted and despised, and for that reason – other possible causes of insomnia aside – could not afford to close their eyes for an instant. In the 'Flâneur' chapter of his work on Baudelaire, Benjamin quotes a passage from *Les Heures parisiennes* by Alfred Delvau,[vii] in which he states that, while the person of this new era might still be allowed to rest from time to time, he no longer has the right to sleep.[50]

In the era of high capitalism, the city becomes a place of eternal wandering [*ewiger Umgang*]. Altenberg's noctambulism is easily a match for Baudelaire's; the poet becomes a professional 'nighthawk' [*Draher*]. The poor performing bears he sees one night bicycling on a harshly lit vaudeville stage remind him so immediately of his own fate that he lends them his voice, and so the talking bears ventriloquize what the poet himself could scarcely have expressed: 'They have dragged us out of the dark woods and made us learn something which is no use for our lives.'[51] This lament applies to the bears' fate just as much as the conditioning inflicted, for the purposes of civilization, on every human child. The only consolation after this midnight performance, for the bears as for the noctambulant poet, is that at least they can sleep away the day 'just like back home',[52] or, as the case may be, in the pre-civilized world of childhood. Perhaps, though, the best image for Altenberg's notorious noctambulism is found in his identification with bats, which – in contrast to those ignorant folk who know nothing of those who fly by night – he sees as eminently useful creatures. Thus he proposes, in order to control the plague of mosquitoes by the Danube at Klosterneuburg, the establishment of a *Fledermauszuchtanstalt* – an institution for the breeding of bats: 'In high airy hangars, on narrow horizontal bars, a million bats would hang sleeping by day, and at night would demolish two hundred midges each: two hundred million mosquitoes!'[53] The benefits are obvious. The bat 'works all night for the whole of humanity, like poets when they happen to be "inspired"'.[54] To be inspired means to be able to fly. No wonder, then, that it should be Peter Altenberg – whose whole life, according to Lina Loos, 'gave the impression of something free-floating'[55] – who at night on the Graben would attempt to take flight, beating faster and faster with his arms until 'strangely weightless, he seemed to be borne aloft by sheer willpower and longing alone.'[56] In keeping with this demonstration of the human capacity for metamorphosis, it is fitting that one of the models for the *pneumatikos* [man of air] Altenberg should be the Flying Dutchman. In *Was der Tag mir zuträgt* [*What the Day Brings Me*], having himself a marked penchant for flowing capes and pelerines, he describes that strange airborne voyager as the dream of all beautiful women – 'swathed in a wide dark cloak, like wings that cover the world, with his mysterious eyes and his fate to wander the world eternally'.[57]

The figure of the eternal wanderer or wandering Jew, a variant of the Flying Dutchman, brings us to the subject which Altenberg, who had converted to Catholicism in 1900, always ignored: that of his own Jewish origins. Nonetheless his own almost emblematic figure exemplifies, more clearly than many an explicit discussion of the topic, the issues and uncertainties surrounding Jewish life in *fin de siècle* Vienna. Although he never travelled far, Altenberg contrived, with his eccentric outfits, to give himself the air of someone newly arrived from far-off lands, or on the point of departing for them. One of his most important props was his walking staff [*Wanderstab*], or rather his walking stick or cane [*Spazierstock*], the most trusty companion of every true traveller. In a prose piece entitled 'Der Spazierstock' ['The Walking Stick'] he foresees a time when his walking stick will be his only means of support: 'Forest, lake, spring, winter, woman, art – all fade away, and there's only one still thrilling thing left: your lovely walking stick!'[58] A vision of old age, true, but also of a benighted future, in which the allegorical figure of the last wanderer, cast out from a society grown alien from itself and nature, tries to make his way in a no less alien region without path or direction. Kafka's wanderer K. and Beckett's Molloy will later perform what Peter Altenberg's singular act prefigures. For Adorno, Mahler was someone who, like Kafka, seemed to have anticipated by decades the coming of fascism, and it is precisely this sense of foreboding, he suggests, that is likely to have been behind 'the despair of the wayfarer whom two blue eyes sent out into the wide world'.[59] Altenberg is none other than this wayfarer. In Vienna, he is already rehearsing survival in a strange land: he procures a 'permit to peddle mixed goods from door to door' and begins to trade in bracelets and necklaces of his own manufacture.[60] Even if he is not entirely serious about this – Altenberg is likely to have hawked his wares not so much from door to door as from his favourite coffee-house table – the gesture is still a telling one, indicating that perhaps, in the hard times to come, one will be forced to have recourse once more to the ancient Jewish occupation of *dorfgeher* [peddler] who travels about the world with an assortment of goods in his heavy pack which – as a story by Karl Emil Franzos makes clear – includes absolutely everything: 'straw hats, leather belts, clasp-knives ... flowers, ribbons, corals, love philters ... linen, tallow, hardware, images of the saints, charms, wax-candles, needles and thread ... prayer books, old trousers and kaftans, new "tefillin" and "mezuzahs" for [...] his fellow believers, snuff, almanacs, last week's newspapers, fine materials for the priests and nobility, spirits, playing cards, smuggled cigars and other items for the cavalry officers, in fact everything. Everything!'[61] Like one of the legendary righteous souls,[viii] the *dorfgeher* carries the world on his back. And Altenberg, too, has more to offer than just necklaces and bracelets, since his books, which, as Gisela von Wysocki writes, are rather reminiscent of a peddler's tray, present an almost complete array of notions and odds and ends – everything one needs to live on. Altenberg is equipped for a long trip, but – as already mentioned – the time is not yet at hand; our wayfarer is still sitting in the waiting room of the Vienna coffee house, and in the meantime what he performs is – as we now know, and as Adorno writes of Mahler's music – the prelude to emigration.[62]

It goes almost without saying that Altenberg's lack of interest in matters Jewish by no means detracts from the fact that the singular figure he cut precisely epitomized the difficult position of the Jewish community in Vienna. The class into which the Jewish population of Vienna aspired to assimilate was a bourgeoisie whose upper strata, at the turn of the century, continued to derive its ethos from the dominant culture of the aristocracy, a culture which, not entirely without justification, regarded the bourgeois virtues of good housekeeping, of both money and emotions, with a certain amount of scepticism. Once middle-class Jewish families had, in the process of assimilation, attained the upper echelons of society, their discomfiture at the bourgeois way of life generally took on a more radical form than among the non-Jewish bourgeoisie. The most famous names of Viennese culture of the *fin de siècle* – Hofmannsthal, Schnitzler, Kraus, Herzl, Wittgenstein and, slightly later, Broch – are, almost without exception, prime examples of this phenomenon. For Altenberg's father, Moritz Engländer, too, proprietor of a business importing basketware from Croatia who had worked his way up from the Leopoldstadt to the 1. Bezirk, reading the novels of Victor Hugo – to which he devoted himself day after day, sitting in a dark red armchair easily adjustable via a mechanism of screws and knobs – was, in the end, more important than the business he had built up.[ix] In order to be assimilated into this milieu, the sons of this generation, filled with higher aspirations, had to make a name for themselves not only in business but also in culture, which – given that the places on Mount Olympus are limited in number – led to the emergence of a *bohème* parasitically clinging to the coat-tails of the bourgeoisie. In his darker moments, when he grew tired of always playing the fool,[63] Altenberg was aware that being a poet is a very ephemeral affair, and that, as a living example of this *bohème*, he was condemned to an unworthy and dependent existence. The fear of *déclassement* – that he might at some point irrevocably cross the line between fly-by-night and vagabond – haunted him all his life, notwithstanding the fact that up to the age of fifty-three he had a regular income of 240 crowns from his father's, later his brother's, business, which was, after all, equivalent to the income of an army captain. And even in later years, after his brother had gone bankrupt, Altenberg was, by one means or another, always able to find a way of coming by his share. There is no need to rehearse here the countless well-known *schnorrer* anecdotes from Altenberg's life, other than perhaps the one that relates how once, in Gmunden, he took all his money to the bank because there had been a burglary in the hotel, and immediately afterwards sent a telegram to his brother: 'Dear Georg, have taken all my money to the post-office savings bank and am now in imminent danger of starving to death.'[64]

Altenberg's relationship with money was complicated in the extreme; he spent it without a second thought, especially if it was not his own, but was at the same time capable of putting it prudently to one side, and indeed to such good effect that he himself forgot all about it and, convinced he stood on the brink of ruin, continued to prevail upon the generosity of others with a good conscience. Those whom Altenberg repeatedly asked for contributions will have had an idea at the time that he was not really as poor as he liked to claim. Schnitzler, for example, learns while playing tennis with two Fräuleins Kraus – nieces, as he puts it, of the 'Fackel-Kraus' – 'that P.A. is apparently well off, indeed rich, and while he was ill hid his money under his pillow – for which reason he did not want to get up. All his begging', Schnitzler suggests, 'would thus be a product of his complete and utter morbid miserliness.'[65] Whether Altenberg's behaviour was actually motivated by pathological miserliness must remain a matter for speculation. At any rate, after his death it became clear how successful his strategy had been. The starving poet, who in his last years had increasingly been supported by his friends, left behind the not insubstantial fortune of 100,000 crowns, which – perhaps in order to redeem his blackened soul – he had bequeathed to the Kinder-Schutz- und Rettungsgesellschaft [Society for the Protection and Rescuing of Children]. In Altenberg's attitude to money, there is something which harks back to a pre-bourgeois era, perhaps an instinctive reaction against the principles of the despised middle class to which he, as an assimilated Jew, belonged. Some of Joseph Roth's most endearing characters, too, are those of his Jewish protagonists not yet corrupted by bourgeois business acumen. Altenberg offers a similar vista of an existence less compromised by society in the passage where he recalls, not without emotion, how, in the summer, his father would happily leave his business to go and live 'dressed as a "woodcutter" in a hut on the "Lakaboden" on the lower pastures of the Schneeberg. He would get up at four in the morning, make himself some *Sterz* [porridge] and go and watch the blackcocks at their mating dances.'[66] For all his rapturous nature worship, Altenberg did not go to quite such lengths. He knew that there was no returning to lost time. The first page of his first book tells the story of Rositta and Margueritta, two very well-brought up children aged nine and eleven, one of whom, according to her mother, is of a philanthropic bent, while the other is so in love with nature that she wants to learn to play the zither and become a dairymaid up on the Patscherkofel, which her more urbane sister finds excessive. As the peerless irony of this vignette shows, Altenberg was all too aware that he would have cut no less outlandish a figure as a woodcutter on the Lakaboden than the young lady on the Patscherkofel, and that, for us, nature ultimately only remains nature insofar as it can be redeemed in and by civilization. For that reason, he has settled in the city, as a *paysan de Vienne*, fully aware of the contradiction between nature and society. The paradoxical nature of such an existence was evident in his ever-changing costumes, from the tweed suits and check flannels of the English travelling gentleman to Austrian provincial *Tracht* [regional costume], from cycling capes to refined elegance, from pyjamas to a clown's costume – pretty much every variation imaginable. Altenberg's disguises were a kind of barometer for the inner state of mind of one who, due to the constellation into which he was born, never knew which way to turn, and who would therefore perform the most extravagant stunts within the small space he could call his own, rather like the great Blondel [sic = Blondin][x] whom he so admired making himself an omelette on the tightrope above Niagara Falls.

Like Baudelaire's before him, Altenberg's life as a poet was destined from the outset to end in ruin, if not financial, then at least physical. In *Mein Lebensabend* [*My Twilight Years*] he describes how, in the Grabenhotel,[xi] where like K. [in *The Castle*] he awaits his end in the maids' quarters, from his window he watches the roofers pursuing their perilous occupation. The routine way in which they carry out their vertiginous exploits, with no safety apparatus whatsoever, shows that 'they are already very familiar with the simple concept that life, everywhere and in every respect, hangs only by the thinnest of threads.'[67] Altenberg has an elective affinity with such *luftmenschen*,[xii] for – as he writes elsewhere – 'ten years more or less really makes no difference to the civilized melancholic.'[68] The third of the Five Orchestral Songs[xiii] which Alban Berg composed in 1912 on picture-postcard texts by Peter Altenberg can be seen as the micrograph of a life cut short.[xiv] 'Über die Grenzen des Alls blickest du sinnend hinaus. Hattest nie Sorge um Hof und Haus. Leben und Traum von Leben' ['Over the bounds of the universe you gaze pensively out. / For house and home you had never a care. / Life and the dream of life'] – thus the lines across which Berg, starting from a now famous twelve-tone complex, spans a truly unprecedented arc of sound which then, with the words 'plötzlich ist alles aus' ['suddenly all is gone'], falls away into absolute tonelessness. In his book on Mahler, Adorno recalls that psychoanalysis ascribes to music the capacity to resist paranoia.[69] Here, though, the abrupt dying away of the notes throws the door wide open to it. Peter Altenberg had long anticipated such a turn for the worse. 'Dearest Georg,' he writes to his brother as early as 1909, 'my end is approaching with giant steps. My melancholic disposition is eating me alive!'[70] The feeling of despair expressed here is that of 'spleen', a feeling 'corresponding to catastrophe in permanence' which Benjamin also diagnosed in Baudelaire.[71] Altenberg was no stranger to the idea of hanging himself from the window frame.[72] 'A proper, decent, honest "balance sheet of life" is something only suicides draw up,' he writes in *Semmering 1912*,[73] but matters are not so easily arranged. 'Many reach for the Browning, but many do not.'[74] Peter Altenberg, for whatever reason, was one of the latter, and so he had no option but to continue with the dressage act he had committed himself to, and for which he finds the perfect metaphor when, one evening at the circus, he watches the antics of the performing ape Peter, his namesake[75] – perhaps the very same creature who inspired Kafka to write his *Bericht an eine Akademie* [*Report to an Academy*]. This story, which, as Max Brod observed early on, may also be read as a gloss on the process of assimilation, describes in a key passage how the ape Rotpeter can only overcome the inhibitions preventing him from becoming human when he raises the schnapps bottle to his lips. Under the heading 'Alkohol' ['Alcohol'] in *Prodromos*, Altenberg conjectures that being drunk may fill 'the terrible gulf between what we are and what we would like to be, ought to be, should become'. In the same passage he writes – in exact analogy to Kafka's text – that 'when the ape realized that he could become human, he took to the bottle, in order to wash away the pain of his still-being-an-ape.'[76] This story encapsulates the whole aetiology of Altenberg's own alcoholism, which facilitated his imaginary metamorphoses night after night. It was alcohol, consumed in enormous quantities for years on end, whose effects he believed he could control with, ultimately, up to forty times the recommended dose of the soporific paraldehyde, which afforded him, as he writes as early as *Prodromos*, 'plenty of time to decide to commit suicide'.[77] Nor was he under any illusion that this regime could lead to anything other than complete derangement and to confinement in the most diverse institutions. The hydropathic establishment in Sulz bei Mödling, the Fango Institute in Vienna, the psychiatric hospitals in Inzerdorf and Am Steinhof – these were the stations along the way mapped out by his postponement strategies. They represented, for him, an 'exile within four walls' to which he was consigned since 'people don't like to witness a slow death'[78] – an exile in which, when visitors are announced, the apathetic invalid is 'rudely awakened from his beneficial rest, washed, and shaved', so that in his freshly laundered sheets he looks for all the world 'as if it was his birthday'.[79] In view of such disagreeable experiences, Altenberg came to the conclusion that it would make more sense if the sick were to lock away the well, 'so that they can't subject them to any more indignities'.[80]

It was thanks to Altenberg's extraordinary resilience, and the intercessions of his friends, that he did not in fact – as he might perhaps in some ways have wished – simply fade away in one or other of these institutions in the year 1913.[xv] What such a twilight existence might have looked like is something he himself describes in a sketch from Inzersdorf: 'In a dark ground-floor room opening on to the garden, Graf C. and Herr D. sit side by side, as they have done for years, in ancient leather armchairs, without speaking, without moving, like waxworks, for hours and hours on end, until someone comes and puts them to bed. Never ever do they express a wish, never smoke, are never bored, waiting out the days, the months, the years, like old trees at peace in nature.'[81] But such a passing into the eternal peace of nature as these lines evoke, a form of simple, natural existence in which, like a tree, there would no longer be any need to move, was a fate that Altenberg – unlike Baudelaire, who, robbed of the power of speech by a stroke, passed away in a private clinic – was not to be granted. Rather, in May 1913, in a coup organized by Alfred Loos, he was spirited away by his friends to freedom and a long summer sojourn in Venice. Here, at the age of fifty-five – on his first ever long trip – he sees the sea for the first time from the balcony of the Hotel Excelsior in Trieste. In October he returns from Venice to Vienna to take up the struggle of daily existence once more. In the war years that follow, which at least at times give another direction to his thoughts, he once again demonstrates his extraordinary indestructibility. Even when, in 1918, calamity strikes and, as he says, 'for months on end', with a double hand fracture, he lies 'without eating, without washing', in his 'coffin-chamber' in the Grabenhotel,[82xvi] he still from time to time manages to rouse himself sufficiently to boost his morale in self-accusatory outbursts whose phrasing is strangely reminiscent of the late tirades of Thomas Bernhard. 'Only you, you alone must, can, will rescue yourself from the abysses you have expressly dug yourself! No one else, no allegedly sympathetic doctor, no good-natured friend! Just you, you, you alone, you yourself! Your fate depends only on your own efforts, not on either the – as far as you are concerned, naturally – completely uncomprehending megalomaniac doctors nor your – just as naturally – uncomprehending well-meaning friends, who with the best of intentions thrust you back into your own depths!'[83] In his *Nachlass*, which shows that he carried on scribbling frenetically on the margins of his life right up to the end, there are passages which show that Altenberg – who had always been borne along on the wings of his own narcissistic pathos – begins, in view of the approaching end, to take himself severely to task. He speaks of the 'awful disaster' of his 'completely pathological brain due to the disgrace of Mama and Papa! Such exceptional creatures of whatever kind should simply not be allowed to bring children into the world, children in whom of course the mental–spiritual–physical curse of being different from all the millions surrounding one immediately becomes exaggerated out of all proportion, into the most tragic – because most innocent – dimensions, and unbridgeable chasms open up all over the place, in all areas, and must somehow be the death of you!'[84] This passage, bearing all the hallmarks of paranoia, is dated 23 December 1918. At Epiphany, on the twelfth night after the festival of light, his long period of suffering is at an end, and 'the greatest of sinners P.A.'[85] died the martyr's death towards which he had held course for so long.

Altenberg's great passion was, of course, seeing. His first book, entitled *Wie ich es sehe* [*As I See It*], contains a sketch which describes the gradations of colour in the Höllengebirge as day turns to evening. At five o'clock the mountains appear as 'shining transparency'; at six they become 'like pink glass', at six-thirty 'like amethyst', and at seven they grow pale beyond the grey waters of the lake where copper-red and bottle-green stripes shimmer.[86] Here is someone who has spent a long time looking. Pure seeing [*reines Schauen*] was something Altenberg started to practise early on. And when snow falls on the Semmering, he wants nothing more than to 'look, look, look' at it, to 'drink it in' as he writes 'with my eyes for hours on end until it is absorbed in my soul'.[87] The most wonderful and purest view, though, is that from the uppermost heights. For Altenberg, the heraldic beast which symbolizes this longing is the albatross, which also has an emblematic role in the poetry of Baudelaire. 'Like albatrosses', writes Altenberg, 'we waddle along the shore – – – but in the air?!' The dashes stand for the moment of drawing breath and lifting off from the earth, opening out undreamed-of poetic possibilities and vistas, and containing a promise only fulfilled in disappearance. The albatross becomes its true self only 'when he has lifted off from the shore and is no longer there – – – then he IS!!! One should live in eternal silence with this noble soul who left his lifeless body with us on the shore, in order to fly away into his own world, and there to BE!'[88]

The Law of Ignominy

Authority, Messianism and Exile in Kafka's *Castle*[i]

In Kafka's work – and in *The Castle* in particular – ugliness and deformity appear to be occasioned by the presence of an irrational power which cannot in any way be vindicated. Nowhere does the novel extend to us conclusive information about the actual goings-on inside the Castle, about the origin and purpose of this untouchable organization; yet nowhere is it maintained that the Castle is inscrutable – the domain of supernatural beings. Conjectures along those lines remain mere fragments of our interpretation. We are, however, repeatedly and quite unmistakably told that the Castle is powerful, this being the cruel lesson which K., in spite of all his initial defiance, will have to learn. Thus, at the beginning of the novel, the humble landlord informs K. that even Schwarzer's father, although only 'Unterkastellan'[ii] and one of the lowest at that, is in a position of power; as for K. himself, however (towards whom the landlord affects after all a kind of awe, if not reverence), he is not considered as being in the least bit powerful. K. points out that even if his mission were doomed, he would still feel the satisfaction 'frei vor einem Mächtigen gesprochen zu haben' ('of having spoken freely to a great and powerful man').[1] And the fable-like simile of the eagle and the blindworm, through which K. — at one of the turning points of the novel — visually comprehends the relationship between Klamm and himself, also implies the distinction between power and impotence. Soon after, K. compares the formal, barely tangible power which Klamm exercises in his assumed function as a land surveyor with the concrete power through which Klamm appears to make himself felt even in K.'s bedroom. Pursuing reflections of this kind, K. begins to abandon himself to the acknowledgement of a power that relentlessly obtrudes upon him until he finally admits 'that the difference in strength between the authorities and himself was so enormous that all the guile of which he was capable would hardly have served appreciably to reduce the difference in his favour' (p. 158). K. has now perceived his own impotence. He recognizes in it the hub of his forlorn predicament, the part allocated to him by the powers that be.[iii]

It is, I think, generally accepted that the only possible rationalization of power is to seize upon it in order to exploit it for a creative purpose. Accordingly, the claims of great works of art to dominate and subjugate the individual imagination are counterbalanced, and thereby made acceptable, by their critical achievements. The power of the Castle authorities, however, is anything but creative; it is completely sterile and its sole aim seems pointless self-perpetuation. The condition of its continued survival is the identification of those who are powerless with the principles of their repression. The Castle's lasting power is therefore less an absolute quality than the product of a symbiosis through which its subjects are fused with it once the experience of impotence has become second nature to them. It is for this reason that Kafka's inexorable portrayal of power defines it, in the first instance, as parasitic rather than powerful. And it is precisely the parasitic features that provide an explanation for the strangely listless, hypersensitive and noisome nature of the officials. Resembling each other to an uncanny degree and with few individual traits, they appear to have regressed to an earlier stage of evolution. Not unlike insects, they are of a limited mobility and their unplanned industry seems, as K. at one point remarks, no more than the ludicrous confusion of primitive organisms. In their helplessness they depend on the habitual assistance of less degenerate beings. Thus Barnabas's father, while still serving with the fire brigade, had to carry the obese Galater from the Herrenhof, although the alleged risk of a fire was largely a figment of the official's over-apprehensive mind. Similarly the vampiric lasciviousness with which the functionaries of the Castle are wont to demand virginal sacrifice and public prostitution appears in its true light only if seen in the context of their parasitic condition.

In the train of such hypotheses one begins to appreciate the significance of the observations which Pepi, in the course of the final chapter, intimates to K., observations concerning the Brückenhof's official guests: that they leave their rooms in such a state 'that not even the Flood could wash them clean' and that 'one had to make a great effort to overcome one's disgust so as to be able to clean up after them' (p. 275). It seems that only the most oppressed inhabitants of the village, the maids, deprived as they are of almost all rights and destined to dwell in subterranean haunts, have some inkling of the true degradation of those in power; but as the maids are, at the same time, furthest removed from them, they do not constitute any immediate threat. They only know the excrement of power, not power itself.

This is Kafka's critical insight into the perfected machinery of the societal system. It anticipates in a number of respects the fragmentary 'Theorie des Unrats' which Christian Enzensberger has provided in his *Grösserer Versuch über den Schmutz*.[iv] In this treatise we are reminded:

> that power and filth invariably go together . . . Faced with power one bows one's head, one shrinks, one goes on one's knees, grovels in the dust, turns into a wriggling worm, into a mere nothing; throughout one's being one is subject to contractions, even in a physiological sense, including excessive perspiration and humiliating defecation. In the presence of power a person will withdraw into himself, feel incapable of preserving his unity and the principles of his structural organization are turned upside down.[2]

Furthermore Enzensberger points to such phenomena as the juxtaposition of scatological tendencies and the craving for power as exemplified in the works of de Sade, to the functional relationship, in other words, that exists between order and ordure: 'The more rigid a system of order, the greater is the amount of filth it generates . . . some systems turn man himself into waste and filth.'[3] And later:

> Those in power banish to the confines of their systems as many forms of behaviour as possible, even though they may have been hitherto quite acceptable, declaring them to be marginal infringements and thus mere filth. The point is that such prohibitive orders increase the terror which they wish to see engendered. Even the most willing of subjects cannot, in the end, comply with all the demands made on him, is overtaken by guilt and henceforth in need of exoneration. The more violent power is claimed, the greater, as a rule, the

clamour for order and propriety. That this generates even more filth is a fact which those in power are at pains to conceal. In reality their one wish is for a universal pig-sty; their true desire is not to increase hygiene but to cleanse themselves. The exercising of power, according to all that has gone before, is thus a dirty business in the real sense of the word.[4]

These sentences furnish an abstract analogy to Kafka's novel and hardly require further interpretation. The filth and debris which parasitic power entails are allotted to the people who live under its sway as their fateful inheritance. Although power, in the last resort, is seen as the source of depravity, this depravity is associated less with the fact of oppression than with the lives of the oppressed. In this state of affairs we recognize the objective correlative of ugliness and deformity in Kafka's works, an ugliness and deformity which paradoxically grow more cruel in proportion to the distance between the victims and the centre of power. One would not go far wrong if one were to interpret this insight as Kafka's knowledge of the temptations of beauty – illustrated in *Das Schweigen der Sirenen* (*The Silence of the Sirens*) – and conversely as his hopeful conjecture that in ugliness we behold our inborn relation to an abstract, powerless deity, to a deliberately constructed counterpart of power and dominion.

To revolutionize a system in which power and impotence almost purposefully complement each other is a logical impossibility. This problem, which ever since Kleist and Büchner has had its place in the more radical works of German literature, was repeatedly considered by Kafka, most perceptively perhaps in the parable of the rusty old toy-guns nobody is prepared to pick up.[5] Kafka's way of representing the dilemma seems to imply that a revolution is nevertheless necessary and that it is all the more imperative the more impossible it becomes to translate its idea into practice. This reflection marks the median point between societal reality and utopia. Given these circumstances which show power and impotence to be invariable, ahistorical, mythical categories, dialectical reasoning at length begins to toy with ways of transcending this hopeless situation. One of the most complex examples of such abstract designs can be recognized in messianism, the aspirations and weakness of which form a central issue of the Castle novel.

Jewish messianism, of which Christology represents but a variant, is a diffuse and immensely variable phenomenon which I cannot hope to describe here even in outline. Suffice it to say that its implications are political as well as metaphysical and that in cases of messianic movements it is usually difficult to distinguish between sedition and surrender. Messianism knows no dogma and indeed has never developed a theology except when it felt historically discredited as, for instance, by the apostasy of Sabbatai Zwi. Apart from such examples, however, messianism remained a tradition in the authentic sense of the word, that is to say unsystematic, contradictory and unstable. Consequently the image of the messiah can hardly be ascertained. It oscillates between that of the king and that of the beggar, between the Zaddik, the epitome of justness, and the criminal, between the representative and the outsider. The contradictions cannot be resolved, not even under the aspect of ethics. Revelation and confidence trick, merit and guilt, submission and violence – such distinctions are of little relevance where messianic striving is the dominant factor. The only invariable and decisive feature is the concept of hope as the guiding principle in a maze of illusions.

The Castle comprises a number of visual and reflective reminiscences of the messianic tradition and frequently the parallels are so pronounced as to suggest that the author may quite consciously have attempted to represent and analyse the messianic idea. Even K.'s arrival in the village reminds one of characteristic features of messianic lore. Like K., about whose looks and origin we never learn anything conclusive, the messiah is of uncertain provenance and his physiognomy is indistinct. In hassidic tales[v] which gave the messianic figure perhaps its most vivid expression one encounters the unknown wanderer – his insignia the knapsack and the walking stick – traversing the country or sitting in wayside inns uttering truth upon truth.[6] He turns up unexpectedly, as a guest perhaps for the *seder*, in the uniform of one pressed into lifelong military service in the czarist army, and disappears without a trace as soon as the community has recognized him. The archetypal experience of the exile informs his elusive persona – the image of one who has come far from his native land, of a God, fallen from grace, as portrayed by Döblin, with all the defects of desperation, in his *Babylonische Wandrung (Babylonian Travels)*.

Without much difficulty, one can discern in K. an incarnation of this kind of figure. A variant of the opening of the novel (which Kafka rejected) tells us that the 'Fürstenzimmer'[vi] of the Brückenhof has been prepared for K., who is not so much announced as always expected; it is this irrational expectation of the stranger which, if we can take K.'s irritation at its face value, penetrates his incognito and endangers his mission. Although far from unambiguous the scene betrays too much of K.'s possible identity – which may be why Kafka chose a less explicit opening. The beginning of the novel as we now know it offers rather more sparse hints, so that it is almost exclusively the term 'land surveyor' itself which gives rise to speculations. The Hebrew word for land surveyor, *moshoakh*, is but one unwritten vowel removed from *moshiakh*, the Hebrew word for messiah. Kafka employed ciphers such as this one in order to conceal a meaning which direct presentation would have deprived of its resonance. The secret code which turns Kafka's texts into palimpsests was based on his belated exercises in Hebrew and his love of Grimm's Dictionary, a synthesis of poles so disparate that one can infer from it the tension which Kafka attempted to live out.

The urgency of K.'s mission is evident from those numerous instances where the text of the novel refers to the protagonist's determination and to his readiness to fight. Right at the beginning we are informed that K. has not ventured into the Castle world by chance; he had *expected* efficient arrangements, even if the existence of a telephone somewhat surprises him. K. mentions to Olga that he thinks he had a fairly clear notion of the place even before his arrival. And now he is in the village to risk a duel which, he believes, is agreed to by the Castle with no more than a smile. Nor does the crucial letter omit to mention 'the fact that if it should come to a struggle K. had had the hardihood to make the first advances' (p. 30). How much K. is conscious of this strained situation is shown by a passage where he reflects on the risk he is running and finally reminds himself that he had not, after all, come to the village simply 'to lead an honoured and comfortable life' (p. 146). And later on he affirms once again: 'I came here of my own accord, and of my own accord I have settled here' (p. 187). However unfavourable the actual conditions may have proved to be, they cannot alter K.'s determination to force the Castle into a confrontation – an aim which had crystallized even before his arrival. 'I have come to fight,' he explains in a variant of the beginning; about the nature of this confrontation, however, the text remains largely silent.

At best we know that it is not K.'s immediate objective to assist those oppressed by the Castle; he has come 'to fight for himself'. If one takes into consideration the novel as a whole, the 'for himself' is likely to refer to the principles which K. represents rather than to his person. According to the teleology of Jewish messianism this principle could perhaps be defined as the liberation not of an individual or of a particular group but of the entire community of the oppressed.

This could also explain why K. cannot redeem any of the hopes invested in him. There are the peasants 'mit ihren förmlich gequälten Gesichtern' ('with their literally tortured faces'), which appear to have been formed 'im Schmerz des Geschlagenwerdens' ('in the pain of beating'). K. initially believes that their exaggerated interest in him is designed to hamper his freedom of movement, but then asks himself whether they might not have hoped to find in him an advocate of their inarticulate desires. When K. evades what thus approaches him, he seems to become guilty of ignoring the urgent demands of a specific group of people, a striking parallel to the dilemma of the revolutionary who in the interest of the general cause cannot afford to show his compassion towards any particular case. Thus Frieda and Pepi too must inevitably be disappointed by their liberator and the Barnabas family, who for so long had been waiting for somebody to reverse developments in the village, equally begin to fear that K. will not be capable of taking upon himself this crucial task. For Olga the glimpse of light which K.'s arrival has brought into the world of the Castle is already a fading memory:

> A Land Surveyor had come and I didn't even know what a Land Surveyor was. But next evening Barnabas . . . came home earlier than usual . . . drew me out into the street, laid his head on my shoulder, and cried for several minutes. He was again the little boy he used to be. Something had happened to him, and he could not bear the joy and the anxieties of all this newness. It was as if a whole new world had suddenly opened to him. (p. 214)

The subjunctive 'as if a whole new world had suddenly opened to him' is a token of the desperate disparity between the messianic promise and its actual achievement. The insufferable tension between the deprivations of this world and the longed-for *Parousia* propels those who believe that the renewal is imminent into self-negation. Characteristic of this is a passage which Kafka rejected in which Olga implores K., '"Take away my fear and you possess me utterly." "What kind of fear", asked K. "The fear of losing you."' Olga's life consists entirely of the apprehension that her hope might be ill-founded. Through the eyes of this utterly reduced creature we finally recognize that K., in his failure to fulfil any of their dreams, is ultimately identical with the downtrodden and the powerless.

This, however, holds true only if we overlook the dialectical insight of the young boy Hans who has a better, more differentiated judgement of K. Though Hans seeks to emulate K., he certainly knows of K.'s present abjectness; but he has also had occasion to note how other people in search of help seem to have been attracted by K. 'because nobody in the old environment had been able to help'. These contradictions had engendered in him the belief that though for the moment K. was wretched and looked down on, yet in an almost unimaginable and distant future he would excel everybody. Accordingly, Hans looks on K. 'as on a younger brother whose future would reach further than his own, the future of a very little boy' (p. 144). This paradox is meaningful only if one sees K. not as a person but as the embodiment of a principle exempt from the passage of time. K., 'the eternal Land Surveyor', as the text at one point tells us, is a cipher for a future that perpetually retreats ahead of a disheartening reality, a cipher of hope, deeply engrained in privation and never redeemed. Even if this principle is forlorn in its own unreality there remains the desire for its realization, the moral dimension, which is anathema to empire and oppression.

That K. represents a threat to the Castle is suggested several times in the text. Although Kafka refrained from unambiguous hints in the novel itself, it is perhaps significant here that an embryonic sketch contained in the diaries describes the wanderer who drifts into the village as possessing a revolver.[7] And when K., in the last chapter, is about to disappear it is said of him that he is either a fool or a child or a very wicked person. Similarly, when K.'s intention to address himself directly to Klamm is mentioned, the landlady attempts to dissuade him. K.'s retort ('you don't fear for Klamm, do you?') exposes the apprehension concealed in this request. Can we not infer that the Castle authorities, for reasons of self-preservation, seek to avoid a direct confrontation with the intruder K.? The landlord of the Herrenhof is convinced that the officials are unable and unprepared to endure the sight of a stranger. In one of the variants, K. learns from an official that Klamm was forced to postpone his departure for two hours as he could not bear to confront K., whereupon K. examines the face of the secretary 'as though trying to discover the law to which one's features had to conform if Klamm was to be able to endure them'. K.'s tactics, to attempt to force his way into the centre of power, thus appear justified, particularly if one considers Momus's remark about 'Klamm's extreme sensitivity'. And is it not the case with power in general that the more exalted it is, the more vulnerable it becomes? Only after due preparations and adequate warning are the powerful in a position to face the challenge of the powerless (cf. p. 267). The litigant's chance is therefore to come 'unannounced in the middle of the night', like a thief. 'Every lock', a hassidic story tells us, 'has its own key . . . but there are strong thieves who know how to open without keys: they break the lock.'[8] This exactly describes K.'s intention. Were he to succeed in confronting the powers that be, in presenting them with his message, they might dissolve before his eyes and *ten* words, as K. indicates in the memorandum he entrusts to Barnabas, would suffice to usher in a new law.

Parallel with such possibilities, however, a final and perplexing irony is being developed: K. is not in a fit state to seize the opportunity when at last it offers itself. Even in the first chapter we read that K. feels, 'at the wrong time', 'really tired', 'the consequences of his exertion making themselves felt' (p. 17). Furthermore he is well aware of the pressure of a discouraging environment, of his growing resignation to disappointment[,] 'the pressure of the imperceptible influences of every moment' (p. 30). The difficulties facing K. are in fact a paradigm of those encountered in the process of Jewish assimilation. And it is unlikely that K. will succeed in resisting its insidious influence – so much so that we may speculate whether the ruling power was not in a position to anticipate his final capitulation all along. Weariness and adaptation, the traditional sins of exile, infringe upon K.'s determination and, at the decisive moment, outweigh his willpower and banish the threat he represents to the system. The image of K.[vii] overcome by the temptations of sleep in Bürgel's room illustrates this turn of events; it is a preliminary sketch for the novel's conclusion when K. is visited by the mysteriously old-fashioned figure of the landlady, an allegory of death.[9] Kafka's imagination quite explicitly conceived of this sombre female as the representation of powerlessness. One of Kafka's notebooks contains the following passage:

> Yesterday I was visited by a swoon. She lives in the house next door. I have quite often seen her disappearing in through the low gate-way, bent down, in the evenings. A tall lady in a long flowing dress and a broad-rimmed hat with feathers on it. Very hastily, with rustling skirt, she came through my door, like a doctor who is afraid he has come too late to a patient whose life is flickering out.[10]

Just as K. submits to a sudden attack of fatigue, so too the narrator of this passage is the victim of a strange kind of *Ohnmacht* (swoon) which prefigures an imminent death. Messianism has only a short step left to take. And yet one is surprised by the daring, extravagant and uninhibited confession in which Bürgel discloses the crucial secret. It is almost as if power desired its own annihilation, as if power too stood in need of redemption.

That messianism is doomed to miss the fulfilment of its hopes by a hair's breadth appears to be the mark of its calamitous origin. If K. embodies messianism then the family of Barnabas represents the state of exile, the *Galut* which prompted the revival of messianic hope and zeal. It is hardly necessary to recall the deprivations this ostracized family has to endure; nor do we have to quote here the numerous instances where Kafka, exposing the irrationality of the whole business, provides us with some of the most profound literary marginalia on the psychology of anti-Semitism. The fate of the Barnabas family is a synoptic sociology of the Jewish people. In its most radical consequences their subsidiary drama demonstrates the attempt of an oppressed minority to rationalize their situation by trying to see themselves from the point of view of their oppressors, i.e. in the language of the Castle. Thus the charges levelled against them are internalized and become part of the minority's own view of themselves.

K. recognizes, at least subliminally, his own predicament in the Barnabas family and its twofold disaster. It is as if this recognition preoccupies his subconscious, as if he only just fails to articulate it. Right at the outset he believes that the Barnabas family will have to accept him without reservations, and we further read: 'He had no feeling of shame where they were concerned' (p. 37). A secret unexposed identification characterizes their relationship and seems to be the cause of their mutual attraction and of the intimate rapport K. and Olga enjoy in their extended conversations. This correspondence strikes one as simple and yet complex, for one can see in K. the representation of a dream, 'the dream', in Jakob Wassermann's words, 'of a secret emperor which exiles sometimes nurture out of a perverse love of their own misfortune'.[11]

Wassermann's phrase intimates the emergence of hope out of despair, a process which we see embodied in the Barnabas family's attitude towards K. And as K. begins to realize the secret of his own origin in the despairing hopes of this family, it dawns on him that what impedes his progress is a constitutional, inbred weakness. The origins of messianism in despair are the inherent cause of its unavoidable failure and incongruity. 'The Messiah', one of Kafka's notebooks relates, 'will come only when he is no longer needed, he will come only one day after his arrival, he will not come on the last day, but on the last day of all.' Philosophically this well-nigh absurd answer implies that the questions messianism raises will always turn back on themselves; historically it means that each messianic figure actually implicated in the scenario of human affairs – be it Bar Kochba, Sabbatai Zwi or Jakob Frank – necessarily bears the stigma of an imposter. Small wonder therefore if K.'s messianic identity seems – as Richard Sheppard has recently pointed out[12] – fictive and merely assumed. This would be the decisive argument against the spirit of messianism in general and against Kafka's novel in particular, were it not for the fact that the fundamental weaknesses have in both cases been consciously acknowledged and weighed in the balance. These weaknesses are deemed to be the irrefutable proof of a truth otherwise stifled and obscured by an oppressive reality. Seen in this light even the false messiah with all his failures acquires the positive function which Buber describes in one of his hassidic tales:

> When God saw that the soul of Israel was sick he clothed it in the searing shroud of exile in order that it might endure. He laid the sleep of numbness upon it. Lest this sleep should destroy it, he wakens it at times with false hopes of the messiah and lulls it back to sleep till the night is over and the true Messiah appears.[13]

Conceivably the true messiah mentioned towards the end of this passage will also turn out to be a charlatan. But this is beside the point. What is important in messianic thought is solely the viability of what Ernst Bloch called *das Prinzip Hoffnung*, 'the Hope Principle', a principle which to Franz Rosenzweig appeared to be *der Stern der Erlösung*, 'the Star of Salvation'.

A further purposeful element in Kafka's delineation of messianism seems to be the peculiar intensity that governs K.'s relationship with Amalia and Barnabas. As has variously been mooted, Amalia's presence provides the only positive counterpart to the Land Surveyor K. We are told of her pride, of her craving for solitude and her strange elevated manner. Kafka was painstakingly explicit in describing Amalia's attitude and yet its significance remains uncertain. We know that Amalia undermines K.'s confidence and determination; one of the rejected passages goes so far as to call her 'an evil obstacle'. If K. fails to win her over he will remain 'in the dark', trying to build a house without foundations. It is difficult to ascertain precisely what these hints suggest, but it seems feasible to argue that Amalia stands for the decisive obstacle which messianism has to overcome in trying to fulfil its own yearning. One is almost tempted to say that Amalia embodies the static counterpart of the dynamic principle represented in K. Kafka discussed a similar relationship in a note of 18 January 1922 dealing with the alternatives of courage and fearlessness: 'Fear means unhappiness but it does not follow from this that courage means happiness; . . . not courage then, but fearlessness with its calm, open eye and stoical resolution.'[14] These sentences have their bearing on Amalia and K. as well as on a conflict which has always played an important role in determining Jewish self-esteem. Ultimately they imply the question of whether a hostile reality ought to be opposed actively or passively. Amalia's attitude is passive, the attitude of traditional Jewish exclusiveness.

To begin with, Amalia may have been horrified at the expression of sexual greed in Sortini's persistent gaze, she may have recognized the ratified power of men over women and perhaps too the violent and base determination with which those in power approach their victims. In turning away from all this, Amalia becomes the object of persecution and it is through this transformation that she gains an insight into the pitiless fate of those who do not belong to the community. Her happiness can only be ephemeral, that of a temporary respite, but it is also untinged by any compromise with power. In a slim book published in Paris in 1947 under the title *Kafka ou le mystère juif*, André Nemeth summed up this kind of experience in a brief formula. 'Persécutés, ils se savent déjà élus. Voilà le paradoxe de leur condition' (p. 20).[viii]

The destiny of the outsider, mediated by the idea of vocation, takes on the quality of exclusiveness, a kind of self-assertion that can be traced back to the books of the prophets and to Isaiah in particular. Combined with the historical reality of exile this makes for an image of Judaism of which Amalia, an outcast of high estate, is a reflection. In an essay entitled *Galut* which appeared in Berlin as late as 1936, Jizchak Fritz Baer outlined the traditional meaning of life in the diaspora. 'The unobtrusive influence of the Jewish can be likened to the mystery of the seed-grain which must seemingly disintegrate and perish in order to assimilate and translate the surrounding matter' (p. 26). It almost seems too much of a coincidence that Kafka, according to Gustav Janouch, should have considered this problem in almost identical terms:

> The Jewish people is scattered, as a seed is scattered. As a seed of corn absorbs matter from its surroundings, stores it up, and achieves further growth, so the destiny of the

Jews is to absorb the potentialities of mankind, purify them, and give them a higher development. Moses is still a reality. As Abiram and Dathan opposed Moses with the words '*Lo naale!* We will not go up!' so the world opposes him with the cry of anti-Semitism.[15]

It is of little importance whether Kafka actually spoke sentences to this effect or whether they are merely – as the sceptical would surely maintain – Janouch's invention; what matters is rather that in Amalia we possess the image of a traditional moralistic attitude which vindicates and justifies a whole way of life, a way of life so completely opposed to the idea of political dominion that it failed to create an earthly domicile for itself.

Compared with Amalia's moral determination, with her almost tragic composure, K.'s political restlessness seems a token of the pathological origin of messianism. Where exile can no longer be endured, messianism emerges as the vision of its annihilation. Not prepared to acknowledge the positive function of the *Galut*, messianism sees in it but a grievous stage preceding redemption. Whereas Amalia in a situation of utter despair still exemplifies human dignity and offers the guilty community around her a chance to come to know the idea of justice, K. for his part intends to break out of this confinement by transcending her merely static confrontation with the powers that be. Pressing for a solution, the messianic figure is the agent of the unceasing endeavour of man to revolutionize his situation.

One of the most carefully planned features in Kafka's novel is the way K. comes face to face, in the Barnabas family, not only with his origin and a critical alternative to his own pursuits but also with the image of his futile exertions. The passages which describe K.'s encounters with Barnabas all but reveal the closely guarded emotions of the author, for the simple reason perhaps that in Barnabas K. recognizes a brother who – like himself – attempts to instigate a new departure in a case that for too long has remained unresolved. K., of course, is not aware of this when he first meets Barnabas. But Kafka with unparalleled artistic discretion induces in us the gradual realization that Barnabas appears to K. as an epiphany, as the longed-for companion of one who feels himself to be on his own. The aura surrounding Barnabas is that of an angel, epitomized in his smile whose radiance cannot be dimmed; this impression is reinforced in his answer to K.'s enquiry: '"Who are you" – "My name is Barnabas. I am a messenger."' The illusion in which K. is here allowed to place his trust for a brief moment encourages the hope that there may be a connection between the sordid real world and his better vision. It is in the proximity of such hopeful radiance that theology is inclined to dwell as a foil to the 'ausdrucksbildende Kraft der Finsternis'[16] ('expressive power of darkness') which Martin Walser noticed in Kafka's works.

K.'s intention parallels that of theology: the dispersing of darkness. It is therefore quite consistent that he should entertain precise, if inarticulate notions concerning the messengers of light. I have in mind here the strange passage where K. tutors that poor girl Pepi. The position in the taproom, he tells her, 'is a job like any other, but for you it is heaven, consequently you set about everything . . . with exaggerated eagerness, trick yourself out as in your opinion the angels are tricked out – but in reality they are different' (p. 291). This negative piece of information about the angels makes us wonder if they might not be figures like Barnabas, creating a feeling of humaneness in a hostile environment. In any case, there is here no definite indication, merely a mirage of supernatural forces. Kafka's image of the angel has nothing to do with metaphysics and pertains rather – not unlike the teaching of Plato, Philo or Aquinas – to the ontological realm. It is therefore of great visual consequence that the hopeful manifestation at the beginning of the novel dissolves as Barnabas strips off his messenger's garb. This does not, however, impair the validity of his first appearance representing man as an incomplete angel; an idea which Paul Klee once described in sentences that could well have been Kafka's own. 'This creature', Klee wrote in January 1905, 'born in contrast to divine beings with only one wing, makes ceaseless attempts to fly. Thereby his limbs are broken and yet he remains true to his idea.'[17] Klee's figure *Der Held mit dem Flügel*, the Winged Hero, embodies, in his ruinous state, precisely the distinction between vision and reality which Kafka's novel critically implies by making K. and Barnabas dependent upon one another. The rest is resignation to a pointless striving which neither of them can abandon because they are identical with it.[ix] Beckett's *Molloy* contains a similar constellation of 'agent' and 'messenger', of the narrator of the story and a certain Gaber whose memory is as rudimentary as that of Barnabas is phenomenal. The analogy, significant in many respects, cannot be pursued further here. Let me end therefore with a quotation in which the agent, the figure corresponding to K., ponders with characteristic scepticism the fate he shares with the messenger:

> That we thought of ourselves as members of a vast organisation was doubtless also due to the all too human feeling that trouble shared, or is it sorrow, is trouble something, I forget the word. But to me at least, who knew how to listen to

the falsetto of reason, it was obvious that we were perhaps alone in what we did. Yes, in my moments of lucidity I thought it possible. And, to keep nothing from you, this lucidity was so acute at times that I came even to doubt the existence of Gaber himself. And if I had not hastily sunk back into my darkness I might have gone to the extreme of conjuring away the chief too and regarding myself as solely responsible for my wretched existence. For I knew I was wretched, at six pounds ten a week plus bonuses and expenses. And having made away with Gaber and the chief (one Youdi), could I have denied myself the pleasure of – you know. But I was not made for the great light that devours, a dim lamp was all I had been given, and patience without end, to shine it on the empty shadows.[18]

A Kaddish for Austria

On Joseph Roth

> Und der Graf fragte den Juden: 'Salomon, was hältst du von dieser Erde?' – 'Herr Graf,' sagte Piniowsky, 'nicht das Geringste mehr.'
>
> Joseph Roth, 'Die Büste des Kaisers'

> And the Count asked the Jew, 'Solomon, what do you count on in this world?' '*Herr Graf*,' said Piniowsky, 'I no longer count on anything at all.'
>
> Joseph Roth, 'The Bust of the Emperor'[i]

In May 1913, at the Deutsches Gymnasium in Brody, the young Joseph Moses Roth drew a neat line under his by no means carefree childhood and youth, graduating with the distinction '*sub auspiciis imperatiori*' as the best in his year in the *Matura* [school-leaving examination]. He was about to set out, via Lemberg [Lviv] and Vienna, for the wider world, and he does not, at the time, appear to have had any regrets about turning his back on his homeland, although what he gave up along with it would later come to symbolize all the loss-making enterprises [*Verlustgeschäfte*] of which life consists. Only in hindsight did Galicia reveal itself to him: a far-off crown land of longing, beyond history, it came to take the place of the lost *Heimat*, destroyed by war, which vanished from the maps for ever with the dissolution of the Empire. Roth, who as time went on found it harder and harder to come to terms with this obliteration, recalls in a piece written in 1929 that mythical moment when the Empire of the Habsburgs sank 'into the oceans of time . . . with all its powers and the might of its weapons so completely, so finally, as the miserable childhood of one of its subjects, not to be compared with the Empire!'[1] This equating of lost empire with lost childhood makes Roth's characteristic melancholic identification with the experience of loss and defeat very clear. If there is such a thing as a promised land, then it lies far back in the past; the words 'so completely, so finally', which set the emotional tone in the quotation above, not only refer to the moment of disappearance, but also represent a last faint glimmer of the glory that once was and is no more. The future, by contrast, is nothing but a mirage. Although, as it says in *Hiob* [*Job*], Mendel Singer 'took his children's word for it, that America was God's own country, New York a city of miracles, and English the most beautiful language in the world', and although he tells himself that soon men will fly like birds, swim like fishes, foresee the future like prophets, live in eternal peace and harmony, and build skyscrapers to touch the stars,[2] he convinces neither himself nor the reader, since travesty is inscribed into the utopian project from the start. It is thus scarcely surprising when, barely a page later, the 'few miserable stars', 'scattered from the main design of the heavens', which Mendel is able to make out against the reflected light from the city awaken in him memories of 'the clear, starry nights at home, the deep blue of the great spanning heavens, the softly curving sickle of the moon, the dark rustle of the forest firs, and the voices of crickets and the frogs'.[3] Memories such as these recur time and time again in Roth's work, and almost always feature the earth's wide horizons, mankind gazing upwards and the starry canopy of the heavens. Their specific form thus recalls Hebrew nature poetry, about which Hermann Cohen notes '[that it] always embraces the universe as a whole, both life on earth and the radiant vaults of the heavens'.[4ii] What, in such Hebrew poetry, might still have been a reflection of the monotheistic world order is in Roth's work inspired by the cold wind of homelessness that blows across the fields of exile.

For Joseph Roth, who had grown up in a town where a large majority of the population was Jewish, and which, as David Bronsen points out, Kaiser Joseph II called the New Jerusalem,[5] the experience of exile began with his arrival at the Nordbahnhof [North station] in Vienna, with his rented room in the Leopoldstadt, and his encounters with the *deutschnational* [German nationalist] students and teachers at the University of Vienna. The First Republic, with its increasingly rabid anti-Semitism, was, for a young Jewish writer, decidedly unsafe territory; and Berlin in the 1920s, which Roth soon moved to, was not exactly designed to make him feel at home either. In his important essay *Juden auf Wanderschaft* [*The Wandering Jews*], first published in 1927, where the trend to westwards migration is described as a wrong turning, Roth suggests that, for the newcomers, a 'no less dismal [. . .] ghetto offers its own brand of darkness', once they 'have barely managed to escape the clutches of the concentration camps'.[6] The date, as mentioned above, is 1927, and one must assume that with the term *Konzentrationslager* Roth is referring to the reception and transit camps – intended purely as charitable measures – in which, until the late 1920s, Jewish emigrants from the former Austrian territories who fetched up in the West were accommodated. Whatever Roth may have meant by the 'Schikanen des Konzentrationslagers' ['clutches of the concentration camps'], the term resonates far beyond what was originally intended, not only because the reader knows what was to come, but also because few people foresaw things as clearly and as farsightedly as Joseph Roth. If Berlin permitted him the illusion of being able to pass, unnoticed, as a cosmopolitan, with every trip to the provinces he realizes more clearly how appalling and uninhabitable his host country has become; it is no coincidence that he mostly abbreviated its name to the virtually soundless consonant sequence 'Dtschlnd.', which appears almost like a metaphor for uncharitableness. On his trip to the Harz mountains in 1931, sitting in an inn in Halberstadt, he feels obliged for reasons of camouflage to drink a beer, smoke a cigar and read the *Amtsanzeiger*, a paper in which democracy is ridiculed. 'The opinion of the paper', writes Roth, 'reassures them' – that is to say the gentlemen at the next table – 'as to my own. And one of them seems so satisfied with me that he raises his glass to me. I respond seriously – and in a flash decide to make good my escape.'[7] Roth's sarcasm barely conceals the fact that he can already see the death threat in his neighbour's eyes. Bronsen notes that after his experiences in Halberstadt and Goslar, Roth commented to his cousin, 'You have no idea how late it is. These towns are only five minutes from the pogrom.'[8] Much of what Roth set down on paper in the next seven years – at once his most difficult and most productive – is dedicated to the symbolic salvation of a world he already knew to be doomed. The literary snapshots from Europe's eastern provinces which Roth bequeaths to us correspond to the photographs Roman Vishniac took in the Jewish communities in Slovakia and Poland immediately before the so-called outbreak of war. In all of them can be seen portents of the approaching end, and in their moving beauty they give perhaps the most accurate idea of the amoral indifference of those who were even then gearing up for their work of extermination.

It has been variously argued that Roth, in his literary restitution of the *Heimat*, was in thrall to an illusionism which verges on the sentimental. Nothing, however, could be further from the truth. While it is true that Roth, in articles for a paper like *Der Christliche Ständestaat* written from purely strategic political motives, is not above resorting to cheap journalism, his literary works – even the less successful ones – are without exception characterized by an anti-illusionistic tendency. Even *Radetzkymarsch* [*The Radetzky March*], generally considered his masterwork, is – as the story of an irreversible downfall – without a shadow of a doubt a novel of disillusionment. At most, the father of the hero of Solferino is still allowed to live out his days 'in arärischer Traulichkeit' ('governmental homeyness');[iii] by contrast, the firmly established world view of the ennobled hero is shaken to the core by the distortion – sanctioned from on high and completely incomprehensible to him – of the simple truth into a mendacious tale for the edification of schoolchildren. Von Trotta, the District Captain representing the next generation, believes he will be able to protect himself from the vicissitudes of life by adopting a highly ritualized set of behaviours, and is only thrown off course by the increasingly evident *malheur* [*Unglück*] of his son.

The latter, the unfortunate Carl Joseph, in his Galician border garrison is gradually going to rack and ruin from love of women, the rules and regulations of the world of men, the interplay of *rouge et noir*, homesickness and the bottles of 90% proof liquor which help him to forget it all. What drives the plot is the favour of the ruler, which, more a curse than a blessing, rests upon the Trotta dynasty like 'a load of cutting ice'.[9] The whole story is an extremely macabre dance of death. 'We are all no longer alive'[10] – with these words Graf Chojnicki reveals to the District Captain the terrible secret of the age, and at the end of the famous passage where Roth has the Corpus Christi procession in Vienna parade before our eyes, it is evident that this performance, simulating a kind of metaphysical life, has already attracted the circling vultures. On the face of it, everything is still the same as before. The infantry marches past, and the artillery, the Bosnians, the gold-decked Knights of the Golden Fleece and the red-cheeked municipal councillors. A half squadron of dragoons follows, and then a fanfare sounds and the principal character in this ostentatious display of might and right, the King of Jerusalem and Kaiser of the Apostolic Realm, appears, clad in a snow-white tunic, and with an enormous crest of green parrot feathers on his hat, which – thus Roth – swayed gently in the wind. Just like young Lieutenant Carl Joseph, witness to this spectacle, we, the readers, are dazzled by the gleaming radiance of the procession, and, like him, we would not hear 'the dark beatings of the vultures' wings', those 'brotherly foes' of the two-headed eagle of the Habsburgs,[11] had they not been expressly brought to our attention. Indeed, the narrator has a particular affinity with birds. A faint, hoarse croaking is heard in the sky when the wild geese leave their summer haunts early, before the outbreak of war – as if, as Chojnicki says, they could already hear the gunfire. To say nothing of the ravens, those prophets among the birds, now sitting motionless in the trees in their hundreds announcing the catastrophe [*Unglück*] with loud croaks. Bad times are coming. Soon 'the shots of the hasty executioners of hasty sentences' will ring out from 'the church squares of hamlets and villages . . . The Austrian army's war', the narrator comments, 'had begun with court-martials. For days on end genuine and supposed traitors hung from the trees to terrify the living.'[12] Looking at their bloated faces, Trotta recognizes them as victims of that same corruption of the law and the flesh that he has for so long sensed in himself. There is nothing in this novel, stripping away as it does every illusion one by one, that would suggest a transfiguration of the Habsburg Empire; on the contrary, *Radetzkymarsch* is a thoroughly agnostic work, whose dismal events, so it seems to Leutnant von Trotta, are fitted together 'in a sombre mosaic as if manipulated by some powerful, hateful, invisible wire puller'.[13] Who this antinomian character refers to is not explained. What is certain is that, at the end of the novel, while the relentless rain shrouds both the castle of Schönbrunn and the Steinhof Insane Asylum, where the prophetic Count Chojnicki is now an inmate, the apostolic order and sheer insanity amount to one and the same thing.

What, though, does the concept of *Heimat* – without doubt the most frequently recurring concept in Roth's work – mean for the disillusioned consciousness which alone could produce a novel like *Radetzkymarsch*? In one way or another, Roth's characters all yearn for home. Sometimes *Heimat* is 'the dark-green shadows of the chestnut trees in the town park filling the room with the entire mellow and powerful calm of the summer',[14] sometimes a place one has left, or, as in the case of the long-serving gunner Eibenschütz, the army, which, as the narrator informs us, was his 'second and perhaps his actual Nikolsburg'.[15] It can be a house, like that of Josephine Matzner where Mizzi Schinagl[iv] felt so at home and superior to every man, or the depths of the ocean to which Nissen Piczenik is drawn by his insatiable love of coral.[v] For the wandering Jews, however, among whose number Roth counts himself, and whose graves, as he writes, are everywhere, *Heimat* is nowhere – and thus the epitome of utopia. Roth has distilled it out of the utter desolation of history, and with the lightest of artistic touches he incorporates it into the depiction of this very desolation. His prose is full of minute turns of phrase, expressions, undertones and cadences which seem to hint that, beyond the incontrovertible historical catastrophe [*Unglück*], there must lie something other. Without in any way detracting from his truly merciless criticism of the comatose Habsburg system, Roth evokes this other world – surrounded by a strange iridescent radiance – in an almost casual allegory of the many-coloured and multifarious Empire. The form the allegory assumes is a map of the monarchy on which, in the imagination of the District Captain, the various crown lands appear merely as 'large variegated forecourts of the Imperial Palace'.[16] The use of the term *Vorhöfe* [forecourts] in connection with the array of colours suggests that this map shows not the real world but the Elysian fields, revealed only to an eschatological vision, and whose best-known topos is the Heavenly Jerusalem. There is, too, a second allegorical transposition in the novel: the figure of the Kaiser who, as the young Trotta conjectures, seemed to have aged suddenly, within a single day, within a very specific hour and who 'since that hour . . . had remained locked in his eternal, silvery and dreadful senility as in an armour of awe-inspiring crystal'.[17] And, so the passage continues, 'the years did not dare approach him. His eyes kept growing bluer and harder.' Walter Benjamin offers a description of the emblematic function of the corpse in baroque tragedy. Only with the corpse, he claims, can the allegorization of the *physis* [body] be achieved.[18] We find a similar process of allegorization in the transformation of Franz Joseph into a body removed from time, existing only in a kind of ceremonial afterlife. By comparison with the vast, multifarious and many-coloured political body of the monarchy, this *corpus*, the Imperial body, reduced almost to an inorganic substance, assumes the status of a holy relic, an object for the cultivation of remembrance. Roth believed in the power and efficacy of such relics. It was thus logical that he should give credence to a plan whereby at the last minute Austria might still, perhaps, be saved if the heir to the throne were to be brought to Vienna in a coffin.[19]

One of the most striking features of Roth's work is the way that, at a time when the novel was developing into a hypertrophic genre, it restores storytelling to its rightful place. The art of storytelling, Benjamin writes, derives primarily from the ability to listen, in a state of self-forgetfulness, to the ground note which runs through everything[20] – perhaps that gentle whispering which Franz Josef too believes he can hear as he nears his end. This is the sound which dictates the rhythm of work, and only when the storyteller succeeds in becoming completely absorbed in his task does the strange impression arise that the gift of storytelling comes to him all by itself.[21] Ulrich Greiner has pointed out that in *Hiob* [*Job*], for example, the art of narrating, as it were 'from within', is so radical that one could imagine the story of Mendel

Singer is being related by a higher being that might, perhaps, be described as a blessed super-ego, even as an accompanying guardian angel.[22] Indeed, there are passages in Roth's work over which the spirit of the storyteller still seems to hover, as if he were only just discovering the right words for his tale. There is Taittinger, Captain of Horse, standing facing Mizzi Schinagl in prison, suddenly deeply moved by her cropped head, as little able to know what to do with his emotions as we with ours. There is melancholic Anselm Eibenschütz gazing up at the stars, to which he has previously never given a second thought and which now, in his misery [*Unglück*], appear to him as very distant relations. And a few hours before his audience with his imperial double, the District Captain [von Trotta] stands at the window like a man standing on the shore, waiting for morning as if for a homecoming ship. Passages like this, which give us a glimpse of 'the edges of eternity',[23] are examples of an art which, despite its apparent unassuming simplicity, is never satisfied with the merely superficial. Of course, it is not easy to discover the secret formula underlying the wonderfully light touch of Roth's prose. It is possible that the narrative trance Roth was clearly able to enter had something to do with the strong spirits he consumed, or indeed with his aversion to eating. As Brónsen informs us, Roth set store by the impression that he lived by intellect alone. 'I have not eaten a meal for the last three years,' he is said sometimes to have claimed.[24] Even if – in common with many of Roth's statements about himself – this did not strictly correspond to the truth, it was certainly more than mere affectation. At the latest after what happened to Friederike,[vi] Roth knew that he was not long for this world. The 1930s, in which the greater part of his literary works were written, was also the last decade of his life. In 'The

Storyteller' ['Der Erzähler'], Benjamin attempts to fathom the connection between storytelling and the proximity of death:

> Just as a sequence of images is set in motion inside a man as his life comes to an end – unfolding the views of himself under which he has encountered himself without being aware of it – suddenly in his expressions and looks the unforgettable emerges and imparts to everything that concerned him that authority which even the poorest wretch in dying possesses for the living around him. This authority is at the very source of the story.[25]

Certainly this applies to Roth's stories, in which a great deal of dying goes on, and where Death is already crossing his haggard, invisible hands over the glass beakers from which the living are still toasting each other's health.[26]

What is being thematized under such auspices is not so much history as the course of the world, which – as Benjamin also remarks – is outside of all real historical categories.[vii] The other epoch in the history of the world, the one which matters to the chronicler watching the round years roll by, one by one,[27] is the period of naïve poetry;[viii] and it is this with which, as a storyteller, Roth keeps faith, for which reason 'his eyes do not stray from that dial in front of which there moves the procession of creatures of which, depending on circumstances, Death is either the leader or the last wretched straggler'.[28] Indeed, dials and clock faces, timepieces of every kind, have a special significance in Roth's work. The voice of the narrator is barely audible above their constant hasty ticking, already reminiscent of the deathwatch beetles in the woodwork. For Leutnant von Trotta, it is not a good omen that his friend Max Demant, killed in a duel, leaves him his watch.[ix] There are too many incontrovertible sayings with regard to time and the end. *Ultima multis*, the last of many. *Ultima necat*, the last one kills, and more in that vein. Bronsen notes that Roth haphazardly collected clocks and watches, and that his preoccupation with them in later years became something of an obsession.[29] What so fascinated him about clocks is summarized by Roth in unforgettable fashion in one of his very last pieces – appearing in the *Pariser Zeitung* on the first weekend of April 1939.[x] The text, scarcely two pages long, is entitled 'Beim Uhrmacher' ('At the Watchmaker's'), and is dedicated to the mystery of time passing and time past. There was, the narrator begins, only one watchmaker in the little town in which he spent his childhood, and at the time, he continues, a clock face was for him 'a round and rather uncanny riddle', which the grown-ups claimed to use to measure time – time which for him still stretched ahead like a boundless ocean. In the course of this rehearsal for his own end, as wondrous as it is prosaic, the child – the author's representative – for whom clocks are still out of reach, comes to suspect that there is a connection between the constant desire of the grown-ups

> to know the time, and the utter terror with which they spoke of sickness, death and the dead. They fell silent as soon as I began to listen, they hid death from me like the clocks, and my mother forbade me to play at funerals. For that reason the small cemetery, whose wall I was often led past and in which, as I knew, a great-uncle was buried, remained a desired and secret goal which I was determined one day to reach. A strange, cool shiver ran through me, a shiver of curiosity and premonition. And there was only *one*

place in the town where a similar nameless, inexplicable premonition touched me, and which I was sometimes allowed to enter: the watchmaker's shop.[30]

This sense of premonition which gripped the child in the darkness of the watchmaker's shop, with its thousand voices whispering and ticking away, is probably what Roth wished to recreate as a storyteller. There he sat, his lens jammed to his eye like the watchmaker, gazing into the broken miracle of the tiny wheels and cogs, 'as if he were peering through a black-rimmed hole into a distant past'.[31] Like the watchmaker, the writer lives in hope that one minuscule intervention is all it will take to restore everything to the rightful order, as was intended from the beginning.

Set against this messianic ideal, much of what he wrote must have necessarily appeared to Roth as inadequate and misbegotten. From time to time he would take himself severely, indeed scrupulously, to task. The work on *Radetzkymarsch*, in particular, caused him almost unassuageable doubts. 'One day everything has worked fine and the next it is all rubbish. Everything is tricky and deceptive . . . I fear I'm nothing but a botcher.'[32] Roth's fear is that, like Nissan Piczenik in the story *Der Leviathan* [*The Leviathan*],[xi] he might end up trading in false goods. He knows that the temptation is great, that the writer's handiwork, exactly like that of the confidence trickster,[xii] consists of finding a 'formula' that will allow him to live beyond his means.[33] In the realm of aesthetics, then, in the end it is always a matter of ethics. Not for nothing do the celluloid corals imported by the lame Jenö Lakatos from Hungary burn with a bluish flame, 'the same colour as the ring of purgatorial fire that burns around Hell'.[34]

Benjamin was of the opinion that the true storyteller owes his allegiance not to history but to natural history.[xiii] Thus it is not surprising that Roth was dissatisfied with *Radetzkymarsch*. The fact that in this novel, for the sake of what he – with evident distaste – calls his 'composition', he was obliged to borrow from history is something he finds 'shabby and mendacious'.[35] In this context it is instructive to consider his *Geschichte der 1002. Nacht* ['The Story of the 1002nd Night', translated as *The String of Pearls*], in which the narrative technique he so despised, a mere working up of noteworthy events, is thematized in the story itself. In the closing pages of this account – suffused by a fairytale sense of hopelessness – of the downfall of Captain Taittinger, the new World Bioscope Theatre, a Viennese cabinet of curiosities, promises to show, in lifelike verisimilitude, in four scenes:

1. The arrival of the great Shah with his aides at the Franz-Joseph Station (Royal train not to scale).
2. The Harem and Chief Eunuch of Teheran.
3. The Viennese concubine, a child of the people from Sievering, conducted to the Shah by important public figures, and subsequently enthroned as the ruler of the harem in Persia.
4. The remaining retinue of the Shah of Persia.[36]

The Viennese concubine is played by Mizzi Schinagl, named as the co-owner of the World Bioscope Theatre, for which enterprise, in an attempt to redeem the guilt he feels towards her, Taittinger has advanced the last of his money. And the four scenes announced on the poster are none other than a synopsis of the fateful time when Taittinger's life took a wrong turning. For Taittinger, the second coming of his own calamitous history is a source of horror, not least because it is played out in life-size; only the royal train is necessarily reduced in scale. Indeed, it is the life-sized dimensions which are truly disturbing, since although small puppets or dolls may, it is said, harbour a soul, life-sized waxwork figures are soulless monsters. Tino Percoli, the old Italian showman who supplies the waxwork figures for the World Bioscope Theatre, knows all about the effects of the mysterious differences in dimension. He closes the story of the 1002nd Night with the words: 'I might be capable of producing figures that have heart, conscience, passion, emotion and decency. But there's no call for that at all in the world. People are only interested in monsters and freaks, so I give them their monsters. Monsters are what they want!'[37]

In contrast to a number of his famous literary contemporaries, engaged upon projects on a monumental scale, Roth's literary ambitions were focused on the shorter form, which, he believed, alone permitted him to maintain a certain amount of integrity. His ideal form had the proportions of a good anthology piece. 'I would like to write in such a way', he is alleged to have said, 'that I am included in a *Lesebuch* [reader or primer].'[38] Perhaps that is why many of his prose works, always written in neat copperplate, and for preference in school exercise books, turned out to be absolutely model examples of *Lesestücke* [anthology pieces]. Not the least among these could be reckoned those pages at the start of *Radetzkymarsch* concerning the distortion of the truth sanctioned by a minister of education. Whether or not they have yet been included in the schoolbooks I do not know. In any case, the historical fantasy constructed around the 'Hero of Solferino' demonstrates Roth's scepticism towards all fictionalization – including his own. If art is about anything, then – or so one might summarize Roth's aesthetics, insofar as they can be teased out – it is about faithful attention to detail. With what dimensions true artistic workmanship operates is illustrated in the wonderful report on the Glashütte [Glassworks] clockmaking factory near Dresden. Because the instruments are so minute, Roth writes, the watchmaker operates 'with the precise touch and poetic sensibility of a blind man. One files away at invisible coils and polishes the points of steel needles which are not there unless one searches for them with a magnifying glass. That is exactly the borderline between work and creation'[39] – the very same borderline that was so crucial for Roth as an author, too, since overcoming it amounted at least in a virtual sense to a release from exile and a return to the lost *Heimat*. From here, a line can be traced to the poetic vision of Austria as Roth always imagined it. It is a vision, it seems to me, from which any claim to power and all imperialist traits are absent. What interested Roth, in his model idea of Austria, were at most the lost opportunities of history. Perhaps, the ancient Herr von Maerker muses at the end of *Der stumme Prophet* [*The Silent Prophet*], there really was still the possibility 'of making a homeland for all out of the old monarchy. It could have been the miniature model of a great future world':[40] 'das kleinere Vorbild einer großen zukünftigen Welt'. The emphasis is not on the great future world – which Roth knows to be long since forfeit – but on the 'miniature model' illuminated by the gleam of past glories. Roth's emotional attachment to his own model [*Modell*] of an ecumenical Reich – hopelessly anachronistic when compared to the actual politics of the day – resembles the relationship of Herr Frohmann from Drohobycz to the model of the Temple of Solomon[xiv] he has constructed from balsawood, papier mâché and gold paint, in exact accordance with the description in the Bible. Herr Frohmann, who travels with his creation from ghetto to ghetto, and sometimes even as far as Berlin, regards himself as a guardian of tradition. He claims to have spent seven years building this miniature temple, where 'every single curtain, courtyard, crenellation, and altarpiece' is clearly visible,[41] and Joseph Roth, who is telling the story of Herr Frohmann, believes him, for, as he says, 'to rebuild a temple demands just as much time as love.'[42]

Una montagna bruna

On Hermann Broch's 'Mountain Novel'

[*Bergroman*][i]

Am Anfang Prophet,
am Ende Zauberer.

Jüdisches Sprichwort

In the beginning a prophet,
In the end a magician.

Jewish saying[ii]

One of the peculiar things about Hermann Broch's oeuvre is that the high regard in which it is held – assiduously promoted by the dutiful dogsbodies of *Germanistik* – is not necessarily borne out by a critical reading. It is telling that, in the context of Austrian literature in particular, his position remains far from assured. Although the author of the *Bergroman* [mountain novel], the main focus of this article, was already hailed by his first editor as an 'überösterreichischer Heimat-dichter'[1] [a supra-Austrian *Heimat* author], this rapturous reverence did not prevail. Thus, for example – unlike, say, Roth,

Musil and Wittgenstein – Broch is not included in the two volumes of *Österreichische Porträts* [*Austrian Portraits*][iii] edited by Jochen Jung in 1985. Clearly there are, then as now, certain difficulties with the critical reception of his work, and it is these difficulties I wish to address here, since they precisely reflect my own problematic relationship with Broch.

I still clearly remember the feeling of admiration which the cool objectivity of *Pasenow* [*The Romantic*][iv] produced in me when, years ago, I read it for the first time – but also my increasing sense of disappointment and unease at the way in which the analytic flow of the narrative is slowed down and interrupted by the overwrought theoretical constructs with which Broch attempts to bring about a synthesis between the divergent forces in his work. While the individual insights arising from the story of the protagonist Hugenau – an example of a completely functionalized individual – are of a degree of acuity otherwise only attained by Musil, the theory of the deterioration of values [*Wertzerfall*] extrapolated from the narrative remains, in the end, somewhat vague, being governed by a pathos incompatible with the novel's ironical stance. Admittedly, the way the author privileges his own powers of perception in the trilogy *Die Schlafwandler* [*The Sleepwalkers*], prioritizing the system over and above empirical detail, is already established in the first volume in the author's consciously 'transcendental' perspective. While this position can, on the one hand, be seen as an attempt to approach everything once more from an independent perspective, on the other it is accompanied by a gradual and chronic loss of reality – something which may, perhaps, account for the strangely hollow and unreal quality of Broch's later prose. Broch's miscalculation lay in the assumption that the blindness of the whole, which takes precedence over subjective perceptions, could still be tackled by means of higher reason. In this, Broch, who considered himself one of the foremost novelists of his day, turns out to be downright traditionalist, since the integrative process of higher reason generally transforms the decisive insights regarding the course of so-called reality into mythology, which is more likely to contribute to blindness than to insight. By the time of *Hugenau* [*The Realist*], Broch has already reached the limits of abstraction where the desire for knowledge and insight abruptly dissolves into vague lyricism and pure mystification, something which would prove as decisive as it was fateful for Broch's later career as a novelist.[2]

When, in the summer of 1935, in the 'capital of the Movement',[v] Broch sets down the first version of the first volume of the *Bergroman*, he is again working on a project of gigantic proportions, even if the next two volumes never get under way. The book, which he mostly refers to in correspondence of the time as 'der große Roman' [the big novel], aspires to be nothing less than a 'new form of totality',[3] and is intended to present an analysis of the now manifest collective madness — all set against the background of a rhapsody, epic in breadth and scope, to the Soul of nature and mankind ['die Beseeltheit der Natur und des Menschen']. This intention alone, with its boundless possibilities, suggests a shapeless outcome, and thus it is not particularly surprising that Broch should be plagued by recurring doubts as to the whole business of 'Dichterei und Erzählerei' ['all this poeticizing and storytelling'][4] — and this not merely on account of the depressing conditions of the times. His dilemma arises from his sense of ethical and didactic responsibility, the feeling that nothing should be left unsaid. Unlike Wittgenstein, who held a discursive differentiation of the ethical assumptions underpinning our existence – in whatever form – to be an impossibility, and who therefore restricted himself to the clear outlines of pure logic, Broch is apparently of the view that large problems can be overcome by means of grand ideas, and indeed later too he repeatedly conceives of projects of positively vertiginous dimensions, all the way up to his idea of a democratic world state.[5] Working on the *Bergroman*, Broch soon finds himself – in accordance with Wittgenstein's prognosis – passing from the unsayable to the unspeakable. The abstract construct of a novel of rural life, with its unspecified Alpine setting, throws up aesthetic and ethical problems the nature of which ought to have made clear to Broch – who had after all thought a great deal about the correlation between these central components of artistic creation – just how overblown and unrealistic his concept was.

The plot itself is relatively straightforward. A wanderer of southern appearance, one Marius Ratti, whom the secondary literature on Broch, on the basis of a variety of verifiable evidence, is inclined to identify with certain fascist leader figures, turns up unannounced in a mountain village and, partly through his reactionary statements about the degenerate times and the need for a great cleansing, in part merely through his own malign presence, causes the population to take leave of its senses. Symptoms of mass psychosis begin to spread, culminating in the 'highly dramatic' scene in which a young girl named Irmgard is killed by the village butcher Sabest at the Cold Stone. The entire village, including the narrator – the country doctor – is present at this 'ritual', which is soon enough forgotten. Opinions may differ as to the suitability of such a plot as a vehicle for a critique of fascism. Although containing not a shred of plausibility, it nevertheless incorporates a set of traits which make it appear viable as a case study of fascist collective behaviour. The problems, then, lie less in the storyline than in the way it is related.

For a start, the character of Ratti is so over-freighted with contradictory symbolic signifiers as to remain an almost completely abstract figure. The melancholic associations of the wanderer, traditionally a disconsolate figure of no fixed abode – one need only think of Schubert's *Winterreise*, of Kafka's novel *Das Schloss* [*The Castle*], of Chaplin or of Joseph Roth – are scarcely compatible with the allegory of evil which Broch places centre-stage in the figure of the sinister Ratti. What is more, the inexplicable visitation on the villagers of this diabolic figure turning up out of the blue suggests that he may vanish as unexpectedly as he appeared. Indeed, the closing chapters of the novel place the ominous episode of the human sacrifice in the wider context of an indifferent nature, in whose serenity it makes scarcely a ripple. The spiritual condition of the country doctor, whose interpretation of events has, as far as one can make out, the approval of his author, corresponds almost exactly to that of, say, Hans Carossa taking comfort in the refuge of nature, remote from the terrible events of the day. This attitude is broadly in accord with the *Naturphilosophie* so characteristic of authors such as Lehmann, Loerke and Wiechert, which still remained influential on many aspects of German post-war literature.[6] The ethical dilemma of inner emigration, in other words of passive resistance – which in practice is indistinguishable from passive collaboration – is not explored by Broch, nor are its implications understood as the crucial dilemma of his narrator. Rather, it appears that, in the *Bergroman* – while making complicated arrangements for the preservation of his self-respect – he has retreated from the urbane life which formerly defined him into that extreme mental provincialism which characterized literary life under Austro-fascism,[7] thereby assimilating principles which lay much further to the right of his better judgement than he was prepared to admit to himself. It was not, as the defenders of Broch's posthumous fame like to claim, merely 'törichter Unsinn' ['ridiculous nonsense'][8] that Broch should from time to time be mentioned in connection with fascistic tendencies. The fact that Broch himself for a while inclined more to the left, and that after the *Anschluß* he was arrested by the fascists, in a kind of Bad Aussee farce as ludicrous as it was malicious, as a Jewish *Kulturbolschewist*, in no way refutes the in many ways extremely disconcerting implications of the *Bergroman*. There was, in the Austria of the 1930s, not exactly any shortage of opportunities to move to the right, given the intense competition at the time between the various fascistoid denominations fighting for space at this end of the political spectrum. The particular value of literature, especially bad literature, is that it permits us to reconstruct precisely these kinds of – frequently unconscious – accommodations. Naturally, the aim here is not to accuse Broch of crypto-fascism, but to understand his particular misfortune at the time, namely that when – as we have on good authority – he really did become completely nauseated by the anti-Semitic machinations, and when it would have long since been time to prepare for exile, he was still attempting to hold on to his 'natural' *Heimat* as some kind of inalienable possession. In fact, had things been a little different, Broch's refocusings of his own position during his work on the *Bergroman* which, among other reasons, led him to remain in Austria, could easily have cost him his life.

In the autumn of 1935, Broch continued to work on the *Bergroman* in the vicinity of Seefeld in Tyrol. He has now, as he writes to his publisher's wife, found 'an ideal place to work. Absolute seclusion, complete isolation, just me all alone in a farmhouse, and out of my window I have a view of the whole length of the Inn valley 600 metres below me, all the way up to the Arlberg . . . It is so indescribably beautiful that I am almost worried that I will only look out of the window and not get any work done at all.'[9] The programme Broch has set himself, however, demands that he should *not* gaze out of the window at the 'indescribable beauty' but rather lower his eyes and commit it to paper, for the work is urgent, 'not least because of the coming war',[10] as Broch notes in a letter of 4 November 1935. Yet the landscape scenes in the novel are not – as one might expect under the circumstances – dominated by a sense of loss; rather, they are presented with a gesture of affirmation, determined by the dubious ideological function of nature in the context of this text. Whereas Broch's *Sleepwalkers* still moved through a world almost devoid of landscape, the frequency of landscape depictions in the *Bergroman* borders on the inflationary. All the registers of seasons and weather are rehearsed, and yet, despite this epic extravagance, the images remain clichés. 'The rain had started again. The woods smoked and white wisps of fog drifted along the slopes. But the rain had thinned, the cloud cover had lifted, the birches and pines glistened luminously in the moistness, and from time to time there even was a break in the clouds, so that a band of rain appeared as a singing golden veil in the rays of the sun'[11] – a dubious sort of prose, hovering between meteorological observation and vapid lyricism. In better times, Broch was allergic to this kind of 'art'. 'Evening atmosphere in the woods', mocks the sometime reviewer of the collected works of the long-since forgotten *Goldschnittpoet* [gilt-edged poet] Heinrich von Stein, 'mists drift like sadness, the lake is silent, and sometimes it speaks.'[12] The mountain is silent, and sometimes it speaks – one can hardly imagine a more accurate synopsis of the descriptions of nature Bloch now cultivates. In a few passages in the text, these images do indeed succeed in giving rise to the intended vista of 'eternity'; the embarrassing moments, on the other hand, are legion. When, towards the end of his report, the doctor climbs up into the woods, where Mother Gisson – the good counterpart to the evil Ratti – has retreated to die, we read the following:

> this is how I return homeward to the pines and the spring, thus pines and spring return to me, homestead [*Heimat*] that I recover and which recovers my own self, and as the landscape all around slowly ceases its motion and my feet once more are able to notice the mossy gravelly forest soil beneath, I come in sight of the Mother, resting next to the spring, she sees me and nods for me to approach.[13]

The artificial pathos here shows the equation Nature = Mother = *Heimat* to be mere mumbo-jumbo; the aesthetic deficit points to an ethical one, and this is true not only in this sole instance, but of the construction of the text as a whole.

The way direct speech is manipulated, with continual markers such as 'he said', 'he asked', 'he grunted', 'I reply', 'came the answer in Pluto's eyes' (the butcher's dog!), 'the young husband ventured', 'Peter interjected', and so on and so forth,[14] can scarcely be surpassed when it comes to unsophisticated narrative technique. The bloated accumulation of adjectives and adverbs – in a passage of no more than eight lines we find the following: 'southerly', 'not young', 'unmanly', 'gray', 'dappled gloom', 'ivory-colored', 'porcelain', 'starry-eyed', 'star-glittering', 'gray-eyed', 'moody', 'cloud-shrouded', 'radiant' and 'thought-laden'[15] – has its equivalent in a no less dubious arsenal of hollow abstractions like 'death', 'darkness', 'nothingness', 'love', 'knowledge', 'joy', 'sacrifice', 'eternity' and 'truth' – all taken from one single short paragraph[16] – which are invariably brought into play at those points where there is a need to restate what the poetic idiom has failed adequately to express. All of this is then further heightened by rhapsodic, would-be rhythmical sequences which, after pages of pseudo-musical composition [*Satzführung*], often culminate in a really quite extravagant display of bombast, for example in the passage where the doctor surmises that, despite his isolation, things are growing ever lighter around him:

> Piercing with my glance through all the shells of my own self, as I sit here sealed up in my flesh and in my life, listening to the music of the light departing the mountain peaks, I, enraptured and looking outward from the inconceivable of my own being into the even less conceivable of ever more extending realms, seeing and yet seen by myself, I apprehend the interwoven texture of all knowledge, I apprehend the apprehension of myself being both mountain and hill, myself being both light and landscape, unreachable because it is my own self and yet forever striven for, goal which I shall reach in spite of everything when in the deepest depths of the oceans, of the mountains, and of the sunken islands, when on the golden bottom of darkest darkness the great oblivion will overtake me one day.[17]

The greater the effort expended on the superstructure, the less stable the whole construct becomes – a law evidently governed by the same set of rules as, at the base, the devaluation of money, which is, after all, something Broch must have had an idea of. The characteristic feature of an inflationary aesthetic is, however, tautology. The 'Gedanken im Meer des Gedachten' ['thought in a sea of thoughts'], the 'heilige Heiterkeit' together with the 'heitere[n] Heiligkeit' ['holy serenity'; 'serene holiness'], the 'holde Scham des Herbstes, enthüllt und verhüllt vom kommenden Schnee' ['fair bashfulness of autumn, both bared and shrouded by the coming snow'], 'das Erfassende' and 'das Erfaßte' ['the perceived and that which perceives'][18] – these are just a few examples of a process of reification which Broch himself explained in his theory of values. Business is business, orders are orders, art is art, a rose is a rose, holiness is serene and serenity holy. The logical function of tautology, in the field of aesthetics as in that of genetics or machine theory, is that it contains *no* information whatsoever; its counterpart, on an ethical level, is defeatism. That Broch, who was the first to go deeper into the complexities of kitsch – kitsch, he wrote, is the evil in the value system of art, and the producer of kitsch not merely a dilettante or incompetent, but a reprobate and a criminal, or, in less histrionic terms, in Broch's own words, a swine[19] – that Broch of all people, despite his radical aversion to kitsch, should himself become a purveyor of the genre, is a tragedy of a quite particular kind. Its title is 'La trahison des clercs' and it was one performed very frequently in the 1930s and '40s. When the doctor, in the forest scene referred to above, gazes into the 'ever-recurrent birth of the spring' and when it seems to him

> as if there were also an ever-recurrent flow and counter-flow between the hither and the beyond, so incessant that no boundary remains between the two, and that this flow need only touch my head as well in order to open me up altogether, flowing into my heart, encircling my heart like a silvery band, penetrating to my deepest and most unattainable core, that core that had been patiently waiting since all beginnings to transcend all boundaries[20]

what we feel is not the intimations of transcendence that great moments in literature — and perhaps life — can give rise to, but merely a surfeit of sheer banality. In this sense, Broch's 'great novel' turns out to be a complete debacle. Broch was no doubt right to identify the loss of the sense for aesthetic unities as the chief symptom of the crisis of the late bourgeois era, and it is perhaps only now that we can grasp the full implications of his theory, in following, for example, Gregory Bateson's theories on the subject of aesthetics–evolution–epistemology, according to which the successive loss of our 'natural' affinity with aesthetic structures is described as an epistemological 'mistake' whose consequences cannot yet be guessed at.[21] Kitsch is the concrete manifestation of a loss of aesthetic sensibility; it is the result of the misprogramming of utopia, a misprogramming that ushers in a new age in which substitutes and surrogates take the place of what — in both nature and natural development — was once real. However, the deficit must be compensated for, hence the urge — to which the author of the *Bergroman* also succumbs — to legitimize this ersatz world; hence the constant references to an ancient knowledge of all things that have existed, and the 'archaic' veneer in the most 'profound' passages of the novel, with its philosophizing reflections on 'the . . . sources of thought and speech, the no longer comprehensible chthonic powers sucking and drawing us down to the dark roots of all harvests'.[22]

The suspicion that he might have 'conformed to an ideological concept of mythology' is rejected out of hand in the secondary literature on Broch as an 'unjust misunderstanding'.[23] This is not particularly surprising, given that critical interventions in the case of an already canonical 'great author' have never gone down well in the world of *Germanistik*. The professional ethos of an in many ways still very backward branch of knowledge demands of its practitioners – and this too is an example of tautology in operation – that they concern themselves less with understanding the work than with legitimizing it via the exhaustive elicitation of its sources and references. From the writings of the church fathers down to Frazer, Bachofen, Robert Graves, Klages, C. G. Jung and a whole host of yet more obscure mythographers and historians of religion – to say nothing of Broch's literary predecessors – almost everything Broch read before and during his work on the novel is brought to bear.[24] The fact that none of this is proof of a coherent concept is overlooked, and thus the real problem remains undiscovered, namely that Broch here makes use of exactly the same eclectic methods that he had so persuasively ruled out in his theory of the decline of values. If, as Broch argues, no authentic style can be derived from an assemblage of heterogeneous elements (Ringstraße architecture!),[vi] then, by analogy, nor can a new myth such as Broch may have had in mind be created out of a miscellaneous collection of mythological elements. What Broch manages to create, in the reiterative presentation of the positive matriarchal world view with which he counters the maleficent notions of Ratti, is at best an example of the derivative mythologizing so characteristic of the time in which he wrote: a desperate attempt to make up for a chronic deficit of meaning by attempts to create meaning and systems of meaning, which of course ultimately always leads, at the first sign of a crisis, to those now overly replete with meaning, like the Gadarene swine[vii] in St Matthew's gospel, stampeding precipitately down a steep slope in order to drown in the sea.

In a lecture on 'Freud's Position in the History of Modern Thought' ['Die Stellung Freuds in der modernen Geistesgeschichte'], which Thomas Mann – who had learned a thing or two during the Weimar years – gave at the university in Munich in 1929, he stresses that the 'reversion to the good old times' by reactionary philosophies and mythologies is necessarily a false trail.'[25] In this context, Thomas Mann is referring expressly to the chthonic fantasies of Bachofen and Klages, and thus to precisely that new irrationalism which Broch has fallen prey to in his *Bergroman*. The crux of this ill-fated constellation is that, as Blumenberg notes, attempts at re-mythicization originate in the 'longing for the compelling quality of those supposedly early discoveries of meaning', but that they regularly founder 'on the unrepeatability of the conditions of their genesis'.[26] Blumenberg explains that 'significance' [*Bedeutsamkeit*] intended to result from '"thought-up" valences' [*ausgedachte Wertigkeiten*] will always break down. This is particularly true, he writes, of the phenomenon of the simulated new myth. 'Where it appears, it makes use of the established repertory of procedures by which to secure an objective foundation, and dresses its creation up in a more or less ritualized scientific manner, as for example [Houston Stewart] Chamberlain, [Ludwig] Klages, or Alfred Rosenberg did, and before them perhaps most clearly Bachofen.'[27] This goes straight to the heart of the difficulties with the *Bergroman*. The mythological formula 'wants' to fill the vacuum created by the loss of values and meaning with significance, however 'equipping something with significance is not something that we can choose to do'[28] – as is repeatedly demonstrated in literature, the *Bergroman* being no exception. The figure of Mother Gisson, intended to evoke something like reverence in the reader, has unintentionally comic features, and the philosophy she stands for becomes a travesty of what was intended. Nor is it clear what, if anything, the name Gisson has to do with the idea of gnosis, with which it is anagrammatically linked, despite the considerable fuss made about this coincidence in the secondary literature. Gnostic philosophy is 'the expression of a universal and great disappointment with the cosmos',[29] and as such committed to a heretical way of thinking, whereas Broch's dire Tyrolean *Urmutter* represents a philosophy of life which affirms everything – including the evil Marius Ratti.

> As urban wastes discharge into a river and, cleansed once more in its flow, are carried off into the sea, all misery and woe, having become once again transparent and pure, turn back into life and revert to what they have been and what they are and will always remain: life, part of the whole, no longer identifiable in the totality, absorbed by it, unrecognizable and submerged in the immutable.[30]

In the end it almost seems as if the sacrificial death of Irmgard has not been in vain, since it too was a part of the everlasting purification process of life and death, which evidently is being described not just by the narrator figure of the doctor, but also by the author who wields his pen.

Many facets of the *Bergroman*, then, do indeed point to a highly suspect ideology. What distinguished Broch from those peddlers of fascism convinced of their cause, who in their pamphlets and poetry completely corrupt the idea of *Lebensphilosophie*, was perhaps his good faith, coupled with a bad conscience with regard to the inner qualities of what he had written. Hence, then, the endless revisions, the long working days, up to seventeen hours long, during which Broch bends the text of his *Bergroman* this way and that without much discernible effect on its substance, form or execution. Broch's martyrdom, in his last years, to his enormous daily workload, under often very adverse conditions, literally led him to die at his desk. He was working on what was probably the final version of the *Bergroman*, and broke off at the description of an Alpine landscape. As Koebner's study relates, he then packed a suitcase for a journey. That was in the early hours of 30 May 1951. At around six o'clock in the morning Broch suffered a ruptured aorta. Over-exertion of the heart is Koebner's view.[31] Entirely possible. What we do know is that the iceman – almost a character from a play by Raimund[viii] – found him lying dead on the floor of his final rather down-at-heel apartment in New Haven, with a peaceful, serene expression on his face. Exile, according to a saying in the Babylonian Talmud, atones for all sins. Perhaps Broch, who had been considering returning to the Jewish faith, did at the last after all ascend Mount Nebo, to look down, like Moses in Deuteronomy,[ix] into the promised land of Canaan which he himself was not allowed to enter.

A Lost Land

Jean Améry and Austria

> Es ist wieder der alte Kampf mit dem alten Riesen. Freilich, er kämpft nicht, nur ich kämpfe, er legt sich nur auf mich wie ein Knecht auf den Wirtshaustisch, kreuzt die Arme oben auf meiner Brust und drückt sein Kinn auf seine Arme. Werde ich dieser Last standhalten können?
>
> Franz Kafka, *Hochzeitsvorbereitungen auf dem Lande*

> It is once again the old fight with the old giant. True, he does not fight, only I fight, he only sprawls over me as a labourer does on the tavern table, crosses his arms on the upper part of my chest and presses his chin on his arms. Shall I be able to endure this load?
>
> Franz Kafka, *Wedding Preparations in the Country*[1]

In Ingeborg Bachmann's story 'Drei Wege zum See' ['Three Paths to the Lake'], thinking back over her past and her career as a photojournalist, Elisabeth, the photographer who represents the author, recalls the scepticism with which, in the time immediately following the Algerian war, her lover Trotta would challenge her professional commitment to objectivity and truth. 'Years later,' it says in the text, 'she happened to read an essay entitled "On Torture" by a man with a French name who was Austrian and lived in Belgium, and afterward she understood what Trotta had meant: for the essay said what she and all journalists couldn't say.'[1] The essayist in question was of course Jean Améry, who only appeared briefly on the horizon of the literary scene of those years – as in these rather uneven lines by Bachmann – in order to make his grave pronouncements before taking his, as he put it, all too often delayed leave. Whether Améry himself approved of being described here as 'an Austrian' is open to doubt. For Améry, Austria and Austrian identity were something of which he had been forcibly deprived, and for which, after his experiences of exile, torture and mass extermination, he no longer felt any desire. Immediately after the end of the war – having only just returned from the dead, after his evacuation from Auschwitz in January 1945, the forced march to Gleiwitz, transport in an open rail carriage to Saxony, reinternment in Buchenwald-Mittelbau and, in April, another open transport to Bergen-Belsen – Améry did indeed consider a return to Vienna, where Leopold Langhammer had invited him to assist in the 'rebuilding of the state education system'; but evidently neither this offer nor, later, his relatively regular trips to Austria suggest to him that it might be possible to settle there once more. The feeling persists that, after all that had happened, he would be better off elsewhere, and Améry persists in it. At the very least, he is unwilling to relinquish the right to resentment [*Ressentiment*][ii] towards his unwholesome homeland [*ungute Heimat*].[iii] In 1972, and again in 1974, he refuses attempts on the part of his Austrian friends to secure him, respectively, the title of professor and the honour of a medal.[2]

Not that Améry ever denied his connection with Austria; he only wished to make it plain that the Hanns Mayer who left his *Heimat* in 1938 and eventually had to telegraph home from the station post office in Antwerp – in bad school French, as he remembers with bitterness – 'heureusement arrivé' was a very distant figure, someone who did not actually exist any more; and that the later Jean Améry could not just simply go back to a time before the difficult lessons life had since taught him. This also is the reason why, in the volume *Örtlichkeiten* [*Localities*],[iv] he re-evoked the environs of his childhood – the Salzkammergut – with a singular blend of nostalgia and black humour. In retrospect, he recognized what Horváth – those crucial few years older at the time of the impending debacle – had already realized, namely how hollow, even then, were the idyllic-seeming provinces. In Bad Ischl, where Améry spent his childhood in the years after the First World War, a ghost play is being performed. The marzipan Kaiser, as Améry calls him, has not come to take the summer air for many a long year, but on the esplanade along the Traun a 'portly Herr Konzertdirektor, squeezed into a frock coat so tight he could hardly breathe, year in year out conducts medleys from the "Walzertraum", "The Merry Widow", the "Rastelbinder" or [. . .] "Gräfin Mariza"'.[3] The audience, too, has scarcely changed; the front row is still largely composed of the Jewish bourgeoisie from the capital, who once upon a time used to follow the Kaiser to [Bad] Ischl, since one was surely entitled to feel safe and legitimate in the presence of a ruler who, as Améry recalls, could not bear anti-Semites. Nothing better illustrates the illusion, created by the glow or afterglow of Imperial tolerance, of feeling one was finally at home better than the anecdote related by Friedrich Torberg, in which Herbert Eisenbach, one of the great Viennese character actors at the turn of the century, appears in his annual role as a regular summer visitor at Bad Ischl. Eisenbach 'set out for the same walk day after day: towards a rather distant hilltop with a rustic restaurant and lookout which was named, in honor of Archduchess Sophie and the panoramic view opening out in two directions, "Sophie's Double Vista"'. During one summer, unusually wet even for Bad Ischl, Eisenbach had for weeks on end been the only guest in the café, when one afternoon he noticed a stranger standing gazing helplessly at the mist surrounding him on all sides. Eisenbach went up to him and revealed the veiled mystery with the words: 'From here, Sir, the old Jews used to see the Dachstein.'[4] In this story, myth and social reality are intertwined in the most inscrutable fashion. Is Austria the Promised Land, and the Dachstein Mount Nebo, or is the viewpoint, with – in view of the weather conditions – its potentially comic name, merely one more stage in an endless odyssey? Be that as it may, Améry's reflections on Bad Ischl clearly show that *Heimat*, as it presented itself to him, was nothing more than a mirage, and it is this disillusioned gaze that Améry, towards the end of his life, casts back upon the region he came from, which allows him some of the most notable reflections on the theme of *Heimat* in recent literature. Améry defines *Heimat*, the home country, as that which one has less need of the more of it one has, which in turn means that any positive pronouncements on the subject are inherently suspect from the start, and that only in exile, *ex negativo*, is it possible to experience what *Heimat* truly means – or could have meant.

These ideas are all the more remarkable given that Améry's own relationship to the region in which he spent his childhood and youth was, at first, a completely intact one. He did not experience that disorienting sense of otherness and difference which so many Jewish autobiographies report. For him, there was evidently no reason to identify with the Jewish minority, whose annual appearance in Bad Ischl meant nothing more to him than the beginning of the summer holidays. Even the occasional visits of his grandfather, a serious gentleman of the Mosaic confession[5] who had concerns about his grandson's education, did not disturb his unquestioning sense of belonging, defined by the horizons of Bad Ischl and Gmunden. The fact that his mother owned an inn, and the modest economic and social circumstances occasioned by the fact that his father had fallen in 1917 as an Imperial rifleman [*Kaiserjäger*], may have increased his adolescent sense of being one of the so-called *Volk*. Even when Améry later arrived in Vienna, where the more vulgar forms of anti-Semitism had been the order of the day for at least a quarter of a century, by his own account this scarcely affected him. Only towards the end of the Republic did the ever more virulent and increasingly organized hostilities make it clear to him that he too was meant. Améry recalls in particular the day in 1935 when he realizes, reading in a coffee-house newspaper that the Nuremberg Laws have just been enacted, that this means his right to exist has thereby been annulled.

Looking back, what Améry found most puzzling was the complete lack of protest with which the Jews, himself included, went along with everything. They 'didn't make a fuss, were happy their next-door neighbour with the Alpine-sounding name still returned their greeting'.[6] Despite the very real threat from 'next door' [Germany], despite the economic misery and clerico-fascism in their own country, the Jews, almost without exception, remained. 'Their patriotic idiocy knows no bounds,' writes

Améry.[7] Even when emigrants from the [Third] Reich start arriving daily in increasing numbers, 'telling horror stories of concentration camps, of boycotts of Jewish businesses, of what over there is called *Gleichschaltung* [forcible coordination] . . . they still stay put, out of a dull apathetic mixture of fear and trust.'[8] In *Unmeisterliche Wanderjahre* [*Unmasterly Journeyman's Years*],[v] Améry declares his own position during this time as inexcusable. 'That I did not hear the drums by night and in the daytime, that the thunder of the brawling in the meeting halls did not reach my ears, that I did not see the uniforms nor the unspeakable faces of the riff-raff marching determinedly towards us – for that, I know, there can be no pardon.'[9]

Améry blames his institutional blindness [*Betriebsblindheit*] on the confused Austrocentric world view to which he had become acclimatized. The idea that Austria was a place apart, chosen for a higher calling than the heathen Reich beyond its frontiers, was one which really did cause not a few otherwise rational minds to take leave of their senses. Legitimizing notions, such as Leopold von Andrian in particular had been purveying since the end of the monarchy, now formed the political programme of a state forced into a hopelessly defensive position. 'Austria's existence', declared Schuschnigg on 10 February 1935, 'finds its legitimation in the fact that it is the last part of the West in the world.'[10] In complete contrast to this purely ideological separatism, whose phrasing is almost reminiscent of Herzmanovsky-Orlando, there stood a political practice which attempted, by means of Thomistic attempts at differentiation on the extreme right, to cling on to a last shred of independence – while in reality already long since beholden to German fascism.

In fact, as Améry's recollections of his own origins show, the much invoked '*österreichisches Wesen*' ['Austrian essence'] had for years been infiltrated by what was being marketed in Germany as the new *Nationalkultur* [national culture]. In *Unmeisterliche Wanderjahre*, with a mixture of retrospective wry amusement and embarrassment, Améry lists the late unlamented mentors from whom he derived his first notions of literature: Ludwig Finckh, Will Vesper, Börries Münchhausen, 'the fat lady Agnes Miegel'.[11] That things could only go downhill from there was fairly obvious, but for someone like himself, under the spell of a culture descending into total provincialism, it was, as Améry assures us, not clear at all. For him, Wildgans and Waggerl, Suso Waldeck, Ernst Scheiblreiter [sic] and Hans Brečka-Stiftegger simply were the norm. Améry's first literary and, in some sense, political education was a backwoods literature [*Holzwegliteratur*] peddling an utterly reactionary concept of *Heimat*. At the heart of this concept was the idea of the direct connection between the Austrian people and the surrounding landscape. In his book *Die Wahrheit über Österreich* [*The Truth about Austria*], published in exile in 1938, Guido Zernatto, one of the key proponents of the cultural movement within Austrofascism, sums up the theory of the higher meaning of *Heimat* in the equation, as simple as it is revealing, that 'For the National Socialist, what counts is the law of blood; for the Austrian it is the law of landscape.'[12] Sleights of hand [*Winkelzüge*] of this kind, in which identities are passed off as polar opposites, were, in the 1920s and '30s, not just the prerogative of the intellectual champions of the *Ostmark*; rather, they were absolutely representative of a large proportion of post-Kakanian culture – or, as the case may be, of the process which, long before the *Anschluß*, had made possible the subordination of the so-called *österreichisches Wesen* to the so-called German one. The power of this reactionary ideology of landscape was such that, in the 1930s, even authors as critically inclined as Hermann Broch fell victim to it.

Thus it is not surprising that the young Jean Améry should have taken comfort in similar ideas. For what can we call our own, if not our home country [*Heimat*]? It seemed to him absolutely inalienable. For its sake he cannot, will not leave. 'One summer evening', as he writes in the volume *Örtlichkeiten*, 'the young would-be writer Hanns Mayer is walking with a friend through the woods around Rax, gazes at the Semmering range rendered immortal by Peter Altenberg, puts a sentimental arm around his companion and says: No one can take us away from all this – "Uns bringt keiner weg von hier."'[13] Améry is at one with the *Zeitgeist*. An amalgam of 'Erfahrenem und Angelesenem' [lived and literary experience], 'landscape', as Améry himself notes, defined the horizons of the imagination. It is composed of 'forest, hills and valleys, field tracks, sunken paths, false trails [*Holzwege*],[vi] cliffs, heathland, the jagged black line of the mountain ridge, the crescent moon and the evening star'.[14] The whole thing is an artificial construct, like the 'northern birchwoods of Jens Peter Jacobsen, where a shot rang out in the mist, forests, black and silent forests, *Waldeinsamkeit* [romantic solitude of the forest] – the magic of the eternal one and only symbol – forest'.[15] This almost all-encompassing German metaphor ultimately made clear to Améry the origins of the notion of landscape to which he subscribed at the beginning of his *Unmeisterliche Wanderjahre*. 'Niels Lyhne's "birch wood" [*Birkenwald*]', he now realizes, as he tries to account for it to himself, 'was right next to Buchenwald [literally 'beech wood']'.[16]

Améry's awakening began, hesitantly and gradually, after the National Socialists seized power in the Reich. As news of boycotts of Jewish businesses, book burnings and internment camps seep across the border, so the gradual transformation of the *Heimat*, the home country, into a *Feindesland* [enemy country] makes itself felt.[17] Améry has to find a new *Heimat*, and for him the new *Heimat* is the Wiener Kreis [Vienna Circle], in the airless vacuum of true, irrefutable principles. From now on, he counters the aesthetics of irrationalism with the aesthetics of logic,[18] as if in this way it were possible to defend himself against the ever-proliferating rule of injustice. 'The mad game to whose rules he submitted' — thus Améry's comment on his new, completely abstract defensive position — 'was perhaps not so much thought itself, as the misconception that there was some kind of competition between those whose thoughts were good and the others whose deeds were evil.'[19] Améry's hope that, through the philosophy of Schlick and Wittgenstein, he was 'armed against the nationalistic *Folklore* which did not for an instant take itself seriously'[20] remained a pious one, for the disaster continued on its course regardless of all right thinking. The Alpine dream, long since over, 'rolled on as an Alpine nightmare over the capital and extinguished all its glory'.[21] The whole country was stylized into nothing more than 'an Alpinesque theme park'.[22] In this manner does the idea of Austria reach its peripeteia. One of the clearest signs of its victory march was what Guido Zernatto approvingly calls 'the extension of rural *Tracht* [traditional costume] even into Vienna in the last years of the *Ständesstaat* [Corporate State]', something he emphasizes as being highly significant.[23]

Améry recalls that Kurt von Schuschnigg 'liked to appear before the people in national costume'.[24] One of Schuschnigg's most memorable appearances in this get-up, as depicted in the memoirs of another Jewish émigré, took place at the famous

Fasching [Carnival] Ball 'Kirtag in St Gilgen' in 1938, a few weeks before the Germans marched in. George Clare relates how, for this event of the season, the whole of the Konzerthaus had been transformed by Vienna's best stage designers into the landscape of the Salzkammergut. The Weißes Rößl [White Horse Inn] had been recreated as a real-life stage set; there was not only a village square, maypole and all, but also barns, stalls and stables with real cows and horses. The only thing missing was the Wolfgangssee. Every kind of music was represented, from brass bands and operetta to Cole Porter and Irving Berlin, and the festivities reached their climax when Chancellor Schuschnigg, in his Tyrolean costume, appeared like a *deus ex machina* in the presidential box, to the accompaniment of the frenetic, indeed hysterical applause of the assembled *Narrenvolk*.[vii] During the ovation, which lasted several minutes, Schuschnigg, his glasses glinting in the light of the stage lamps trained upon him, bowed repeatedly from the waist in his stiff mechanical manner.[25]

Thus the 1938 'Kirtag in St Gilgen', the fake enactment of a thoroughly counterfeit and misappropriated *Heimatgefühl* [sentimental attachment to the idea of *Heimat*], became the provisional last act of the Austrian national and political melodrama [*Haupt- und Staatsaktion*], for neither the State nor the *Heimat* would survive this tour de force staggering wildly between tragedy and farce. The dissolution of Austria was already scheduled. Whether Améry himself was present at the 'Kirtag in St Gilgen' may reasonably be doubted. But that, for him, the day of the '*Anschluß*' meant the irrevocable destruction of his *Heimat* is something he explicitly comments on: 'Everything that had filled my consciousness – from the history of my country, which was no longer mine, to the landscape images, whose memory I had suppressed – had become intolerable to me since that morning of the 12th of March 1938, on which the blood-red cloth with the black spider on a white field had waved even from the windows of out-of-the-way farmsteads.'[26] In similar vein, Ingeborg Bachmann recalled the day Hitler's troops entered her home town of Klagenfurt as the day which forever shattered her childhood, when for the first time she felt mortal fear.[27] And yet there is a decisive difference. For Améry, it was not so much the invasion of Hitler's troops that destroyed his *Heimat* as the readiness with which the country welcomed the invasion, given that the flags must have been ready and waiting for quite some time. A further difference from Bachmann's statement was the fact that, for Améry, on the day of the *Anschluß*, it was not only his *Heimat*, childhood and youth that were destroyed, but also, *de jure*, his own identity: a person who was no longer called Hanns Mayer, but Hanns Israel Mayer. 'I was a person who could no longer say "we" and who therefore said "I" merely out of habit, but not with the feeling of full possession of my self.'[28] Comparing the fate of Jewish exiles with that of other displaced persons, Améry writes:

> They lost their possessions, homestead, business, fortune, or perhaps only a modest job; beyond that, they lost the land, meadows and hills, a forest, a silhouette of a city, the church in which they had been confirmed. We lost all this too, but we also lost the people: the schoolmate from the same bench, the neighbor, the teacher. They had become informers or bullies, at best, embarrassed opportunists.[29]

In this context, one might also note that the betrayal Améry speaks of in the lines quoted above was motivated not by opportunism alone, but by the positively perverse ambition to be ahead of the Germans when it came to the expulsion of the Jews. If an Austrian general complained – in a speech to his officers reported in Karl Kraus's *Die letzten Tage der Menschheit* [*The Last Days of Mankind*] that what the Austrians lacked was organization, whereas the Germans – one couldn't begrudge them that – were just very organized, now the Austrians could show that the General's wish that 'That must be your ambition, each and every one of you, to introduce organization here'[30] had not been uttered in vain. In the twenty months leading up to December 1939, almost three-quarters of the 220,000 Jews living in Vienna had been deported via the 'deportation factory' at Prinz-Eugen-Straße 22, organized by one Adolf Eichmann from Linz – a system that was to set a precedent, and for which the chief of the Reichssicherheitsamt [Reich Security Head Office] in Berlin, Reinhard Heydrich, did not fail to show his esteem.[31] One of the over 150,000 deportees was Jean Améry, who left Austria in late 1938. The circumstances of his departure meant that his love of his country [*Heimatliebe*] was transformed into hatred [*Heimathass*]. Améry, who knew the meaning of *ressentiment*, knew also that hatred of one's country ultimately turns into self-hatred, and that separation becomes *déchirure*. Where what one most loves becomes taboo, the damage is irreparable.

Améry's comments on his continued nostalgia for his home country, long after he had consciously dissociated himself from Austria, reveal the intensity of the emotions this loss provoked. In his essay 'Wieviel Heimat braucht der Mensch?' ['How Much Home Does a Person Need?'], he relates how, when during the darkest days a Polish Jew once asked him, in Yiddish, 'V'n wie kimt Ihr?' ['Where do you come from?'] he could not really give a proper response. Wilna, that might have been an understandable answer, or Amsterdam. But what was a Polish Jew, 'for whom wandering and expulsion were just as much family history as for me a permanence of abode that had become meaningless',[32] to do with the mention of Hohenems, or Ischl and Gmunden? He could not even explain to others in his situation what Austria had meant to him. The territory so well known that it was taken for granted had become a more incomprehensible point of reference than even the most foreign of regions. *Heimat* had become, for him, the epitome of irreality. And yet, Améry writes, you could not be rid of it, it pursued you, and from time to time caught up with you unexpectedly. There were, for example, real-life shocks, like the occasion when an SS man, his uniform jacket unbuttoned, his hair dishevelled, one afternoon appears at the door of the flat in Brussels in which Améry's resistance group produce their flyers. And it is precisely in the dialect of Améry's immediate native region that this man demands peace and quiet for himself and his comrades, tired out from night duty, so that Améry, 'in a paradoxical, almost perverse emotional state of trembling fear and, at the same time, surging intimate cordiality',[33] for one crazy moment feels an urge to answer him in his own language. It was, though, not only in such concrete confrontations that *Heimat* was liable to ambush one, but also in the diffuse, abstract form of a *mal du pays* which could be triggered by the tiniest detail, and which can perhaps best be compared with the searing phantom pain felt in an amputated limb. 'Homesickness, a nasty, gnawing sickness which does not have a folksong-like, homey quality, nor at all one sanctioned by emotional conventions, and of which one cannot speak in the Eichendorff tone. I felt it piercingly for the first time', wrote

Améry, 'when I stood at the exchange counter in Antwerp with fifteen marks fifty, and it has left me as little as the memory of Auschwitz, or torture, or of my return from the concentration camp, when once again I was back in the world, with a live weight of forty-five kilograms, wearing a striped prisoner's suit [. . .]'[34] And right up to the end of his life Améry was so afflicted by homesickness that for him — paradoxically, as it may seem to some — a return was out of the question.

Améry, then, took upon himself what has been called the vice of the Jewish people, *être ailleurs* [being elsewhere], and became 'ein gelernter Heimatloser' [a qualified homeless person].[35] However, he intensified this expatriation still further, into a radical intellectual position of extraterritoriality. Améry's uncompromising moral integrity, his adherence to justified *ressentiments*, had to do with his sense of pride, and thus in turn with his courage and determination to resist: those particular and rare qualities which he possessed to such a high degree. The dialect maxim with which Améry summed up his relationship to his *Heimat* ran like this: 'In a Wirtshaus, aus dem ma aussigschmissn worn is, geht ma nimmer eini'[36] [roughly, 'never go back into a pub you have been thrown out of']. The gnawings of homesickness [*Heimweh*], though, were not assuaged by such a conscious statement of position, given that it is one of those emotional impulses through which the past can be retrieved and what is irreversible protested. In that sense, of course, Améry's homesickness was at one with his wish for a revision of history, a wish that only increased with the passing of the years. Naturally Améry could not know, when, early in 1939, at Kalterherberg [= cold hostel] — never did a place have a more fateful name — he crossed the Belgian border into exile, just how hard the tension between the

Heimat growing ever stranger and the foreign country growing steadily more familiar would be to bear. In the end, though, he knew. That Améry in 1978 should have broken off, apparently without warning, a reading tour which had taken him from Hamburg, Kiel, Neumünster and Oldenburg to Marburg, and which was set to continue to Mannheim, Heidelberg, Karlsruhe, the Frankfurt Book Fair, Stuttgart and Schwäbisch Hall, in order to travel to Salzburg, where, in the Hotel Österreichischer Hof, he took his own life – this in many ways ostentatious means of taking the way out[viii] in the end also had something to do with finding a solution to the insoluble conflict between *Heimat* and exile, or, as Cioran says somewhere, *entre le foyer et le lointain*.[ix]

Améry's death, about which naturally much has been written, much of it slanderous – it was of course an absolute gift even for the *BILD-Zeitung*, where a certain Gustav Jandek, under the headline 'Suicide poet Améry found dead in hotel – poisoned!' saw fit to report that Améry, before he killed himself, had been working for thirty-three years on the book *Hand an sich legen*[x] [*On Suicide*][37] – this death was in the end the subject of a commentary by another writer from Salzburg, Thomas Bernhard, in an interview in the Hotel Ambassador in Vienna reported in the journal *Theater Heute*.[38] There, mid-tirade, Bernhard recalls how in 1975 he had sat in the bar of the Frankfurter Hof with 'that Améry'[xi] because 'that Améry' wanted to talk to him about his book *Die Ursache* [*An Indication of the Cause*][xii] which had just appeared. According to Bernhard, Améry had lectured him about how one should not and could not write about Salzburg and its inhabitants in the way that he had in *Die Ursache*. After all, 'that Améry' is supposed to have said, not everyone from Salzburg had been a Nazi. Bernhard then continues his tale, manipulating his memories in the most cavalier fashion, relating how he had just then been really incredibly annoyed by Améry's review in *Merkur*, because 'that Améry had understood nothing at all, absolutely nothing about *Die Ursache*',[39] and how he, Bernhard – still enraged about this in his opinion completely uncomprehending review – then sees on the television that 'that Améry' has only gone and killed himself in Salzburg. It is, perhaps, not relevant that one part of this scene takes place in 1975 and the other in 1978, nor that the two temporally distant events had become fused, as it were synoptically, in Bernhard's recollection; what is remarkable, however, is how here two writers, each bound to their *Heimat* in the most ambivalent way, are completely incapable of finding any understanding for the position of the other. Bernhard, with his customary deliberate and hyperbolic offensiveness, evidently perceived Améry's wilful – as he saw it – return to Salzburg as an act of tactlessness, even of usurpation. From Améry's perspective, though, the story will almost certainly have looked rather different. If it were possible to get to the bottom of the relationship between a place and two writers, one a moralist, the other an amoralist, one might come close to understanding something of the inner dynamics of literature. In any case, the constellation was a supremely Austrian one; indeed the story could not have had a more Austrian ending, which is why the final inn[xiii] Améry was at last allowed to enter after his long winter's journey is a grave of honour in the Zentralfriedhof in Vienna.

In an Unknown Region

On Gerhard Roth's Novel *Landläufiger Tod*
[*A Common or Garden Death*]

> Wenn unser körperliches Leben – ein Verbrennen ist, so ist wohl auch unser geistiges Leben eine Kombustion (oder ist dies gerade umgekehrt?). Der Tod also vielleicht eine Veränderung der Kapazität.
>
> Novalis, *Fragmente*

> If our corporeal life is a burning to ashes, so doubtless our spiritual life is also a combustion (or is it in fact the other way round?). Thus is death perhaps a transformation of capacity.
>
> Novalis, *Fragments*[i]

In his narratives, Gerhard Roth always has his characters experiment with flight from the environment which constitutes our consciousness. The winter journey of the schoolteacher Nagl,[ii] which, after a number of melancholy erotic excursions, took him to the far north, all the way to Fairbanks, Alaska, was one such example. But stories of this kind, notwithstanding their all-pervasive and far-reaching sense of longing, still remained committed to a thoroughly conventional narrative position which at times demoted the author to a mere stagehand shifting the scenery that forms the backdrop to his own fantasies. In the novel *Der Stille Ozean* [*The Ocean of Silence*], however, there are increasing signs that Roth's aim is to break the bounds of mere realistic description. Ascher, the doctor whose career is in doubt on account of a professional faux pas, moves to the country, where he gradually abandons himself to neglect and dissolution. Now, bent over his microscope, trying to fathom the workings of nature, he comes to realize the full strangeness and intransigence of life – his own included. But it is only in the novel *Landläufiger Tod* [*A Common or Garden Death*],[iii] where Ascher reappears as a marginal figure, already lost, that Roth, using a new technique, truly succeeds in making visible the hidden side of the picture, uncovering the secrets which lie scattered, as it were flattened, beneath the gaze of our perception.[1] This new technique involves the dissolution of narrative reason via the intensity of poetic imagination. Roth demonstrates how a heightened capacity for experience means that Ascher's path increasingly departs from the gravitational pull of reality as legitimized by reason. Lying in bed for hours on end with his eyes closed, Asher can picture every detail of the house, can flit like a bat through the rooms or linger in them as if he were himself an object – exercises in renunciation, or attempts to transcend, through the practice of empathy, the ultimate boundaries which define our existence. A doctor stands before the body of a child suddenly deceased. Completely naked, it lies on the kitchen table. No one wants to believe it. And the relatives plead with him to try everything. So – and this, like Lenz's attempt at resuscitation,[iv] is already a sign of *dérangement* – the doctor takes the dead child home in his black bag and lays it on his bed, and the longer he looks at it, the less he can understand why he should not be able to bring it back to life. Once he has grasped – in the face of the immovable other side of life – the fundamental impossibility of his own existence, he rules himself out of life and draws ever nearer to the idea of death, which he will soon inflict upon himself.

With the death of Ascher, there exits the last of Roth's protagonists in whom an identification, in the conventional sense, between the author and his representative the narrator was still possible. This now vacant position is occupied by the mute son of the beekeeper, from the perspective of whose much stranger consciousness – as measured against normal reason – Roth's magnum opus unfolds. The fact that he cannot speak, but writes down everything which goes on in his head, all his trains and leaps of thought, every perception and observation, takes the story to a rarefied plane, where the merely literary can no longer breathe and where, as Jean Paul demanded of inspired prose, the truly immense, eerie feeling takes effect 'with which the mute spirit stands as if stunned and alone in the wild gigantic mill of the universe'.[2] Roth's mute protagonist, an epitome of disturbance [*Verstörung*], allows the reader to become aware of the gap between the tautological truth of so-called reality and that which does not accord with it. 'There are men' – Jean Paul again – 'who torment themselves with broken and confused organs of speech and say something other than they wished.'[3] As the beekeeper's son discovers in the asylum, all of them have long stories within them and belong – as does he himself – to the long-lost breed of people of the forest and the night, passive genii to whom – as it says in the *Vorschule der Ästhetik* [*Preschool of Aesthetics*] – fate has denied the power of speech. But when the mute son in the lunatic asylum — and with him the author, who lends him his words — uses writing to protest against fate, against oblivion, against loneliness, because he wants to gain the upper hand against the voices and return to the village,[4] this logically takes place in a language which displaces the search for sense into nonsense. The resulting notes and jottings to a great extent consist of long lists of highly idiosyncratic axiomatic statements, such as — to choose one example from many hundreds — that on the day of the stag the thunderstorm is honoured with an embroidered flag.[5] Despite their hermetic nature, many of these *Grund-Sätze* [literally basic sentences; axioms, principles] are of considerable suggestive power, and one often has the feeling that if only it were possible to understand what is being said, each could give rise to a new way of looking at the world, indeed to a whole new world — a world in which, to stay with the example quoted, the stag, the hunted animal, the hunt, the hunter, the flag of the marksmen's association and the atmospheric phenomena stand in a relationship to each other completely different from the order imposed by the logic of discursive language. This discrepancy means, too, that any attempt to interpret dream images inevitably involves distortion, as the beekeeper's son points out to the doctor treating him. Only in the dream itself, were he but capable of it, could he set down in words what he had dreamed. Anything else, any attempt to recapitulate the dream while awake, is, he says, a falsification [*Schwindel*], since setting down a dream in words already implies imposing order on it according to precisely those laws without which humankind — apostrophized in this passage as universal lawyers — could not bear reality. The distinction Roth draws here, in the section entitled 'Traumlogik' ('Dream Logic'),[6] between the autonomous meaning of dreams and our desperate attempts at interpretation [*Sinngebung*], is the central defining strategy of his narratives, since for him what matters is to go back, as far as possible, to a time predating not only the teachings of psychology but civilized thought as a whole. The method he uses to achieve this, in order to arrive at a place 'where the gates around the whole horizon of reality stay open the entire night without one's knowing what strange figures fly in through them',[7] entails a deconstructing of his own consciousness, not in the sense of a suspension [*Aufhebung*] of the capacity for language [*Sprachvermögen*], but in the sense of a regeneration of the substance of language itself, analogous to that which can be brought about only in the paradoxical realm of creativity.

The catalogues of difficult, at times incomprehensible phrases and sentences which the beekeeper's son sets down on paper – the section 'Das Alter der Zeit' ['The Age of Time'][v] alone comprises 697 imagistic aphorisms of this kind – are thus at the same time *études* or exercises which, running counter to the system of writing and the syntactic ordering of potentially meaningful [*sinnfällig*] elements, attempt to instigate a decentralization of language by means of dissociation and dislocation. Against the terrifying evidence of the inadequacy of language ultimately attested to in the statement that one must be silent about that whereof one cannot speak – that puritanical abstinence which made Wittgenstein the most enigmatic of philosophers[8] – Roth sets the attempt to let language speak and babble for itself, in order then to follow it along all its truly infinite meanderings. Whereas, in his earlier novels, Roth in the main contented himself with describing what he had seen in New York, Naples or Venice – the author as travel guide often cutting rather a poor figure – now he, and we with him, unexpectedly arrives in regions unknown where no one has ever been, where the rabbits frozen in their hutch watch over the memories of the children, and where the bride only removes her veil when the blind man scatters the scales of the fish eaten on Friday from the rooftops.[9] The most remarkable thing about these mottos and devotional sayings conjured from the magician's black box is the fact that, despite contradicting all teleology, they are, nevertheless, the best of all possible signposts in the undiscovered country which Roth spreads out before us in this, his great *Heimatroman* [*Heimat* novel], since the involuntary precision of the almost preverbal linguistic reflexes – short circuits of meaning between the most disparate words – could only arise from a profound knowledge, acquired over a long period and bordering on the fantastical, of the conditions of life in a natural and social environment, a knowledge which has few equals in the literature of recent times.

Roth's mythopoetic method also evinces a certain archaizing tendency, in the sense that it is clearly determined by a process of accumulation in which every found object, every fragment from nature and every last shard from the ruins of history the author can come by becomes a building block in the reconstruction of a way of life vanishing ever more rapidly. In this way, the novel becomes a kind of laboratory of the most extraordinary forms and deformities, in which, although nothing is categorized or organized, at any moment the apparently most worthless object can become the brood cell for a poetic process of evolution, initiated at the moment when two completely disparate elements are joined with an equals sign to become the first link in a chain in which everything is connected to everything else. Like the *pensée sauvage* described by Lévi-Strauss, the creative instinct at work here pursues the goal of arriving at a general understanding of the universe via the shortest possible route. Just as, in the mythical world view, the hare with the cleft palate is related to the twin, and the south wind to the dragon fish, the same applies in the *orbis* which Roth reveals to us. How else could he arrive at the sentence that for the storks the sea of fog represents eternity, or that the gendarme protects the swollen combs of the cockerels?[10] The inventiveness evident in such fusions uncovers those hidden qualities of reality not accessible to our acquired knowledge; what is otherwise separate is here combined in binary, serial operations, according to the principle that one thing always leads to another and this to a third thing, to form connections as incredible as they are revealing. Thus the beekeeper's son contemplates the question as to whether he should open the beehive by imagining the chain reaction set in motion by this act. 'If I open the beehive, the cat will begin to dream, with the cat's dream the foetus in the young woman's belly will move, with the kicking of the foetus it will begin to rain, the rain will make the old lady's glasses fall to the ground and break, through the shattering of the glass a leaf falls from the chestnut tree, as the leaf drifts to the ground one of the inhabitants of the village dies, at the last breath of the dying man his pendulum clock stops, the stopping of the clock makes the tightrope walker lose his balance . . .'[11] and so on and so forth, right down to the memories of the General which cause the sacristan to start praying, whereupon H., who has donned women's clothing, gets an erection, which leads to a tile working loose on the roof. The tile, which falls from the roof apparently for no reason, strikes and kills . . . Here the train of thought breaks off with the question 'Should I really open the beehive?'[12] The hypothetical exploration of the consequences of our actions clearly suggests a pronounced scrupulantism [*Skrupulantismus*], a pathological phenomenon well known to psychiatry which, however, seen from another angle, could lead to the conclusion that we all harbour far too few anxieties, take far too few precautions and all too readily disturb the fragile equilibrium on which our existence depends. Roth's stories, which are aimed at a resensitizing of our long-buried perceptive capabilities, can be read as demonstrations of the theory that it is less important to identify problems reductively than to reconceive them imaginatively. The art which must be learned for this purpose involves a continual change of perspective, a technique by means of which, for example, an apple can become the subject of a didactic tale. 'An apple', it says in the forty-ninth of the *Märchen* [folk- or fairytales] set down by 'the brothers Franz and Franz Lindner', 'found it too boring hanging there on the tree, he threw his life away and found himself on the grass. There he felt himself possessed of new strengths. He no longer had to look down on everything from above and discuss it with the other apples. No longer did the wind wake him in the morning, and the leaves no longer blocked his view. Now he could see the rabbit, the cat, the ants; and the child too he saw from close by, and at night he could look up to the heavens and imagine them as a shining apple tree.'[13] The moral of life and death set out in the remainder of this tale of the metamorphosis of the apple forms part of a mythology which bestows equal rights on everything that exists, relinquishing the concept of domination and hierarchy in favour of a vision of reconciliation. From this perspective, even the most far-fetched and outlandish stories have the same status as the concept of the novel overall, which is itself only constituted from the ever-changing kaleidoscope of fables. Moreover, as Lévi-Strauss has repeatedly emphasized, in 'mythic narrative' even what to us appears 'false' makes transparent the hidden reality beneath; the more 'false' the tale appears to be, the more intense the effect.[14] In similar fashion, in the eccentric proliferations of Roth's stories, deviation becomes the agent of a new form of knowledge [*Erkenntnis*] which permeates the text of the novel even in those passages where the latter makes use of more realistic narrative models. The destructuring of narrative which Roth – paradoxically – achieves in writing opens up undreamed-of possibilities of expression. There are in this book countless examples where the words appear in exactly the right place, with a beauty and absolute clarity, as unexpectedly as if they had that moment been invented, so that as one reads a shiver runs down one's spine because one can suddenly visualize it all so clearly.

When, on receiving the news of his father's death, the narrator's friend returns to the village, his uncle is already waiting under the apple tree in the yard, wearing a black velvet hat. 'My father', the description continues,

> was lying in the office on a bed which had been brought down from the attic and covered with a sheet. He was wearing a black suit and a dark tie, and the sheet reached to the ground, so that he looked like a figure levitating in a magic trick.[vi] His cheeks were pale and hollow, and his nose emerged sharp and pointed from his face, as if he had been arguing with someone immediately before his death. A pair of patent leather shoes was placed in front of the bed, and he held a small bunch of primroses in his folded hands. My uncle had removed his hat when we entered the room, and placed it on the desk next to the window. For reasons I cannot explain, this reassured me.[15]

The absolute rightness of the details and of the emotions of the narrator, which make visible the surreal fringes of reality, is in keeping with the unspoken principle of the mythopoetic technique which, as Lévi-Strauss noted, never waits until 'transcendental deduction has intervened to produce its effects' – in the context of the novel, this would mean explanatory interventions on the part of the author, such as occur with disconcerting frequency in Roth's earlier novels – but which provides, in the poetic images themselves, the algorithms of an empirical deduction whose constituent parts combine to create the vast combinatory apparatus that each and every mythic system amounts to.[16]

Rural Styria, over which the narrative system of *Landläufiger Tod* spans its starry firmament, is here a mythical domain bordering directly on eternity. In many ways it is reminiscent of the singular region which Bruno Schulz describes in *The Republic of Dreams*.[vii] Like a crater, or a dried-out lake, governed by silence, down there where the map already has a very southern feel, isolated and solitary, full of undiscovered paths, it has become an enclosed microcosm, a world of its own cut off from the outside.[17] The inhabitants of this *Heimat*, suspended in the vastness of the universe, have, like an Indian tribe, acquired a totemic name of their own. They are known as *Gelbfüßler* [Yellowfeet], because in their region is found a breed of chickens after whose yellow-coloured feet they are named.[18] Like the chickens hypnotized by the ringmaster in the circus, who next morning are pecking around for food in the meadow as if nothing had happened, they too are barely aware of what goes on above their heads. We, the readers, though, soon understand that they are not only light years away from the idyll of rural life – which in any case has never existed in reality – but are indeed in danger of extinction, representing, in their endangered collective existence, an anthropological paradigm of the end of the history of mankind. Part of the false consciousness of those affected – which it falls to us to decipher as their myth – is, significantly enough, the memory of past catastrophes which they have survived, but from which they are unable to derive any lessons – unless it be the one our own culture always suppresses, namely that the next catastrophe too will arrive without warning, just like the earthquake which, back then, broke the eggs in the table drawer and sent glasses and pitchers crashing to the ground, so that people came rushing out into the open, where for a moment they saw the landscape pitching up and down as if they were on a huge ship heading out towards the glowering horizon.[19] Terrifying, too, was the appearance of the Northern Lights in the summer of 1939, when a red cloud rose behind the mountain peaks and dissolved in the red glow of the sky. 'Our hands and faces', as the beekeeper's son's aunt recalls, 'seemed to be dripping with blood, the red light stained fields, meadows, houses, birds and dogs red, and we gazed at each other like people who have committed a crime.' It was thought a fire had broken out and was destroying the forests, and the fire brigades 'sat mute with wide staring eyes in their vehicles as they raced along'.[20] Human life thus appears extremely precarious, since from one day to the next everything can have gone up in flames, the land ripped apart, swallowed up by snow or overrun by war – and indeed in the end it makes little difference whether the catastrophe is caused by nature or by the workings of history, which consumes and engulfs everything in exactly the same way as fire or water. One of the consistent theses of Roth's novel is that he conceives of human history as merely a particularly virulent phase, perhaps the final phase, of natural history: the already faltering equilibrium disrupted further to precisely the degree in which humanity is hurtling headlong towards collective disaster [*Unglück*] through the organization of some great enterprise, affecting even the remotest regions, which, seen from their perspective, strikes just as much out of the blue as ever a lightning bolt did from the clearest of skies. While it is true that there are attempts to derive lessons from the recurrent patterns of catastrophe – such as the fact that, at the end of every war, executions take place at the brickworks[21] – these hopelessly isolated insights into the regularly recurring debacle can do nothing to alter the ongoing process of dissolution. The depictions of the outcomes of war thus come to epitomize the behaviour of a hopelessly destabilized species. Those fleeing are everywhere trying to pick a path through the rubble, the children perched on wheelbarrows look like old people, and at the far end of the village one can see the priest scurrying off towards the woods carrying a small black bag.[22] The parades and pilgrimages, pageants and processions organized in times of peace are merely an alternative expression of the drives and instincts [*Triebstruktur*][viii] of a species characterized by a fundamentally disturbed relationship with nature, and whose internal deficit is constantly accumulating.

Roth's novel, in which instances of destruction and self-destruction, massacres, suicides, killing sprees and the most diverse forms of insanity are presented like a catalogue of symptoms of an omnipresent sickness, shows how even the most eccentric acts are nothing more than attempts to regain this lost equilibrium. But what could be a more eccentric act than such a novel which, in displaying the most artfully mounted taxonomic specimens of nature – fish, and birds, and vine leaves, and gourds, and the whole monstrosity that is humanity – under a bell jar in a simulacrum of life, attempts to create or redeem a homeostatic model which would, in theory at least, be safe from the destructive tendencies now grown endemic in our civilization. The construction of such a model goes far beyond what is normally considered artistic judgement. It is a completely passionate work of *bricolage*, a labour of love whose instructions are derived from the hieroglyphs of sunken histories, such as for example appear on minutely prepared microscopic slides;[23] animated, then, by the hope of natural philosophy, long and wrongly discredited, that there are vital messages to be discovered in the fern-like tunnellings of bark-beetle larvae, the tracery of frost flowers or the distribution of iron filings in a magnetic field. Thus the author, like the schoolteacher, sits behind closed curtains, utterly rapt, 'a magnifying glass to his eye, bent over the crystalline forms of moss, muttering Latin names to himself',[24] because he knows that in the sphere of nature there is no difference between the smallest mystery and the greatest. Accordingly, it comes as no surprise when a star falls from the night sky in the region of Untergreith and buries itself deep in the forest floor. The fallen star – which, as the mad seismologist relates, everyone soon goes to see in order to marvel at the forms enclosed within it, strange plants and animals in shapes and colours such as did not exist on earth – as it were encapsulates the catalogue of a past life; and, in the same way, the marvellous book in which this story is related contains within the synchronicity of its narrative timeframe the whole diachronic spectrum of human imagination and thought, from the mythopoetic animistic world view, via the speculations of science, right down to the point we find ourselves at today, when even our scientific knowledge no longer appears to be adequate. The recapitulation of the natural history of human thought brings to light many things which appear before us as erratic phenomena, like the shipwreck which the glacier one day gives up, with the officers, frozen into an immense block of ice, still sitting at breakfast exactly as in the moment when the disaster overtook them a hundred years before. The specific *choc* these stories of Roth's convey is the insight into the age of time, into a life which has outlived itself. Perhaps — as Roth has one of his characters reflect — things would not be so bad 'if humans only lived to the age of twenty'.[25] In contrast to such a utopian notion of a much reduced, and thus less harmful, presence of mankind in the world, we however, due to our capacity for thought, keep ourselves alive well beyond our allotted span; and the older we get, the more we use our experiences for our own advantage and the exploitation of others, systematically preventing ourselves from becoming at one with and a part of nature. In this way we resemble, both individually and as a species, no one so much as the General von Kniefall,[ix] well over a hundred years old, whose bodily exterior has almost disintegrated, or rather become so bonded with his splendid uniform that in the end nothing is left of him but his own outer case.

The capacity for thought as the instrument of survival is the compulsion [*Zwang*] we are continuously subjected to; in accordance with its function, it contains within itself the danger of endless proliferation; indeed, hypertrophic reflection, a restlessness on the verge of paralysis, is the defining condition of mankind — and who could know more about this than the author. It is probably for this reason that the arsonist one day appears in the beekeeper's parlour and states that the human brain has developed to the point where it can no longer abide itself.[26] And indeed it is difficult, reading the stories in *Landläufiger Tod*, to avoid the impression that the aetiology of the countless acts of violence which occur ought, surely, to indicate an inflammation of the brain which is rampant in these parts like rabies. It is a disease of the head which drives people to seek, in death, a way out of the ever more unendurable miscalculations of life. The beekeeper's son knows, though, that our sums will not add up even in death. Although it is true, he says to his father, that only death can create, for a few moments, the illusion of absolute precision – even harmony – there then immediately begins 'that opposite life, life after point zero as it were, in which another mechanism is set in motion and completely and utterly destroys this precision'.[27] Thus death as an alternative is discredited, exposed as the illusion which Kafka also had in mind when he wrote: 'Unsere Rettung ist der Tod, aber nicht dieser' ['Our salvation is death, but not this one'].[28] For life does not go gently into the stillness of death; death spreads like wildfire with brutal violence in the midst of life. Roth's novel provides us with many parables of this. And so in the end the bloody corpse of Korradow, the Russian sailor with total recall who turned up in the village during the first war, lies among the slaughtered chickens in the snow. It seems doubtful whether he is not now better off than during his lifetime, when he often felt as if he were already at the bottom of the sea. Korradow's murderers, who thought his incredible powers of memory a provocation, bury him behind the cowshed. Ten years later a drunken gravedigger finds the skeleton, which the president of the veterans' association places in the attic. Shortly before the second war it fetches up in the school, where it serves the children as a natural history lesson – the story of a death thus becomes an allegory of never-to-be-found peace and unassuaged guilt.[29] The life of Karl Gockel – who, although one of the poorest and most unremarkable inhabitants of the village, as a young man gets caught up in the wheels of history and finally ends up in the camp at Mauthausen – is also one which contradicts the idea of the utopia of death, since the destroying of the prisoners in the granite quarries is an example of that dystopian symbiosis in which death enters into life, but not the other way round.

The fact that Roth, notwithstanding this consciously antimetaphysical awareness, refuses to renounce metaphysical speculation – indeed persists in it – is, in both the ethical and the aesthetic sense, one of the most productive contradictions in his novel. The metaphysical experience is one which mostly comes about through complete absorption in the act of looking [*selbstvergessenes Schauen*]. The beekeeper's son's aunt relates how, even though she has given birth to three sons, she had never been so moved as when, the first time she left the area of her immediate *Heimat*, she stood with his uncle on the Schneeberg where she spent a long time gazing far down into the valleys. 'I've often dreamed about it since,' she exclaims, 'how we are standing at the top of the Schneeberg, oblivious to everything else, just gazing in wonder.'[30] The metaphysical moment of vision and overview derives from a profound fascination in which our relation to the world is temporarily turned upside down. In looking, we sense how things are looking at us, and we understand that we are not here in order to penetrate the universe, but to be penetrated by it.[31] One of the prerequisites of such an experience, as the aunt's report from the Schneeberg shows, is the ability completely to forget oneself, indeed to forget everything – the distancing of the self from the world, then, by means of looking [*Schauen*], for, according to a theory of Lévi-Strauss,[x] if one can only achieve sufficient distance, the mythic field, whose confusing and disturbing details so confound us, appears completely empty and can mean, potentially, anything at all.[32] The medium from which the metaphysical panorama then emerges is that of colours, their quiet whisperings the overture to another world. Thus, too, the beekeeper's son makes the following entry in his diary, under the number 1374: 'What occupies me most are colours. For hours on end I gaze out of the window at the yellow sky with black clouds which look like holes (through which it might be possible to enter the cosmos).'[33] The pathos expressed here, the yearning for something beyond the unsettling horizons of home – a pathos which the writer of the diary himself punctures with the postscript 'as long as you take an umbrella' – is the response to the boundless sense of regret that nothing can ever be as we would wish it. The reason for this fundamental disparity is discovered, by the most radical of all metaphysical hypotheses, in human existence. For this reason, transcendental landscapes, like the plains of Baku described by Jean Paul, across which a blue fire runs at night which neither injures nor ignites, while the mountains loom dark against the heavens,[34] are always empty of people, which gives rise to the question – as in many passages in Roth's work where people stand lost in contemplation – as to whether there is not a nature 'which exists only when there is no human, and which he anticipates?' – 'When, for example,' as Jean Paul speculates, 'the dying man is already laid alone in that dark desert, around which the living stand far away on the horizon like low clouds, like sunken lights, and he lives and dies alone in the desert; then we can learn nothing of his last thoughts and visions. – – But poetry shines like a white shaft of light deep into the desert, and we can gaze into the last hour of that lonely soul.'[35]

The poetic images which are sent out to sound the depths of meaning behind the meaning we otherwise ascribe to the world have their origins in the knowledge that what Saussure called the anagrammatic potential of the significant whole is inexhaustible – and yet, if successful, such images form ephemeral models of precisely this potential. As with many forms of 'savage', pre-scientific thought, they shed light on the fact that the nature of things is not as we like to imagine it. The secret autonomy of things – that which we are not – thus only reveals itself to the extent to which we are able to preserve the world we live in from the interference caused by our existence. Lévi-Strauss has shown that the inventors of Indian myths feared nothing so much as the contamination of nature by mankind. The resulting understanding of the world has as its central lesson that what matters most is to erase all traces of our existence. It is a lesson of unassuming modesty, diametrically opposed to the one our culture has chosen to follow. Our cultural ideals are still typified by works on a monumental scale, those of mythopoetic thinking by the most diminutive possible experiment of at best provisional validity. Whereas our ill-fated forebears, the Romans – as Lévi-Strauss also explains[36] – were intoxicated by proliferating rows of multiplication, and enthralled by visions of the future in which days add up to months, months to years, years to decades and decades to centuries, at the end of which there inevitably opened up the eschatological vision of the millennium, mythopoetic calculation sets itself against the violence of large numbers, seeking salvation in the relativizing and revocation of human existence. Elias Canetti, who was the first to think about the danger of ever-mounting numbers,[xi] associates the possibility of redemption with the ability to become smaller. In a related sense, the truth of Roth's large-scale novel project lies in the fact that nowhere does it spill over into megalomaniac fantasies, but rather manifests itself in a completely unwavering loyalty to every last, minute detail. The moral thus announced is in accordance with the morality of myth, and in direct opposition to that propagated by our civilization. In an age in which, as Lévi-Strauss writes, 'man is actively destroying countless living forms of life . . . it has probably never been more necessary to proclaim, as do the myths, that sound humanism does not begin with oneself, but puts the world before life, life before man, and respect for others before self-interest.'[37] In the interests of what one oneself is not, it seems to me that the novelist Gerhard Roth, who in his earlier work so often placed himself in the foreground of the narrative, has, in *Landläufiger Tod*, placed himself as far in the background as possible, an example of discretion which restores to the art of writing much of its dignity – a dignity which has to do with resolutely holding out in hopeless positions, and not letting go of superstitions, since in these there is no less knowledge than there is credibility in science. So, too, the author of this essay, who as a child saw his grandfather raise his hat to an elder bush, here once more permits himself to use Jean Paul's words to say that he is 'glad for his part to have spent . . . his early years in a village, and thus to have been brought up in some superstition, in which memory he now tries to find comfort'.[38]

Across the Border

Peter Handke's *Die Wiederholung* [*Repetition*]

> Die Fahrten des Menschen sollen dahin gehen, woher er gekommen ist.
>
> Schlomo von Karlin

> The stages of man shall take him to where he has come from.
>
> Shelomo of Karlin[i]

There can be few clearer instances of the distorted relationship between culture and the culture industry [*Kulturbetrieb*] in recent years than the example of Peter Handke. Until around the time of his return to Austria, it almost went without saying that this author, who from the beginning had been the focus of public attention, was one of the foremost representatives of contemporary literature in German. The fascination of the particular narrative genre he had developed lay in the absolutely innovative linguistic and imaginative precision with which, in stories such as *Die Angst des Tormanns* [*The Goalkeeper's Anxiety*][ii] or *Wunschloses*

Unglück [*A Sorrow Beyond Dreams*], he relates and reflects upon the silent catastrophes continually occurring in the inner life of mankind. What is remarkable about these stories, particularly in retrospect, is the way that they were able to cater to the demands of the market without in the least compromising their literary qualities. The secret of this success lay, I suspect, in the fact that Handke's stories, which without a shadow of a doubt bear all the hallmarks of his consummate artistry and genuine sensibility, offered little resistance to what the critics were willing or able to understand as literature. Handke's texts were accessible; even on a superficial reading, they lent themselves to all manner of progressive speculation. Nor did Handke's work present any particularly great obstacles to academic study. Very soon there appeared a plethora of articles, studies and monographs,[1] and Handke's oeuvre was systematically incorporated into the canon.

However, starting with the publication of the four books which comprise *Langsame Heimkehr* [*Slow Homecoming*],[iii] the interest in Handke was already beginning to falter.[2] Far more hermetic, far more difficult to describe than his earlier work, these texts, with their different way of looking at the world, seem to me almost deliberately designed to throw a spanner in the works of critics and academics alike. Having thus succeeded – whether unintentionally or deliberately – in securing the right to a certain discretion with regard to his works even after publication, the author naturally paid a high price for such presumption. More than anything else, however, the critics were disconcerted by Handke's new, one might say programmatic concept of making visible, by the power of words alone, a world more beautiful than this one. Even when confronted with the many truly wonderfully constructed textual arcs in *Kindergeschichte* [*Child Story*] or *Die Lehre der Sainte-Victoire* [*The Lesson of Mont Sainte-Victoire*], neither critics nor academics could do much more than declare them examples of the outlandishness, passing all normal understanding, of Handke's most recent phase to date. Meanwhile the readers – such as they were – have moved on, the academics have as far as I can see on the whole liquidated their investment, and the critics who, naturally enough, were most exposed felt obliged to publicly renounce their faith in Handke.[3] In recent years, things have come to such a pass that, while new works by Handke are still reviewed, the reviews are on the whole characterized by an open or thinly veiled hostility, and even the few positive comments are characterized by a curious helplessness and a distinct sense of unease. All of this fails to make any mention of the metaphysical ideas Handke develops in his recent work, which seek to translate what has been seen and perceived into the written word. Nowadays there is evidently no longer any discursive context in which metaphysics can claim a place as of right. And yet art, wherever and whenever it comes into being, is most intimately connected to the realm of metaphysics. In order to explore this relationship, the writer must have recourse to an unprecedented degree of courage, whereas of course for criticism and science, which now only regard metaphysics as a kind of lumber room, it is easy to get away with the general remark that the air is thin in the higher regions and the risk of falling great. In what follows, I do not intend to trace in detail this progressive distancing from Handke, nor do I wish to succumb to the – admittedly considerable – temptation of outlining the psychology and sociology of that parasitic species to which literature plays host; rather, I want to try to explore a few aspects of the book *Die*

Wiederholung [*Repetition*] which, when I first read it in 1986, made a profound, and as I now know, lasting impression on me.

Die Wiederholung is the report of a journey across the border to Slovenia undertaken in the summer of 1960 or '61 by a young man named Filip Kobal in the footsteps of his missing elder brother Gregor. The narrator and author of the report is Filip Kobal himself, looking back on that time a quarter of a century later. The more we learn from him about the young Filip Kobal, the less the now middle-aged narrator is inclined to divulge about his present self. For this reason it is almost as if he himself – whom we know only through his words – is the lost brother on whose trail the younger Filip Kobal sets out. The positive effect on the reader of the quest that Handke describes is due in no small measure to this constellation: the way in which the young Kobal is guided at every turn by the elder brother whom he seeks, and the fact that protagonist and narrator, divided by nothing but the passing of time, are as closely related as the two brothers who are the subject of Handke's tale.

Immediately after his last school examination, Filip Kobal leaves his home, his aged father, his ailing mother and his confused sister, and travels across the border to that legendary land on the far side of the Karawanken mountains whence the Kobal family originally hailed, and where, in the mid-1930s, before he was drafted into the German army, Gregor went to learn the art of fruit cultivation at the agricultural college in Maribor. Crossing the border introduces Filip to a whole new realm. Although the industrial city of Jesenice, the first stage on his journey, 'gray on gray, squeezed into a narrow valley, shut in between [. . .] shade-casting mountains',[4] in no way corresponds to the image Filip had of that realm beyond as a collection of cities resplendent with colour spread out over a wide plain all the way to the sea,[5] it still – as the narrator expressly points out – 'fully confirmed my anticipation'.[6] Jesenice is indeed the gateway to a new world. Filip is struck by the way that the 'swarms' of people in the streets, quite unlike those in the small towns back home, 'took notice' of him 'now and then, but never stared' at him, and the longer he looks around, the more certain he becomes 'that this was a great country'.[7] In the station restaurant he dreams of being accepted among the inhabitants of this great other country, accepted by a people whom he imagined 'on an unceasing, peaceful, adventurous, serene journey through the night, a journey in which the sleeping, the sick, the dying, even the dead were included'.[8] This realm which Filip Kobal sees himself entering – in this passage steeped in darkness, but otherwise mostly flooded with light – is as different as can possibly be imagined from the false *Heimat* which – according to the synopsis of his previous life – 'after almost twenty years in a non-place, in a frosty, unfriendly, cannibalistic village'[9] he has managed to escape. As the narrator notes, for Filip Kobal the feeling of liberation is a concrete one, since, by contrast to his 'so-called native land', the country on whose threshold he now stands makes no claims on him 'in the name of compulsory education or compulsory military service'; on the contrary, the narrator continues, he feels he could lay claim to it 'as the land of my forefathers, which thus, however strange, was at least my own country'.[10] 'At last', the narrator exclaims with hindsight, 'I was stateless: instead of being always present, I could be lightheartedly absent.'[11] The foreign country as the land of his forefathers and of absence: it is strangely moving how, in these passages, the imagery of a realm of freedom and the realm of shades [*Schattenreich*] overlap, a connection which is not necessarily obvious. And yet it is fitting, inasmuch as both realms, the realm of freedom and that of shades, are places of expectation where no living soul has ever been. The narrator recalls that, whenever there was talk of her Slovenian homeland, his mother could recite the names of the main towns – Lipica, Temnica, Vipava, Doberdob, Tomaj, Tabor, Kopriva – as if they were places in 'a land of peace where we, the Kobal family, would at last recapture our true selves'.[12] This land of peace, imagined by both mother and son, is at once a metaphysical and a political concept. No doubt the metaphysics of a realm beyond [*Jenseits*], where one will rejoin one's ancestors, implies a certain tendency to resignation, since liberation can only ever be a liberation from life; at the same time, however, the things the son remembers his mother saying are characterized by a resolute resistance to any enforced assimilation, and by a clearly articulated resentment towards Austria. The talk of a possible altered state thus not only refers to an easeful death, but is also of actual social relevance. The land of peace conjured up by the mellifluous Slovenian names is the absolute opposite of the unwholesome *Heimat* Austria and the horrors of a society narrowly organized around federations and associations. The text is absolutely unequivocal on this score. What delights Kobal most about the crowd on the streets of the Yugoslavian cities 'was what it lacked, the things that were missing: the chamois beards, the hartshorn buttons, the loden suits, the lederhosen: in short, no one in it wore a costume'.[13] It is thus not so much the passive losing oneself in an anonymous other which gives Filip Kobal – far from home among the shadowy passersby of Jesenice – the feeling of finally being among his own kind as the absence of any sort of traditional costume [*Tracht*], of insignia, of everything overdetermined. The dialectical mediation between the metaphysical and the political here brings about a reversal of positions. The more alive the hunched shades of Jesenice become, the more the costume wearers [*Trachtler*] go around like malevolent, unquiet and dead souls. Wearing national costume is – if this observation may be permitted – by no means the same thing as a desire to preserve the *Heimat*; rather, it is the unmistakable sign of a kind of opportunism fully capable of combining the promulgation of the idea of *Heimat* with the destruction of the *Heimat* itself. Moreover, such folkloric costume-wearing ultimately implies the negation of the outside world. Whereas in the nineteenth century the idea of *Heimat* evolved alongside the increasingly unavoidable experience of foreign parts, the ideological appropriation of *Heimat* in the twentieth century – likewise inspired by a fear of loss – taken to its logical conclusion leads to the attempt to expand the *Heimat* as far as possible, if need be by violent means and at the expense of the homelands of others. The word *Österreich* [Eastern Reich] as the designation for the Alpine republic left over after the dissolution of the Empire may be seen as emblematic of this paranoid concept of *Heimat*, whose gruesome consequences extend far into the post-war period in which Filip Kobal grew up. When he returns home at the end of his journey on foot through the karst, spurred on perhaps by the hope of being able to bring home his many and varied experiences abroad, he is at first happy to see Austria again. 'On the way from the border station to the town of Bleiburg . . . as I walked, I vowed to be friendly while demanding nothing and expecting nothing, as befitted someone who was a stranger even in the land of his birth. The crowns of the trees broadened my shoulders.'[14] But barely has he arrived in the town with the ominous-sounding name [Bleiburg = leaden castle] than he is struck by the 'guilty, hangdog ugliness and formlessness'[15] of his Austrian contemporaries who, 'fashionably dressed . . . gleaming badges on their lapels [and hats]'[16] form a suspicious *Volk* whose sidelong glances make the twenty-year-old realize 'that not a few members of this crowd were [. . .]

people who had tortured and murdered, or at least laughed approvingly, and whose descendants would carry on the tradition faithfully, and without a qualm'.[17] This remembered realization, as well as the narrator's complete silence regarding how he fared afterwards in his inhospitable homeland, makes it clear why, twenty-five years after he first left the country, he had to repeat his departure from Austria.

Setting out for the imagined true home on the far side of the mountains is an attempt, not just at personal liberation, but at an escape from exile [*Durchbrechung des Exils*] in all the wide-ranging meanings of that term. The Kobal family – who in many ways can be compared to the Barnabas family in Kafka's *Castle* – although resident in Rinkenberg for many years and considered indigenous by their fellow villagers, have, so the narrator says, obstinately remained strangers in the village.[18] By contrast to the other Rinkenbergers, they possess and guard the memory of a more dignified way of life than their present lowly station among the corrupt Austrian *Volk*. For this reason, his father and mother cannot but help look back on that earlier time as if the two of them, cut off from their Slovenian origins, had been sentenced to a life in Austria against their will and were thus really 'prisoners and exiles'.[19][iv] Their family legend, in which the story of the banishment of the Kobals is preserved, and said to be rooted in a historical event, tells of one Gregor Kobal, the instigator of the Tolmin peasants' revolt,[v] whose descendants were driven out of the Isonzo valley following his execution. Since that far-off time, the Kobals have become a tribe of hirelings and itinerant workers [*Knechte und Waldarbeiter*],[vi] foresters spread over a wide area extending as far as Carinthia. The text makes no secret of the fact that the mythological conjecture, on the part of an oppressed people, about being descended from rebellious ancestors condemned to a shameful death, is intended to suggest a renewed revolt against '[their] exile, [their] servitude, and the suppression of [their] language'.[20] The father, in particular, 'with all his strength, especially the strength of his obstinacy [. . .] was intent on redemption for himself and his family',[21] although he has no idea as to 'the form the redemption of his family here on earth might take'.[22] In accordance with the mythological scheme of things, the task of redemption falls upon the sons. Gregor, the lost brother, who bears the name of his rebel ancestor, and who appears in his parents' stories as a king cheated out of his throne,[23] was the first to set out in the 1930s to rediscover the land to the south, and now it is the turn of the younger brother, whom the mother calls the 'rightful heir',[24] to take up the long-lost quest and go to a place where there are cities quite unlike 'our Klagenfurt', cities like Gorizia where, according to the father, 'There are palm trees in the parks and there's a king buried in the monastery crypt.'[25] The path out of exile is the road to Jerusalem, and the one who treads it, the young Filip Kobal, has to be an innocent. Unlike his contemporaries, who had almost all met with a serious accident, lost a finger, an ear or a whole arm, he is still unmarked, and during his years at the seminary his 'youth had passed but [he] had never for one moment known the experience of youth'.[26] Now he, the holy fool, who himself recognizes 'the mentally deranged and feeble-minded' as his 'guardian angels',[27] is sent out, away from the misfortune/s [*Unglück*] of his family, to discover whether the other world beyond, which appears in the dreams of the exiles, might not, perhaps, be real after all.

It is hard to overlook the fact that the 'secret royalty' of the Kobal family bears traits of Handke's own family history, at least as related in *Wunschloses Unglück* [*A Sorrow Beyond Dreams*].[vii] The fictional transpositions in *Die Wiederholung* [*Repetition*] may thus be read as so many desires for redemption on the part of the author. The key aspect of Handke's rewriting of his *Familienroman* [family novel] is that it cannot, in any straightforward way, be described as an idealization – the Kobal family is in many ways an extremely bleak and self-destructive association; rather, in the reworking, what matters to Handke is the elimination of one particular element, involving as radical a distancing as possible from his father's German origins, which, it seems to me, were the cause of some of the greatest tribulations in the psychological and moral development of the writer Peter Handke. The Kobals have nothing in common with the Germans, nor even, at bottom, with the Austrians. Their privilege and sovereign right [*Fürstenpatent*] is to be the *others*, who had no part in the violence starting with the fear of the fathers and spreading across the entire continent of Europe. The ideal image of a more humane mode of coexistence, which one might extrapolate from the family bonds of the Kobals – where seen in a more positive light – is of a society in which fathers play at most a subordinate role. His mother's dream, the narrator tells us, would have been to run a 'big hotel, with the staff as her subjects'.[28] The extended household of this dream is, like the utopia inscribed in the narrative as a whole, a decidedly matriarchal one. Thus in the narrator's recollection it also seems as if his 'mother spoke with the voice of a judge',[29] and the maxim which Felix Kobal adopts, after serving a kind of apprenticeship as a hired hand to his hostess in the karst, is 'Get away from your father.'[30] Whereas in the patriarchal order everyone is as isolated as the narrator – despite knowing better – clearly still feels himself to be, in a matriarchal regime, where the bonds of kinship are much more loosely woven, each is almost a brother to the other. Something of this shines through in Filip Kobal's encounters with other male characters in the archaic landscape of the karst. One might name here the young soldier from Vipava, who appears to Filip Kobal as his own *Doppelgänger*, as well as the figure of the waiter from the Wochein [Bohinj],[viii] whom Filip imagines to be from a smallholder's family like his own. This waiter, whose portrait is drawn with the utmost devotion, is a veritable imago of the ideal of *fraternité*. Constantly attentive and only 'seemingly lost in some faraway dream', in actual fact he has an overview over the 'whole realm'.[31]

Handke's portrayal, in three or four pages, of the story of the waiter is one of the most evocative passages in literature in German of the last decade. Deeply impressed by this epitome of true obligingness, who lights even the cigarettes of the drunks with complete seriousness, the next day Felix Kobal can think of no one else. He now realizes, says the narrator, that 'it was a kind of love'[32] – not a desire for contact, only to be near him. The silent encounter between these two young men – not a single word passes between them – on Filip Kobal's last day at the Gasthof zur Schwarzen Erde [Black Earth Hotel] takes a strange turn. On his way up to his room just before midnight, Filip Kobal passes the open door of the kitchen and sees 'the waiter sitting by a tub full of dishes, using a tablecloth to dry them. Later,' the text continues, 'when I looked out of my window, he was standing in his shirt-sleeves on the bridge across the torrent, holding a pile of dishes under his right arm. With his left hand, he took one after another and with a smooth graceful movement sent them sailing into the water like so many Frisbees.'[33] This scene is not commented on in any way, merely related and left to stand in its own right. It is this very absence of comment which makes the waiter, ending his working day in the strangest way imaginable, such an unforgettable figure for the reader. And the plates sailing out into the darkness become, like the narrator's no less beautifully constructed sentences arching across a dark abyss, messages of true fraternity.

A notable feature of traditional exile literature are the consolatory dreams in which a long series of messianic figures emerge from the as yet unredeemed world. There is scarcely any age, even in the worst of times, when one of the righteous does not walk the land. The task, though, is to recognize him. By contrast to the Christian doctrine of *Heilsgeschichte* [salvation history], which systematically and repeatedly suppressed any recurrent and resurgent hopes of redemption, the Judaic form of messianism, which is ready to see the longed-for redeemer in every unrecognized stranger, contains, alongside the theological dimension, a potential political one. Even if the father cannot say what 'form the redemption of his family here on earth might take',[34] it is clear that it must encompass both redemption in this world and the redemption of an entire community. It is no coincidence that the mythical ancestor of the exiled family is a rebel. The tendency to insurrection, the anti-authoritarian sentiment, is fundamental to the dynamics of the messianic imagination — which does not, however, mean that the form the redeemer will assume is in any way fixed or predetermined. Rather, the figure of the messianic redeemer is characterized by its mutability. With his one eye, Gregor, the elder brother who has gone before Filip into the other country, is already marked out as the king among the blind in exile. Although, as the narrator tells us, despite often coming close to it he 'never actually became an insurrectionary',[35] he embodies a trait the narrator claims to have otherwise encountered only in a few children, namely piety.[36] The disappearance in time of war of this son, in whom the hopes of the Kobal family live on, and for whom 'holy', one of his favourite words, was connected not with 'any other place outside the world'[37] but with rising early and the routine activities of everyday life – for the exiles, this loss of the bearer of their hopes represents a trauma which can scarcely be overcome. Even 'twenty years after my brother's disappearance', the narrator remembers, our house 'was still a house of mourning',[38] in which the lost brother left the family 'no peace; every day he died again for them'.[39] It is this unassuaged and unassuageable grief which gives rise, on the part of the otherwise very distant parents, to the shared dream of their son's return. As the text says, both parents worshipped their missing son, each in their own way, to such an extent 'that at news of his coming she [the mother] would immediately have prepared "his apartment", scrubbed the threshold, and hung a wreath over the front door, while my father would have borrowed a neighbour's white horse, harnessed it to the spit-and-polished barouche, and, with tears of joy running down his nose, driven to meet him' to the ends of the earth.[40]

The Kobal family epitomizes the exiles' superior sense of self-assurance. In future, of this the mother is certain, 'after our return home, our resurrection from a thousand years of servitude',[41] the village of Kobarid in the Isonzo valley, where, according to tradition, the Kobals hail from, will be renamed Kobalid. All it takes for the messianic adjustment of the world is the tiniest slip of the tongue. That the village of Kobal is called in German Karfreit [*Karfreitag* = Good Friday] is a further indication of the mission of redemption, on the part of its sons, to bring about their transformation from an oppressed existence to an attitude of indomitable pride. According to their family mythology, the Kobals are the chosen representatives of the Slovenian people, who, like the Jews – the paradigmatic example of a people in exile – are composed of those 'who had been kingless and stateless down through the centuries, a people of journeymen and hired hands'.[42] Moving among these people on the streets of the Yugoslavian cities, Filip notices how, from this anonymous collective, which has 'never set up a government',[43][ix] a force emerges which is opposed to all authority. 'We children of darkness' – thus the narrator, including himself in their midst – 'were radiant with beauty, self-reliant, bold, rebellious, independent, each man of us the next man's hero.'[44] The unique status the narrator ascribes to the Slovenian people is a reflection of the changing awareness of Filip Kobal, who, like Amalia in Kafka's *Castle*, is learning to bear his enforced fate of exile as a mark of distinction. One of the least understood characteristics of the Jewish people in the diaspora is, as Hannah Arendt explains, the fact that 'the Jews never really knew what power was, even when it was almost in their grasp, nor did they ever really have any interest in power.'[45] In *Die Wiederholung*, the Slovenian people are described in very similar terms, as a people without power: 'without aristocracy, without military marches, without land',[46] they have remained uncorrupted and – again almost like the Jewish people – recognize as their only king the legendary hero who, the saying goes, wanders about in disguise, showing himself only briefly before disappearing again.[47] Like his brother before him, Filip Kobal is destined to assume the role of this secret king. His messianic disguise is that of the guest who appears unexpectedly on the threshold,[x] a role allotted to him at an early age by his mother and sister who, when he came home from school, would, for example – with the readiness to serve which had become second nature — set down a cup before him as if he were 'an unexpected noble guest'.[48] And on his journeyings, this smallholder's son — someone who 'had no origins at all'[49] — becomes truly aware of the magnitude of his task. Just as, in an early version of the opening of *Das Schloß* [*The Castle*], the best room [*Fürstenzimmer* — 'prince's room'][xi] is made ready for the wanderer K. when he arrives in the village, so too Filip Kobal finds that he is offered a large room in the inn Zur Schwarzen Erde 'with four beds, enough for a whole family'.[50] And when in the evening he is sitting in the inn, no one, 'not even the militia on its constant rounds, asked [his] name; everyone called [him] "the guest".'[51] Filip, for whom since his last days at school journeying and travelling have been his true home, and whose journey south, on which he embarks with a blue sea bag and a hazel wand, is a further rehearsal for his allotted role, is, as the guest from foreign parts sitting quietly by, the one from whom redemption is awaited. He himself needs a long time — a whole quarter of a century — before the task assigned to him at the time becomes clear to him in the repetition. To begin with, he is only searching for his brother. However, it is significant that when, in a kind of evocation of ancestors, for a moment, as it says, he catches a glimpse of his brother's likeness, he is unable to endure it. At the sight of the hallucinatory apparition, with eyes set so deep in their sockets 'that his white blindness remained hidden',[52] Filip is completely overcome, and can only leave the site of the apparition immediately, taking refuge in the torrent of passers-by as he goes on his way once more. In the messianic tradition, it is less important that those separated should finally sink into each other's arms than that the effort should continue, that the younger should succeed the elder, the pupil become a teacher, and that the pious wish for redemption, the hope Gregor expressed in his letters from the front that they would travel together in the festive Easter vigil carriage into the Ninth Country, should find its earthly 'fulfilment [. . .]: in writing'.[53][xii]

The text of *Die Wiederholung* constitutes this fulfilment. The book *is* the Easter carriage in which the scattered members of the Kobal family are assembled once more. Writing is thus anything but a secular affair. The narrator is clear from the outset about the difficulty of the task before him. Accordingly, he recalls how his mother 'whenever I had been out of the house for any length of time, in town or alone in the woods or out in the fields, assailed me with her "Tell me"',[54] and how, at the time, at least before her illness, he was never able to tell her anything. The fact that it is his mother's illness which finally helps him overcome this inhibition implies that one of the main tasks of storytelling, in the sense meant here, is the alleviation of suffering. One of the prerequisites for the exercise of such a healing art, closely related to the doctor's vocation, is the willingness to keep a vigil through the dark watches of the night. Even for the schoolboy Kobal, it is the 'one lighted window in the teachers' house',[55] and not the feeble flickering flame on the altar, which represents the true eternal light that keeps alive the possibility of redemption. In Handke's work, teaching and learning are ways of preserving the world. This is exemplified in *Die Wiederholung* in the elder brother's Slovenian notebooks, particularly those relating to the cultivation of fruit, which Filip takes with him on his journey and which become, for him, a textbook and manual for living. From his brother's studies and notes he realizes that, 'unlike the great mass of those who speak and write', those who have the gift of 'bringing words and through them things to life',[56] and who are ready constantly to practise this strange art, can exercise a healing effect. His brother's disappearance without trace in the war, though, also demonstrates how cruelly so-called circumstances can, almost without fail, cut short the possibilities set out in even the most beautifully wrought text. The narrator's fear that he too could be obliterated just as easily as his brother before him haunts his recollections as a feeling of helplessness. The timeframe of his report however suggests that he has already managed to hold out for a good number of years. It has been a quarter of a century since the young Filip Kobal discovered his own inner storyteller. Looking back on this time, however, the narrator, now aged forty-five, also realizes that at the time he would not have been capable of telling anyone the story of his *Heimat*. The process of gestation by which apparently irrelevant *trouvailles* from one's own life are transformed into worthwhile images is a lengthy one; and even when the fragments from times past appear to be assembled in meaningful patterns, the narrator is still beset by doubts, never quite allayed, as to whether what he now holds in his hands is not merely 'the last remnants, leftovers, shards of something irretrievably lost, which no artifice could put together again'.[57] The fact that, despite such doubts and difficulties, there are many passages in *Die Wiederholung* which, like the one about the midnight waiter quoted above, convey a sense almost of levitation is a measure of the exceptional quality of this story, whose secret aim is one of lightness. Not that the narrator is lighthearted or free from care; but, instead of talking about what burdens him, he turns his attention to producing something which helps both him and the reader – who is perhaps equally in need of solace – to withstand the temptations of melancholy. The model Filip Kobal chooses for his work of storytelling is that of the road mender, responsible for the upkeep of the local roads and paths, who, like the writer in his cell, lives in a 'one-room house . . . suggesting the porter's lodge of a nonexistent manor house'.[58][xiii] This road mender, who, like the scribe, day by day carries out his laborious work, at times unexpectedly metamorphoses into a sign painter, standing at the top of a ladder above, say, the entrance to the inn at the centre of the village. 'As I watched him' – thus the narrator – 'adding a shadowy line to a finished letter with a strikingly slow brushstroke, aerating, as it were, a thick letter with a few hair-thin lines, and then conjuring up the next letter from the blank surface, as though it had been there all along and he was only retracing it, I saw in this nascent script the emblem of a hidden, nameless, all the more magnificent and above all unbounded kingdom.'[59] I can think of no more beautiful image to capture the enforced relationship between thankless drudgery and ethereal magic, so characteristic of literary art in particular, than this page of *Die Wiederholung* dedicated to the road mender and sign painter. It is significant, too, that the work of the narrator's chosen teacher takes place out of doors; that instead of enclosing the landscape in a frame – as is usual in art – both road mending and sign painting are adapted to the landscape. The exceptional openness of the text of *Die Wiederholung* stems from the fact that the outdoor scenes are far more important than those which take place indoors. Accordingly, the model for the true place of the storyteller – as Filip Kobal recognizes in hindsight – is his father's shed in the corner of the field where, as a boy, having 'gone directly to the fields from school' he would sit 'at the table with my homework'.[60] This hut or shelter, he now realizes, was and is 'the centre of the world, where the storyteller sits in a cave no larger than a wayside shrine and tells his story'.[61] Like the sukkah [*Laubhütte*, literally 'leafy hut'][xiv] in a different tradition, the hut in the field [*Feldhütte*] the narrator has in mind here represents a resting place on the journey through the wilderness, and its periodic re-erection in the midst of a civilization circumscribing ever more narrowly the natural origins of mankind is a ritual recollecting a life in the open air. And in allowing the particular light which filters through the leaves of the canopy or the canvas of a tent to shine through from time to time between the words placed with often astonishing care and precision, Handke, in *Die Wiederholung*, succeeds in making the text itself a place of refuge among the arid zones which, even in the culture industry, are encroaching further by the day. The book of a journey on foot through the Karst landscape, with the notorious bora blowing hard across it, thus also comes to resemble one of those low-lying hollows or *dolinas* below the level of the wind which, fringed by trees all bent at the same angle, are, at the bottom, islands of calm where, as the narrator relates, the stubbly grass barely trembles, the beanstalks and potato plants hardly sway and in whose depths, 'without fear of one another, the beasts of the Karst could assemble, a stocky little roe deer along with a hare and a herd of wild pigs'.[62] Inscribed into this image of a peaceable kingdom, reminiscent of the Ark, is the hope that, despite the unfavourable circumstances, some small part of our natural *Heimat* may yet be saved after all.

Notes

Part One

To the Edge of Nature – An Essay on Stifter

1 [Adalbert Stifter,] *Sämtliche Werke*, Briefwechsel vol. 7, Reichenberg, 1939, p. 37.
2 Quoted in U. Roedl, *Adalbert Stifter*, Reinbek, 1965, p. 74.
3 Cf. Roedl, op. cit., pp. 52f. [sic = pp. 152f.].
4 Cf. [J. P. Stern,] *Re-Interpretations*, New York, 1964, p. 361.
5 Apart from the biographical works by A. R. Hein (*Adalbert Stifter. Sein Leben und seine Werke*, 2nd edn, Vienna, Bad Bockler, Zurich, 1952), U. Roedl (*Adalbert Stifter. Geschichte seines Lebens*, 2nd edn, Berne, 1958) and H. Augustin (*Adalbert Stifters Krankheit und Tod*, Basel, 1964), only the study by F. Gundolf (*Adalbert Stifter*, Halle, 1931), [J.] P. Stern's piece in *Re-Interpretations* (New York, 1964) and the monographs by H. A. Glaser (*Die Restauration des Schönen*, Stuttgart, 1965) and G. Mattenklott (*Sprache der Sentimentalität. Zum Werk Adalbert Stifters*, Frankfurt am Main, 1973) are particularly worthy of note. The critical rehabilitation of Stifter set in motion by the last-named works in particular has, of course, borne some strange fruits of its own, as demonstrated in the most recent work by H. J. Piechotta ('Ordnung als mythologisches Zitat. Adalbert Stifter und der Mythos', in *Mythos und Moderne*, ed. K. H. Bohrer, Frankfurt am Main, 1983) where critical jargon takes on truly abstruse dimensions.

6 [Franz Kafka,] *Forschungen eines Hundes*, in *Erzählungen*, Frankfurt am Main, 1971, p. 323; 'Investigations of a Dog', in *The Great Wall of China and Other Short Works*, tr. Malcolm Pasley, London: Penguin, 2002, p. 141 (translation adapted).

7 [Stifter,] *Sämtliche Werke*, vol. III/3, p. 164; 'The Ancient Seal', in Adalbert Stifter, *Tales of Old Vienna and other Prose*, tr. Alexander Stillmark, Riverside, CA: Ariadne, 2016, pp. 21–70 at p. 55. Cf. also J. P. Stern, *Re-Interpretations*, op. cit., p. 266.

8 Ibid., p. 185; 'The Ancient Seal', tr. Stillmark, p. 70 (translation slightly adapted); cf. also *Re-Interpretations*, p. 268.

9 On this, see H. and H. Schlaffer, *Studien zum ästhetischen Historismus*, Frankfurt am Main, 1975, p. 115.

10 Glaser, op. cit., p. 20.

11 See the essay on Stifter and Handke in this volume, above p. 193.

12 [Stifter,] *Die Mappe meines Urgroßvaters*, *Sämtliche Werke*, vol. XII, pp. 274f.

13 [Stifter,] *Sämtliche Werke*, vol. XIII/1, pp. 175f. ['Prokopus'].

14 One of the clearest examples of this topos, which recurs frequently from the Romantics onwards, occurs in Robert Walser's story *Kleist in Thun*: 'Below him lies the lake, as if it had been hurled down by the great hand of a god, incandescent with shades of yellow and red, its whole incandescence seems to glow up out of the water's depths. It is like a lake of fire. The Alps have come to life and dip with fabulous gestures their foreheads into the water. His swans down there circle his quiet island, and the crests of trees in dark, chanting, fragrant joy float over – over what? Nothing, nothing. Kleist drinks it all in. To him the whole sparkling lake is the cluster of diamonds upon a vast, slumbering, unknown woman's body.' Robert Walser, *Romane & Erzählungen*, vol. V, Frankfurt am Main, 1984, pp. 11f.; 'Kleist in Thun', in Robert Walser, *Selected Stories*, tr. Christopher Middleton et al., Manchester: Carcanet, 1982, pp. 17–26 at p. 22.

15 Cf. 'Mein Leben' in Adalbert Stifter, *Die fürchterliche Wendung der Dinge*, ed. H. J. Piechotta, Darmstadt and Neuwied, 1981; 'My Life: An Autobiographical Sketch', in *Tales of Old Vienna*, pp. 154–65. (Cf. *Re-Interpretations*, pp. 352–8, where the short text is reproduced in German with parallel English translation.)

16 On this cf. G. Mattenklott, *Der übersinnliche Leib*, Reinbek, 1982, pp. 84f.

17 [G. Bachelard,] 'Der Mythos der Verdauung', in *Die Bildung des wissenschaftlichen Geistes*, Frankfurt am Main, 1978 (= 'Le Mythe de la digestion', ch. IX in *La Formation de l'esprit scientifique – Contribution à une psychanalyse de la connaissance objective*, J. Vrin, 1967); 'The Myth of Digestion', in *The Formation of the Scientific Mind: A Contribution to a Psychoanalysis of Objective Knowledge*, tr. Mary McAllester Jones, Manchester: Clinamen, 2002.

18 [Stifter,] *Sämtliche Werke*, vol. XII, p. 9 ['Die Mappe meines Urgroßvaters'].

19 [Stifter,] *Sämtliche Werke*, vol. XII, p. 257 ['Die Mappe meines Urgroßvaters'].

20 [Stifter,] *Sämtliche Werke*, vol. XIII/1, p. 198 ['Prokopus'].

21 [Georg Simmel,] In *Philosophische Kultur*, Leipzig, 1911, p. 150 [and p. 152]; Georg Simmel, 'The Alps', tr. Margaret Cerullo, *Qualitative Sociology* 16.2 (1993), 179–84 at pp. 181, 182, https://doi-org.uea.idm.oclc.org/10.1007/BF00989749.

22 Ibid., p. 154; 'The Alps', p. 184.

23 Cf. U. H. Peters, *Hölderlin*, Reinbek, 1983.

24 [Stifter,] *Sämtliche Werke*, vol. I/2, pp. 290 and 292 [*Der Hochwald*]. [An alternative translation may be found in: *Der Hochwald* (*The High Forest*), in *Four Obscurities from the Borderlands: Works by Werner Bergengruen, Maria von Ebner-Eschenbach, Joseph Roth and Adalbert Stifter, 1842–1942*, tr. Edwin K. Tucker, Amazon, 2018, pp. 174–278 at pp. 248 and 250). I have chosen to use my own translation here.]

25 I owe the reference to this constellation to a lecture by Z. [sic = J.] Reddick with the title *Mystification, Perspectivism and Symbolism in Der Hochwald* held at a Stifter Colloquium in London [= John Reddick, 'Mystification, Perspectivism and Symbolism in *Der Hochwald*', in *Adalbert Stifter Heute: Londoner Symposium 1983*, ed. Johann Lachinger, Alexander Stillmark and Martin Swales, Linz: Adalbert-Stifter-Institut, 1985, pp. 44–74].

26 [Stifter,] *Sämtliche Werke*, vol. VI/1, pp. 261 and 284; Adalbert Stifter, *Indian Summer*, tr. Wendell Frye, New York: Peter Lang, 1985, pp. 139–40 and 151.

27 Cf. [Simmel,] *Die Mode* in op. cit.; Georg Simmel, 'Fashion', *American Journal of Sociology* 62.6 (May 1957), 541–58, http://www.jstor.org/stable/2773129.

28 [Walter Benjamin, *Gesammelte*] *Schriften*, vol. V/1, Frankfurt am Main, 1982, p. 130; *The Arcades Project*, tr. Howard Eiland and Kevin McLaughlin, Cambridge, MA: Belknap Press, 1999, p. 79 ('B9.1').

29 [Stifter,] *Sämtliche Werke*, vol. III/3, pp. 157f.; 'The Ancient Seal', pp. 49–50: the translation of the first passage here follows Martin and Erika Swales, *Adalbert Stifter: A Critical Study*, Cambridge: Cambridge University Press, 1984, p. 81 (punctuation adapted); cf. also *Re-Interpretations*, op. cit., p. 266.

30 [Sigmund Freud,] *Drei Abhandlungen zur Sexualtheorie*, in Freud, *Studienausgabe*, Frankfurt am Main, 1970, p. 63 [p. 64]; *On Sexuality: Three Essays on Sexuality and Other Works*, tr. and ed. James Strachey, vol. 7, ed. Angela Richards, Harmondsworth: Penguin, 1977 (repr. 1991), p. 66.

31 [Stifter,] *Sämtliche Werke*, vol. III/3, pp. 163 and 164; 'The Ancient Seal', p. 54.

32 [Stifter,] *Sämtliche Werke*, vol. XIII/1, p. 203 ['Prokopus'].

33 [Stifter,] *Sämtliche Werke*, vol. XII, p. 210 ['Die Mappe meines Urgroßvaters'].

34 Ibid., pp. 213f.; this passage is translated slightly differently in Swales and Swales, op. cit., p. 121.

35 Ibid., p. 216; the latter part of this translation (from 'Sir') follows Swales and Swales, op. cit., pp. 121, 122.
36 [Kafka,] *Hochzeitsvorbereitungen auf dem Lande*, Frankfurt am Main, 1980, p. 64; Franz Kafka, *Wedding Preparations in the Country and Other Posthumous Prose Writings*, tr. Ernst Kaiser and Eithne Wilkins, London: Secker & Warburg, 1954 (repr. 1975), p. 85 (24 November 1917).

The Horror of Love – On Schnitzler's *Traumnovelle* [*Dream Story*]

1 Cf. [Gert Mattenklott,] *Der übersinnliche Leib*, Reinbek, 1982, pp. 155ff.
2 On this subject cf. Georg Simmel, 'Zur Philosophie der Geschlechter', in *Philosophische Kultur*, Leipzig, 1911, esp. p. 112; Georg Simmel, *On Women, Sexuality, and Love*, tr. Guy Oakes, New Haven/London: Yale University Press, 1984, p. 142.
3 Cf. Niklas Luhmann, *Liebe als Passion – Zur Codierung der Intimität*, Frankfurt am Main, 1982, and Michel Foucault, *La Volonté de savoir*, Paris, 1976; Niklas Luhmann, *Love as Passion: The Codification of Intimacy*, tr. Jeremy Gaines and Doris L. Jones, Cambridge: Polity, 1986, and Michel Foucault, *The History of Sexuality*, vol. 1: *The Will to Knowledge*, tr. Robert Hurley, London: Penguin, 1981 (repr. 1998).
4 Walter Benjamin's essay on [Goethe's] *Die Wahlverwandtschaften* [*Elective Affinities*] and Heinz Schlaffer's study on Goethe's 'Der Bräutigam' ['The Bridegroom'], in *Der Bürger als Held*, Frankfurt am Main, 1976, could serve as examples here.
5 Nike Wagner's book *Geist und Geschlecht – Karl Kraus und die Erotik der Wiener Moderne*, Frankfurt am Main, 1982, is the most nuanced and intelligent commentary on this.

6 Even then, Freud's first letter to Schnitzler was only occasioned by the congratulatory speech which Schnitzler delivered to Freud on the occasion of his fiftieth birthday in 1906.

7 On this, cf. Katharina Rutschky (ed.), *Schwarze Pädagogik – Quellen zur Naturgeschichte der bürgerlichen Erziehung*, Frankfurt am Main/Berlin/Vienna, 1977, pp. 318f.

8 Schnitzler, *Die Erzählenden Schriften*, vol. II, Frankfurt am Main, 1961, p. 434; *Dream Story*, tr. J. M. Q. Davies, London: Penguin, 1999, p. 3.

9 Ibid., p. 441; *Dream Story*, pp. 13 and 14.

10 Cf. for example 'Bruchstücke einer Hysterie-Analyse', in *Freud-Studienausgabe*, vol. VI, Frankfurt am Main, 1971, pp. 83ff.; 'Fragment of an Analysis of a Case of Hysteria', in *Standard Edition of the Complete Psychological Works of Sigmund Freud*, vol. VII, tr. James Strachey, pp. 7–122 (the case is better known in English as 'Dora': cf. Freud, *Case Histories I: 'Dora' and 'Little Hans'*, tr. Alix and James Strachey, Penguin Freud Library, vol. 8, ed. Angela Richards, London: Penguin, 1990, pp. 31–164).

11 Cf. *Freud-Studienausgabe*, vol. IX, Frankfurt am Main, 1974, p. 352; Freud, 'Totem and Taboo', tr. James Strachey, in *The Origins of Religion*, Penguin Freud Library, vol. 13, ed. Albert Dickson, London: Penguin, 1990, pp. 43–224 at p. 118.

12 Schnitzler, op. cit., p. 444; *Dream Story*, p. 18.

13 Ibid., p. 445; *Dream Story*, p. 18.

14 Ibid., p. 443; *Dream Story*, p. 16.

15 Ibid., p. 445; *Dream Story*, p. 19.

16 Ibid., p. 436; *Dream Story*, p. 6.

17 Fridolin too counts himself lucky that 'a charming and lovable woman was there at his disposal, and that he could have another one, many others, if he so desired'. Ibid., p. 446; *Dream Story*, p. 21.

18 [Roth, *Das falsche Gewicht*,] Reinbek (rororo), 1981, p. 7; Joseph Roth, *Weights and Measures*, tr. David Le Vay, London: Peter Owen, 1982 (repr. 2002), p. 10.

19 Schnitzler, op. cit., p. 448; *Dream Story*, p. 23.

20 Ibid., p. 478; *Dream Story*, p. 65.

21 Ibid., p. 435; *Dream Story*, p. 4.

22 Edmund Bergler, 'Zur Psychologie der Hasardspieler', *Imago* XXII.4 (1936), p. 439; cf. Edmund Bergler, *The Psychology of Gambling*, New York: Hill & Wang, 1957, a greatly expanded book-length version of the original and successive articles.

23 Cf. for example Werner Sombart, *Liebe, Luxus und Kapitalismus*, Berlin, 1983 [= Werner Sombart, *Luxury and Capitalism*, tr. W. R. Dittmar, Ann Arbor, MI: University of Michigan Press, 1967]; Steven Marcus, *The Other Victorians*, London, 1966; Heinrich Grün, *Prostitution in Theorie und Wirkllichkeit*, Vienna, 1907.

24 Walter Benjamin, *Das Passagen-Werk*, *Gesammelte Schriften*, vol. VI [sic = V.1], Frankfurt am Main, 1982, p. 637; Benjamin, *The Arcades Project*, tr. Howard Eiland and Kevin McLaughlin, Cambridge, MA/London: Belknap Press, 1999, p. 511 ('O II, a, 4').

25 [Schnitzler,] *Jugend in Wien*, Vienna/Munich/Zurich, 1968, pp. 308f.; Arthur Schnitzler, *My Youth in Vienna*, tr. Catherine Hutter, London: Weidenfeld & Nicolson, 1970, pp. 260, 261.

26 [Schnitzler,] *Erzählende Schriften*, vol. II, p. 450; *Dream Story*, p. 26.

27 *Jugend in Wien*, p. 86; *My Youth in Vienna*, p. 71.

28 Ibid., p. 104; *My Youth in Vienna*, p. 83.

29 Ibid., p. 176; *My Youth in Vienna*, p. 146.

30 Luhmann, op. cit., p. 93; *Love as Passion*, p. 73.

31 [Schnitzler,] *Erzählende Schriften*, vol. II, p. 451; *Dream Story*, p. 28.

32 Ibid., p. 455; *Dream Story*, p. 33.

33 Ibid., p. 458; *Dream Story*, p. 38.

34 Ibid., p. 464; *Dream Story*, p. 46.

35 Ibid., p. 470; *Dream Story*, p. 53.

36 Ibid., p. 456; *Dream Story*, p. 35.

37 Ibid., p. 495; *Dream Story*, p. 87.

38 Ibid., p. 500; *Dream Story*, pp. 93–4.

39 Peter Sloterdijk, *Kritik der zynischen Vernunft*, vol. II, Frankfurt am Main, 1983, p. 490; Peter Sloterdijk, *Critique of Cynical Reason*, tr. Michael Eldred, Foreword by Andreas Huyssen, Theory and History of Literature, vol. 40, Minneapolis: University of Minnesota Press, 1987, p. 266.

A Venetian Cryptogram – Hofmannsthal's *Andreas*

1 Cf. Nike Wagner, *Geist und Geschlecht – Karl Kraus und die Erotik der Wiener Moderne*, Frankfurt am Main, 1982, p. 135.

2 Martini's study of *Andreas* was published in *Hugo von Hofmannsthal – Wege der Forschung*, ed. S. Bauer, Darmstadt, 1968. The passages quoted are from pp. 315ff.

3 [Hugo von Hofmannsthal,] *Andreas*, vol. XXX of the critical edition published by the Freies Deutsches Hochstift, Frankfurt am Main, 1982, p. 108 [N 71]. The idiosyncratic punctuation and at times also orthography of the passages cited follow the usage in Hofmannsthal's manuscript, which has fortunately been retained uncorrected in the critical edition. [English translation: 'Andreas', in Hugo von Hofmannsthal, *Selected Prose*, tr. Mary Hottinger and Tania and James Stern, London: Routledge & Kegan Paul, 1952, pp. 3–125 at p. 97. (Quotations in English follow this edition where possible. This translation represents 'A comprehensive revision by her (Hottinger) of her translation published in 1936 by J. M. Dent and Sons, London.' The latter translation forms the basis for *Andreas*, tr. Marie D. Hottinger, London: Pushkin, 1998 (repr. 2001).)]

4 Cf. ibid., p. 99 [N 64]; *Selected Prose*, p. 97.

5 Ibid., p. 146 [N 180]; *Selected Prose*, p. 116.

6 Ibid., pp. 64 and 115 [N 87]; *Selected Prose*, pp. 32 and 102.

7 Freud, *Studienausgabe*, vol. VI, Frankfurt am Main, 1971, p. 77; Sigmund Freud, 'The Aetiology of Hysteria', in *The Standard Edition of the Complete Psychological Works*, tr. James Strachey, vol. 3: *Early Psycho-Analytic Publications*, London: Hogarth Press, 1962, pp. 191–221 at p. 217.

8 *Andreas*, p. 99 [N 63]; *Selected Prose*, p. 9.

9 [Baudelaire,] *Œuvres Complètes*, vol. 2, Paris, 1925, p. 404 [*L'Art romantique*: 'Madame Bovary']; cf. '*Madame Bovary* by Gustave Flaubert', in Baudelaire, *Selected Writings on Art and Artists*, tr. with an introduction by P. E. Charvet, Cambridge: Cambridge University Press, 1972, pp. 244–55 at p. 252.

10 [Benjamin,] *Gesammelte Schriften*, vol. VI [sic = V.1], Frankfurt am Main, 1982, p. 432; Benjamin, *The Arcades Project*, tr. Howard Eiland and Kevin McLaughlin, Cambridge, MA/London: Belknap Press, 1999, p. 342 ('J 64, 1').

11 Quoted in Wagner, op. cit., p. 32.

12 This photograph is reproduced in W. Volke, *Hofmannsthal* (rororo monographie 127), Reinbek, 1967, p. 98.

13 *Andreas*, pp. 51f.; *Selected Prose*, p. 17 (translation adapted, to reflect differences between critical edition cited by WGS and the edition the translation is based on).

14 Ibid., p. 41; *Selected Prose*, p. 4.

15 Edmund Bergler, 'Zur Psychologie des Hasardspielers', *Imago* XXII.4 (1936), 441 [sic = 409–10]. Cf. Bergler, *The Psychology of Gambling*, New York: Hill & Wang, 1957.

16 *Andreas*, p. 179 [N 270].

17 Ibid., p. 68; *Selected Prose*, p. 37.

18 Olga Schnitzler, *Spiegelbild der Freundschaft*, Salzburg, 1962, p. 84.

19 Hugo von Hofmannsthal/Eberhard von Bodenhausen, *Briefe der Freundschaft*, ed. Dora von Bodenhausen, Düsseldorf, 1953, p. 149 [letter dated Rodaun, 21 January 1913].

20 Cf. Volke, op. cit., p. 31.

21 *Andreas*, p. 160 [N 220].

22 Ibid., p. 23 [N 35].

23 Mario Praz, *The Romantic Agony*, Oxford/New York, 1983, p. 61 [cited in English in the original].

24 *Andreas*, p. 165 [N 233].

25 Ibid., p. 113 [N 82]; *Selected Prose*, p. 83.

26 Ibid., p. 150 [N 189]; *Selected Prose*, p. 122.

27 Cf. ibid., p. 113 [N 82]; *Selected Prose*, p. 83.

28 Ibid., p. 56; *Selected Prose*, p. 23.

29 Ibid., p. 59; *Selected Prose*, pp. 26–7 (translation adapted).

30 Ibid., p. 58; *Selected Prose*, pp. 24–5.

31 Ibid., p. 57; *Selected Prose*, p. 34.

32 Quoted Praz, op. cit., p. III [sic = p. 111]. [Quoted in French by WGS following Praz. English version: F. R. de Chateaubriand, *Atala – René*, tr. Rayner Heppenstall, London: Oxford University Press, 1963, p. 48.]

33 *Andreas*, p. 55; *Selected Prose*, p. 21.

34 Ibid., p. 56; *Selected Prose*, p. 23.

35 Ibid., pp. 20 and 201 [N 30, N 336]; cf. *Selected Prose*, p. 86 (the second note not included in the published translation).

36 Cf. ibid., p. 151 [N 191]; *Selected Prose*, p. 113.

37 Cf. Praz, op. cit., pp. 205f.

38 *Andreas*, p. 18 [N 25]; cf. *Selected Prose*, p. 88.

39 Cf. ibid., p. 9 [N 3]; *Selected Prose*, p. 87.

40 Ibid., p. 20 [N 28 and N 30]; *Selected Prose*, pp. 90 and 92.

41 Ibid., p. 19 [N 25]; *Selected Prose*, p. 88.

42 Cf. [Alewyn,] 'Andreas und die wunderbare Freundin', in *Über Hugo von Hofmannsthal*, Göttingen, 1958, p. 135: 'The meaning of this apparently playful prop and its relationship to the motif of the dog, which frequently recurs in Hofmannsthal and elsewhere in *Andreas*, cannot be determined with any certainty.'

43 *Andreas*, p. 62; *Selected Prose*, p. 31.

44 [Goncourt,] *Journal*, vol. II (30 August 1866), Paris, 1956, p. 275 [quoted in French in the original].

45 *Andreas*, p. 64; *Selected Prose*, p. 33.

46 Ibid., p. 65; *Selected Prose*, p. 34.

47 [Baudelaire,] Op. cit., p. 96 [quoted in French in the original]; 'The Painter of Modern Life', in Charles Baudelaire, *The Painter of Modern Life and Other Essays*, ed. and tr. Jonathan Mayne, London/New York: Phaidon, 1965 (repr. 2001), pp. 1–41 at p. 32 ('In Praise of Cosmetics').

48 *Andreas*, p. 138 [N 154]; *Selected Prose*, pp. 105–6.

49 [Flaubert,] Letter to Louise Colet of 7/8 July 1853, *Correspondances*, vol. II, Paris, 1923, pp. 84f. [quoted in French in the original]; cf. Gustave Flaubert, *Selected Letters*, tr. Geoffrey Wall, London: Penguin, 1997, pp. 218–22 at p. 220.

50 *Andreas*, pp. 45f.; *Selected Prose*, p. 10 (translation adapted to reflect difference between edition quoted by WGS and that on which published translation based).

51 [Baudelaire,] Quoted Benjamin, op. cit., p. 422; *Arcades Project*, p. 334 ('J 59, 4').

52 *Andreas*, p. 167 [N 237].

The Undiscover'd Country – The Death Motif in Kafka's *Castle*

[Translator's Notes, designated in the main text by a capital letter, [1A], [7B] and so on, relating to Sebald's endnotes to this chapter, can be found at pp. 478–80.]

1 F. Kafka, *The Castle*, p. 297. All quotations from *The Castle* are from the Penguin edition, Harmondsworth, Middlesex, 1964.

2 Ibid., p. 11.

3 Translated from Th. W. Adorno, *Schubert*, pp. 25f., in *Moments Musicaux*, Frankfurt am Main, 1964.

4 Cf. Johann von Tepla (von Saaz), *Der Ackermann aus Böhmen*.

5 *The Castle*, p. 295.

6 Adorno, op. cit., pp. 26f.

7 Walter Benjamin, *Über einige Motive bei Baudelaire*, pp. 231f., in *Illuminationen*, Frankfurt am Main, 1961.

8 Cf. *Handwörterbuch des deutschen Aberglaubens*, ed. H. Bächtold-Stäubli, vol. IV, col. 198, Berlin, 1938–41.

9 *The Castle*, p. 17.

10 Quoted by Adorno in *Zweimal Chaplin*, p. 89, in *Ohne Leitbild. Parva Aesthetica*, Frankfurt am Main, 1969. The quotation comes from an early piece entitled *Repetition* which Kierkegaard wrote under a pseudonym.

11 G. Janouch, *Gespräche mit Kafka*, Frankfurt am Main, 1969, p. 217.

12 *The Castle*, p. 221. The German original reads here: '. . . dieses Fleisch, das manchmal den Eindruck machte, als sei es nicht recht lebendig'. The Muirs' translation '. . . this puppet . . .' seems unjustifiably free at this point. I have retained the imagery of the original. Cf. in this context also the following remark by the maid Pepi about the officials of the Castle: 'Truly, they were exalted gentlemen, but one had to make a great effort to overcome one's disgust so as to be able to clear up after them' (ibid., p. 275).

13 Ibid., p. 237.
14 Ibid., pp. 43f.
15 Ibid., p. 177.
16 Cf. Th. Mann, *Doktor Faustus*, Stockholmer Ausgabe, Frankfurt am Main, 1967, p. 248.
17 *The Castle*, p. 177.
18 Ibid.
19 Ibid., pp. 203f.
20 Ibid., p. 204.
21 Towards the end of a very vivid description Döblin tries to subsume what he has witnessed under some category: 'It is something horrifying. It's something primitive, atavistic. Has it anything to do with Judaism? They are the living remnants of ancient ideas. The residue of a fear of the dead, fear of the souls that wander without finding rest. A feeling that has been handed down to this people with their religion. It is the remnant of another religion, animism, a death cult' (A. Döblin, *Reise in Polen*, Olten und Freiburg im Breisgau, 1968, pp. 92f.).
22 *The Castle*, p. 34.
23 Adorno, *Minima Moralia*, Frankfurt am Main, 1962, p. 150.
24 *The Castle*, p. 49.
25 W. Benjamin, 'Franz Kafka', p. 259, in *Angelus Novus*, Frankfurt am Main, 1966.
26 Cf. *Handwörterbuch des deutschen Aberglaubens*, vol. IV, col. 196. B. v. Regensburg's original reads: 'die hell ist enmitten. dâ daz ertrîche aller sumpfigest ist.'
27 *The Castle*, p. 22.
28 Ibid., p. 215.
29 Ibid., p. 191.
30 Ibid., p. 176.
31 Ibid., pp. 272f.

32 Ibid., p. 140.

33 F. Kafka, *Hochzeitsvorbereitungen auf dem Lande*, Frankfurt am Main, 1950, pp. 228f.

34 *The Castle*, p. 144.

35 Ibid., p. 146.

36 Cf. *Die Zimtläden*, Munich, 1968, p. 78.

37 *The Castle*, pp. 252f.

38 Ibid., p. 250.

39 Ibid., p. 254.

40 Ibid., p. 254.

41 Kafka, *The Diaries, 1910–1923*, 25 December 1911.

42 Kafka, *Letters to Milena*, New York, 1953, p. 219.

43 Cf. *Handwörterbuch des deutschen Aberglaubens*, vol. IX, col. 987. In German folklore the devil's tavern is known by the name of 'Nobiskrug' and as the 'Grenzwirtshaus auf dem Passübergang Jenseits'. The etymology of 'nobis' appears to be 'en obis', 'en âbis', 'in abyssum'.

44 *The Castle*, p. 227.

45 Cf. M. Proust, *À la recherche du temps perdu*, *Le Coté de Guermantes*, Pléiade, Paris, vol. II, p. 133. Having described at length the miraculous possibilities brought about by the invention of the telephone Proust continues: 'Nous n'avons, pour que ce miracle s'accomplisse, qu'à approcher nos lèvres de la planchette magique et appeler . . . les Vierges Vigilantes dont nous entendons chaque jour la voix sans jamais connaître le visage, et qui sont nos Anges gardiens dans les ténèbres vertig[i]neuses dont elles surveillent jalousement les portes; les Toutes-Puissantes par qui les absents surgissent à notre côté, sans qu'il soit permis de les apercevoir; les Danaïdes de l'invisible qui sans cesse vident, remplissent, se transmettent les urnes des sons; les ironiques Furies qui, au moment que nous murmurions une confidence à une amie, avec l'espoir que personne ne nous entendait, nous crient cruellement: "J'écoute"; les

servantes toujours irritées du Mystère, les ombrageuses prêtresses de l'Invisible, les Desmoiselles du téléphone!' Cf. also the remarkably similar passage by W. Benjamin in *Berliner Kindheit um 1900*, in *Illuminationen*, pp. 229f.

46 Cf. *The Castle*, p. 249: 'Well, yes, you are not familiar with conditions here,' Bürgel says to K. in the course of the interview, 'but even you must, I suppose, have been struck by the foolproofness of the official organization. Now from this foolproofness it does result that everyone who has any petition or who must be interrogated in any matter for other reasons, instantly, without delay, usually indeed even before he has worked the matter out for himself, more, indeed even before he himself knows of it, has already received the summons.'

47 Cf. *Handwörterbuch des deutschen Aberglaubens*, vol. IV, col. 194.

48 R. Gray, *Kafka's Castle*, Cambridge, 1956, p. 131.

49 5th Duino Elegy, lines 88–94. It is perhaps interesting to note here that the 5th Elegy was written in the spring of 1922 at about the same time as *The Castle*. Cf. in this context also an entry dated 22 May 1912 in Kafka's Diary: 'Yesterday a wonderfully beautiful evening with Max ... Cabaret Lucerna. *Madame la Mort* by Rachilde'. (Rachilde, pseud. for Marguerite Valette, 1862–1935, French novelist and playwright.)

50 Gray, *Kafka's Castle*, p. 132.

51 *The Castle*, pp. 132f.

52 Jean-Paul [sic], *Ueber das Leben nach dem Tode, oder der Geburtstag*, in *Ausgewählte Werke*, Berlin, 1848, vol. XV, p. 251.

Summa Scientiae – Systems and System Critique in Elias Canetti

1 Canetti, *Masse und Macht*, Hamburg, 1960, p. 510; Elias Canetti, *Crowds and Power*, tr. Carol Stewart, Harmondsworth: Penguin, 1984, p. 515.

2   Another case which would illustrate this complex is that of the Viennese writer Arthur Trebitsch (1879–1927), who was associated with Ludendorff and who, along with Ernst von Salomon and Arnolt Bronnen, may be counted among the propagandists of national socialism. In his day, Trebitsch wrote around twenty books as well as countless essays. He is also thought to be one of the co-propagators of the notorious *Protocols of the Elders of Zion*, one of the most influential fakes in history, which played a central part in the development of anti-Semitism as a political ideology. Trebitsch believed he had been chosen to save the German people from the Jews. His anti-Semitism, directed against his own origins, developed the theory of a Jewish–capitalist conspiracy into an all-encompassing *Wahnsystem* [system of madness]. Trebitsch feared the rays and gases emanating from his enemies, and believed he was exposed to their magnetic influence. He surrounded his study with insulating wires and finally slept in a glass house erected for this purpose in his garden, from where he could be sure of surveying everything. The translation of his *Wahnsystem* into political practice was something he did not live to see. (On this, cf. Theodor Lessing, *Jüdischer Selbsthaß*, Berlin, 1930; *Jewish Self-Hate*, tr. Peter C. Appelbaum, New York: Berghahn, 2021.)

3   [Canetti,] *Die gespaltene Zukunft*, Munich, 1972, p. 8; 'Hitler according to Speer', in Elias Canetti, *The Conscience of Words*, tr. Joachim Neugroschel, New York: Continuum, 1979, pp. 145–52 at p. 146.

4   [Canetti,] *Aufzeichnungen, 1949–1960*, Munich, 1970, p. 82; Canetti, *The Human Province*, tr. Joachim Neugroschel, London: André Deutsch, 1985, p. 161.

5   Cf. *Die gespaltene Zukunft*, p. 8; *The Conscience of Words*, p. 146.

6   *Aufzeichnungen, 1949–1960*, p. 82; *The Human Province*, p. 19.

7 Cf. [Canetti,] *Die Blendung*, Frankfurt am Main, 1965, p. 351; Canetti, *Auto-da-Fé*, tr. C. V. Wedgwood, Harmondsworth: Penguin, 1965, p. 443.

8 Ibid., p. 30; *Auto-da-Fé*, pp. 40–41.

9 Ibid., p. 330; *Auto-da-Fé*, pp. 417–18.

10 *Masse und Macht*, p. 520; *Crowds and Power*, p. 524.

11 Cf. [Bernhard,] *Prosa*, Frankfurt am Main, 1967, p. 44 ['Ist es eine Kömödie?']; 'Is it a comedy? Is it a tragedy?', in Thomas Bernhard, *Prose*, tr. Martin Chalmers, London/New York/Calcutta: Seagull Books, 2010, pp. 47–64 at p. 64 (WGS adapts the quotation slightly, translation adjusted to fit).

12 *Masse und Macht*, p. 526; *Crowds and Power*, p. 530.

13 *Aufzeichnungen, 1942–1948*, Munich, 1969, p. 144 [1947]; *The Human Province*, p. 104.

14 Franz Jung, *Der Weg nach unten*, Berlin/Neuwied, 1961, p. 119.

15 *Aufzeichnungen, 1942–1948*, p. 145 [1947]; *The Human Province*, p. 105.

16 Ibid., p. 99; *The Human Province*, p. 69.

17 Cf. *Die Blendung*, p. 353; *Auto-da-Fé*, p. 447.

18 *Aufzeichnungen, 1942–1948*, p. 9 [1942]; *The Human Province*, p. 1.

19 *Aufzeichnungen, 1949–1960*, p. 124 [1960]; *The Human Province*, p. 186.

20 *Aufzeichnungen, 1942–1948*, pp. 107f. [1946]; *The Human Province*, p. 75.

21 Ibid., p. 135 [1947]; *The Human Province*, p. 97.

22 *Aufzeichnungen, 1949–1960*, p. 10; *The Human Province*, p. 114.

23 *Aufzeichnungen, 1942–1948*, p. 107; *The Human Province*, p. 75.

24 Ibid., p. 109; *The Human Province*, p. 76 (the alternative translation quoted here is from 'Elias Canetti: Notebooks, 1942–1948', tr. Margaret Woodruff, *Dimension* 1.3 (1968), 420–41 at p. 435).

25 [*Aufzeichnungen, 1949–1960*], p. 30 [1951]; *The Human Province*, p. 127.

26 Ibid., p. 101 [1957]; *The Human Province*, p. 172.

Wo die Dunkelheit den Strick zuzieht
[Where Darkness Draws Tight the Noose] –
Some Marginal Notes on Thomas Bernhard

[Original article in English; quotations and footnotes in German. Sebald added two late notes, 13a and 30a; that numbering has been retained.]

1 Quoted after Urs Jenny, 'Österreichische Agonie', in *Über Thomas Bernhard*, ed. Anneliese Botond, Frankfurt am Main, 1970, p. 107.
2 [Thomas Bernhard,] *Der Keller – Eine Entziehung*, Munich, 1979, p. 87; 'The Cellar: An Escape', in Thomas Bernhard, *Gathering Evidence: A Memoir*, tr. David McLintock, New York: Knopf, 1985, pp. 143–213 at p. 193.
3 [Handke,] *Als das Wünschen noch geholfen hat*, Frankfurt am Main, 1974, p. 74.
4 Theodor W. Adorno, *Prismen*, Munich, 1963, p. 262; Adorno, *Prisms*, tr. Samuel and Sherry Weber, Cambridge, MA: MIT, 1981, p. 260 ('Notes on Kafka', pp. 243–71).
5 Cf. Christian Enzensberger, *Größerer Versuch über den Schmutz*, Munich, 1970.
6 [Bernhard,] *Verstörung*, Frankfurt am Main, 1976, p. 118; Thomas Bernhard, *Gargoyles*, tr. Richard and Clara Winston, New York: Knopf, 1970, p. 125.
7 Ibid., p. 119; *Gargoyles*, p. 126.
8 Ibid., pp. 109f.; *Gargoyles*, p. 116.
9 Ibid., p. 114; *Gargoyles*, p. 121.
10 Ibid., p. 118; *Gargoyles*, p. 125.
11 On this, see Benjamin's differentiation between bloody and non-bloody, human and divine violence, in 'Zur Kritik der Gewalt', in *Angelus Novus*, Frankfurt am Main, 1966, p. 42 [and] passim; 'Critique of Violence', tr. Edmund Jephcott, in Walter Benjamin, *Selected Writings*, vol. 1: *1913–1926*, Cambridge, MA/London: Harvard University Press, 1996, pp. 236–52 at p. 236 and passim.
12 *Verstörung*, p. 123; *Gargoyles*, p. 131.

13 Ibid., p. 122; *Gargoyles*, p. 129.

13a Ibid., p. 115; *Gargoyles*, p. 122.

14 [Bernhard,] *Frost*, Frankfurt am Main, 1972, pp. 305f.; *Frost*, tr. Michael Hofmann, New York: Vintage, 2008, p. 270.

15 [Franz Kafka,] 'Forschungen eines Hundes', in *Erzählungen*, Frankfurt am Main, 1961, [pp. 333–71 at] p. 346; Kafka, 'Investigations of a Dog', in *The Great Wall of China and Other Short Works*, tr. and ed. Malcolm Pasley, London: Penguin, 1991, pp. 141–77 at pp. 153–4.

16 [Bernhard,] *Ungenach*, Frankfurt am Main, 1975, p. 17.

17 Cf. Franz von Baader, *Evolutionismus und Revolutionismus*, in *Gesellschaftslehre*, Munich, 1957, p. 216.

18 [Bernhard,] *Frost*, p. 153; *Frost* (English), p. 140.

19 Ibid., p. 154; *Frost* (English), p. 140.

20 *Verstörung*, pp. 63f.; *Gargoyles*, p. 66 (Bernhard's emphasis).

21 Ibid., p. 117; *Gargoyles*, p. 124.

22 [Bernhard,] *Das Kalkwerk*, Frankfurt am Main, 1976, p. 70; Bernhard, *The Lime Works*, tr. Sophie Wilkins, New York: Knopf, 1973, p. 75.

23 Ibid., p. 66; *The Lime Works*, p. 70.

24 *Verstörung*, p. 169 [this sentence is omitted from *Gargoyles*, pp. 180–81].

25 Cf. [Benjamin,] *Karl Kraus*, in *Illuminationen*, Frankfurt am Main, 1961, p. 385; Benjamin, *Selected Writings*, vol. 2, pp. 433–57, tr. Edmund Jephcott, at p. 441.

26 On this cf. Winfried Kudszus, 'Literatur, Soziopathologie, Double Bind', in *Literatur und Schizophrenie*, ed. W. Kudszus, Munich, 1977, p. 135 [and] passim.

27 [Benjamin, *Karl Kraus*,] Op. cit., p. 395; Benjamin, *Selected Writings*, vol. 2, p. 448.

28 [Karl Kraus,] *Die letzten Tage der Menschheit*, vol. II, Munich, 1964, p. 234; Karl Kraus, *The Last Days of Mankind*, tr. Fred Bridgham and Edward Timms, New Haven/London: Yale University Press, 2015, p. 509 (Act V, scene 54).

29 [Bernhard,] *Der Stimmenimitator*, Frankfurt am Main, 1978, p. 51; Thomas Bernhard, *The Voice Imitator*, tr. Kenneth J. Northcott, Chicago/London: Chicago University Press, 1997, p. 27.

30 *Verstörung*, p. 142; *Gargoyles*, p. 152 ('the world at bottom is a carnival').

30a [Bakhtin,] In *Literatur und Karneval*, Munich, 1969, p. 47 [and] passim; cf. Mikhail Bakhtin, *Rabelais and his World*, tr. Hélène Iswolsky, Bloomington: Indiana University Press, 1984.

31 [Kafka,] *Erzählungen*, p. 145 ['Die Sorge des Hausvaters', pp. 144–5]; Kafka, 'The Worries of a Head of Household', in Franz Kafka, *Metamorphosis and Other Stories*, tr. Michael Hofmann, New York: Penguin, 2007, pp. 211–12.

32 [George Orwell,] 'Politics vs Literature: An Examination of Gulliver's Travels', in *Inside the Whale and Other Essays*, Harmondsworth, 1974, p. 137.

33 *Die Zeit*, Nr. 27, 29 June 1979.

34 [Orwell,] Op. cit., p. 142.

Beneath the Surface – Peter Handke's Story of the Goalkeeper's Anxiety

1 Cf. here in particular Claus [sic] Conrad, *Die beginnende Schizophrenie – Versuch einer Gestaltanalyse des Wahns*, Stuttgart, 1966 – a study which had a decisive influence on the concept of Handke's story. [English summary: Aaron L. Mishara, 'Klaus Conrad (1905–1961): Delusional Mood, Psychosis, and Beginning Schizophrenia', *Schizophrenia Bulletin* 36.1 (January 2010), 9–13, https://doi.org/10.1093/schbul/sbp144.]

2 Cf. H. Kipphardt, *März*, Reinbek, 1978; *Leben des schizophrenen Dichters Alexander M. – Ein Film*, Berlin, 1976. In the film, especially, and in the play in similar vein premiered in Düsseldorf in 1980, Kipphardt lapsed into a cheap heroicization of mental illness, decked out with Christological

ornament, as has become common from Expressionism onwards. The artistic 'fashioning' of the theme is thus in glaring contrast to Kipphardt's aims of enlightenment, and in particular to the respect which Ernst Herbeck's work, so freely made use of by Kipphardt, deserves.

3 [Peter Handke,] *Die Angst des Tormanns beim Elfmeter*, Frankfurt am Main, 1972, p. 23; Peter Handke, *The Goalkeeper's Anxiety at the Penalty Kick*, tr. Michael Roloff, London: Penguin, 2020, p. 14.

4 Ibid., p. 84; *The Goalkeeper's Anxiety*, p. 65.

5 Leo Navratil, *Gespräche mit Schizophrenen*, Munich, 1978, p. 19.

6 [Ernst Herbeck,] *Alexanders poetische Texte*, ed. Leo Navratil, Munich, 1977, p. 113.

7 *Die Angst des Tormanns*, p. 7; *The Goalkeeper's Anxiety*, p. 1.

8 Ibid., p. 9; *The Goalkeeper's Anxiety*, p. 3.

9 [Peter Handke,] *Das Gewicht der Welt*, Frankfurt am Main, 1979, p. 224 [20 October 1976]; Peter Handke, *The Weight of the World*, tr. Ralph Manheim, New York: Farrar, Straus & Giroux, 1984, pp. 189–90.

10 Cf. *Die Angst des Tormanns*, p. 38: 'Wieder kam es Bloch vor, als schaue er einer Spieluhr zu; als hätte er das alles schon einmal gesehen.' Cf. *The Goalkeeper's Anxiety*, p. 26: 'Again it seemed to Bloch as if he were watching a music box [earlier edition has "a musical clock"]; as though he had seen all this before.'

11 Ibid., p. 21; *The Goalkeeper's Anxiety*, p. 13.

12 Ibid., p. 31; *The Goalkeeper's Anxiety*, p. 21.

13 Cf. [Stanislaw Lem,] *Imaginäre Größe*, Frankfurt am Main, 1981, p. 62; Stanislaw Lem, *Imaginary Magnitude*, tr. Mark E. Heine, London: Secker & Warburg, 1985, pp. 52f. [Polish original: *Wielkość urojona*, 1973. Note that the examples given in the English translation differ from those in the German translation.]

14 Ibid., p. 200; *Imaginary Magnitude*, pp. 165–6.

15 *Die Angst des Tormanns*, p. 108; *The Goalkeeper's Anxiety*, pp. 86–7.

16 *Imaginäre Größe*, p. 56; *Imaginary Magnitude*, p. 47.

17 Ibid., p. 57; *Imaginary Magnitude*, p. 47.

18 *Die Angst des Tormanns*, p. 93; *The Goalkeeper's Anxiety*, pp. 73–4.

19 Cf. ibid., p. 42; *The Goalkeeper's Anxiety*, p. 30.

20 Ibid., p. 51; *The Goalkeeper's Anxiety*, p. 38.

21 Ibid., p. 68; *The Goalkeeper's Anxiety*, p. 52.

22 Ibid., p. 63; *The Goalkeeper's Anxiety*, p. 47, which however omits the detail of the leaf.

23 Ibid., pp. 70f.; *The Goalkeeper's Anxiety*, p. 54.

24 Cf. Rudolf Bilz, *Wie frei ist der Mensch? – Paläoanthropologie*, vol. I/i, Frankfurt am Main, 1973, p. 327.

25 Ibid., p. 201.

26 Ibid., p. 165.

27 *Die Angst des Tormanns*, pp. 36f.; *The Goalkeeper's Anxiety*, p. 25.

28 Ibid., p. 32; *The Goalkeeper's Anxiety*, p. 22.

29 Ibid., p. 102; *The Goalkeeper's Anxiety*, p. 81.

30 Rudolf Bilz, *Studien über Angst und Schmerz – Paläoanthropologie*, vol. I/ii, Frankfurt am Main, 1974, pp. 9ff.

31 Bilz, *Wie frei ist der Mensch?*, p. 166.

32 *Die Angst des Tormanns*, p. 35; *The Goalkeeper's Anxiety*, p. 24.

33 Ibid., p. 62; *The Goalkeeper's Anxiety*, p. 47.

34 Ibid., p. 107; *The Goalkeeper's Anxiety*, p. 86.

35 *Das Gewicht der Welt*, p. 204 [29 September 1976]; *The Weight of the World*, p. 173.

A Small Traverse – The Poetry of Ernst Herbeck

1 Ernst Herbeck 'was born in Stockerau in 1920. He attended a normal state school and one year of Handelsschule [business school], then worked for a haulage company and an arms factory, and was called up

for a short time during the war. Because of a palate defect, he underwent several operations between the ages of seven and eighteen. Since the age of twenty he has suffered from schizophrenic psychosis, and after three temporary stays in hospital he has been permanently hospitalized since 1946.' These details about Ernst Herbeck's life are taken from Leo Navratil's volume *Gespräche mit Schizophrenen* [*Conversations with Schizophrenics*], published in Munich in 1978.

2 [Ernst Herbeck,] *Alexanders poetische Texte*, ed. Leo Navratil, Munich, 1977, pp. 83 ['Der Rabe'] and 73 ['Die Treue'].

3 On this, cf. note 2 to the essay 'Unterm Spiegel des Wassers' ['Beneath the Surface', p. 432 of this volume].

4 [Walter Benjamin,] *Angelus Novus*, Frankfurt am Main, 1966, pp. 212f.; Walter Benjamin, 'Surrealism', tr. Edmund Jephcott, in Walter Benjamin, *Selected Writings*, vol. 2: *1927–1934*, ed. Michael W. Jennings, Howard Eiland and Gary Smith, Cambridge, MA/London: Harvard University Press, 1999, pp. 207–21 at p. 216.

5 Leo Navratil, *Gespräche mit Schizophrenen*, p. 25.

6 Sigmund Freud, *Das Unbewußte* in *Ges.[ammelte] Werke*, vol. X, London, 1940, p. 302; Sigmund Freud, *The Unconscious*, tr. Graham Frankland, London: Penguin, 2005, pp. 84–5.

7 *Alexanders poetische Texte*, pp. 75 ['Die Mütterliche'] and 105 ['Die Dame ohne Unterleib'].

8 Quoted in Freeman/Cameron/McGhie, *Studie zur chronischen Schizophrenie*, Frankfurt am Main, 1969, p. 92; English original: Thomas Freeman, John L. Cameron and Andrew McGhie, *Chronic Schizophrenia*, London: Tavistock, 1958, p. 82.

9 Ibid.

10 *Alexanders poetische Texte*, p. 7.

11 Konrad Lorenz, *Die Rückseite des Spiegels – Versuch einer Naturgeschichte menschlichen Erkennens*, Munich, 1977, pp. 47f.; *Behind the Mirror: A Search*

for a Natural History of Human Knowledge, tr. Ronald Taylor, London: Methuen, 1977, p. 29.

12 Alexanders poetische Texte, pp. 84 ['Die Gans'] and 156 ['Der Lebenslauf'].
13 Rudolf Bilz, Studien über Angst und Schmerz, Frankfurt am Main, 1974, p. 292.
14 Quoted after Bilz, p. 290 [= Nietzsche, Fröhliche Wissenschaft, III #224]; Nietzsche, The Gay Science, tr. Walter Kaufmann, New York: Vintage, 1974, p. 211.
15 Alexanders poetische Texte, p. 98 ['Die Poesie' (prose poem)].
16 Ibid., p. 129 ['Der Erfolg'].
17 Ibid., p. 61 ['(83) Alexander'].
18 [Claude Lévi-Strauss,] Das wilde Denken, Frankfurt am Main, 1973, p. 29; Claude Lévi-Strauss, The Savage Mind (La Pensée Sauvage), (translator not named,) London: Weidenfeld & Nicolson, 1972 (repr. 1976), pp. 16–17.
19 Ibid., p. 30; The Savage Mind, p. 17.
20 Ibid., p. 35; The Savage Mind, p. 22.
21 Alexanders poetische Texte, pp. 132 ['*Übung am Klavier!* (nach Rainer Maria Rilke)'] and 135 ['*Zwei Segel!* (nach Conrad Ferdinand Meyer)'].
22 Das wilde Denken, p. 30; The Savage Mind, p. 17.
23 Alexanders poetische Texte, p. 128 ['Meine Freunde, die hier in der Anstalt sind'].
24 Navratil, Gespräche mit Schizophrenen, p. 15.
25 Cf. Bilz, Die menschheitsgeschichtlich ältesten Mythologeme, in Studien über Angst und Schmerz, p. 276 [and] passim. Also Herbert Read, Icon and Idea, London, 1955.
26 Alexanders poetische Texte, p. 65 ['Die Sprache']; cf. also Ernst Herbeck, Everyone Has a Mouth, tr. Gary Sullivan, Brooklyn, NY: Ugly Duckling Press, 2012, p. 22 ('Language'), https://uglyducklingpresse.org/publications/everyone-has-a-mouth/.
27 Ibid., p. 150 ['Ein Brief an meine Frau'].
28 Ibid., p. 106 ['Worte, die mir einfallen'].

29 Ernst Jandl, *Laut und Luise*, Neuwied/Berlin, 1971, p. 74 [sic = p. 44].

30 *Alexanders poetische Texte*, pp. 126–7 ['Ein Erlebnis'].

31 Ibid., p. 82 ['Adolf'].

32 Ibid., p. 159; Herbeck, *Everyone Has a Mouth*, p. 20 [the first four lines of this poem are cited in Sebald's article 'Des Häschens Kind, der kleine Has: Über das Totemtier des Lyrikers Ernst Herbeck', in W. G. Sebald, *Campo Santo*, ed. Sven Meyer, Munich/Vienna: Hanser, 2003, pp. 171–8 at p. 171, and translated by Anthea Bell, '*Des Häschens Kind, der kleine Has*: On the Poet Ernst Herbeck's Totem Animal', in Sebald, *Campo Santo*, London: Hamish Hamilton, pp. 130–39 at p. 130].

33 Ibid., p. 70 ['Die Dame'].

34 Ibid., p. 40 ['(13) Ein schöner Mond'].

35 Gilles Deleuze and Félix Guattari, *Kafka – für eine kleine Literatur*, Frankfurt am Main, 1976, p. 98 – the passages from Kafka's work cited in the quote are from an early draft of a story on the theme of the bachelor; Gilles Deleuze and Félix Guattari, *Kafka: Toward a Minor Literature*, tr. Dana Polan, Minneapolis/London: University of Minnesota Press, 1986 (11th printing, 2016), p. 71.

36 Ibid., p. 99; *Kafka: Toward a Minor Literature*, p. 71.

37 *Alexanders poetische Texte*, p. 80 ['Patient und Dichter'].

38 Ibid., p. 46 ['(31) Der Zwergck'].

39 Ibid., p. 77 ['Die Sonne'].

The Man with the Overcoat – Gerhard Roth's *Winterreise*

1 [Gerhard Roth,] *Winterreise*, Frankfurt am Main, 1979, p. 7; Gerhard Roth, *Winterreise*, tr. Joachim Neugroschel, New York: Farrar, Straus & Giroux, 1980, p. 5.

2 Ibid., p. 8; *Winterreise* (English), p. 8.

3 Ibid., pp. 8f.; *Winterreise* (English), p. 8.

4 Ibid., p. 8; *Winterreise* (English), p. 7.

5 Ibid., p. 59; *Winterreise* (English), p. 72.

6 [Roth,] *Ein neuer Morgen*, Frankfurt am Main, 1976, p. 50.

7 *Winterreise*, p. 29; *Winterreise* (English), p. 10.

8 Cf. ibid., pp. 5–18; *Winterreise* (English), pp. 3–28.

9 Cf. ibid., pp. 69 and 83; *Winterreise* (English), pp. 85 and 103.

10 Ibid., pp. 23f.; *Winterreise* (English), p. 27 [NB the translation has 'she whispered' but the German has 'er' – 'he'].

11 On this cf. S. Sontag, 'The Pornographic Imagination', in G. Bataille, *Story of the Eye*, London, 1979, p. 100.

12 Cf. [John Berger,] *Ways of Seeing*, London, 1978, pp. 45ff.

13 *Winterreise*, p. 53 (emphases WGS); *Winterreise* (English), p. 64.

14 Many examples could be cited here, particularly from the bourgeois *Novelle* tradition from Kleist and Hoffmann to Mann and Schnitzler.

15 [Beatrice Faust,] *Women, Sex and Pornography*, Harmondsworth, 1981.

16 Cf. for example the difficulties B. Faust describes in the marketing of magazines such as *Viva*, which have still not quite succeeded in selling the 'Pin-up guy' to a female audience.

17 One may gain an idea of the scale of the 'female' pornography business from for example the fact that the Canadian publishing house Harlequin Enterprises Ltd, which markets novels for women in eighty countries, was able to sell 125 million copies in 1978 alone.

18 On this cf. George Steiner, 'Night Words', in *The Case against Pornography*, ed. D. Holbrook, London, 1972.

19 At the beginning of *Winterreise*, while Nagl is sitting on the train, the following thoughts go through his head (*Winterreise*, p. 12): 'Outside, the world had perished, the myth of work no longer existed, work, which was full of constraints, which had always basically humiliated him, which had nothing to do with his wishes, his thoughts, his imagination, or his dreams'; *Winterreise* (English), p. 13.

20 *Winterreise*, pp. 79 and 85 respectively; *Winterreise* (English), pp. 85 and 106.

21 [Sontag,] Op. cit., p. 94 [quoted in English in original].

22 Mihail Bachtin, *Die Ästhetik des Wortes*, Frankfurt am Main, 1979, p. 275; cf. Mikhail Mikhaylovich Bakhtin, 'Toward the Aesthetics of the Word', tr. Kenneth N. Brostrom, *Dispositio* 4.11/12 (Summer–Autumn 1979), 299–315, https://www.jstor.org/stable/41491180 (translation here my own).

23 [Sontag,] Op. cit., pp. 106 and 108 [quoted in English in original].

24 Cf. ibid. [*Winterreise*], pp. 22 and 35; *Winterreise* (English), pp. 25 and 42.

25 Ibid., p. 101; *Winterreise* (English), p. 125.

26 Ibid., p. 102; *Winterreise* (English), p. 127.

27 On this cf. Frank Kermode, *The Genius of Secrecy*, Cambridge, MA, 1980, p. 52 [quoted in English in original].

Light Pictures and Dark – On the Dialectics of Eschatology in Stifter and Handke

1 [Adalbert Stifter,] *Der Nachsommer*, vol. 2, *Sämtliche Werke*, vol. VII, Hildesheim, 1972, p. 200 [Book 2, Chapter 3: 'Der Einblick']; Adalbert Stifter, *Indian Summer*, tr. Wendell Frye, New York: Peter Lang, 1985, p. 277 (translation adapted).

2 On this, see also the passage in *Der Nachsommer* in which Stifter explains the principle of watercolour and which closes with the words: 'Immer aber waren die Farben so untergeordnet gehalten, daß die Zeichnungen nicht in Gemälde übergingen, sondern Zeichnungen blieben, die durch die Farbe nur mehr gehoben wurden. Ich kannte diese Verfahrungsweise sehr gut, und hatte sie selber oft angewendet' (*Der Nachsommer*, vol. 1, p. 106 [Chapter 4: 'Die Beherbergung']); 'The colours were always kept subordinate so that the drawings didn't become paintings; they maintained their identity as drawings that were only somewhat improved by colours. I was quite familiar with this method and had used it often' (*Indian Summer*, pp. 62–3).

3 *Der Nachsommer*, vol. 2, p. 200; *Indian Summer*, p. 278.

4 'Mein Leben' in *Die fürchterliche Wendung der Dinge*, ed. H. J. Piechotta, Darmstadt/Neuwied, 1981, p. 8; Adalbert Stifter, 'My Life: An Autobiographical Sketch', in *Tales of Old Vienna and Other Prose*, tr. Alexander Stillmark, Riverside, CA: Ariadne, 2016, pp. 154–8 at p. 156 (cf. also J. P. Stern, *Re-Interpretations*, New York: Basic Books, 1964, pp. 352–8 at p. 355 (parallel German text and English translation)).

5 Ibid., p. 9; *Tales of Old Vienna*, p. 156 (cf. *Re-Interpretations*, p. 355).

6 Ibid.

7 *Der Nachsommer*, vol. 1, *Sämtliche Werke*, vol. VI, p. 23 [Book 1, Chapter 2: 'Der Wanderer']; *Indian Summer*, p. 20 (translation adapted).

8 Ibid., vol. II, p. 197 [mainly Book 2, Chapter 3: 'Der Einblick']; *Indian Summer*, pp. 275–6 (translation slightly adapted).

9 'Mein Leben', p. 11; *Tales of Old Vienna*, p. 158 (cf. also *Re-Interpretations*, pp. 357–8).

10 Cf. [Peter Handke,] *Das Gewicht der Welt*, Frankfurt am Main, 1979, p. 21 [December 1975]; Peter Handke, *The Weight of the World*, tr. Ralph Manheim, New York: Farrar, Straus & Giroux, 1984, p. 12.

11 Ibid., p. 204 [29 September 1976]; *The Weight of the World*, p. 173.

12 [Johann Wolfgang von Goethe,] *Zur Farbenlehre. Didaktischer Teil*, dtv-Gesamtausgabe, vol. 40, Munich, 1963, p. 44 [#119]; *Goethe's Theory of Colours*, tr. Charles Lock Eastlake, London: Frank Cass, 1967 (repr. of 1840 edn), p. 50.

13 Cf. [Werner Heisenberg,] 'Die Goethesche und Newtonsche Farbenlehre', in *Goethe im 20. Jahrhundert*, ed. H. Mayer, Hamburg, 1967, p. 430.

14 [Peter Handke,] *Die Lehre der Sainte-Victoire*, Frankfurt am Main, 1980, p. 9; *The Lesson of Mont Sainte-Victoire*, in Peter Handke, *Slow Homecoming*, tr. Ralph Manheim, New York: Farrar, Straus & Giroux, 1985, pp. 139–211 at p. 141.

15 Cited in Hermann Augustin, *Adalbert Stifter: Krankheit und Tod*, Basel, 1964, p. 96.
16 Ibid.
17 Ibid., p. 97.
18 Ibid., p. 98.
19 No specific page references are necessary here, since these references continue throughout the whole novel. Once the reader has become aware of them, the strangely comic effect becomes hard to overlook.
20 On this see for example Wilhelm Abel, *Massenarmut und Hungerkrisen im vorindustriellen Deutschland*, Göttingen, 1972. From this monograph it emerges that at the time in question a working-class family consumed only three pounds of butter, eight pounds of herring, sixteen pounds of *Quark* [curd cheese] and seventeen pounds of meat per head per year.
21 *Der Condor*, in [Stifter,] *Sämtliche Werke*, vol. I.1, Reichenberg, 1940, pp. 6f.; *The Condor*, in *Tales of Old Vienna*, pp. 1–20 at pp. 2–3.
22 Ibid., pp. 10f.; *Tales of Old Vienna*, pp. 6–7.
23 Ibid., p. 11; *Tales of Old Vienna*, p. 9.
24 Cf. [Goethe,] *Zur Farbenlehre. Didaktischer Teil*, p. 45 [#129]; *Goethe's Theory of Colours*, p. 53.
25 *Aus dem bairischen Walde*, in [Stifter,] *Sämtliche Werke*, vol. XV, Reichenberg, 1935, pp. 338f.
26 Ibid., p. 340.
27 Ibid., p. 344.
28 *Der Nachsommer*, vol. I, p[p]. 184[f.] [Chapter 5: 'Der Abschied']; *Indian Summer*, p. 102 (translation adapted).
29 [Handke,] *Langsame Heimkehr*, Frankfurt am Main, 1979, p. 15; *The Long Way Around*, in Peter Handke, *Slow Homecoming*, tr. Ralph Manheim, New York: Farrar, Straus & Giroux, 1985, pp. 3–137 at p. 7.
30 Ibid., p. 19; *Long Way Around*, p. 10.
31 Ibid., pp. 42f.; *Long Way Around*, pp. 26–7.

32 Ibid., p. 98; *Long Way Around*, p. 65.

33 Ibid., p. 46; *Long Way Around*, p. 29.

34 Cf. [Susan Sontag,] *On Photography*, Harmondsworth, 1979, p. 10.

35 *Langsame Heimkehr*, p. 165; *Long Way Around*, p. 112.

36 Ibid., p. 167; *Long Way Around*, p. 114.

37 Ibid., p. 168; *Long Way Around*, p. 114.

38 *Die Lehre der Sainte-Victoire*, p. 99; *Lesson of Mont Sainte-Victoire*, p. 190.

39 *Langsame Heimkehr*, pp. 190f.; *Long Way Around*, p. 130.

40 Ibid., p. 199; *Long Way Around*, p. 136.

41 Ibid., p. 195; *Long Way Around*, pp. 133–4.

42 On what follows cf. Mircea Eliade, *Schamanismus und archaische Ekstasetechnik*, Zurich/Stuttgart, 1954; Mircea Eliade, *Shamanism: Archaic Techniques of Ecstasy*, tr. Willard R. Trask, New York: Bollingen, 1964.

43 *Die Lehre der Sainte-Victoire*, p. 12; *Lesson of Mont Sainte-Victoire*, p. 143.

44 *Langsame Heimkehr*, p. 200; *Long Way Around*, p. 137.

45 *Die Lehre der Sainte-Victoire*, p. 45; *Lesson of Mont Sainte-Victoire*, p. 160.

46 Ibid., p. 74; *Lesson of Mont Sainte-Victoire*, p. 176.

47 Ibid., p. 41; *Lesson of Mont Sainte-Victoire*, p. 158.

48 [Goethe,] *Geschichte der Farbenlehre*, dtv-Gesamtausgabe, vol. 41, p. 162 [V. Abteilung, 17. Jhdt.; 'Intentionelle Farben'].

49 [Dante,] *Divina Commedia*, ed. E. Laaths [no place, n.d.], pp. 64ff. [Canto I, v. 54]; *The Divine Comedy of Dante Alighieri*, vol. I: *Inferno*, tr. Melville B. Anderson, Oxford: Oxford World Classics, 1921, p. 5.

50 *Die Lehre der Sainte-Victoire*, p. 80; *Lesson of Mont Sainte-Victoire*, p. 179.

51 Ibid., p. 29; *Lesson of Mont Sainte-Victoire*, p. 152.

52 Ibid., p. 48; *Lesson of Mont Sainte-Victoire*, p. 162 (translation adapted).

53 Ibid., p. 66; *Lesson of Mont Sainte-Victoire*, p. 171.

54 Quoted after Ludwig Wittgenstein, *Bemerkungen über die Farben / Remarks on Colour*, ed. G. E. M. Anscombe, tr. Linda L. McAlister and Margarete

Schättle, Oxford: Blackwell, 1977, p. 2 (parallel text German–English: English translation p. 2e).

55 [Wittgenstein,] *Bemerkungen über die Farben*, p. 15; *Remarks on Colour*, p. 15e.

56 Cf. G. Scholem, 'Farben und ihre Symbolik in der jüdischen Überlieferung und Mystik', in *Judaica III*, Frankfurt am Main, 1975; cf. Gershom Scholem, 'Colours and their Symbolism in Jewish Tradition and Mysticism', tr. Johanna Pick Margulies, *Diogenes* 28:109 (1980), 64–76, https://doi.org/10.1177/039219218002810905.

57 Quoted in Augustin, op. cit., p. 108.

58 *Die Lehre der Sainte-Victoire*, p. 122; *Lesson of Mont Sainte-Victoire*, p. 202.

59 Ibid., p. 125; *Lesson of Mont Sainte-Victoire*, p. 203.

60 Ibid., p. 131; *Lesson of Mont Sainte-Victoire*, pp. 206–7.

61 Ibid., p. 133; *Lesson of Mont Sainte-Victoire*, p. 207.

62 Ibid., p. 128; *Lesson of Mont Sainte-Victoire*, p. 205.

63 Cf. [Benjamin,] *Illuminationen*, Frankfurt am Main, 1963, p. 231 ['On Some Motifs in Baudelaire', X]; Walter Benjamin, *Illuminations*, tr. Harry Zohn, London: Fontana, 1992, pp. 152–90 at p. 181.

64 *Die Lehre der Sainte-Victoire*, p. 134; *Lesson of Mont Sainte-Victoire*, p. 208.

65 Ibid., p. 138; *Lesson of Mont Sainte-Victoire*, p. 210.

66 [Jean Paul,] *Leben Fibels* in *Werke*, vol. II, Munich, 1975, p. 539.

67 *Die Lehre der Sainte-Victoire*, pp. 138f.; *Lesson of Mont Sainte-Victoire*, p. 210 (translation adapted).

Part Two

Introduction

1 Cf. W. G. Sebald, *Die Beschreibung des Unglücks*, Salzburg, 1985, p. 85 [sic]. [See Part One of the present volume.]

2 Cf. *Profil* 22/1987, Interview with Georg Pichler.

Views from the New World – On Charles Sealsfield

1   Cf. F. Sengle, *Biedermeierzeit*, vol. III, Stuttgart, 1980, pp. 752ff.
2   Ibid., p. 754.
3   On this point cf. Sengle, ibid. [p. 755].
4   Olms Verlag, Hildesheim/New York.
5   Sengle, op. cit., and W. Weiss, 'Der Zusammenhang zwischen Amerikathematik und Erzählkunst bei Charles Sealsfield', in *Jahrbuch der Görresgesellschaft*, Neue Folge, vol. 8 (1967).
6   [Sengle,] Op. cit., p. 758.
7   Probably Count Lažanski. Cf. V. Klarwill's afterword to Ch. Sealsfield, *Österreich, wie es ist*, Vienna, 1919, p. 206.
8   Castle's theory, that Postl's flight was made possible through connections to the Freemasons, is in every respect plausible. Postl would otherwise scarcely have been able to come by the not insignificant funds needed for the journey. Freemason discretion also goes a long way to explaining why, in later years, Postl said so little about his flight from Austria.
9   Cited in E. Castle, *Der große Unbekannte – Das Leben von Charles Sealsfield (Karl Postl)*, Vienna/Munich, 1952, pp. 137f.
10 Sealsfield, *Das Cajütenbuch oder Nationale Charakteristiken*, Sämtl. Werke, vol. 17, Hildesheim/New York, 1977, p. 23.
11 Sealsfield, *The Indian Chief or Tokeah and the White Rose*, Sämtl. Werke, vol. 5, Hildesheim/New York, 1972, pp. 110f.
12 Stuttgart, 1827, Sämtl. Werke, vol. 1, Hildesheim/New York, 1972, pp. 110f. [*Die Vereinigten Staaten von Nordamerika.*] [Sealsfield's English version, *The United States of North America As They Are* = Sämtliche Werke, vol. 2, Olms. 1972.]
13 On this point cf. G. Winter, 'Einiges Neues über Charles Sealsfield', in *Beiträge zur neueren Geschichte Österreichs*, May 1907, reprinted in Sealsfield,

Austria As It Is, *Sämtl. Werke*, vol. 3, Hildesheim/New York, 1972, especially p. LVI [and] passim. It is noteworthy that none of the secondary literature on Sealsfield makes any attempt to connect this blunder with the inherent qualities of Sealsfield's writings.

14 Probably the most embarrassing howler is the address 'Serene Higness' (sic), which Postl repeats in this form at the end of the letter. Cf. ibid., p. LXI.

15 Freiherr von Neumann, who met Postl in Wiesbaden at Metternich's behest, was at any rate of the opinion 'que cet individu était un aventurier cherchant à nous . . . extorquer de l'argent'. Ibid., p. LXVI.

16 Cf. E. Castle (ed.), *Das Geheimnis des Großen Unbekannten Charles Sealsfield – Carl Postl. Die Quellenschriften*, Vienna, 1943, p. 436.

17 Cf. Castle, *Der große Unbekannte*, pp. 413ff.

18 Cf. ibid., p. 336.

19 The volume itself gives 1828 as the year of publication.

20 Sealsfield, *Österreich, wie es ist*, *Sämtl. Werke*, vol. 3, p. 5 [vol. 3 of the *Sämtliche Werke*] comprises the German text, *Österreich, wie es ist*, prefaced by the English, *Austria As It Is*. [WGS quotes from the German translation but quotations here are taken, where possible, from the English version (*Austria As It Is*, p. v).]

21 Postl was obliged to borrow the money for the journey from Frankfurt to London. Cf. Winter, op. cit., pp. XXVIf., where it is stated that in London Postl 'had to owe money for his board for a fortnight and could not send a map to Cotta because he did not have money for the postage'.

22 Sealsfield, *Österreich, wie es ist*, p. 21; *Austria As It Is*, p. 17.

23 Ibid., pp. 42 and 45; *Austria As It Is*, pp. 40 and 38.

24 Ibid., p. 46; *Austria As It Is*, p. 42.

25 Ibid., p. 67; *Austria As It Is*, p. 66.

26 Ibid., p. 89; *Austria As It Is*, p. 91.

27 Ibid., p. 19; *Austria As It Is*, p. 13 (here I have followed the German text).

28 Cf. ibid., p. 90; *Austria As It Is*, p. 93 (WGS paraphrases in the German: I have quoted here from the English version).

29 Cf. ibid., p. 146; *Austria As It Is*, pp. 153–4.

30 Ibid., p. 131; *Austria As It Is*, p. 139.

31 Ibid., p. 84; *Austria As It Is*, p. 85.

32 Cited in R. Gottschall, *Literarische Charakterköpfe*, Leipzig, 1870, reprinted in T. Ostwald (ed.), *Charles Sealsfield*, Brunswick, 1976, p. 81.

33 Cf. Castle, *Der große Unbekannte*, p. 479.

34 Erhard was Sealsfield's publisher in Stuttgart.

35 Cited in Castle, *Der große Unbekannte*, pp. 513f.

36 Ibid., p. 517.

37 This diagnosis is that of the liberal literary historian Julian Schmidt. Cited here after Castle, ibid., p. 574.

38 Cf. Castle, ibid., p. 356.

39 Sealsfield, *Das Cajütenbuch*, *Sämtl. Werke*, vol. 17, p. 378; Charles Sealsfield, *The Cabin Book: Or, National Characteristics*, London: Ingram, Cooke, 1852 [1871]; reprint Eakin Pr (1 October 1985), Frankfurt am Main: Outlook, 2022; translations are quoted from the 1871 edition at https://archive.org/details/cabinbookornatio0sealgoog, pp. 268, 269.

40 'd'une blancheur éclatante': F. R. de Chateaubriand, *Œuvres romanesques et voyages*, vol. 1, Paris, 1969, p. 40 [sic = p. 88]; Chateaubriand, *Atala – René*, tr. Rayner Heppenstall, London: Oxford University Press, 1963, p. 48 ('of a dazzling white').

41 'statue de la virginité endormie', ibid., p. 89; *Atala – René*, p. 48 ('a statue of Virginity Sleeping').

42 H. B. Stowe, *Three Novels*, New York, 1982, p. 486.

43 Chateaubriand, op. cit., p. 71; *Atala – René*, p. 38 ('the triumph of Christianity over savage life').

44 Ibid., p. 68 [sic = p. 65]; *Atala – René*, p. 32 ('carrying the now unlighted lantern on the end of a stick').

45 Sealsfield, *Tokeah*, *Sämtl. Werke*, vol. 4, p. 75 [quoted in English in original. Sealsfield's punctuation here reads: 'their blood is no longer to be seen; their lands are no more their own'].

46 Sealsfield, *Tokeah*, *Sämtl. Werke*, vol. 5, pp. 200f. [The translation here quotes the English which WGS translates/paraphrases in German.]

47 Ch. Darwin, *Gesammelte Werke*, vol. 5, Stuttgart, 1899, p. 174; Charles Darwin, *The Works of Charles Darwin*, ed. Paul H. Barrett and R. B. Freeman, vol. 21: *The Descent of Man and Selection in Relation to Sex* (Part 1), London: Pickering, 1989, p. 162.

48 Cf. D. Sternberger, *Panorama oder Ansichten vom 19. Jahrhundert*, Frankfurt am Main, 1974, p. 88; Dolf Sternberger, *Panorama of the Nineteenth Century*, tr. Joachim Neugroschel, New York: Urizen/Oxford: Blackwell, 1977, p. 80. [Quoted here from English translation. WGS paraphrases but does not quote.]

49 Cf. *Tokeah*, *Sämtl. Werke*, vol. 5, p. 104. [The translation here quotes the English which WGS translates/paraphrases in German.]

50 [Gottschall,] Op. cit., p. 84.

51 Ibid.

52 Ibid.

53 Castle, *Der große Unbekannte*, p. 249.

54 Cf. ibid., p. 356.

55 [Gottschall,] Op. cit., p. 87.

56 Castle, *Das Geheimnis des Großen Unbekannten*, p. 134.

57 Sealsfield, *Cajütenbuch*, *Sämtl. Werke*, vol. 16, p. 27; *The Cabin Book* (1871), p. 13.

58 [Sengle,] Op. cit., p. 767.

59 Cited in Castle, *Der große Unbekannte*, p. 476.

60 F. Kürnberger, *Der Amerikamüde*, Frankfurt am Main, 1986, pp. 169ff.

61 Cited in Castle, *Der große Unbekannte*, p. 359.

62 Cf. ibid., p. 361.

63 On this, cf. H. St. Foote, *Texas and the Texans; or, Advance of the Anglo-Americans to the South West*, Philadelphia, 1841, and Hermann Ehrenberg, *Texas und seine Revolution*, Leipzig, 1843.

64 *Cajütenbuch, Sämtl. Werke*, vol. 16, p. 8 [not included in English translation].

65 Ibid., p. 275; *The Cabin Book*, p. 109.

66 *Cajütenbuch, Sämtl. Werke*, vol. 17, pp. 101f.; *The Cabin Book*, p. 159.

67 Ibid., p. 113; *The Cabin Book*, p. 164.

68 Ibid., p. 115; *The Cabin Book*, p. 164.

69 Ibid.; *The Cabin Book*, p. 164.

70 *Cajütenbuch, Sämtl. Werke*, vol. 16, pp. 42f.; *The Cabin Book*, pp. 27–8.

71 Ibid., pp. 57f.; *The Cabin Book*, p. 25.

72 Ibid.; *The Cabin Book*, p. 25.

73 Ibid., p. 84; *The Cabin Book*, p. 35.

74 [*The Indian Chief,*] *Sämtl. Werke*, vol. 5, p. 65 [quoted in English in original].

75 *Cajütenbuch, Sämtl. Werke*, vol. 16, pp. 23ff.; *The Cabin Book*, p. 12.

76 Stephan Gutzwiller, the so-called (by Postl) Washington from the Basler Land, noted this characteristic of Postl's as early as the [18]50s. Cf. Castle, *Der große Unbekannte*, pp. 551f.

77 Max Brod, *Der Prager Kreis*, Stuttgart, 1966, p. 24.

78 *Der große Unbekannte*, pp. 386f. and 566f.

79 Ibid., p. 611.

80 Ibid., p. 581.

81 Brussels and Leipzig, 1864.

Westwards – Eastwards: Aporia of German-Language Tales from the Ghetto

1 Cf. W. Iggers (ed.), *Die Juden in Böhmen und Mähren*, Munich, 1986, p. 148; Wilma Iggers (ed.), *The Jews of Bohemia and Moravia: A*

Historical Reader, ed. and tr. Wilma Abeles Iggers with Káča Poláčková-Henley and Kathrine Talbot, Detroit: Wayne State University Press, 1992, p. 154.

2   St Hock, Introduction to L. Kompert, *Sämtliche Werke*, vol. I, Leipzig, 1906, p. xxxvi.

3   Cf. Kompert, *Sämtliche Werke*, vol. 2, Leipzig, 1906, p. 27 [*Der Dorfgeher*]; *The Peddler*, tr. Jonathan M. Hess, in Nadia Valman, Maurice Samuels and Jonathan M. Hess (eds.), *Nineteenth-Century Jewish Literature: A Reader*, Stanford, CA: Stanford University Press, 2013 (ebook), pp. 25–64 at p. 44.

4   Ibid., p. 32; *Peddler*, p. 47.

5   Ibid., p. 21; *Peddler*, p. 40.

6   Ibid., p. 22; *Peddler*, p. 40.

7   Kompert, *Sämtl. Werke*, vol. 1, pp. 130f. [*Die Kinder des Randars*]; cf. *The Randar's Children*, in Leopold Kompert, *Scenes from the Ghetto: Studies of Jewish Life*, London: Remington, 1882, pp. 77–280 at p. 159, https://archive.org/details/ldpd_16043324_000 (translation here my own).

8   Cf. [Susan Sontag,] *On Photography*, Harmondsworth, 1979, p. 80.

9   Cf. Kompert, *Sämtl. Werke*, vol. 1, p. 158 [*Die Kinder des Randars*]; cf. *Randar's Children*, p. 194 (translation here my own).

10 Ibid., p. 93; cf. *Randar's Children*, p. 105 (translation here my own).

11 Ibid., pp. 96f. [sic = pp. 93f.]; cf. *Randar's Children*, p. 105 (translation here my own).

12 F[ranz]. Kafka, *Sämtl[iche]. Erzählungen*, Frankfurt am Main, 1961, p. 9; 'Children on the Country Road', in Franz Kafka, *The Transformation ('Metamorphosis') and Other Stories*, ed. and tr. Malcolm Pasley, London: Penguin, 1992, pp. 10–14 at p. 13.

13 Kompert, *Sämtl. Werke*, vol. 1, p. 221 [*Die Kinder des Randars*]; *Randar's Children*, p. 279 (translation here my own).

14 M[ax]. H[ermann]. Friedländer, *Tieferet Jisrael – Schilderungen aus dem innern Leben der Juden in Mähren in vormärzlichen Zeiten*, Brno, 1878, p. 54.

15 Franzos, *Die Juden von Barnow*, Leipzig, 1880, p. 258 [*Das Christusbild*]; *The Picture of Christ*, in Karl Emil Franzos, *The Jews of Barnow: Stories*, tr. M. W. MacDowall, London: Appleton, 1882, pp. 259–98 at p. 263, https://catalog.hathitrust.org/api/volumes/oclc/17458388.html: *The Picture of Christ*.

16 Ibid., p. 12 ['Der Shylock von Barnow']; 'The Shylock of Barnow', in *The Jews of Barnow*, pp. 1–58 at p. 13.

17 Cf. ibid., p. 310 ['Ohne Inschrift']; 'Nameless Graves', in *The Jews of Barnow*, pp. 299–341 at p. 318.

18 Ibid., p. VIII; 'Preface' in *The Jews of Barnow*, p. vii.

19 Ibid.; *The Jews of Barnow*, p. vi.

20 Franzos, *Aus Halb-Asien – Kulturbilder aus Galizien, der Bukowina, Südrußland und Rumänien*, vol. 1, Stuttgart/Berlin, 1901, p. 183.

21 Franzos, *Vom Don zur Donau*, quoted from the selection *Halb-Asien*, ed. E. J. Görlich, Graz/Vienna, 1958, p. 75 ['Die Gezwungenen'].

22 Franzos, *Die Juden von Barnow*, p. 53 ['Der Shylock von Barnow']; *The Jews of Barnow* ('The Shylock of Barnow'), p. 57 (translation adapted).

23 Ibid., p. 185 ['Esterka Regina']; 'Esterka Regina', in *The Jews of Barnow*, pp. 173–236 at p. 183.

24 Ibid., p. 38 ['Der Shylock von Barnow']; *The Jews of Barnow* ('The Shylock of Barnow'), p. 42.

25 'Schiller in Barnow', quoted from the collection *Halb-Asien*, p. 38; 'Schiller in Barnow', tr. Ritchie Robertson, in Robertson (ed.), *The German–Jewish Dialogue: An Anthology of Literary Texts, 1749–1993*, Oxford: Oxford University Press, 1999, pp. 110–20 at p. 114.

26 Cf. L. von Sacher-Masoch, *Jüdisches Leben*, Mannheim, 1892, p. 105 [and] passim ['Der Buchbinder von Hort']; 'The Bookbinder from Hort', in Leopold von Sacher-Masoch, *Jewish Life: Tales from Nineteenth-Century Europe*, tr. Virginia L. Lewis, Riverside, CA: Ariadne Press, 2002, pp. 59–68 at p. 65.

27 Franzos, *Halb-Asien*, vol. I, pp. 102 and 185.

28 'Die kk. Reaktion in Halb-Asien', ibid., pp. 85–127, where Franzos characterizes the Austrian regime as a mixture of tragedy and farce.

29 Ibid., p. 102.

30 Cf. for example Franzos, *Die Juden von Barnow*, pp. 41, 58 and 318; *The Jews of Barnow*, pp. 45, 63, 326.

31 Ibid., p. 258 [*Das Christusbild*]; *The Picture of Christ*, in *The Jews of Barnow*, p. 292 (translation adapted).

32 Ibid., p. 289 [*Das Christusbild*]; *The Picture of Christ*, in *The Jews of Barnow*, p. 295.

33 Cf. [L. Goldmann,] 'Sur la peinture de Chagall', in *Structures mentales et création culturelle*, Paris, 1976, p. 419.

34 Franzos, *Die Juden von Barnow*, p. 296 ['Ohne Inschrift']; 'Nameless Graves', *The Jews of Barnow*, p. 302 (translation adapted).

35 Ibid., p. 301; 'Nameless Graves', p. 308.

36 Ibid.; 'Nameless Graves', p. 308.

37 Ibid.; 'Nameless Graves', pp. 308–9 (translation adapted).

38 Ibid., p. 297; 'Nameless Graves', pp. 303–4.

39 Cf. Sacher-Masoch, *Souvenirs*, Munich, 1985, pp. 15ff. ['Meine Herkunft'].

40 Ibid., p. 16.

41 Cf. M. Farin, 'Sacher-Masochs *Jüdisches Leben*', in Leopold von Sacher-Masoch, *Jüdisches Leben*, Dortmund, 1985 (repr. of the Mannheim 1892 edn), pp. 357f. [not included in translation].

42 [Sacher-Masoch,] *Jüdisches Leben*, p. 12; *Jewish Life*, p. 4.

43 Cf. 'Galizien', in Sacher-Masoch, *Souvenirs*, pp. 32f.

44 Published as *Das Vermächtnis Kains*, Stuttgart, 1870.

45 Cf. F. Kürnberger, 'Vorrede zum Don Juan von Kolomea', in Sacher-Masoch, *Don Juan von Kolomea – Galizische Geschichten*, ed. M. Farin, Bonn, 1985, pp. 188f.

46 Ibid., pp. 191f.

47 [Sacher-Masoch,] *Jüdisches Leben*, p. 362 [not included in translation].

48 Ibid., p. 14; *Jewish Life*, pp. 4–5.

49 Cf. ibid., p. 197 [where it illustrates the story 'Mascheve'].

50 [Joseph Roth,] *Das falsche Gewicht*, Reinbek, 1981, pp. 5f.; Joseph Roth, *Weights and Measures*, tr. David Le Vay, London: Peter Owen, 2002, p. 8.

51 Ibid., p. 14; *Weights and Measures*, p. 19.

52 Ibid., pp. 64 and 32; *Weights and Measures*, pp. 79 and 40.

53 Ibid., p. 83; *Weights and Measures*, p. 103.

54 Ibid., p. 120; *Weights and Measures*, p. 148.

55 Ibid.; *Weights and Measures*, p. 148.

56 R. Vishniak, *Die verschwundene Welt*, Munich, 1984; cf. Roman Vishniac, *The Vanished World*, Foreword by Elie Wiesel, New York: Farrar, Straus & Giroux, 1983.

57 [Roland Barthes,] *La Chambre claire*, Paris, 1984 (Section 40), pp. 151–2; Roland Barthes, *Camera lucida: Reflections on Photography*, tr. Richard Howard, London: Fontana, 1984, p. 97.

Peter Altenberg – *Le Paysan de Vienne*

1 Altenberg, *Mein Lebensabend*, Berlin, 1919, p. 150 ['Ort Altenberg'].
2 Th. W. Adorno, *Mahler*, Frankfurt am Main, 1969, pp. 190f.; Theodor W. Adorno, *Mahler: A Musical Physiognomy*, tr. Edmund Jephcott, Chicago: University of Chicago Press, new edn 1996, p. 152.
3 Cf. ibid., p. 209; *Mahler: A Musical Physiognomy*, p. 161.
4 Cf. [Altenberg,] *Wie ich es sehe*, 16.–18. Aufl., Berlin, 1922, p. 36 ['Seeufer, Landpartie'].
5 Altenberg, *Mein Lebensabend*, p. 237 ['Gmunden'].
6 Altenberg, *Vita Ipsa*, Berlin, 1918, p. 265 ['Der Sommer'].
7 Altenberg, *Prodromos*, Berlin, 1906, p. 126 ['Dichterliebe'].
8 Altenberg, *Mein Lebensabend*, p. 237 ['Gmunden'].
9 Ibid., pp. 262f. ['Der 60-Jährige'].
10 [Baudelaire,] *Oeuvres*, vol. 2, Paris, 1931/2, p. 536 (translated by W. Benjamin) [= 'Marceline Desbordes-Valmore', in *L'Art romantique*, XIX: 'Réflexions sur quelques-uns de mes contemporains']; 'On Some Motifs in Baudelaire' (Section X), in Walter Benjamin, *Illuminations*, tr. Harry Zohn, London: Fontana, 1992, pp. 152–96 at p. 178.
11 Altenberg, *Mein Lebensabend*, p. 237 ['Gmunden'].
12 C. Schaefer, *Peter Altenberg*, Vienna, 1980, p. 28.
13 Altenberg, *Prodromos*, p. 177 ['Wenn meine wunderbare vergötterte Mama'].
14 Ibid., p. 178.
15 *Nachfeschung*, 10th edn, Berlin, 1919, p. 304 ['Splitter'].

16 Cf. ibid., p. 284 ['Splitter'].

17 Cf. Altenberg, *Mein Lebensabend*, p. 225 ['Wiener Rathauspark'].

18 Cf. Altenberg, *Wie ich es sehe*, p. 231 ['Landstädtchen. Die Frauen'].

19 Cf. Altenberg, *Mein Lebensabend*, p. 275 ['Rathauspark'].

20 Quoted in Schaefer, p. 7.

21 Cf. Altenberg, *Vita Ipsa*, p. 204 ['Angst'].

22 Altenberg, *Was der Tag mir zuträgt*, 7.–8. Aufl., Berlin 1919, p. 290 ['Ein Wiener'].

23 *Ashantee*, in *Wie ich es sehe*, pp. 298ff. ['Der Hofmeister']; 'The Private Tutor', in *Telegrams of the Soul: Selected Prose of Peter Altenberg*, tr. Peter Wortsman, New York: archipelago books, 2005, pp. 60–64.

24 Ibid., p. 311 ['Ein Brief aus Accra'].

25 Ibid.

26 Altenberg, *Mein Lebensabend*, p. 66 ['Frauenschicksal'].

27 Cf. Altenberg, *Wie ich es sehe*, pp. 8, 60 ['Neunzehn', 'Im Stadtgarten'].

28 Cf. Benjamin, 'Zentralpark', *Gesammelte Schriften*, vol. I.2, Frankfurt am Main, 1971, p. 681; 'Central Park', in Walter Benjamin, *Selected Writings*, vol. 4, ed. Howard Eiland and Michael W. Jennings, Cambridge, MA / London: Harvard University Press, 2003, pp. 161–91 at p. 182.

29 H. Malmberg, *Widerhall des Herzens – Ein Peter Altenberg-Buch*, Munich, 1961, p. 157.

30 Cf. [Schäfer,] op. cit., p. 75.

31 Altenberg, *Neues Altes*, Berlin, 1911, p. 192 ['Peter Altenberg als Sammler']; 'Peter Altenberg as Collector', in *Telegrams of the Soul*, p. 88.

32 Altenberg, *Prodromos*, p. 58 ['Er besass ein kleines Taschentuch . . .'].

33 Cf. Altenberg, *Vita Ipsa*, p. 198 ['Liebe'].

34 Altenberg, *Feschung*, 5.–6. Aufl., Berlin, 1918, p. 170 ['Die "unglückliche" Liebe'].

35 Quoted in Benjamin, op. cit., p. 689; Benjamin, 'Central Park', p. 190 (first line of Baudelaire's poem 'Spleen III').

36 Altenberg, *Semmering, 1912*, Berlin, 1913, p. 55 ['Mein grauer Hut'].

37 [Benjamin,] Op. cit., p. 670; 'Central Park', p. 172.

38 See, for example, the diaries of Arthur Schnitzler, who visited the panorama with some regularity.

39 Altenberg, *Neues Altes*, p. 183 ['Rückkehr vom Lande'].

40 Ibid.

41 Cf. Benjamin, *Charles Baudelaire – Ein Lyriker im Zeitalter des Hochkapitalismus, Gesammelte Schriften*, vol. I.2, p. 543; 'The Paris of the Second Empire in Baudelaire', tr. Harry Zohn, in Benjamin, *Selected Writings*, vol. 4, pp. 3–66 (Section II, 'The Flâneur', p. 22).

42 Cf. [Spitzer,] *Wiener Spaziergänge*, 2 vols., Vienna, n.d.

43 G. Wysocki, *Peter Altenberg*, Frankfurt am Main, 1986, p. 54.

44 Altenberg, *Prodromos*, pp. 87f. ['Die Sohlen meiner Schuhe beginnen zu reissen'].

45 Altenberg, *Vita Ipsa*, p. 23 ['Ich'].

46 Benjamin, op. cit., p. 550 ['Der Flaneur']; Benjamin, *Selected Writings*, vol. 4, p. 26.

47 Cf. ibid., p. 621; Benjamin, 'On Some Motifs in Baudelaire' (Section V), in *Illuminations*, tr. Zohn, p. 164 [= *Selected Writings*, vol. 4, p. 322].

48 Cf. ibid., p. 550 ['Der Flaneur']; Benjamin, *Selected Writings*, vol. 4, p. 26.

49 According to Schäfer, op. cit., p. 89, Schnitzler's relationship to Altenberg was decidedly ambivalent. He finds 'much that is delightful, perhaps genius' in his work, but thinks his 'prophet pose' 'deeply impure and inauthentic' (*Tagebücher, 1913–1916*, Vienna, 1983, 15 March 1916). Kraus, too, sees Altenberg both as 'the first poet in the German language' and as 'the worst scribbler' (cf. Schäfer, op. cit., p. 10). There are complex reasons for the aversion thus expressed. Altenberg embodied something like a travesty of the outsider, and made the dangers of *déclassement* all too evident to authors from the

bourgeoisie. More significant, though, are the deprecating terms '*Schmierer*' [scribbler] and '*unrein*' [impure, unclean], which imply feelings of disgust. Schnitzler and Kraus probably found Altenberg's *Schnorrerei* [scrounging] 'Jewish, all-too Jewish'; they possibly found his openness regarding his erotic feelings no less embarrassing. In this context, there is an interesting entry in Schnitzler's diary on 1 August 1914: 'Letter from Hofrath Zuckerkandl, i.a. [*inter alia*], that Austria has been designated for this year's literature Nobel Prize, and that they are thinking of splitting it between me and Altenberg, which Olga finds far more annoying than I do – (not for financial reasons – but because the Nobel Prize for literature has NEVER been shared to date).' The tone of this passage also betrays that, in fact, it was not the sharing of the prize which so bothered Schnitzler so much as the embarrassing prospect of being associated with Altenberg.

50 Cf. [Benjamin,] op. cit., p. 553; Benjamin, 'Paris in the Second Empire of Baudelaire', *Selected Writings*, vol. 4, p. 28.

51 Altenberg, *Nachfeschung*, p. 233 ['Splitter'].

52 Ibid.

53 Altenberg, *Mein Lebensabend*, p. 45 ['Die "Gelsen"'].

54 Ibid., p. 46.

55 Quoted in H. Ch. Kosler (ed.), *Peter Altenberg*, Frankfurt am Main, 1984, p. 130.

56 Ibid.

57 Altenberg, *Was der Tag mir zuträgt*, p. 137 ['Der "Fliegende Holländer"'].

58 Quoted in Kosler, pp. 20f. [sic = pp. 208f.]; cf. Altenberg, 'The Walking Stick', in *Telegrams of the Soul*, pp. 90–91 at p. 90.

59 Adorno, *Mahler*, p. 51; Adorno, *Mahler: A Musical Physiognomy*, p. 34.

60 Cf. Wysocki, *Peter Altenberg*, p. 82.

61 K. E. Franzos, *Die Juden von Barnow*, Leipzig, 1880, p. 64 ['Nach dem höheren Gesetz']; Karl Emil Franzos, 'Chane', in Franzos, *The Jews of Barnow: Stories*, tr. M. W. MacDowall, Edinburgh/London: William Blackwood & Sons, 1882, p. 68 (translation adapted to match the German quotation).

62 [Adorno,] Op. cit., p. 192; Adorno, *Mahler: A Musical Physiognomy*, p. 148.

63 Cf. e.g. Peter Altenberg, *Der Nachlass*, Berlin, 1923, p. 75 ['Geselligkeit'].

64 Quoted in E. Randak, *Peter Altenberg*, Graz/Vienna, 1961, p. 160.

65 A. Schnitzler, *Tagebücher, 1910–1913*, Vienna, 1981 (4 July 1910).

66 Altenberg, *Mein Lebensabend*, p. 5 ['Mein Vater'].

67 Ibid., p. 39 ['Die Dachdecker'].

68 Ibid., p. 284 ['Erziehung'].

69 [Adorno,] Op. cit., p. 39; *Mahler: A Musical Physiognomy*, p. 25.

70 E. Fridell (ed.), *Das Altenbergbuch*, Leipzig/Vienna/Zurich, 1921, p. 52.

71 [Benjamin,] Op. cit., p. 660; Benjamin, 'Central Park', *Selected Writings*, vol. 4, p. 164.

72 Cf. Altenberg, *Märchen des Lebens*, Berlin, 1908, p. 218 [sic – no such page!]. Cf. 'Das Hotelzimmer', p. 51; 'The Hotel Room', in *Telegrams of the Soul*, p. 78.

73 Altenberg, *Semmering, 1912*, p. 114 ['Bilanz'].

74 Altenberg, *Mein Lebensabend*, p. 353 ['Der 13. Dezember 1918 5 Uhr morgens'].

75 Cf. Altenberg, *Neues Altes*, pp. 73f. ['Der Affe Peter'].

76 Altenberg, *Prodromos*, pp. 119f. ['Alkohol'].

77 Ibid., p. 118 ['Alkohol'].

78 Altenberg, *Semmering, 1912*, p. 106 ['Abschied'].

79 Ibid., p. 107 ['Kranken-Toilette'].

80 Altenberg, *Feschung*, p. 27 ['Nachtrag zu Prodromos'].

81 Altenberg, *Neues Altes*, p. 141 ['Wie ich gesundet bin'].

82 Altenberg, *Mein Lebensabend*, p. 287 ['Brief an die Tänzerin'].

83 Ibid., pp. 356f. ['14.12.1918'].

84 Altenberg, *Der Nachlass*, p. 140 ['23.12.1918'].

85 Ibid., p. 142 ['Nachts, 27. Dezember 1918'].

86 Altenberg, *Wie ich es sehe*, p. 96 ['Am Lande'].

87 Altenberg, *Semmering, 1912*, p. 245 ['Winter auf dem Semmering'].

88 Altenberg, *Was der Tag mir zuträgt*, pp. 51f. ['Eine schweigende Runde. Dem Andenken an Friedrich Mitterwurzer als "König Philipp" geweiht'].

The Law of Ignominy – Authority, Messianism and Exile in Kafka's *Castle*

1 The Muirs' translation of this passage ('of having spoken my mind freely to a great man', p. 53) is misleading. In order to render the 'mächtig' [powerful] more accurately it is probably advisable to use a combination of words like 'great and powerful'. Page references to quotations from *The Castle*, if they are not my own [translations], refer to Franz Kafka, *The Castle*, tr. Willa and Edwin Muir, Harmondsworth, 1971 (1957).

2 Christian Enzensberger, *Grösserer Versuch über den Schmutz*, Munich, 1970, p. 49.

3 Ibid., p. 39.

4 Ibid., p. 51.

5 Cf. [Kafka,] *Wedding Preparations in the Country*, ed. Max Brod, London, 1954, pp. 60f.

6 Cf. Martin Buber, *Die Erzählungen der Chassidim*, Zurich, 1949, p. 418.

7 'Temptation in the Village', *The Diaries of Franz Kafka*, ed. Max Brod, Harmondsworth, pp. 280ff.

8 Buber, op. cit., p. 201.

9 Cf. my article on 'The Undiscover'd Country: The Death Motif in Kafka's *Castle*', *Journal of European Studies* 2.1 (1972), pp. 22–34 [pp. 82–102 in the present volume].

10 *Wedding Preparations in the Country*, p. 58.
11 Jakob Wassermann, *Mein Weg als Deutscher und Jude*, Berlin, 1921, p. 36.
12 In his *On Kafka's Castle*, London, 1973, pp. 81 and 213.
13 Buber, op. cit., p. 365.
14 [Kafka,] *The Diaries*, p. 400.
15 Gustav Janouch, *Conversations with Kafka*, 2nd rev. and enlarged edn, London, 1971, p. 110.
16 Martin Walser, *Beschreibung einer Form*, Frankfurt am Main/Berlin, 1972, p. 18.
17 [Paul Klee,] *Tagebücher*, Cologne, 1957, p. 172.
18 S. Beckett, *Molloy*, London, 1966, pp. 115f.

A Kaddish for Austria – On Joseph Roth

1 'Die k. und k. Veteranen', quoted D. Bronsen, *Joseph Roth*, Cologne, 1974, p. 21 [*Frankfurter Zeitung*, 18 June 1929 and *Prager Tagblatt*, 25 June 1929; = Roth, *Werke*, vol. III: *Das journalistische Werk, 1929–39*, Cologne: Kiepenheuer & Witsch, 1991, pp. 64–70 at p. 65].
2 J. Roth, *Romane, Erzählungen, Aufsätze*, Cologne, 1964, p. 256; Joseph Roth, *Job: The Story of a Simple Man*, tr. Dorothy Thomson, London: Granta, 2000, pp. 139, 140.
3 Ibid., p. 257; *Job*, p. 141 (WGS paraphrases in German but I have quoted from the published English translation).
4 H. Cohen, *Schriften*, vol. II, Berlin, 1924, pp. 45f.
5 [Bronsen,] Op. cit., p. 45.
6 Roth, *Romane, Erzählungen, Aufsätze*, p. 561; Roth, *The Wandering Jews*, tr. Michael Hofmann, London: Granta, 2001, p. 8.
7 'Halberstadt, Tannhäuser, Schach', in Roth, *Werke*, vol. III, Cologne, 1976, p. 697 [*Frankfurter Zeitung*, 4 September 1931].
8 [Bronsen,] Op. cit., p. 421.

9 Roth, *Radetzkymarsch*, Reinbek, 1967, p. 54; Roth, *The Radetzky March*, tr. Joachim Neugroschel, London: Penguin, 1995, p. 70.

10 Ibid., p. 119; *Radetzky March*, p. 161.

11 Ibid., p. 149; *Radetzky March*, pp. 193–4 (WGS's quote does not exactly match the German text).

12 Ibid., p. 234; *Radetzky March*, p. 317.

13 Ibid., p. 190; *Radetzky March*, p. 256.

14 Ibid., p. 27; *Radetzky March*, p. 33.

15 Roth, *Das falsche Gewicht*, Reinbek, 1981, p. 7; Roth, *Weights and Measures*, tr. David Le Vay, London: Peter Owen, 2002, p. 10.

16 Roth, *Radetzkymarsch*, p. 93; *Radetzky March*, pp. 125–6.

17 Ibid., p. 54; *Radetzky March*, p. 70.

18 Cf. W. Benjamin, *Ursprung des deutschen Trauerspiels*, Frankfurt am Main, 1963, p. 246; Walter Benjamin, *Origin of the German Trauerspiel*, tr. Howard Eiland, Cambridge, MA/London: Harvard University Press, 2019, p. 236.

19 Cf. Bronsen, op. cit., p. 177; translated in *Joseph Roth: A Life in Letters*, tr. Michael Hofmann, London: Granta, 2012, pp. 220–21 (#168, 28 October 1932).

20 [Benjamin,] 'Der Erzähler', in Benjamin, *Illuminationen*, Frankfurt am Main, 1961, p. 417; 'The Storyteller', in Walter Benjamin, *Illuminations*, tr. Harry Zohn, London: Fontana, 1992, pp. 83–106 at pp. 90–91.

21 Cf. ibid.; 'The Storyteller', p. 91.

22 Cf. [U. Greiner,] 'Joseph Roth', in *Österreichische Porträts*, vol. II, ed. J. Jung, Salzburg, 1985, p. 375.

23 Roth, *Radetzkymarsch*, p. 168; *Radetzky March*, p. 226.

24 Bronsen, op. cit., p. 373.

25 [Benjamin,] Op. cit., pp. 420f.; 'The Storyteller', p. 93.

26 Cf. Roth, *Radetzkymarsch*, p. 98; *Radetzky March*, p. 132.

27 Cf. ibid., p. 9; *Radetzky March*, p. 6.

28 Benjamin, op. cit., p. 424; 'The Storyteller', p. 96.

29 Cf. [Bronsen,] op. cit., p. 247.

30 Roth, *Werke*, vol. IV, Cologne, 1976, pp. 893ff. ['Beim Uhrmacher', *Pariser Tageszeitung*, 2/3 April 1939].

31 Ibid., p. 895.

32 Quoted Bronsen, op. cit., p. 395 [to Stefan Zweig, 'Sonntag 1932'].

33 Cf. 'unveröffentlichte autobiographische Notizen', quoted in Bronsen, op. cit., p. 138.

34 Roth, *Werke*, vol. III, p. 281; Roth, 'The Leviathan', in *Collected Shorter Fiction of Joseph Roth*, tr. Michael Hofmann, London: Granta, 2002, pp. 259–91 at p. 284.

35 Cf. Bronsen, op. cit., p. 397.

36 Roth, *Romane, Erzählungen, Aufsätze*, p. 503; Roth, *The String of Pearls*, tr. Michael Hofmann, London: Granta, 1999, pp. 242–3.

37 Ibid., p. 509; *String of Pearls*, p. 256.

38 Cf. Bronsen, op. cit., p. 357.

39 Roth, *Werke*, vol. III, p. 709 ['Glashütte', *Frankfurter Zeitung*, 24 May 1925].

40 Roth, *Der stumme Prophet*, Reinbek, 1968, p. 129; Roth, *The Silent Prophet*, tr. David LeVay, London: Peter Owen, 1979, p. 207 (translation adapted).

41 Roth, *Romane, Erzählungen, Aufsätze*, p. 595; Roth, *The Wandering Jews*, p. 73.

42 Ibid., *Wandering Jews*, p. 73 (translation slightly adapted).

Una montagna bruna – On Hermann Broch's 'Mountain Novel' [*Bergroman*]

1 Cf. F. Stössinger's Afterword to *Der Versucher* [*The Spell*; literally 'The Tempter'], Zurich, 1953, p. 569. *Der Versucher* is a compilation of the three versions of the *Bergroman*. My investigation is based on the text of the first version of the four-volume critical edition by

Frank Kress and Hans Albert Maier, published in Frankfurt am Main in 1969.

2 On this cf. A. Bowie, 'The Novel and the Limits of Abstraction: Hermann Broch's *Die Schlafwandler*', *Journal of European Studies* 3 (1984). In this excellent article Bowie stresses that, while the novel at times thematizes the gulf between empirical experience and constructive historical awareness, in the end it becomes a victim of the crisis which it aims to discuss.

3 Letter to Daniel Brody of 19 October 1934, quoted in *Brochs Verzauberung*, ed. P. M. Lützeler, Frankfurt am Main, 1983, pp. 38f.

4 Ibid., p. 71.

5 Broch mentions this 'project' in his first years of exile in the United States in a group consisting of a few European émigrés, among them Thomas Mann, Giuseppe Antonio Borgese, Siegfried Marck and Hans Meisel.

6 Cf. on this subject Th. Koebner, 'Mythos und Zeitgeist', in Lützeler, op. cit., p. 180.

7 Cf. on this subject F. Aspetsberger, *Literarisches Leben im Austrofaschismus*, Königstein, 1980.

8 Cf. J. Strelka, 'Broch heute', in *Broch heute*, ed. J. Strelka, Bern, 1978, p. 13.

9 Lützeler, op. cit., p. 48.

10 Ibid., p. 50.

11 H. Broch, *Bergroman*, pp. 291f.; *The Spell*, tr. H. F. Broch de Rothermann, London: Picador, 1988, p. 255 (this is a translation of *Die Verzauberung*, which is the first, and only completed, version of the 'mountain novel'. As such, it varies in places from the edition cited by WGS).

12 Hermann Broch, *Werkausgabe*, ed. P. M. Lützeler, Frankfurt am Main, 1974–81, vol. 9/1, p. 41.

13 Broch, *Bergroman*, p. 425; *The Spell*, p. 369.

14. All examples from ibid., p. 11; *The Spell*, pp. 11–12.
15. Ibid., p. 220; *The Spell*, p. 187.
16. Ibid., p. 364; *The Spell*, pp. 316–17.
17. Ibid., p. 96; *The Spell*, p. 83.
18. Ibid., pp. 344 and 379; *The Spell*, pp. 300 and 330 (translation slightly adapted).
19. *Werkausgabe*, vol. 9/2, pp. 94f.
20. *Bergroman*, p. 422; *The Spell*, p. 366.
21. Gregory Bateson, *Mind and Nature*, London, 1980, p. 28.
22. *Bergroman*, p. 247; *The Spell*, p. 218.
23. Cf. *Brochs Verzauberung*, p. 176 [Koebner, 'Mythos und Zeitgeist'].
24. In the spirit of *Germanistik*, Lützeler in particular has done such sterling work that it is not always easy to see the wood for the trees. Cf. *Brochs Verzauberung*, especially pp. 259–74 ['Religions- und mythologiegeschichtliche Aspekte', in Lützeler, 'Forschungsbericht'].
25. Th. Mann, *Das essayistische Werk – Schriften und Reden zur Literatur, Kunst und Philosophie*, vol. I, Frankfurt am Main, 1968, p. 385; 'Freud's Position in the History of Modern Thought', tr. Helen Lowe-Porter, in Thomas Mann, *Past Masters*, London: Martin Secker, 1933, pp. 167–98 at p. 198.
26. H. Blumenberg, *Arbeit am Mythos*, Frankfurt am Main, 1981, p. 178; Blumenberg, *Work on Myth*, tr. Robert M. Wallace, Cambridge, MA: MIT, 1988, p. 161.
27. Ibid., pp. 77f.; *Work on Myth*, p. 68 (WGS uses 'zerfällt' instead of 'entfällt').
28. Ibid., [p. 78]; *Work on Myth*, p. 68.
29. Ibid., p. 389; *Work on Myth*, p. 357.
30. *Bergroman*, p. 344; *The Spell*, p. 300.
31. Koebner, *Hermann Broch*, Bern/Munich, 1965, p. 119.

A Lost Land – Jean Améry and Austria

1 I. Bachmann, 'Drei Wege zum See', in *Werke*, vol. 2, Munich/Zurich, 1978, p. 421; 'Three Paths to the Lake', in *Three Paths to the Lake: Stories by Ingeborg Bachmann*, tr. Mary Fran Gilbert with an introduction by Mark Anderson, New York/London: Holmes & Meier, 1989, pp. 117–212 at p. 145.

2 The details in this passage are thanks to the biographical information on Améry which F. Pfäflin published in the *Marbacher Beiträge* [sic = Friedrich Pfäfflin (ed.), *Améry. Unterwegs nach Oudenaarde*, Marbacher Magazin 24/1982, Stuttgart/Bad Cannstatt: Deutsche Schillergesellschaft, 1982].

3 J. Améry, *Örtlichkeiten*, Stuttgart, 1980, p. 10.

4 F. Torberg, *Die Tante Jolesch oder der Untergang des Abendlandes in Anekdoten*, Munich, 1975, p. 106. There is, incidentally, a certain amount of overlap between the chapter 'In der Sommerfrische' ('Summer Vacation') in this book and the chapter 'Bad Ischl – Wien' ('Bad Ischl – Vienna') in *Örtlichkeiten*, suggesting that Améry must have had Torberg's text in mind while writing his recollections of Bad Ischl. Cf. Friedrich Torberg, *Tante Jolesch or the Decline of the West in Anecdotes*, tr. Maria P. Bauer, Riverside, CA: Ariadne, 2006, pp. 60–61.

5 Cf. Améry, *Örtlichkeiten*, p. 13.

6 Ibid., p. 17.

7 Ibid., p. 23.

8 Ibid., p. 24.

9 Améry, *Unmeisterliche Wanderjahre*, Stuttgart, 1971, p. 28.

10 *Österreichs Erneuerung. Die Reden des Bundeskanzlers Kurt von Schuschnigg*, ed. Österreichischer Bundespressedienst, vol. 2, Vienna, 1936, pp. 154f.

11 Améry, *Unmeisterliche Wanderjahre*, p. 11.

12 [Guido Zernatto, *Die Wahrheit über Österreich*,] New York/Toronto, 1938. Quoted here after Friedbert Aspetsberger, *Literarisches Leben im Austrofaschismus*, Meisenheim, 1980, p. 88.

13 Améry, *Örtlichkeiten*, p. 25.
14 Améry, *Unmeisterliche Wanderjahre*, p. 14.
15 Ibid., [p. 15].
16 Ibid., [p. 15].
17 Cf. ibid., p. 33.
18 Cf. ibid., p. 38.
19 Ibid., p. 48.
20 Ibid., pp. 37f.
21 Ibid., p. 10.
22 Ibid., p. 38.
23 Cf. Aspetsberger, op. cit., p. 112.
24 Améry, *Unmeisterliche Wanderjahre*, p. 47.
25 Cf. G. Clare, *Last Waltz in Vienna*, London, 1982, pp. 171f.
26 Améry, *Jenseits von Schuld und Sühne*, Stuttgart, 1977, p. 78; Jean Améry, *At the Mind's Limits: Contemplations by a Survivor on Auschwitz and its Realities*, tr. Sidney Rosenfeld and Stella P. Rosenfeld, published in association with the United States Holocaust Memorial Museum, Bloomington and Indianapolis: Indiana University Press, 1980, pp. 43–4.
27 'There was a particular moment which shattered my childhood. Hitler's troops marching into Klagenfurt. It was something so terrible that my memories begin with this day: a pain experienced much too early, stronger perhaps than any I felt afterwards. Of course I did not understand all that in the sense that an adult would understand it. But this appalling brutality, that was palpable, this yelling, singing and marching – the first time I felt mortal fear . . .' Quoted from an interview with Gerda Bödefeld in A. Hapkemeyer (ed.), *Ingeborg Bachmann, Bilder aus ihrem Leben*, Munich/Zurich, 1983.
28 Améry, *Jenseits von Schuld und Sühne*, p. 78; *At the Mind's Limits*, p. 44.
29 Ibid., pp. 75f.; *At the Mind's Limits*, p. 42.

30 K. Kraus, *Die letzten Tage der Menschheit*, Munich, 1966, vol. II, p. 27 [sic = Act II, scene 27]; Karl Kraus, *The Last Days of Mankind*, tr. Fred Bridgham and Edward Timms, New Haven/London: Yale University Press, 2015, p. 221.

31 Cf. J. Riedl, 'Geht doch in die Donau – Über den österreichischen Anteil am Holocaust', in J. Riedl, *Versunkene Welt*, Jewish Welcome Service, Vienna, 1984.

32 Améry, *Jenseits von Schuld und Sühne*, p. 78; *At the Mind's Limits*, p. 44.

33 Ibid., p. 85; *At the Mind's Limits*, p. 49.

34 Ibid., pp. 76f.; *At the Mind's Limits*, p. 43.

35 Cf. ibid., p. 92; *At the Mind's Limits*, p. 54.

36 Améry, *Örtlichkeiten*, p. 89.

37 Cf. *BILD-Zeitung*, 19 October 1978.

38 Cf. *Theater Heute*, No. 1, 1986.

39 Ibid., p. 1.

In an Unknown Region – On Gerhard Roth's Novel *Landläufiger Tod* [*A Common or Garden Death*]

1 Lévi-Strauss outlines a similar set of difficulties in the method of description when he recalls how a new epistemological model, that of structuralism, which made it possible to abstract from the notorious philosophical subject, led to a disproportionately deeper understanding. Cf. *Mythologica*, vol. IV/2, Frankfurt am Main, 1975, p. 808; Claude Lévi-Strauss, *The Naked Man: Introduction to a Study of Mythology: 4*, tr. John and Doreen Weightman, London: Cape, 1981, p. 687.

2 Jean Paul, *Vorschule der Ästhetik*, in *Werke*, vol. IX, Munich, 1976, p. 96; *Horn of Oberon: Jean Paul Richter's School for Aesthetics*, tr. Margaret R. Hale, Detroit: Wayne State University Press, 1973, pp. 66–7.

3 Ibid., p. 52; *Horn of Oberon*, pp. 31–2.

4 Cf. G. Roth, *Landläufiger Tod*, Frankfurt am Main, 1984, p. 134.

5 Ibid., p. 141.

6 Ibid., pp. 507ff.

7 Jean Paul, op. cit., p. 97; *Horn of Oberon*, p. 67.

8 For what, we may ask ourselves, may have going through his mind when, sitting in the front row of a Cambridge cinema, he would watch a Western while eating pork pies.

9 Roth, op. cit., p. 190.

10 Ibid., pp. 186 and 184 [#604 and #571].

11 Ibid., p. 206.

12 Ibid., p. 207.

13 Ibid., p. 716.

14 C. Lévi-Strauss, *Das wilde Denken*, Frankfurt am Main, 1968, p. 280; Claude Lévi-Strauss, *The Savage Mind (La Pensée Sauvage)*, [translator not named,] London: Weidenfeld & Nicolson, 1972 (repr. 1976), p. 242.

15 Roth, op. cit., p. 203.

16 Cf. Lévi-Strauss, *Mythologica*, vol. IV/2, pp. 654f.; Lévi-Strauss, *The Naked Man*, p. 559.

17 Cf. B. Schulz, *Die Republik der Träume*, Munich, 1967, p. 17; cf. Bruno Schulz, 'The Republic of Dreams', tr. Walter Arndt, *Chicago Review* 40.1 (1994), pp. 66–72.

18 Roth, op. cit., p. 23.

19 Ibid., pp. 92f.

20 Ibid., pp. 94f.

21 Cf. ibid., p. 217.

22 Cf. ibid., p. 496.

23 Cf. ibid., p. 253.

24 Ibid., p. 283.

25 Ibid., p. 226.

26 Ibid., p. 227.

27 Ibid., p. 274.

28 F. Kafka, *Hochzeitsvorbereitungen auf dem Lande*, Frankfurt am Main, 1980, p. 90; Franz Kafka, *Wedding Preparations in the Country and Other Posthumous Prose Writings*, tr. Ernst Kaiser and Eithne Wilkins, London: Secker & Warburg, 1954 (repr. 1975), p. 116.

29 Cf. Roth, op. cit., pp. 347ff.

30 Ibid., pp. 10f.

31 On this see M. Merleau-Ponty, *L'Oeil et l'Esprit*, Paris, 1964, p. 31; Maurice Merleau-Ponty, 'Eye and Mind', tr. Michael B. Smith, in *The Merleau-Ponty Aesthetics Reader: Philosophy and Painting*, ed. Galen A. Johnson, Evanston, IL: Northwestern University Press, 1993, pp. 121–49 at p. 129.

32 Cf. [Lévi-Strauss,] *Mythologica*, vol. III, p. 206; Claude Lévi-Strauss, *The Origin of Table Manners: Introduction to a Study of Mythology: 3*, tr. John and Doreen Weightman, London: Cape, 1978, p. 195.

33 Roth, op. cit., pp. 766f.

34 Jean Paul, op. cit., p. 98; *Horn of Oberon*, p. 68.

35 Ibid., p. 40; cf. *Horn of Oberon*, pp. 22–3 (I have chosen to use my own translation here).

36 Cf. [Lévi-Strauss,] *Mythologica*, vol. III, p. 459; *Origin of Table Manners*, pp. 430–31.

37 Ibid., p. 546; *Origin of Table Manners*, p. 508.

38 Jean Paul, op. cit., p. 95; cf. *Horn of Oberon*, p. 66 (translation adapted).

Across the Border – Peter Handke's *Die Wiederholung* [*Repetition*]

1 In 1982 the list of secondary literature already consisted of around 200 titles.

2 While the tide of secondary literature did not dry up in the 1980s, much of what has been written on Handke in the last decade [the 1980s] is concerned with his earlier work. In addition, a considerable proportion of what has been published about Handke's more recent work tends to be of a polemic nature. Thus there exists scarcely any objective appraisal of one of the most important of contemporary authors. Cf. J. Lohmann, 'Handke-Beschimpfung oder der Stillstand der Kritik', *Tintenfaß* 2 (1981). On the academic front, this increasingly distant stance is exemplified in, for example, Manfred Durzak's 1982 study *Peter Handke und die deutsche Gegenwartsliteratur*. Clearly unconvinced by the ideas Handke develops across the four books of *Langsame Heimkehr*, Durzak criticizes the solitary or reclusive aspects of the work, its lack of reference to social reality, and in particular its 'stylistic pointillism, which endlessly compiles details without discernible motivation and without the poetic vision that would create a coherent whole'. (Quoted from N. Honsza (ed.), *Zu Peter Handke – Zwischen Experiment und Tradition*, Stuttgart, 1982, p. 108.)

3 Cf. for example B. Heinrichs, 'Der Evangelimann. Glücksmärchen, Wanderpredigt, Lesefolter: *Die Wiederholung*', in *Die Zeit*, 3 October 1986.

4 P. Handke, *Die Wiederholung*, Frankfurt am Main, 1986, p. 126; Peter Handke, *Repetition*, tr. Ralph Manheim, London: Penguin, 2020, p. 79.

5 Cf. ibid.; *Repetition*, p. 79.

6 Ibid.; *Repetition*, p. 79.

7 Ibid., p. 12; *Repetition*, p. 5.

8 Ibid., p. 18; *Repetition*, p. 9.

9 Ibid., p. 119; *Repetition*, p. 74.

10 Ibid.; *Repetition*, p. 75.

11 Ibid.; *Repetition*, p. 75.

12 Ibid., p. 77; *Repetition*, p. 48.

13 Ibid., p. 131; *Repetition*, p. 82.
14 Ibid., p. 323; *Repetition*, p. 210.
15 Ibid., p. 325; *Repetition*, p. 211.
16 Ibid.; *Repetition*, pp. 210–11 (where, however, the reference to the hats is omitted).
17 Ibid.; *Repetition*, p. 211.
18 Cf. ibid., p[p]. 67[f.]; *Repetition*, p. 41.
19 Ibid., p. 68; *Repetition*, p. 41.
20 Ibid., p. 71; *Repetition*, p. 44.
21 Ibid., p. 72; *Repetition*, p. 44.
22 Ibid.; *Repetition*, p. 44.
23 Cf. ibid., p. 20; *Repetition*, p. 10.
24 Ibid.; *Repetition*, p. 11.
25 Ibid., p. 77; *Repetition*, p. 47.
26 Ibid., p[p]. 46[f.]; *Repetition*, p. 27.
27 Ibid., p. 53; *Repetition*, p. 31.
28 Ibid., p. 20; *Repetition*, p. 10.
29 Ibid., p. 40; *Repetition*, p. 23.
30 Ibid., p. 306; *Repetition*, p. 198.
31 Ibid., p. 228; *Repetition*, p. 147.
32 Ibid., p. 229; *Repetition*, p. 148.
33 Ibid., p. 231; *Repetition*, p. 149.
34 Ibid., p. 72; *Repetition*, p. 44.
35 Ibid., p. 181; *Repetition*, p. 115.
36 Cf. ibid.; *Repetition*, p. 115.
37 Ibid., p. 182; *Repetition*, p. 116.
38 Ibid., p. 69; *Repetition*, p. 42.
39 Ibid.; *Repetition*, p. 42.
40 Ibid., p. 185; *Repetition*, p. 118.
41 Ibid., p. 73; *Repetition*, p. 45.

42 Ibid., p. 132; *Repetition*, p. 83.

43 Ibid., p. 200; *Repetition*, p. 129.

44 Ibid., p. 132; *Repetition*, p. 83.

45 H. Arendt, *Elemente und Ursprünge totalitärer Herrschaft*, vol. I: *Antisemitismus*, Frankfurt am Main/Berlin/Vienna, 1975, p. 54; cf. Hannah Arendt, *The Origins of Totalitarianism*, London: Penguin, 2017, p. 30 (NB the German edition quoted by WGS, translated by Arendt, differs from Arendt's English original).

46 Handke, *Die Wiederholung*, p. 201; *Repetition*, p. 128.

47 Cf. ibid.; *Repetition*, p. 128.

48 Ibid., p. 56; *Repetition*, p. 33.

49 Ibid., p. 59; *Repetition*, p. 35.

50 Ibid., p. 150; *Repetition*, p. 95.

51 Ibid., pp. 226f.; *Repetition*, p. 146.

52 Ibid., p. 127; *Repetition*, p. 80.

53 Ibid., p. 317; *Repetition*, p. 206.

54 Ibid., p. 15; *Repetition*, p. 7.

55 Ibid., p. 36; *Repetition*, p. 20.

56 Ibid., p. 215; *Repetition*, p. 138.

57 Ibid., p. 284; *Repetition*, p. 184.

58 Cf. ibid., p. 49; *Repetition*, p. 29.

59 Ibid., p. 50; *Repetition*, p. 29.

60 Ibid., p. 288; *Repetition*, p. 187.

61 Ibid., p. 289; *Repetition*, p. 187.

62 Ibid., p. 276; *Repetition*, p. 179.

Translator's Notes

Part One

Foreword

i The reference here is to Jean Paul, *Vorschule der Ästhetik* or 'Pre-School of Aesthetics', in *Werke*, vol. IX, Munich: Carl Hanser, 1976.

ii See the essay on Charles Sealsfield in Part Two of the present volume (above p. 227).

iii Those who disappear (*Verschollene*) – a reference to the title of Kafka's *The Man Who Disappeared* (also known as *America/Amerika*).

iv As note iii above; the *Naturtheater* is also referenced in *After Nature*.

v The title of Peter Handke's tetralogy (see the final essay in Part One of the present volume, above p. 193).

vi The Church of Our Lady before Týn on the main square in Prague's Old Town.

vii A reference to the title of the volume, *Die Beschreibung des Unglücks*. The German *Unglück*, the opposite of *Glück* (happiness, luck, good fortune), can be variously rendered as unhappiness, misery, misfortune, or indeed as accident, disaster or catastrophe. Where Sebald uses the term, all of these meanings resonate. The translator is obliged to select a meaning, or meanings, according to context.

viii A reference, presumably, to Joseph Roth (see the essays 'Westwards – Eastwards' and 'A Kaddish for Austria' in Part Two of the present volume (above pp. 253 and 327).

ix Kafka, *Letters to Milena*, tr. Philip Boehm, New York: Schocken, 1990, p. 223 (German: *Briefe an Milena*, Fischer, 1983, pp. 301–32), end March 1922.

x *Unglück* – see note vii above.

xi As note vii.

xii As note vii.

xiii 'Sieh ins Buch. Wenn man hineinguckt, weint man nicht.'

xiv As note vii.

To the Edge of Nature – An Essay on Stifter

Text:

'Bis an den Rand der Natur – Versuch über Stifter', in *Österreichische Porträts*, ed. Jochen Jung, Salzburg: Residenz, 1985, vol. I, pp. 232–55. An English translation by Anthea Bell, 'To the Edge of Nature: An Essay on Stifter', appeared in *Southern Humanities Review* 39.4 (Fall 2005), 305–24.

i *Vormärz*: the period before the failed March revolutions of 1848.

ii *Der Nachsommer* has been translated as *Indian Summer* by Wendell Frye (New York: Peter Lang, 1985). The recurrent phrases highlighted by Sebald are translated slightly differently there as the occasion demands.

iii Thomas Bernhard, *Gargoyles*, tr. Richard and Clara Winston, New York: Knopf, 1970.

iv 'Le Mythe de la digestion', in Bachelard, *La Formation de l'esprit scientifique – Contribution á une psychanalyse de la connaissance objective*, ch. IX, Paris: J. Vrin, 5th edn, 1967.

v 'Heerwagen' (chariot) is according to *Grimms Wörterbuch* another term for the constellation 'Himmelswagen' = Ursa Major or the Plough.

vi In German the word 'Scho(o)ß', for the skirt or hem/train of the dress, also means lap or womb. It is unclear whether this allusion is deliberate on Stifter's part; it seems probable that it is on Sebald's.

vii Here Sebald misquotes Freud's 'Lieben' (love) as 'Leben' (life).

viii The reader may note a marked resemblance to Jäger (Hunter) Schlag's disappearance in 'Ritorno in patria' towards the end of *Vertigo*, one of the many examples of intertextual reference and overlap in Sebald's fictional work.

ix Quoted in English in the original.

x *Schwermütiger*: literally heavy spirited, i.e. melancholic.

The Horror of Love – On Schnitzler's *Traumnovelle* [*Dream Story*]

Text:
'Das Schrecknis der Liebe – Zu Schnitzlers "Traumnovelle"', in *Merkur* 39.2 (February 1985), 120–31.

i Epigraph: Léon Bloy, *Exégèse des Lieux Communs*, Paris: Mercure de France, 1902, pp. 152–3, No. 82: 'Tuer le temps'. 'Killing time ... When the Bourgeois has fun, we're entering the realm of the eternal. For Bourgeois entertainments are like death' (Léon Bloy, *Exegesis of Commonplaces*, tr. Louis Cancelmi, Belmont, NC: Wiseblood Classics, 2021, p. 132).

ii *Das weite Land* (*The Vast Domain*) is the title of a 1911 drama by Schnitzler, also adapted as *Undiscovered Country* by Tom Stoppard in 1979.

iii Otto König, Austrian ethnologist/behaviourist and photographer, student of Konrad Lorenz (b. Vienna 1914; d. 1992, Klosterneuburg).

iv Schnitzler's 1895 play *Liebelei*, filmed by Max Ophüls in 1933; adapted e.g. as *Dalliance* by Tom Stoppard (1986); as *Loveplay* by Lawrence Leibowitz (1987); and as *Sweet Nothings* by David Harrower (2010).

A Venetian Cryptogram – Hofmannsthal's *Andreas*

Text:

'Venezianisches Kryptogramm – Hofmannsthals "Andreas"' appeared after or simultaneously with *Die Beschreibung des Unglücks* in the volume *Fin de Siècle Vienna*, ed. G. J. Carr and Eda Sagarra, Proceedings of the Second Irish Symposium in Austrian Studies, Trinity College, Dublin, 28 February–2 March 1985, Dublin: Trinity College, 1985, pp. 143–60.

i Fritz Martini, 'Hugo von Hofmannsthal: "Andreas oder die Vereinigten"', in *Hugo von Hofmannsthal: Wege der Forschung*, ed. Sibylle Bauer, Darmstadt: Wissenschaftliche Buchgesellschaft, 1968, pp. 311–51; Richard Alewyn, 'Andreas und die "Wunderbare Freundin". Zur Fortsetzung von Hofmannsthals Romanfragment und ihrer psychiatrischen Quelle', ibid., pp. 352–401.

ii 'Hysteria! Why should this physiological mystery not constitute the basis and substance of a work of literature, this mystery, [unsolved as yet by the Faculty,] which takes the form, in women, of a feeling of rising and choking oppression (to mention only the main symptom), and which produces, in men of nervous temperament, every form of impotence and also a capacity for all kinds of excess?' ('*Madame Bovary* by Gustave Flaubert', in Baudelaire, *Selected Writings on Art and Artists*, intro. and tr. P. E. Charvet, Cambridge: Cambridge University Press, 1972, pp. 244–55 at p. 252).

iii *Passionsweg*: literally 'the stations of the cross of male sexuality' (*Passion* in German means suffering; cf. 'passion of Christ'). *The Arcades Project*, tr. Howard Eiland and Kevin McLaughlin, Cambridge, MA/London: Belknap Press, 1999, p. 342, renders this as 'It is impotence that makes for the bitter cup of male sexuality.'

iv English in original.

v The pseudonym under which Hugo van Hofmannsthal published poems as a teenage prodigy.

vi 'In dem Malteser etwas von Charlus' (Hofmannsthal, *Andreas*, in *Sämtliche Werke*, Frankfurt am Main: Freies Deutsches Hochstift, 1982, vol. XXX, p. 201 (N 337) – a reference to Baron Charlus in Proust's *À la recherche du temps perdu*.

vii 'those marriages of the first-born of men, of those ineffable unions, in which sister was wedded to brother, so that love and brotherly friendship mingled in one heart, and the purity of the one augmented the delights of the other'. F. R. de Chateaubriand, *Atala – René*, tr. Rayner Heppenstall, London: Oxford University Press, 1963, p. 48.

viii 'mit Eifer sucht, was Leiden schafft': an untranslatable pun on 'Eifersucht' (jealousy) and 'Leidenschaft' (passion). *Eifer* = eagerness, zeal; *suchen* = to seek; *Leiden* = suffering; *schaffen* = to create.

ix 'Passion for things doesn't come from their pure goodness or beauty, it comes above all from their corruption. We'll love a woman madly, for her putridity, for the wickedness of her mind, for the crookedness in her head, her heart, her senses; we'll have the deranged taste of a delicacy for its advanced, stinking odour. Basically, what passion does is to give you a taste for beings and things that are on the verge of putrefaction' (tr. Paul Rowe, University of Leeds).

x 'it is she [nature] too who incites man to murder his brother, to eat him, to lock him up and to torture him.' Charles Baudelaire, *The Painter of Modern Life and Other Essays*, ed. and trans. Jonathan Mayne, London/New York: Phaidon, 1965 (repr. 2001), pp. 1–41 at p. 32 ('In Praise of Cosmetics').

xi Cf. the passages on Casanova's incarceration and escape in the 'All'estero' section of *Vertigo*. A number of Hofmannsthal's works also draw on Casanova's memoirs.

xii *L'Homme qui rit* (*The Man Who Laughs*), 1869 novel by Victor Hugo, subject of several film adaptations.

xiii 'and where is the truth more clearly visible than in those splendid exhibitions of human misery?' Cf. Gustave Flaubert, *Selected Letters*, tr. Geoffrey

Wall, London: Penguin, 1997, pp. 218–22 at p. 220. NB the French has 'ces' not 'les'.

xiv 'Images – my great, my primitive passion' (Baudelaire, *Mon coeur mis à nu*).

xv 'there is no greater suffering than to remember happy times – from a state of misery.' Cf. *Andreas*, op. cit. p. 167 (N 237): '[Maria] Malibran in Rossini's *Othello*. Beneath Desdemona's window a gondolier sings. Nessun maggior dolor che ricordarsi del tempo felice – nella miseria.' The Italian quotation is from Dante, *Inferno*, Canto V, 121f.: *The Divine Comedy of Dante Alighieri*, vol. I: *Inferno*, tr. Melville B. Anderson, Oxford: Oxford World Classics, 1921, p. 49 – '[. . .] It is the woe of woes / remembrance of the happy time to keep / in misery [. . .]'

The Undiscover'd Country – The Death Motif in Kafka's *Castle*

Notes numbered [A], [B] and so on comment on the relevant endnote in Sebald's English text.

Text:

'Das unentdeckte Land – Zur Motivstruktur in Kafkas "Schloß"' appeared under the title 'Thanatos – Zur Motivstruktur in Kafkas "Schloß"' in *Literatur und Kritik* 66 (1972), 399–411, and in English under the title 'The Undiscover'd Country – The Death Motif in Kafka's "Castle"' in *Journal of European Studies* 2 (1972), 22–34. This latter version, in Sebald's English, is the one reproduced in the present volume.

The German text has two epigraphs in place of the Beckett quote: 'Der Tod ist vor uns, etwa wie im Schulzimmer an der Wand ein Bild der Alexanderschlacht. – Franz Kafka' ('Death is before us like a picture of the *Alexanderschlacht* [Alexander's battle] in the classroom' – cf. the end of *Nach der Natur (After Nature)*); and 'Di fiss trogn, wo der kop sol run – Jiddisches Sprichwort' ('The feet carry where the head shall rest – Yiddish saying').

The first paragraph of the English text is omitted in the German.

A Note on note 1: Franz Kafka, *The Castle*, tr. Willa and Edwin Muir, with additional material tr. Eithne Wilkins and Ernst Kaiser, Harmondsworth: Penguin, 1957 and reprints.

B Note on note 7: English tr. of essay 'On Some Motifs in Baudelaire', in Walter Benjamin, *Illuminations*, tr. Harry Zohn, London: Fontana, 1992, pp. 152–90 at p. 181.

C Note on note 10: 'Zweimal Chaplin' = 'Chaplin Times Two'.

D Note on note 11: G. Janouch, *Conversations with Kafka*, tr. Goronwy Rees, New York: New Directions, 2nd edn, 2012.

i 'schwarz' = black.

E Note on note 12: 'this flesh, which sometimes gave the impression that it was not really alive'.

ii Rite of spring.

iii Walter Benjamin, 'Franz Kafka. On the Tenth Anniversary of His Death', in *Illuminations*, tr. Harry Zohn, London: Fontana, 1992, pp. 108–35 at p. 126.

F Note on note 33: cf. Kafka, *Wedding Preparations in the Country and Other Posthumous Prose Writings*, with notes by Max Brod, tr. Ernst Kaiser and Eithne Wilkins, London: Secker & Warburg, 1954, p. 222.

G Note on note 36: 'Die Zimtläden': German translation of stories by Polish author Bruno Schulz: *Sklepy Cynamonowe* (*Cinnamon Shops*), included in *The Complete Fiction of Bruno Schulz*, tr. Celina Wieniewska, New York: Walker & Company, 1989, and in *Collected Stories*, Madeline G. Levine, Boston, MA: Northwestern University Press, 2018.

H Note on note 43: 'Grenzwirtshaus auf dem Passübergang Jenseits' = 'inn at the border crossing to the other world'.

I Note on note 45: 'For this miracle to happen, all we need to do is to approach our lips to the magic panel and address our call [. . .] to the

Vigilant Virgins whose voices we hear every day but whose faces we never get to know, and who are the guardian angels of the dizzy darkness whose portals they jealously guard; the All-Powerful ones who conjure absent beings to our presence without our being permitted to see them; the Danaïds of the unseen who constantly empty and refill and transmit to one another the urns of sound; the ironic Furies who, just as we are murmuring private words to a loved one in the hope we are not overheard, call out with brutal invasiveness: "This is the operator speaking"; the forever fractious servants of the Mysteries, the shadowy priestesses of the Invisible, so quick to take offence, the Young Ladies of the Telephone!' (Marcel Proust, *The Guermantes Way*, tr. Mark Treharne, London: Penguin, 2003, p. 130).

Walter Benjamin's text 'The Telephone' can be found in *Berlin Childhood Around 1900*, tr. Howard Eiland, in Benjamin, *Selected Writings*, vol. 3: *1933–1938*, Cambridge, MA: Harvard University Press, 2002, pp. 344–413 at pp. 349–50.

iv Like the motif of the wandering Jew and the Flying Dutchman, a recurring trope in Sebald's work. Cf. the 'All'estero' section of *Vertigo*.

v The German omits the Jean Paul reference and ends with 'diese Reise K.'s in das unentdeckte Land, von des Bezirk kein Wanderer wiederkehrt', the quote from *Hamlet*, III, i, from which the title of the essay is taken ('The undiscovered country from whose bourn / No traveller returns').

Summa Scientiae – Systems and System Critique in Elias Canetti

Text:

'Summa Scientiae – System und Systemkritik bei Elias Canetti', in *Literatur und Kritik* 177–8 (1983), 398–404, as well as in *Études Germaniques* 39.3 (1984), 268–75.

i   In the section 'Rulers and Paranoiacs', the final section of Canetti's *Crowds and Power*.

ii *Wacht am Rhein*: 'Watch on the Rhine' – patriotic German poem set to music by Karl Wilhelm (1854); German military offensive (Operation Watch on the Rhine) in the Ardennes in late 1944 ('Battle of the Bulge').

iii Daniel Paul Schreber, *Memoirs of My Nervous Illness* (1903), tr. Ida McAlpine and Richard A. Hunter, New York: New York Review of Books, 2000.

iv Michel Foucault, *Madness and Civilization: A History of Insanity in the Age of Reason*, tr. Richard Howard, London: Routledge, 1989; French: *Folie et déraison: Histoire de la folie à l'âge classique*, Paris: Gallimard, new edn 1972.

v   Cf. Sebald's 1975 essay 'Strangeness, Integration and Crisis: On Peter Handke's Play *Kaspar*', in *Campo Santo*, tr. Anthea Bell, London: Hamish Hamilton, 2003, pp. 55–67. Kaspar Hauser, subject of Werner Herzog's 1974 film *The Enigma of Kaspar Hauser*, was a favourite subject of Sebald's.

vi Here Sebald has adapted the quote, which in Bernhard (*Werke*, vol. 14, Frankfurt am Main: Suhrkamp, 2018, p. 42) reads 'Die ganze Welt ist eine einzige Jurisprudenz. Die ganze Welt ist ein Zuchthaus', to read 'Die ganze Welt ist eine einzige ungeheure Jurisprudenz. Die Welt ist ein Zuchthaus!'

vii Possibly this refers to William Blake, *The Circle of the Lustful: Francesca da Rimini*, watercolour (1824–7), City Museum and Art Gallery, Birmingham.

viii 'construction': in German 'Bau' with its resonances of Kafka's unfinished story *Der Bau* (*The Burrow*).

ix Here, as frequently occurs, Sebald is paraphrasing or half quoting the text (Canetti, *Die Blendung*, Frankfurt am Main: Fischer, 1965, III, 'Ein Irrenhaus'; *Auto-da-Fé*, tr. C. V. Wedgwood, Harmondsworth: Penguin, 1965, III/3: 'A Madhouse'.).

x   For another translation of this see Canetti, 'Notebooks 1942–1948', tr. Margaret Woodruff, *Dimension* 1.3 (1968), 420–41 at p. 421.

xi   Cf. Canetti, *The Conscience of Words*, tr. Joachim Neugroschel, New York: Farrar, Straus & Giroux, 1984, p. 173.

xii Another translation is in 'Notebooks 1942–1948', tr. Margaret Woodruff.

xiii Also translated as 'To read until the eyelashes are almost audible with fatigue' (Canetti, *The Human Province*, tr. Joachim Neugroschel, London: André Deutsch, 1985, p. 76).

xiv A reference to *Die Blendung*, II, 'Enthüllungen', p. 264; *Auto-da-Fé*, II/5: 'Revelations', p. 274.

xv   These last two quotations are in fact from *Aufzeichnungen, 1949–1960*, Munich: Hanser, 1970, not from *Aufzeichnungen, 1942–1948*, Munich: Hanser, 1969, as Sebald's 'Ibid.' in notes 25 and 26 suggests. The page numbers given are correct.

Wo die Dunkelheit den Strick zuzieht
[Where Darkness Draws Tight the Noose] –
Some Marginal Notes on Thomas Bernhard

Text:
'Wo die Dunkelheit den Strick zuzieht – Zu Thomas Bernhard', in *Literatur und Kritik* 155 (1981), 294–302.

The version reproduced here is an unpublished English version by Sebald discovered in his *Nachlass* in the Deutsches Literaturarchiv Marbach. It is thought to have been given as a conference paper at CUTG (Conference of University Teachers in German) at the University of Sussex in September 1980, where it was entitled 'Anarchy and Satire: Some Notes on Thomas Bernhard' (source: Richard Sheppard, 'W. G. Sebald: A Chronology', in Jo Catling and Richard Hibbitt (eds.), *Saturn's Moons: W. G. Sebald – A Handbook*, Oxford/London: Legenda, 2011, pp. 462 and 628). While the original article is in English, the quotations and footnotes are in German: the English translation of quotations has been appended as footnotes to the text. Where these are from published translations this is referenced as an addition to Sebald's endnotes.

i 'Everything dies. Death must be died. If you don't believe it, ask Vienna in Austria about it' (Abraham a Santa Clara, *Mercks Wienn: 1680*, ed. Werner Welzig, Tübingen: Niemeyer, 1983).

ii Here Sebald inserts a handwritten note in the margin of the typescript: 'Desc. book. uner.[hörte] Begebenh.[eit].' 'Unerhörte Begebenheit' (unprecedented/shocking event) is according to Goethe an essential component of the *Novelle*. The text of the quotation is photocopied and pasted into the typescript.

iii Here again a photocopied cutting is pasted into the typescript.

iv In the typescript Sebald adds the words 'missa finita' here.

Beneath the Surface – Peter Handke's Story of the Goalkeeper's Anxiety

Text:

'Unterm Spiegel des Wassers – Peter Handkes Erzählung von der Angst des Tormanns', in *Austriaca* 16 (1983), 43–56.

There are two versions of the English translation of the Handke text: *The Goalie's Anxiety at the Penalty Kick*, tr. Michael Roloff, London: Methuen, 1977; and *The Goalkeeper's Anxiety at the Penalty Kick*, tr. Michael Roloff, London: Penguin, 2020. There are slight differences between the two editions, e.g. 'building worker' vs 'construction worker'. The translated quotations follow the 2020 Penguin Classics edition.

i Epigraph: Storm, *The White Horseman and Beneath the Flood*, tr. Geoffrey Skelton, London: The New English Library, 1962, p. 107.

ii 'Au' in German also means meadow; 'Schwerhörigkeit' (deafness) literally = hard [heavy]-of-hearingness; but 'Hörigkeit' also means addiction or enslavement.

iii Cf. the end of Paul Celan's poem 'Tübingen Jänner'.

iv 'falsche Bewegung': a probable allusion to the eponymous 1975 film by Wim Wenders scripted by Peter Handke.

A Small Traverse –
The Poetry of Ernst Herbeck

Text:

'Eine kleine Traverse – Das poetische Werk Ernst Herbecks', in *manuskripte* 74 (1981), 35–41.

i Epigraph: from the poem 'Einfach dasein' in the 1972 collection by Nicolas Born, *Das Auge des Entdeckers*. The Herbeck quotation is from the poem 'Der erste Mai' in *Alexanders poetische Texte*, ed. Leo Navratil, Munich: dtv, 1977, p. 110.

ii The term is from Leo Navratil, the director of the psychiatric institute (Centre for Art and Psychotherapy) in Gugging outside Klosterneuburg, now renamed House of Artists. Cf. Outsider Art; Art Brut.

iii 'Allerleihrauh', the title of one of the Grimms' *Märchen*: 'All kinds of fur'. Also the title of a 1971 book of children's rhymes by Hans Magnus Enzensberger, a copy of which Sebald owned.

iv A play on the idiom 'Vom Regen in die Traufe', 'from the frying pan into the fire'.

v An unaccountably popular 'freakshow attraction' at funfairs in German-speaking regions, apparently based on the real case of Antonia Matt, born without legs, who made a career as the 'half lady' Mademoiselle Gabrielle (1878–1958).

vi Cf. Konrad Lorenz, *Behind the Mirror: A Search for a Natural History of Human Knowledge*, tr. Ronald Taylor, London: Methuen, 1977, p. 30: 'If two independent systems are coupled together, entirely new, unexpected system characteristics will emerge, of whose appearance there was previously not the slightest suggestion.'

vii A pun on 'bergab' = downhill.

viii Kurt von Schuschnigg, Chancellor of Austria 1934–8, prior to the *Anschluß*. See also the essay on Jean Améry in Part Two (above p. 367).

ix 'Der Irrsinn ist bei Einzelnen etwas Seltenes, – aber bei Gruppen, Parteien, Völkern, Zeiten die Regel.' Friedrich Nietzsche, *Jenseits von Gut und Böse*, Viertes Hauptstück, Nr. 156, in *Werke*, vol. 3, Cologne: Könemann Verlagsgesellschaft, 1994, p. 93 ('Madness is something rare in individuals – but in groups, parties, peoples, ages it is the rule': Nietzsche, *Beyond Good and Evil*, tr. R. J. Hollingdale, London: Penguin, 1973, rev. 1990, p. 103).

x 'Herr Karl', opportunistic anti-hero of the eponymous satirical and controversial play by Helmut Qualtinger and Carl Merz (1961), who switches political allegiance for his own advantage according to the prevailing wind.

xi The first four lines of this poem are also translated by Anthea Bell in the essay on Herbeck, 'Des Häschens Kind', in *Campo Santo*, pp. 131–2.

xii 'Flammenschrift' (letters of flame), the 'writing on the wall' at Belshazzar's Feast. The fiery lettering is not biblical but comes from Rembrandt's picture and Heine's reading of it in the ballad *Belsazar*.

xiii 'Patentender' – a made-up word, comprising, one may conjecture, 'patent' and the designation for a stag in German, e.g. a 'Sechzehnender' has sixteen tines on its antlers.

xiv In German, nouns are capitalized but not adjectives.

xv 'Laubhütte' literally means leafy hut – this motif recurs several times, e.g. in the essays on 'Westwards – Eastwards' and 'In an Unknown Region' in Part Two of this volume.

xvi A reference to Paul Klee's painting *Villa R* (1919) in the Künstmuseum Basel.

xvii 'Das Schloß', meaning both castle (as in the title of Kafka's novel) and lock, is a neuter noun in German; 'die Schloß' is therefore incorrect.

The Man with the Overcoat – Gerhard Roth's *Winterreise*

Text:
'Der Mann mit dem Mantel – Gerhard Roths "Winterreise"' appeared under the title 'Literarische Pornographie? – Gerhard Roths "Winterreise"' in *Merkur* 38.2 (1984), 171–80.

i Epigraph: tr. Barry Mitchell, 'Schubert's Wanderer: "Erstarrung"'.

ii 'Der stille Ozean' is also the term for the Pacific Ocean.

iii Another reference to Jean Paul's *Vorschule der Ästhetik* – see Foreword above.

iv A medieval allegorical figure of a woman beautiful in front, but unsightly and loathsome from behind. Cf. Konrad von Würzburg, *Der Welt Lohn*. In 'The Undiscover'd Country' (above p. 100), Sebald refers to this figure as 'Mistress World', which I have followed here.

v 'falls er wiederkäme': the published translation (Gerhard Roth, *Winterreise*, tr. Joachim Neugroschel, New York: Farrar, Straus & Giroux, 1980, p. 128) reads 'in case he came back' – translation adapted.

vi As noted above, a recurring motif in Sebald's work, whether configured as the wandering Jew, the Flying Dutchman or Jäger/Hunter Gracchus. Cf. Benjamin's 'poor souls that wander restlessly, but outside of history', often cited by Sebald.

vii English in original.

Light Pictures and Dark – On the Dialectics of Eschatology in Stifter and Handke

Text:

'Helle Bilder und dunkle – Zur Dialektik der Eschatologie bei Stifter und Handke', in *manuskripte* 84 (1984), 58–64.

i   Literally: black stream.

ii *Langsame Heimkehr*: Peter Handke's *Slow Homecoming* comprises the three novels *The Long Way Around/ The Lesson of Mont Sainte-Victoire/ Child Story*. Handke, *Slow Homecoming*, tr. Ralph Manheim, London: Methuen, 1986.

iii The pun on 'Frauenzimmer' (an old word for 'woman' or 'wench', but literally 'woman's room') is untranslatable here.

iv See note ii – the first volume of the trilogy translated as *Slow Homecoming*.

v   'die Wahrheit des Erzählens als Helligkeit': Handke, *Die Lehre der Sainte-Victoire*, Frankfurt, 1980, p. 99; *The Lesson of Mont Sainte-Victoire*, in Handke, *Slow Homecoming*, tr. Ralph Manheim, New York: Farrar, Straus & Giroux, 1985, pp. 139–211 at p. 190.

vi The motif of dream flight is a favourite theme of Sebald's: see for example the final section of *After Nature*.

vii That is, a return to a first-person narrative.

viii A reference to Ludwig Tieck's 1798 Romantic 'artist novel' (*Künstlerroman*) *Franz Sternbalds Wanderungen*.

ix Cf. the Dante epigraph to the first part of *After Nature*, translated by Michael Hamburger as 'my guide, lord, master from this day' ('tu duca, tu signore e tu maestro').

x   'Schreckensbilder': translated by Manheim as 'horror pictures' (*Lesson of Mont Sainte-Victoire*, p. 146).

xi 'Kannitverstan': cf. *A Place in the Country*, tr. Jo Catling, London: Hamish Hamilton, 2013, p. 17, and *Rings of Saturn*, Section II.

Part Two

Introduction

i For an excellent introduction to twentieth-century Austria, see Katrin Kohl and Ritchie Robertson, 'Introduction', in Kohl and Robertson (eds.), *A History of Austrian Literature, 1918–2000*, Rochester, NY: Camden House, 2006, pp. 1–20.

ii See Karl Kraus, *Weltgericht*, vol. I, Frankfurt am Main: Suhrkamp, 1988, pp. 148–51; first published *Die Fackel*, Nr. 445–453, XVIII Jahr, 18 January 1917.

iii Josef Weinheber (1892–1945), Karl-Heinrich Waggerl (1897–1973), Nazi-affiliated popular Austrian writers. Waggerl in particular idealized rural life in his work.

iv H. C. Artmann, *Med ana schwoazzn dintn: gedichta r aus bradnsee*, Salzburg: Otto Müller, 1958 – Artmann's first volume of poems, written in his native Viennese dialect, a copy of which Sebald owned.

v 'Auszug der Grazer': this refers to the Grazer Gruppe (Graz Group), the 'avant-garde' literary movement of the 1960s and 1970s based in the southern Austrian city of Graz. Cf. the book by Peter Laemmle and Jörg Drews, *Wie die Grazer auszogen, die Literatur zu erobern*, Munich: Text + Kritik, 1983, and W. G. Sebald's article 'Damals vor Graz' – see Translator's Introduction and Bibliography.

Views from the New World – On Charles Sealsfield

Text:
'Ansichten aus der Neuen Welt – Über Charles Sealsfield', in *Die Rampe* 1 (1988), 7–18.

i *Vormärz*: the period before the failed March revolutions of 1848.

ii 1919–34.

iii A number of articles appeared however in the wake of a symposium on Sealsfield at Madison in October 1988. It is not clear whether Sebald, whose own article was first published in early 1988 in the Austrian literary journal *Die Rampe*, knew of this conference. The papers are published as *The Life and Works of Charles Sealsfield (Karl Postl), 1793–1864*, ed. Charlotte L. Brancaforte, Madison, WI: Max Kade Institute for German–American Studies, 1993. See also works by Jeffery L. Sammons, e.g. 'Charles Sealsfield: A Case of Non-Canonicity' in *Amsterdammer Beiträge* 31–3 (1990/1), 155–72, and *Ideology, Mimesis, Fantasy: Charles Sealsfield, Friedrich Gerstäcker, Karl May, and Other German Novelists of America*, Chapel Hill/London: University of North Carolina Press, 1998.

iv Coincidentally or not, this name recurs in Bernhard's *Verstörung* (*Gargoyles*): cf. the essay on Bernhard in Part One of this volume (above pp. 118–29).

v The volume cited by Sebald contains both English and German texts which differ subtly from each other. Sebald quotes from the German version; I have referred to the original (and sometimes quirky) English. A more recent edition of the English is Charles Sealsfield, *Austria As It Is, or Sketches of Continental Courts*, ed. with an introduction and Glossary by Todd C. Hanlin, Riverside, CA: Ariadne, 2004.

vi The German text is more effusive here: '40 Meilen weit führt die Straße von Teplitz nach Karlsbad ununterbrochen durch wohlbestelltes Ackerland.'

vii Prague.

viii Here the English version differs from the German; the English reads 'and wandering to the borders of Holland to seek a foreign country'.

ix An untranslatable pun on 'Schattenreich' (literally shadow empire), a euphemism for the underworld often used by Sebald.

x A reference to Prince Alfred I of Windisch-Graetz (1787–1862), descendant of a noble family from the eponymous place in Styria (now

Slovenj Gradec in Slovenia), known for his role in suppressing the 1848 revolutions in the Austrian Reich.

xi Quoted in English in the original.

xii The novel was written in English during Sealsfield's time in the New World.

xiii Hambach Festival: 27–30 May 1832, one of the main public demonstrations (disguised as a country fair at Hambach Castle in the Palatinate) in support of German unity and democracy during the *Vormärz* era.

xiv 'ein weites Feld' – a reference to the end of Fontane's novel *Effi Briest*, echoed in Günter Grass's eponymous 1995 post-*Wende* novel, translated as *Too Far Afield*.

xv I have quoted the English translation here; Sebald lightly paraphrases in German. Charles Sealsfield, *The Cabin Book: Or, National Characteristics*, London: Ingram, Cooke, 1852 [1871]; reprint Eakin Pr (1 October 1985)/ Frankfurt: Outlook, 2022; translations are quoted from the 1871 edition at https://archive.org/details/cabinbookornatiooosealgoog, p. 13.

Westwards – Eastwards: Aporia of German-Language Tales from the Ghetto

Text:
'Westwärts – Ostwärts: Aporien deutschsprachiger Ghettogeschichten', in *Literatur und Kritik*, 233–4 (1989), 161–78.

i Epigraph: Dolf Sternberger, *Panorama oder Ansichten vom 19. Jahrhundert*, Frankfurt am Main: Suhrkamp, 1974, p. 173; *Panorama of the Nineteenth Century*, tr. Joachim Neugroschel, Oxford: Blackwell, 1977, p. 160.

ii W. Iggers (ed.), *Die Juden in Böhmen und Mähren*, Munich, 1986, p. 148 however gives the date as 1867.

iii For an overview of Kompert's life and work, see Wilma A. Iggers, 'Leopold Kompert, Romancier of the Bohemian Ghetto', *MAL* 6.3–4 (1973), 117–38. Ritchie Robertson has published widely in this area, e.g. *The German–Jewish Dialogue: An Anthology of Literary Texts, 1749–1993*, ed. and tr. Ritchie Robertson, Oxford: Oxford University Press, 1999; *The 'Jewish Question' in German Literature, 1749–1939*, Oxford: Oxford University Press, 1999; 'Western Observers and Eastern Jews: Kafka, Buber, Franzos', *Modern Language Review* 83 (1988), 87–105.

iv The English translation changes the metaphor, which in German suggests a hat pulled down over the eyes.

v 'However the novelist may be judged, the portrayer of men and manners demands that his words should be believed.' Karl Emil Franzos, *The Jews of Barnow: Stories*, tr. M. W. MacDowall, London: Appleton, 1882 (https://www.gutenberg.org/files/34617/34617-h/34617-h.htm), p. vi.

vi As noted above, a favourite motif of Sebald's.

vii A reference to Lessing's 1779 play *Nathan der Weise* (*Nathan the Wise*) with its plea for religious tolerance.

viii Sebald writes Goldmann, but the relevant contribution is by Wilhelm Goldbaum: 'Sacher-Masoch, von Wilhelm Goldbaum' contained in Michael Farin, 'Sacher-Masochs Jüdisches Leben: Ein Dossier' (appendix to Leopold von Sacher-Masoch, *Jüdisches Leben in Wort und Bild*, Dortmund, 1985), pp. 358–64. In what follows, Goldmann has been silently corrected to Goldbaum.

ix *Volkston*, cf. *A Place in the Country*, p. 81; *Hausfreund*, cf. the essay on Johann Peter Hebel and his *Schatzkästlein des rheinischen Hausfreunds* (*Treasure Chest of the Rhineland Family Friend*) in *A Place in the Country*, pp. 5–36.

x *Gartenlaube*, a kind of summerhouse or arbour, but also the title of a popular weekly 'illustrated family journal' founded in 1853 which did not cease publication until 1944.

xi 'Schimmel' usually refers to a white horse (cf. Theodor Storm's story *Der Schimmelreiter* (*The White Horseman*)), but can also signify a grey, which is what the English translation of *Weights and Measures* uses (Joseph Roth, *Weights and Measures*, tr. David Le Vay, London: Peter Owen, 1982/2002).

xii 'die letzte Lehre erweisen', a pun on 'die letzte Ehre erweisen' = to show a person the last honour', to pay one's final respects ('Ehre' = honour; 'Lehre' = lesson).

Peter Altenberg – *Le Paysan de Vienne*

Text:
'Peter Altenberg – Le Paysan de Vienne', in *Die neue Rundschau* I (1989), 75–96.

i The subtitle is a reference to the 1926 surrealist novel *Le Paysan de Paris* by Louis Aragon, a book which was also an inspiration for Walter Benjamin's *Passagenwerk* (*Arcades Project*).

ii 'Der Hofmeister': one of Sebald's favourite (teaching) subjects; the eponymous play by J. M. R. Lenz, but also the poet Hölderlin, who worked as a private tutor before his descent into madness.

iii Roland Barthes, *Système de la mode*, Paris: Éditions du Seuil, 1967; *The Fashion System*, tr. Matthew Ward and Richard Howard, New York: Hill & Wang, 1983.

iv 'I have more memories than if I had lived a thousand years' (from 'Spleen II' = *Les Fleurs du mal*, LXXVI), tr. Anthony Hecht in *Baudelaire in English*, ed. Carol Clark and Robert Sykes, London: Penguin, 1997, p. 90.

v 'Gemsjagd-Kaiser-Hütchen'.

vi *Wiener Spaziergänge* is actually the title of the work by Daniel Spitzer; cf. Stifter, *Aus dem alten Wien*, vol. 13 of the Birkhäuser Klassiker edition, ed. Konrad Steffen, Basel/Stuttgart, 1962–72.

vii Alfred Delvau (1825–67); *Les Heures parisiennes* appeared in 1866. Sebald erroneously writes Delvaud here.

viii Cf. *A Place in the Country*, p. 25: 'legendary righteous souls who hold the world in equilibrium'.

ix Cf. Peter Altenberg, 'Autobiography', in *Telegrams of the Soul: Selected Prose of Peter Altenberg*, tr. Peter Wortsman, New York: archipelago books, 2005, p. 3.

x 'Blondel' = Charles Blondin (Jean François Gravelet, 1824–1897. Sebald writes Blondel here.

xi The Grabenhotel in the Dorotheergasse in Vienna (adjacent to the central square known as Graben). 'Graben' = trench, but 'Grab' = grave, a deliberate play on words.

xii A pun on the Yiddish *luftmensch*, 'an impractical contemplative person having no definite business or income' (Merriam Webster); in German it literally means air person ('Luft' = air).

xiii Op. 4, also known as *Altenberg-Lieder*.

xiv The German 'Mikrogramm' (microgram or micrograph) suggests an allusion to Robert Walser's minuscule pencil jottings from his later years: cf. *A Place in the Country*, pp. 140–43, and Robert Walser, *Mikrogramme*, ed. Bernhard Echte and Lucas Marco Gisi, Berlin: Suhrkamp, 2011, translated into English as *Microscripts*, tr. Susan Bernofsky, New York: New Directions, 2010.

xv 1913 is of course a key date in Sebald's *Vertigo* (written at around the same time as this essay), with its locales in Vienna and Venice.

xvi '"Sarg-Kabinette" im Grabenhotel': again the pun on coffin ('Sarg') and grave ('Grab').

The Law of Ignominy – Authority, Messianism and Exile in Kafka's *Castle*

Text:

'Das Gesetz der Schande – Macht, Messianismus und Exil in Kafkas *Schloß*', in *manuskripte* 89–90 (1985), 117–24. First appeared in English as 'The Law of Ignominy – Authority, Messianism and Exile in *The Castle*', in *On Kafka: Semi-Centenary Perspectives*, ed. Franz Kuna, London: Paul Elek, 1976, pp. 42–59. It is this latter version, in Sebald's English, which is reproduced here.

Title: In the first English publication, the title of the essay reads 'The Law of Ignominy – Authority, Messianism and Exile in *The Castle*'. However, at the end of the volume, Sebald gives the title as 'The Law of Ignominy – Authority, Messianism and Exile in Kafka's *Castle*'. This is the title used here.

i   The German version in *Unheimliche Heimat* is prefaced by the following epigraph (in English):

> He's a perverted Jew from a place in Hungary and it was he drew up all the plans according to the Hungarian system. We know that in the castle.
>
> James Joyce, *Ulysses*

ii   In the translation by the Muirs, the terms 'Castellan' and 'under-castellan' are used (pp. 9 and 11). Anthea Bell renders this as 'castle warden' and 'deputy warden' respectively: Kafka, *The Castle*, tr. Anthea Bell, Oxford: Oxford University Press, 2009 (pp. 5 and 7).

iii This sentence is longer in the German: see *Unheimliche Heimat*, p. 88.

iv 'Theory of rubbish'; '*Larger Essay on Filth*'.

v   'hassidic [sic] tales' (cf. note 6): Martin Buber, *Tales of the Hasidim*, tr. Olga Marx, New York: Schocken, 1961.

vi 'Fürstenzimmer', literally prince's room – the best room; cf. the essay on Handke's *Repetition*, p. 408 of the present volume.

vii From 'The image of K.' to the end of the paragraph ('in need of redemption') this paragraph differs from the German version in *Unheimliche Heimat* (pp. 97–8), which omits the reference to Madame Lamort and the quote about the swoon, instead quoting from *Das Schloß*. In general, in the German text Sebald quotes more directly from the novel, whereas in the English version he tends to paraphrase (without giving a page reference).

viii 'Persecuted, they knew themselves already chosen. Here is the (whole) paradox of their condition.'

ix The German text ends here, omitting the Beckett quotation at the end.

A Kaddish for Austria – On Joseph Roth

Text:
'Ein Kaddisch für Österreich – Über Joseph Roth', in *Frankfurter Rundschau*, 27 May 1989. Newspaper piece to commemorate the fiftieth anniversary of Roth's death, with the title 'Ein Kaddisch für Österreich. Über Joseph Roth. Zu seinem 50. Todestag'.

i Epigraph: Joseph Roth, 'Die Büste des Kaisers', in Joseph Roth, *Werke 5: Romane und Erzählungen, 1930–1936*, ed. Fritz Hackert, Cologne: Kiepenheuer & Witsch, 1990, pp. 655–77 at p. 670. Joseph Roth, 'The Bust of the Emperor', in *Hotel Savoy*, tr. John Hoare, London: Chatto & Windus, 1986, pp. 155–83 at pp. 175–6.

Alternative translation of epigraph by Michael Hofmann ('The Bust of the Emperor', in Joseph Roth, *Collected Shorter Fiction*, London: Granta, 2001, pp. 235–58 at p. 251):

> And the Count asked the Jew: 'Solomon, what's your opinion of this world of ours?' 'Count,' replied Piniowsky, 'it has sunk [The world is broken, there is no Emperor].'

ii Cf. Psalm 104.
iii Roth, *The Radetzky March*, tr. Joachim Neugroschel, Penguin, 2000, p. 5.
iv *Die Geschichte der 1002. Nacht – The String of Pearls*, tr. Michael Hofmann, Granta 1999, p. 74.
v   *Der Leviathan* (*The Leviathan*); see note xi below.
vi Friederike (Friedl) Roth, née Reichler (1900–40), married Joseph Roth in 1922; she was committed to Westend psychiatric hospital, Berlin, in 1929 and thereafter to various psychiatric hospitals until murdered by the NS regime in 1940 (https://gailcrowther.com/2020/08/03/lost-lives-invisible-women-friederike-reichler/).
vii 'The Storyteller', in Walter Benjamin, *Illuminations*, tr. Harry Zohn, London: Fontana, 1992, pp. 83–106 at p. 96.
viii A reference to Schiller's essay *Über naïve und sentimentale Dichtung* (*On Naïve and Sentimental Poetry*) in Benjamin, 'The Storyteller', loc. cit.
ix *Radetzky March*, p. 123.
x   Joseph Roth died 27 May 1939.
xi 'The Leviathan', in *Collected Shorter Fiction of Joseph Roth*, tr. Michael Hofmann, London: Granta, 2002, pp. 259–91.
xii The writer as confidence trickster ('Hochstapler' or 'Schwindler') is one of Sebald's favourite motifs. Cf. the German title of *Vertigo*, *Schwindel. Gefühle*.
xiii 'The Storyteller', p. 94.
xiv Cf. also Roth, 'Solomon's Temple in Berlin' (*Neue Berliner Zeitung*, 2 October 1920), in *What I Saw: Reports from Berlin, 1920–33*, tr. Michael Hofmann, London: Granta, 2003, where the protagonist is one Herr Schwarzbach; and, on a somewhat less portable scale, the model of the Temple of Jerusalem in section IX of *The Rings of Saturn*.

Una montagna bruna – On Hermann Broch's 'Mountain Novel' [*Bergroman*]

Text:

'Una montagna bruna – Zum Bergroman Hermann Brochs', in *Frankfurter Rundschau*, 1 November 1986. Newspaper piece to commemorate the hundredth anniversary of Broch's birth, with the title 'Es schweigt der Berg, und manchmal spricht er. Vom Unsagbaren zum Unsäglichen: Zu Hermann Brochs berühmten "Bergroman"'.

i On the title and translations: between 1934 and 1936, Broch worked on a novel published posthumously in 1953 as *Der Versucher*; three versions of it were later published together in four volumes as *Bergroman* (1969), the edition to which Sebald refers. Versions of the novel have also been published as *Demeter* (1967) and *Die Verzauberung* (1976). The English translation, *The Spell: A Novel*, tr. H. F. Broch de Rothermann, New York: Farrar, Straus & Giroux, 1987, is based on *Die Verzauberung* and is the one from which the English quotations here are taken (the page references are to the 1988 Picador edition). Since the *Bergroman* version contains multiple variants on the text, it has sometimes been necessary to adapt the translation to fit.

ii Epigraph: this is probably derived from the story of Balaam, Numbers 22:2–24:25.

iii *Österreichische Porträts*: the volume to which Sebald contributed the essay on Stifter reproduced as the first essay in *Die Beschreibung des Unglücks* (Part One of the present volume). See also my Introduction (above p. xviii).

iv *Pasenow* (*The Romantic*), the first book in Broch's trilogy *Die Schlafwandler* (1931–2) (*The Sleepwalkers*). The three volumes are as follows: *Pasenow oder die Romantik* (1888); *Esch oder die Anarchie* (1903); *Hugenau oder die*

Sachlichkeit (1918). The 1947 English translations by Willa and Edwin Muir (*The Romantic*; *The Anarchist*; *The Realist*) – are reprinted as Penguin Classics: London: Penguin, 2000.

v 'Hauptstadt der Bewegung', an NS propaganda term for Munich.
vi This presumably refers to the eclectic architectural styles (Historicism) on Vienna's famous Ringstraße.
vii Matthew 8:28–34.
viii Ferdinand Raimund (1790–1836), Viennese playwright and actor known for *Volkstheater* and Viennese farce. Anglophone readers may more readily associate the iceman with the title, if not the content, of Eugene O'Neill's 1939 play *The Iceman Cometh*.
ix Deuteronomy 34:1.

A Lost Land – Jean Améry and Austria

Text:
'Verlorenes Land – Jean Améry und Österreich', in *Jean Améry*, ed. Irene Heidelberger-Leonard, Munich: Text + Kritik, 1988, pp. 20–30.

Reference is made to Jean Améry's experience of torture in Breendonck near the beginning of *Austerlitz*.

i Epigraph: 'Fragmente aus Heften und losen Blättern', in Kafka, *Hochzeitsvorbereitungen auf dem Lande*, Frankfurt am Main: Fischer, 1983 (repr. 1995), p. 212; *Wedding Preparations in the Country and Other Posthumous Prose Writings*, tr. Ernst Kaiser and Eithne Wilkins, London: Secker & Warburg, 1954 (repr. 1975), p. 286.
ii 'Resentments', one of the chapter headings in *Jenseits von Schuld und Sühne*, translated as *At the Mind's Limits: Contemplations by a Survivor on Auschwitz and its Realities*, tr. Sidney Rosenfeld and Stella P. Rosenfeld, published in association with the United States Holocaust

Memorial Museum, Bloomington and Indianapolis: Indiana University Press, 1980.

iii In the essay 'How Much Home Does a Person Need?' in *At the Mind's Limits* this is rendered as 'hostile homeland' (p. 52).

iv The Rosenfelds translate this as 'Places and Stations' in their Preface to Jean Améry, *Radical Humanism: Selected Essays*, Bloomington: Indiana University Press, 1984.

v The title *Unmeisterliche Wanderjahre* alludes to Goethe's *Bildungsroman Wilhelm Meisters Wanderjahre (Wilhelm Meisters Journeyman Years)*. The Rosenfelds give this as 'Lean Journeyman Years'.

vi 'Feldweg, Hohlweg, Holzweg': a 'Holzweg', famous from the title of Heidegger's 1950 essay collection translated as *Off the Beaten Track*, colloquially means a dead end or false trail: a path created in the process of woodcutting where wood is often stored, but not leading anywhere. Both literal and metaphorical meanings are relevant here.

vii 'Narrenvolk': the 'Narren' – fools or jesters – are an important part of Carnival celebrations in southern Germany, Austria and Switzerland. The pun is no doubt intended.

viii 'Der Weg ins Freie' ('The Way into the Open', or 'The Road to the Open'), title of a 1908 novel by Schnitzler, but also of the last chapter of Améry's book *Hand an sich legen*, translated as *On Suicide: A Discourse on Voluntary Death*, tr. John D. Barlow, Bloomington: Indiana University Press, 1999.

ix 'between home (the hearth) and far away'.

x 'Hand an sich legen', German title of Améry's *On Suicide* and of the third chapter which in English is translated as 'To Lay Hands on Oneself'. This is also the phrase Sebald uses of Adalbert Stifter at the end of the first essay in the present volume (above p. 35).

xi 'der Améry' – the informal use of the definite article with a proper name in German can have a slightly deprecating effect.

xii *Die Ursache* ('The Cause') is translated as 'An Indication of the Cause' in Bernhard, *Gathering Evidence: A Memoir*, tr. David McLintock, New York: Knopf, 1985/Vintage, 2003.

xiii 'das letzte Wirtshaus' ('the last inn') – see both the dialect maxim quoted above (p. 372) and the essays 'The Undiscover'd Country' (above pp. 91, 99 and 100) and 'Light Pictures and Dark' (above p. 215).

In an Unknown Region – On Gerhard Roth's Novel
Landläufiger Tod [*A Common or Garden Death*]

Text:

'In einer wildfremden Gegend – Zu Gerhard Roths Romanwerk *Der Landläufige Tod* [sic]', in *manuskripte* 92 (1986), 52–7. This essay is also translated by Markus Zisselsberger as 'In a completely unknown region: on Gerhard Roth's novel *Landläufiger Tod*', *Modern Austrian Literature* 40.4 (2007), 29–39.

i Epigraph: Novalis [Friedrich von Hardenberg], 'Fragmente und Studien 1799–1800', #26 in Novalis, *Werke*, ed. Gerhard Schulz, Munich: C. H. Beck, 1969, p. 523. *Pollen and Fragments: Selected Poetry and Prose of Novalis*, tr. Arthur Versluis, Grand Rapids, MI: Phanes Press, 1989, p. 83 (translation slightly adapted).

ii See the essay 'The Man with the Overcoat' in Part One of the present volume (above p. 175).

iii This represents volume III of the seven-volume 'Romanzyklus' *Die Archive des Schweigens* ('The Archives of Silence'), yet to be translated into English.

iv Cf. Georg Büchner's short story 'Lenz' (on J. M. R. Lenz, a contemporary of Goethe's and author of the play *Der Hofmeister*).

v *Landläufiger Tod*, pp. 149–91.

vi   Cf. Sebald's poem 'Ein Walzertraum' ('A Waltz Dream') and the image *Das Land des Lächelns* (*The Land of Smiles*) by Jan Peter Tripp it accompanies.

vii   English translation of the Polish original: Bruno Schulz, 'The Republic of Dreams', tr. Walter Arndt, *Chicago Review* 40.1 (1994), pp. 66–72, https://doi.org/10.2307/25305807.

viii   'Triebstruktur': the German title of Marcuse's *Eros and Civilization* is *Triebstruktur und Gesellschaft*.

ix   'General von Kniefall' – a figure in Roth's *Landläufiger Tod*.

x   Cf. Claude Lévi-Strauss, *The Origin of Table Manners (Introduction to a Study of Mythology: 3)*, tr. John and Doreen Weightman, London: Cape, 1978, p. 195; *Mythologiques 3: L'origine des manières de table*, Paris: Plon, 1968, p. 159.

xi   Cf. Elias Canetti, *Crowds and Power*, tr. Carol Stewart, Harmondsworth: Penguin, 1984, pp. 104 and 217.

Across the Border – Peter Handke's *Die Wiederholung* [*Repetition*]

Text:

'Jenseits der Grenze – Peter Handkes Erzählung *Die Wiederholung*', published for the first time in *Unheimliche Heimat*. Also translated by Nathaniel Davis as 'Across the Border: Peter Handke's *Repetition*', https://thelastbooks.org/wordpress/wp-content/uploads/2020/04/Sebald_Across_the_Border.pdf.

i   Epigraph: Schlomo von Karlin, in Martin Buber, *Die Erzählungen der Chassidim*, Zurich: Manesse, 1994, p. 425 ('Die Fahrten'). Shelomo of Karlin, 'The Stages', in Martin Buber, *Tales of the Hasidim*, tr. Olga Marx, New York: Schocken, 1961, p. 275.

ii   See the essay 'Beneath the Surface' in Part One of the present volume (above p. 133).

iii See the essay 'Light Pictures and Dark' in Part One of the present volume (above p. 193). The four books are the novels *The Long Way Around* (the eponymous *Langsame Heimkehr*, 1979); *The Lesson of Mont Sainte-Victoire* (*Die Lehre der Sainte-Victoire*, 1980); *Child Story* (*Kindergeschichte*, 1981) and the 'Dramatisches Gedicht' ('dramatic poem') *Über die Dörfer* (1981). English editions: *Slow Homecoming: 3 Novels* by Peter Handke, tr. Ralph Manheim, London: Methuen 1985, repr. with an Introduction by Benjamin Kunkel, New York: New York Review Books, 2009; *Walk about the Villages: A Dramatic Poem*, in a Translation for Voice with an Afterword by Michael Roloff, Riverside, CA: Ariadne, 1996.

iv 'Gefangene und Verbannte': Sebald has adapted this; the text actually reads 'Gefangene oder Verbannte': 'prisoners *or* exiles'.

v Tolmin, a town in western Slovenia, site of a peasant revolt against increased taxation in 1713.

vi Again, Sebald misquotes here – Handke's German text has 'Knechte und Wanderarbeiter' (hirelings and itinerant workers) rather than 'Waldarbeiter' (forest workers).

vii Handke, *A Sorrow Beyond Dreams*, tr. Ralph Manheim, New York: New York Review Books Classics, 2002.

viii For the story of the soldier, see *Repetition*, pp. 165–70; the story of the waiter is on pp. 146–9.

ix Sebald adapts the translation here, changing the tense and omitting 'eigene' (of their own).

x Cf. *A Place in the Country*, p. 25.

xi 'Fürstenzimmer': see the essay 'The Law of Ignominy', above p. 312.

xii 'die Schrift' means both writing and Scripture.

xiii Sebald paraphrases the German here; I have quoted from the relevant passage of the English translation.

xiv The recurring motif of the *Laubhütte* or sukkah; cf. in the essays 'A Small Traverse' (above p. 171) and 'Westwards – Eastwards' (above p. 265).

Selected Bibliography

Background and reference

Catling, Jo and Richard Hibbitt (eds.), *Saturn's Moons: W. G. Sebald – A Handbook*, Oxford/London: Legenda, 2011

Kohl, Katrin and Ritchie Robertson (eds.), *A History of Austrian Literature, 1918–2000*, Rochester, NY/Woodbridge, Suffolk: Camden House, 2006

Schütte, Uwe (ed.), *W. G. Sebald in Context*, Cambridge: Cambridge University Press, 2023

Sheppard, Richard, 'W. G. Sebald: A Chronology', in Catling and Hibbitt (eds.), *Saturn's Moons*, pp. 619–59

Sheppard, Richard, 'W. G. Sebald – Primary Bibliography', in Catling and Hibbitt (eds.), *Saturn's Moons*, pp. 447–96: this gives the full publication history of all of Sebald's work; see in particular sections 'D' and 'E'

Works by Sebald in order of German publication

(Details of the first publications of the essays in this volume are given in the *Nachweise* section below; see also the Translator's Notes)

[Nine poems], *ZET* [*Das Zeichenheft für Literatur und Grafik*], 2.6 (July 1974), 13, and 3.10 (June 1975), 18–19; [translations of four poems by Roger McGough], *ZET*, 3.12 (December 1975), 6–8

Carl Sternheim. Kritiker und Opfer der Wilhelminischen Ära [*Carl Sternheim: Critic and Victim of the Wilhelmine Age*], Stuttgart: Kohlhammer, 1969

Der Mythus der Zerstörung im Werk Döblins [*The Myth of Destruction in the Work of Döblin*], Stuttgart: Klett, 1980

Die Beschreibung des Unglücks. Zur österreichischen Literatur von Stifter bis Handke, Salzburg/Vienna: Residenz, 1985

Nach der Natur. Ein Elementargedicht, Nördlingen: Greno, 1988; *After Nature*, tr. Michael Hamburger, London: Hamish Hamilton, 2002

Schwindel. Gefühle., Frankfurt am Main: Eichborn, 1990; *Vertigo*, tr. Michael Hulse, London: Harvill, 2000

'Damals vor Graz – Randbemerkungen zum Thema Literatur und Heimat', in Kurt Bartsch and Gerhard Melzer (eds.), *Trans-Garde: Die Literatur der 'Grazer Gruppe' Forum Stadtpark und 'manuskripte'*, Graz: Droschl, 1990, pp. 141–53

Unheimliche Heimat. Essays zur österreichischen Literatur, Salzburg/Vienna: Residenz, 1991

Die Ausgewanderten, Frankfurt am Main: Eichborn, 1993; *The Emigrants*, tr. Michael Hulse, London: Harvill, 1996

Die Ringe des Saturn. Eine englische Wallfahrt, Frankfurt am Main: Eichborn, 1995; *The Rings of Saturn*, tr. Michael Hulse, London: Harvill, 1998

Logis in einem Landhaus, Munich/Vienna: Hanser, 1998; *A Place in the Country*, tr. Jo Catling, London: Hamish Hamilton, 2013

Luftkrieg und Literatur, Munich/Vienna: Hanser, 1999; *On the Natural History of Destruction*, tr. Anthea Bell, London: Hamish Hamilton, 2003

Austerlitz, Munich/Vienna: Hanser, 2001; *Austerlitz*, tr. Anthea Bell, London: Hamish Hamilton, 2001

Campo Santo, ed. Sven Meyer, Munich/Vienna: Hanser, 2003; *Campo Santo*, tr. Anthea Bell, London: Hamish Hamilton, 2005

Über das Land und das Wasser, ed. Sven Meyer, Munich/Vienna: Hanser, 2008; *Across the Land and the Water: Selected Poems, 1964–2001*, tr. Iain Galbraith, London: Hamish Hamilton, 2011

Other translations of the two 'Austrian' essay volumes (selected)

Pútrida Patria. Ensayos sobre literatura, tr. Miguel Sáenz, Barcelona: Anagrama, 2005

Pátria Apátrida (Ensaiõs sobre literatura austríaca), tr. Telma Costa, Lisbon: Teorema, 2010

La Description du malheur. À propos de la littérature autrichienne, tr. Patrick Charbonneau, Arles: Actes Sud, 2014

Amére Patrie. À propos de la littérature autrichienne, tr. Patrick Charbonneau, Arles: Actes Sud, 2017

Reviews and interviews cited

Hartl, Edwin, 'Fahrten und Erfahrungen: Dichtender Dozent', *Die Presse*, 30 June/1 July 1990

Sebald, W. G., interview on *Night Waves*, BBC Radio 3, 5 October 2001

Sebald, W. G., interview with Uwe Pralle (2001): 'Mit einem kleinen Strandspaten Abschied von Deutschland nehmen', in Torsten Hofmann (ed.), *Auf ungeheuer dünnem Eis*, Frankfurt am Main: Fischer, 2011, pp. 252–63

Silverblatt, Michael, 'A Poem of an Invisible Subject', in Lynne Sharon Schwartz (ed.), *Emergence of Memory*, New York/London: Seven Stories Press, 2007, pp. 77–86

'In This Distant Place: A Conversation with Steve Wassermann (Los Angeles, 2001)': 'Three Conversations with W. G. Sebald', in Catling and Hibbitt (eds.), *Saturn's Moons: W. G. Sebald – A Handbook*, Oxford/London: Legenda, 2011, pp. 364–75

Secondary sources on Sebald as critic and the genesis of the essays

Bartsch, Scott, 'W. G. Sebald's "Prose Project": A Glimpse into the Potting Shed', in Uwe Schütte (ed.), *Über W. G. Sebald. Beiträge zu einem anderen Bild des Autors*, Berlin: De Gruyter, 2017, pp. 99–134

Finch, Helen, *Sebald's Bachelors: Queer Resistance and the Unconforming Life*, Oxford/London: Legenda, 2013

Finch, Helen, '"Die irdische Erfüllung": Peter Handke's Poetic Landscapes and W. G. Sebald's Metaphysics of History', in Anne Fuchs and J. J. Long (eds.), *W. G. Sebald and the Writing of History*, Würzburg: Königshausen & Neumann, 2007, pp. 179–97

Fuchs, Anne, 'Between Pathography and Ethnography: Sebald as a Diagnostic Reader', *Modern Austrian Literature* 40.4 (2007), 109–23

Pages, Neil Christian, 'Sebald, Handke and the Pathological Vision', *Modern Austrian Literature* 40.4 (2007), 61–92

Pages, Neil Christian, 'Tripping: On Sebald's "Stifter"', in Markus Zisselsberger (ed.), *The Undiscover'd Country: W. G. Sebald and the Poetics of Travel*, Rochester, NY: Camden House, 2010, pp. 213–46

Radvan, Florian, 'Vom Sodiumglanz ferner Städte: W. G. Sebalds literarische Erinnerungen an Die Ausgewanderten', in *Im Krebsgang:*

Strategien des Erinnerns in den Werken von Günter Grass und W. G. Sebald, ed. Rüdiger Sareika, Iserlohn: Institut für Kirche und Gesellschaft, 2006, pp. 55–70

Robertson, Ritchie, 'W. G. Sebald as a Critic of Austrian Literature', *Journal of European Studies* 41.3–4 (2011), 305–22

Schmucker, Peter, *Grenzübertretungen. Intertextualität im Werk von W. G. Sebald*, Berlin: De Gruyter, 2012 [in German; 600 pages]

Schütte, Uwe, 'Against *Germanistik*: W. G. Sebald's Critical Essays', in Jo Catling and Richard Hibbitt (eds.), *Saturn's Moons: W. G. Sebald – A Handbook*, Oxford/London: Legenda, 2011, pp. 161–82

Schütte, Uwe, *Interventionen. Literaturkritik als Widerspruch bei W. G. Sebald*, Munich: edition text+kritik, 2014 [in German; 650 pages]

Swales, Martin, 'Theoretical Reflections on the Work of W. G. Sebald', in J. J. Long and Anne Whitehead (eds.), *W. G. Sebald – A Critical Companion*, Seattle: University of Washington Press, 2004, pp. 23–8

Nachweise [= Places of first publication of the essays, often in somewhat abbreviated or different form, included by Sebald at the end of the two German volumes]

Part One (*Die Beschreibung des Unglücks*)

'Bis an den Rand der Natur – Versuch über Stifter' ('To the Edge of Nature: An Essay on Stifter'), in *Österreichische Porträts*, ed. Jochen Jung, Salzburg: Residenz, 1985, vol. I, pp. 232–55

'Das Schrecknis der Liebe – Zu Schnitzlers "Traumnovelle"' ('The Horror of Love – On Schnitzler's *Traumnovelle* [*Dream Story*]'), in *Merkur* 39.2 (February 1985), 120–31

'Venezianisches Kryptogramm – Hofmannsthals "Andreas"' ('A Venetian Cryptogram: Hofmannsthal's *Andreas*') – see Translator's Notes for subsequent or simultaneous publication

'Das unentdeckte Land – Zur Motivstruktur in Kafkas "Schloß"' ('The Undiscover'd Country – The Death Motif in Kafka's "Castle"') appeared under the title 'Thanatos – Zur Motivstruktur in Kafkas "Schloß"' in *Literatur und Kritik* 66 (1972), 399–411, and in English in *Journal of European Studies* 2 (1972), 22–34. It is this latter version, in Sebald's English, which is reproduced here

'Summa Scientiae – System und Systemkritik bei Elias Canetti' ('Summa Scientiae – Systems and System Critique in Elias Canetti'), in *Literatur und Kritik* 177–8 (1983), 398–404, as well as in *Études Germaniques* 39.3 (1984), 268–75

'Wo die Dunkelheit den Strick zuzieht – Zu Thomas Bernhard' ('Wo die Dunkelheit den Strick zuzieht [Where Darkness Draws Tight the Noose] – Some Marginal Notes on Thomas Bernhard'), in *Literatur und Kritik* 155 (1981), 294–302

'Unterm Spiegel des Wassers – Peter Handkes Erzählung von der Angst des Tormanns' ('Beneath the Surface – Peter Handke's Story of the Goalkeeper's Anxiety'), in *Austriaca* 16 (1983), 43–56

'Eine kleine Traverse – Das poetische Werk Ernst Herbecks' ('A Small Traverse: The Poetry of Ernst Herbeck'), in *manuskripte* 74 (1981), 35–41

'Der Mann mit dem Mantel – Gerhard Roths "Winterreise"' ('The Man with the Overcoat – Gerhard Roth's *Winterreise*') appeared under the title 'Literarische Pornographie? – Gerhard Roths "Winterreise"' in *Merkur* 38.2 (1984), 171–80

'Helle Bilder und dunkle – Zur Dialektik der Eschatologie bei Stifter und Handke' ('Light Pictures and Dark – On the Dialectics of Eschatology in Stifter and Handke'), in *manuskripte* 84 (1984), 58–64

Part Two (*Unheimliche Heimat*)

'Ansichten aus der Neuen Welt – Über Charles Sealsfield' ('Views from the New World – On Charles Sealsfield'), in *Die Rampe* 1 (1988), 7–18

'Westwärts – Ostwärts: Aporien deutschsprachiger Ghettogeschichten' ('Westwards – Eastwards: Aporia of German-Language Tales from the Ghetto'), in *Literatur und Kritik* 233–4 (1989), 161–78

'Peter Altenberg – Le Paysan de Vienne' ('Peter Altenberg – *Le Paysan de Vienne*'), in *Die neue Rundschau* I (1989), 75–96

'Das Gesetz der Schande – Macht, Messianismus und Exil in Kafkas *Schloß*', in *manuskripte* 89–90 (1985), 117–24. First appeared in English as 'The Law of Ignominy – Authority, Messianism and Exile in Kafka's *Castle*' in *On Kafka: Semi-Centenary Perspectives*, ed. Franz Kuna, London: Paul Elek, 1976, pp. 42–59. It is this latter version, in Sebald's English, which is reproduced here

'Ein Kaddisch für Österreich – Über Joseph Roth' ('A Kaddish for Austria – On Joseph Roth'), in *Frankfurter Rundschau*, 27 May 1989

'Una montagna bruna – Zum Bergroman Hermann Brochs' ('Una montagna bruna – On Hermann Broch's "Mountain Novel" [*Bergroman*]'), in *Frankfurter Rundschau*, 1 November 1986

'Verlorenes Land – Jean Améry und Österreich' ('A Lost Land – Jean Améry and Austria'), in *Jean Améry*, ed. Irene Heidelberger-Leonard, Munich: Text + Kritik, 1988, pp. 20–30

'In einer wildfremden Gegend – Zu Gerhard Roths Romanwerk *Der Landläufige Tod* [sic]' ('In an Unknown Region – On Gerhard Roth's Novel *Landläufiger Tod* [*A Common or Garden Death*]'), in *manuskripte* 92 (1986), 52–7

'Jenseits der Grenze – Peter Handkes Erzählung *Die Wiederholung*' ('Across the Border – Peter Handke's *Die Wiederholung* [*Repetition*]') – published for the first time in *Unheimliche Heimat*

Acknowledgements

These translations, long in the making and in many ways a labour of love, were commenced during my time as Senior Lecturer in German and European Literature at the University of East Anglia, which I joined as a colleague of W. G. Sebald in 1993. I should like to acknowledge in particular the support of the Faculty of Arts and Humanities and the British Centre for Literary Translation for this project.

The Estate of W. G. Sebald and The Wylie Agency have been unfailingly kind and generous throughout, and I wish to express my gratitude for their unwavering support in sometimes choppy waters. As with *A Place in the Country*, it has been a great privilege to translate these two books of essays.

I am most grateful to the British Academy, the DAAD and the German Auswärtiges Amt for generously financing stays at the Deutsches Literaturarchiv Marbach and the Europäisches Übersetzerkollegium Straelen, as well as to colleagues in both institutions for their always helpful assistance and advice.

Very many thanks to the Santa Maddalena Foundation, Tuscany and the Translation House Looren, Switzerland for their generous support and for providing such incomparably peaceful, idyllic and inspirational surroundings in which to work.

Many thanks too to Simon Prosser and the team at Penguin for seeing the project to fruition; and a special mention to my wonderful, and wonderfully patient, copy-editor Peter James (not forgetting the owls . . .).

Among the many friends, family and colleagues who have so generously contributed suggestions, advice and support, I wish in particular to express my thanks here to the late Anthea Bell, for the suggestion of translating these essays, and to Dr Renate Birkenhauer; Gillian Catling; Margaret Dériaz; Heide Gerland; Dr Richard Hibbitt and colleagues; Luke Ingram; Jennie Juckes (and Pentre Mawr); Catherine Juckes; Richard Juckes; Professor Duncan Large and BCLT; Baronessa Beatrice Monti della Corte and all at Santa Maddalena; Dr Brigid Purcell; Professor Gene Rogers and colleagues; Eva Schestag; Dr Uwe Schütte; Dr Elizabeth Ward; Stephen Watts; Professor Lynn Wolff. Special thanks are due to Hannes Schüpbach for Swiss hospitality and the finding of words and images.

Last but not least I would like to thank the community of Sebald translators, the Sebald-Übersetzergemeinschaft, for all their comradeship and suggestions. In particular I would like to express my appreciation to Patrick Charbonneau, whose beautiful French translations of these essays have been a constant source of inspiration and elucidation.

Jo Catling
Norwich, June 2024